BEST PRACTICES IN OCCUPATIONAL HEALTH, SAFETY, WORKERS COMPENSATION AND CLAIMS MANAGEMENT FOR EMPLOYERS

Best of Luck

BEST PRACTICES IN OCCUPATIONAL HEALTH, SAFETY, WORKERS COMPENSATION AND CLAIMS MANAGEMENT FOR EMPLOYERS

ASSISTING EMPLOYERS IN NAVIGATING "THE ROAD TO ZERO"

LISA GRANGER

Universal-Publishers
Boca Raton

*Best Practices in Occupational Health, Safety, Workers Compensation
and Claims Management for Employers:
Assisting Employers in Navigating "The Road to Zero"*

Copyright © 2010 Lisa Granger

Universal-Publishers
Boca Raton, Florida • USA
2010

ISBN-10: 1-59942-812-1
ISBN-13: 978-1-59942-812-3

www.universal-publishers.com

TABLE OF CONTENTS

INTRODUCTION

General Introduction

The intent of this book is to provide a general understanding of the legislation relevant to health and safety and give some helpful tips on managing both health and safety programs and disability management effectively and efficiently. This information will assist companies in developing and implementing sound disability management practices in order to ensure compliance, cost efficiency and effective business strategies. Cost management is a critical part of efficient business strategies. Developing, customizing and implementing best practices in disability management will help any human resources professional or manager and is necessary in managing costs and human capital effectively. Effective health and safety programs and efficient disability management will provide any company with the following advantages:

- Improved morale
- Decreased frequencies of injuries
- Decreased severity of injuries
- Decreased lost time from injuries
- Decreased potential for penalties and fines for non-conformance to legislation
- Decreased lost productivity
- Increased productivity

- Decreased potential for mandated Workwell audit
- Decreased claims costs
- Increased potential for premium adjustments for workplace injury insurance, including rebates, decreased premiums, etc.
- Tools to achieve health and safety targets and objectives
- Increased investment in labour capital
- Lower employee turnover
- Lower potential of Ministry of Labour visits
- Employee participation in the program(s)
- Tools for accurate project forecasting, including claim costs, surcharges, premiums, etc.
- Increased understanding of legislative requirements and processes
- Access to potential obscure rebates

Introduction to Disability Management

Disability Management is a process in managing human capital, medical intervention, recoveries, restrictions, costs, accommodations and legislation. There are several wage loss benefits programs for workers that require effective disability management practices by companies which include but are not limited to short term disability, long term disability, and workers' compensation. In Ontario, the workers compensation insurance program is dictated by Workplace Safety and Insurance Act (WSIA) and managed by the Workplace Safety and Insurance Board (WSIB). The Ministry of Labour (MOL) enforces the WSIA.

The WSIA mandates that each company report any workplace injuries to the WSIB, and depending on the severity, some injuries also must be reported to the MOL. The WSIA outlines when and how a company is to report an injury as well as the duties and responsibilities of all parties involved in the recovery process. Unfortunately, the WSIA does not explain in detail how companies develop and implement plans to manage what happens after the workplace injury occurs. The information herein will provide a general understanding of best practices in disability management, a general understanding of the workers' compensation programs and the laws of the land.

Introduction to Workers' Compensation

In order to develop and implement a functioning disability management program, there must be some understanding of the workers' compensation program. Learning about the program will help to develop practices that will ensure compliance to legislation, cost efficiency and effective business strategies.

The purpose of a workers' compensation insurance program is to provide wage replacement and coverage of health care costs during the recovery process of a workplace injury. In Ontario, the government administers the workers' compensation program. This program is called the Workplace Safety and Insurance Act (WSIA) of Ontario. It is a mandatory program where the employers pay the premiums for the insurance coverage of the workers.

The WSIA outlines the roles and responsibilities of all the parties involved. One unique condition of this government based insurance program is that the worker forfeits their right to sue the employer for the workplace injury in exchange for the wage replacement and the coverage of the health care costs.

Relevant Legislation

To perform business anywhere in the world, each company has to respect and incorporate the laws of the land in which they operate into the way they do business. In Canada, there are three (3) levels of legislation: federal, provincial, and municipal. Within each of these levels of government, disability management programs are affected by several pieces of legislation.

A company operating a business in Ontario will be subject to legislation governed by the Canadian government like the Canadian Charter of Rights and Freedoms, by the Ontario government like Workplace Safety and Insurance Act (WSIA) and Occupational Health and Safety Act of Ontario (OHSA), and, by the municipal government like municipal taxes.

Some significant pieces of legislation in Ontario that impact disability management programs include but are not limited to:

- Workplace Safety and Insurance Act (WSIA)
- Occupational Health and Safety Act of Ontario (OHSA)
- Regulation 1101 First Aid
- Human Rights Code

- Privacy Act
- Employment Standards Act
- Canada Labour Code
- Pension Act
- Labour Relations Act
- Bill C-45 (outlining executive, management and supervisor responsibilities under the criminal code for gross negligence in a workplace injury)
- Bill 168 (Violence in the Workplace)
- Bill 118 – Prohibiting the use of handheld electronic equipment while driving a vehicle

Business in Ontario

Every business operating in Ontario must register with the Workplace Safety and Insurance Board (WSIB) either as an Independent Operator or as an employer. The WSIB is a provincial government branch responsible for the enforcement and administration of the Workplace Safety and Insurance Act (WSIA). The WSIB administers the workers compensation insurance program to provide payment for wage loss and health care costs incurred for workplace injuries.

A business operating in Ontario that is owned and operated by one person can apply for Independent Operator status with the WSIB. The Independent Operator must complete an Independent Operator questionnaire which can be found on the WSIB website in order for the WSIB to determine if the business is classified as one of an Independent Operator.

In general, according to the WSIA, the Independent Operator is a person who operates a business but does not have any employees whereas, the employer has employees. For more discussion on the independent operator status vs. the employer status, please see the chapter on Independent Operators later in this book.

The employer registers with the WSIB as an employer stating the number of employees. When a business registers with the WSIB, they receive an account number and a firm number. The company is also assigned to a rate group determined by the industry and type of business of the company. Each company may have more than one rate group depending on the type of business they operate.

The WSIB tracks the performance of each company's health and safety program through the number of injuries and the severity of the injuries claimed. The WSIB uses the costs of the claims registered to the company's account number and firm number as a unit of measure for frequency and severity.

The WSIB calculates the average of all the members in the same rate group. The average is then used to measure the performance of each of the companies within the rate group against the rate group as a whole. The rate group's average is referred to as the industry standard for all companies operating like businesses.

For those companies who have performance ratings higher than the industry standard, the WSIB will flag the company as a poor performer. The Ministry of Labour (MOL) will begin to visit those companies listed as poor performers unannounced to audit the company's health and safety program. These visits may result in fines, penalties and various orders to improve the safety standards or procedures in the company.

Those companies who have performance ratings lower than the industry standard will likely not be subject to as many unannounced visits by the MOL. The assumption is that the lower amount of incidents indicates that the company's health and safety program is functioning well and the workers are at less risk of getting injured at the workplace.

Once an employer has an account and a firm number, the WSIB will assign the company to a sector. Each sector is comprised of a team of the WSIB decision makers. Prior to March 2009, the team included Account Manager, Claims Adjudicators, Nurse Case Manager, a Mediator, and an Ergonomist. Some positions like the Mediator and the Ergonomist were shared among a few sectors. In this structure one claims adjudicator would be responsible for making decisions in the claim from start to finish of the claim. The claims were assigned randomly by computer by case load.

However, post March 2009, the WSIB has restructured their administrative services for claims administration. The new structure resembles a division of decision making responsibility according to the different phases in maturity of the claim. There will now be a different adjudicator for each phase of maturity of the claim. For example, the first adjudicator will review the claim for initial entitlement. The second adjudication team will make decisions on the claim from the period of entitlement to 180 days of the life of the claim. Finally, the last adjudication team will make decisions on claims for claims that are post 180 days in life.

The last level of adjudication is the group that determines if the injured workers are assessed for the Labour Marker Re-entry (LMR) program. There will be further discussion on the adjudication team and their responsibilities and impact during the disability management process throughout the course of this book. Best practices start with establishing a good rapport with all the adjudicators of the WSIB. A good relationship and strong communication skills are required in working with the decision makers at the WSIB in order to develop, implement and maintain a well-functioning disability management program.

The WSIA outlines the regulations for the workers compensation insurance program for Ontario. As mentioned before, participation in this program is mandatory for all employers. The employer pays premiums to the WSIB monthly. The premiums are proportional to the amount of payroll paid for the month and the number of employees.

The premiums are used to pay the costs of the claims in addition to all of the administrative costs of the WSIB. Unfortunately, for many years the revenue from only the premiums was not sufficient to cover the administration costs and all of the claims costs. The deficiency of funds to cover all the costs contributed to the rising amount of deficit called the unfunded liability.

The WSIB considered adjusting the premiums for each rate group in order to collect enough money to pay down the cumulative deficit. However the WSIB determined that increasing the premiums would not be sufficient to pay down the deficit. As a result, the WSIB developed and implemented a system of rebates and surcharges based on a company's health and safety program (injury) performance.

The rebates and surcharge program were calculated based on the company's performance against their respective rate group. The development of the rebate/surcharge program has enabled the premium rates per $100 payroll remain relatively stable over time and focus on the companies with poor health and safety performances paying for the deficiencies in the unfunded liability since the poor performers continue to be the major contributors to the rising unfunded liability.

Therefore, every business in Ontario (indeed, the world) should have a functioning and effective health and safety program in order to reduce the number and severity of injuries in their workplace in order to reduce the worker's compensation costs. Strong disability management programs will assist in reducing the worker's compensation costs by managing the costs through return to work programs, independent medical evaluations, cost relief awards, terminating claims appropriately, etc.

Highlights of a comprehensive health and safety program can include the following:

- Health and safety policy clearly outlining the company's (and executive) commitment to the health and safety program and the health and safety of all workers
- Setting targets and objectives for the program for each year
- OHSAS 18001 Certification
- Health and safety risk assessment of our workplace
  - OHSA requirements
  - Ergonomic development into engineering design as well as corrective action
  - Developed and implemented procedures for managing or working with risks identified safely
  - Incident reporting procedure
  - Corrective actions and prevention initiatives
- Joint Health and Safety Committee (JHSC)
- Communication – open door approach
- Training
- Mentoring
- Auditing
- Continuous Improvements
- Completed Ergo training for Industrial and Manufacturing Engineers:
- Intro to Ergonomics
- Ergo Risk Factors and Injuries
- Ergo Design Specifications
- Review of Possible Engineering and Administrative Controls
- Review of Anthropometric Data
- Developed an Ergonomic Design Specification

In addition to satisfying a company's environmental health and safety legal obligations and responsibilities, a well-developed and comprehensive health and safety program including an effective disability management program will allow the company to establish practices of due diligence. These practices will also demonstrate commitment to the health and wellness of all workers.

Similar to a good quality program, an efficient health and safety program can contribute to increased productivity, increased morale, and increased employee retention resulting in profitable business operations. As with all good business practices, it takes some investment to develop and establish the programs that will have the most impact on a long term, sustainable, and profitable bottom line.

Ontario Ministry of Labour
Another branch of the provincial government in Ontario that is a key participant in the health and safety program development, implementation and maintenance is the Ministry of Labour (MOL). The MOL's responsibilities include (but are not limited to):

- Enforcing the Occupational Health and Safety Act of Ontario (OHSA)
- Supporting the Workplace Safety and Insurance Act (WSIA)
- Monitors the health and safety of workers in Ontario
- The WSIB will flag the MOL when a company reports a critical injury, exhibits higher trends of injuries than industry standards, reports suspicious type of injuries, etc.
- Supporting the WSIB through:
  - High risk flagging
  - Increase random visits to the company's workplace
  - Workwell audits activity
  - Critical injuries investigation and follow up including penalties and fines
  - Follow up for long term/latent injuries from occupational illness and disease

- The WSIB provides the MOL with annual reports on all companies who have significant levels of severity and frequency

A representative from the MOL can and will show up at any Ontario workplace at any time of the day or week. The visits may be prompted by an anonymous tip, the WSIB statistics, critical injury, police, health care professional, the company, for no specific reason, etc.

Upon visiting a workplace, the representative from the MOL must identify him/herself with proper identification. The inspector has full authority to enter any workplace in Ontario without a subpoena. The inspector will request to review company records and documents relating to compliance to the Occupational Health and Safety Act (OHSA) and, indirectly, the WSIA. The employer must allow the inspector in and must comply with the inspector's requests.

The MOL can write orders to the company to develop and implement any corrective actions to address deficiencies to compliance to the OHSA. The MOL can also levy fines and penalties for any significant non-compliance and significant infraction to the OHSA. The MOL is interested in reviewing evidence that the company's Internal Responsibility System (IRS) is functioning and effective. The MOL will request to examine documentation supporting the company's commitment to compliance of the law. An inspector will also request evidence that all the workers are not only knowledgeable of law and of the health and safety concerns of their workplace but also that the workers are part of the solution.

The MOL will enter any Ontario business facility at any time without notice. Once on the premises, the MOL representative will ask to speak with the Health and Safety Management Representative as well as the JHSC Co-Chair Worker Representative. In accordance to the OHSA, Section 9, the size of the company will determine the existence and size of the Joint Health and Safety Committee (JHSC).

The company has to comply with all the requests of the MOL inspector. The inspector may request to review such evidence as JHSC meeting minutes, incident reports, the WSIB reports, training records, etc. The MOL will request this documentation as proof that the company has a functioning IRS (Internal Responsibility System) and monitor compliance to OHSA. Failure to comply with the requests of the MOL will result in written orders, fines, penalties, and can go as far as litigation.

It is very important to document all policies, procedures, meeting minutes, training content, training requirements, training certifications, training attendance, communications, postings, etc. Documentation is the strongest evidence for any company to prove attempts at compliance.

Monitoring the results of all training as well as monitoring the application of all training will also provide evidence to the MOL that the company is supporting compliance to the law. Written documentation is always more credible in any legal proceedings compared to reliance on memory.

Evidence of a functioning and effective IRS can be determined by a number of methods including, but not limited to:

- JHSC
- JHSC meeting minutes
- Incident reports
- Interviews with the JHSC
- Interviews with workers regarding the health and safety program and the JHSC
- Minutes from any problem solving meetings including workers (non-management personnel)
- Training records
- New hire orientations
- Health and safety policy
- Risk assessments
- Risk evaluations
- Pre-Start Health and Safety Review (PHSRs)
- Certifications and licenses (ie: forklift operation, skilled trades, etc.)
- WHMIS
- Records of communications regarding health and safety concerns
- Records of management responses to health and safety concerns

When interacting with the MOL, it is important to remain calm, confident and cooperative. The MOL will ask questions regarding what they want to know. The company Representative should be honest, forthright, and informative. Keep the answers concise, simple and relevant to the point. The MOL has a right to get these copies without a subpoena according to the Occupational Health and Safety Act of Ontario.

Sometimes, the MOL will request a tour or to see a specific location in the building. Should the MOL spot a worker violating any part of the OHSA, the company, the Supervisor and/or the worker may be fined depending on the training records available and the violation. For example, a lift truck operator may not be wearing a seat belt while operating the forklift. The MOL may fine the operator $300 on the spot for not wearing the seat belt. The Supervisor may also be fined unless the company can produce training records and discipline records supporting that the operator ought to have known that wearing the seat belt was required.

The documentation will be evidence that the supervisor coached, trained, and disciplined the operator regarding wearing the seat belt. Without this documented evidence, the Supervisor will likely be fined for not enforcing the OHSA. The MOL may fine Executives of the company for allowing this to happen in the facility.

It is important to understand the power and influence the MOL has on developing a sound disability management program. The MOL enforces the compliance of OHSA. Therefore the MOL shapes or influences the company's health and safety program. The health and safety program is the foundation of the disability management program.

OHSA including any Canadian Standards Association (CSA) guidelines viewed by the MOL as enforceable, will shape the development of the best practices of a health and safety program resulting in influencing the development of the best practices in disability management program. A sound health and safety program is heavily interdependent on a sound disability management program.

Injury prevention is the main focus of a sound health and safety program. Best practices in disability management can facilitate the understanding of the nature of the injuries. This understanding will assist in the implementation of corrective actions through the root cause analysis process. The MOL will ask questions on both the company's commitment to health and safety through policies and procedures as well as how the company responds to injuries through their disability management program.

SECTION I

UNDERSTANDING INJURIES

Objectives:

After reviewing this chapter, the reader should be able to understand and explain the following concepts:

1. Define an injury;
2. Understand different types of injuries;
3. Define a critical injury as defined by Occupational Health and Safety Act of Ontario;
4. Understanding the role of the Ministry of Labour in Ontario with respect to critical injuries;
5. Describe and contrast disease, illness, and disability;
6. Explain and contrast short term and long term disability; and,
7. Distinguish between impairment and permanent impairment.

CHAPTER 1
INJURY

There are many different types of injuries. To understand the types of injuries, the definition of an injury must first be discussed. According to Wikipedia, an injury is:

> ... damage or harm caused to the structure or function of the body caused by an outside agent or force, which may be physical or chemical, and either by accident or intentional. (Wikipedia, 2009)

For the purposes of this book, an injury is simply defined as the damage or harm done to any part of the human body whether accidentally or intentionally. The damage or harm can be in many forms such as physical trauma or illness, emotional or psychological trauma, disease, etc. The illness can be viral, bacteria, chemical, or a result of a genetic defect. Illness and disease will be further discussed in the next chapter.

Injuries can be intentional or accidental. An intentional act of harm to another person or to one self, is as it implies, the offender has intended or purposefully inflicted harm on the victim. However, the general understanding of an accidental injury is an injury that is caused from an act which had no intention to cause harm or the injury. The accidental injury is an injury that is an unexpected by-product of an act to accomplish another goal.

Most disability insurance programs make distinctions between accidental and intentional injuries. Private disability or life insurance programs will generally exclude the intentional self-inflicted act of harm such as suicide.

Other forms of deliberate harm and damage may also not be covered depending on the event. The law in Canada and in the United States, indeed, in most developed countries have provisions addressing deliberate or intentional acts of violence on another as a criminal offence or in the very least, a case for damages to be awarded under the civil court system. For further discussion on the legal impact on intentional violence, one should consult a lawyer.

Personal injury also known as non-occupational injury is an injury sustained as a result of personal activities or activities outside of the normal course of employment or work. Short term and long term disability insurance programs address wage replacement for non-occupational injuries usually with the exception of suicide or attempted suicide. In Canada, Canadian Pension Plan (CPP) is also a wage replacement program for people who experience permanent disability so severe that the disability prohibits the person from working.

According to the Workplace Safety and Insurance Act (WSIA) of Ontario, a workplace injury is an injury that happens as a result of a workplace accident. The WSIA (Section 2(1), defines an accident as:

> ...(a) a wilful and intentional act, not being the
> act of the worker,
> (b) a chance event occasioned by a physical or
> natural cause, and
> (c) disablement arising out of and in the course
> of employment; ("accident") (WSIA, 1997)

A workplace injury is defined as an injury that occurs out of the course of employment. Interestingly, the Workplace Safety and Insurance Act (WSIA) does not make a distinction between intentional act or unintentional act. The employer is expected to sort that distinction out and act in accordance with pieces of relevant legislation such as the Occupational Health and Safety Act of Ontario, the Human Rights Code of Canada and of Ontario, the Criminal Code of Canada and of Ontario, the Violence and Harassment in the Workplace amendment to the OHSA of Ontario (Bill 168), etc.

Preventing workplace injuries is one of the most important responsibilities of the employer. However, despite the most effective prevention program, injuries still may occur at the workplace. Workplace injuries can range in severity. They can be as simple as a minor cut to the finger from cutting a box open, to as severe as a fatality from a forklift hitting a pedestrian. The Occupational Health and Safety Act of Ontario (OHSA) and the Workplace Safety and Insurance Act (WSIA) will assist the employer in understanding their role and responsibilities in the workplace injury reporting system. .

The severity of the injury will dictate to the employer the required course of action. Injuries that do not require medical attention should be reviewed by the employer's Internal Responsibility System (IRS) to plan corrective action activities. The course of action required for those injuries that require medical attention will be dictated by the Workplace Safety and Insurance Act of Ontario (WSIA). Should the injury be so severe that the injury falls under the classification of a critical injury, in addition to the requirements of the WSIA, the employer will have additional responsibilities as dictated under the Occupational Health and Safety Act of Ontario (OHSA).

Critical Injury
Under the OHSA of Ontario, a critical injury is an injury that is life threatening. Consistent with the Occupational Health and Safety Act (OHSA), Regulation 834, a company has 48 hours (Section 51(1)) to report a critical injury to the Ministry of Labour (MOL) in addition to the WSIB. The MOL considers an injury to be critical if the injury is classified as one of the following:

> ...A "critical injury" is an injury of a serious nature that,
> (a) Places life in jeopardy,
> (b) produces unconsciousness,
> (c) Results in substantial loss of blood
> (d) involves the fracture of a leg or arm but not a finger or toe,
> (e) involves the amputation of a leg, arm, hand or foot but not a finger or toe,
> (f) Consists of burns to a major portion of the body, or
> (g) Causes the loss of sight in an eye.
> (OHSA, 2009)

In addition to reporting the injury to the MOL, the employer has to investigate the incident causing the injury and develop a corrective action plan to prevent future occurrences. The investigation should include pictures, witness statements, facts, etc. Furthermore, the MOL will require the accident scene to be secured and preserved until an inspector is able to personally inspect the incident. Usually, with a critical injury the MOL will write orders, The MOL will also issue fines and penalties to the employer for violating the OHSA of Ontario. For more on this topic, the chapter on incident reporting and responsibilities will discuss this in more detail.

Critical injuries are only one type of workplace injuries. In personal injuries, critical injuries can occur but the classification of critical is dependent on the diagnosis or prognosis from the medical professional assessing the injury. In addition to calling for professional medical attention for the injured party, if the injured party is not related to the owner of the property where the injury occurs, the property owner should discuss the injury with their property insurance carrier immediately in case there is some legal action taken against the property owner as a result of the injury. Please consult a lawyer for further responsibilities.

As an employer of a worker who suffered an injury outside of work activity, the employer may have a wage replacement insurance program for the worker to assist the worker financially while the injured worker is unable to work. However, in Ontario, an employer is not required by law to provide short term or long term insurance benefits for their workers. Sometimes, this benefit is negotiated between the employer and the workers. For those workers who do not have access to short or long term wage replacement insurance coverage, the Employment Insurance (Sick) program in Canada may provide some benefits.

CHAPTER 2
DISEASE

Generally, illness or disease is harm to the body that comes from infection, genetic mutation, mental health disorders, etc. Disease is defined as:

> ...medical condition is an abnormal condition of an organism that impairs bodily functions, associated with specific symptoms and signs... is often used more broadly to refer to any condition that causes pain, dysfunction, distress, social problems, and/or death to the person afflicted, or similar problems for those in contact with the person. In this broader sense, it sometimes includes injuries, disabilities, disorders, syndromes, infections, isolated symptoms, deviant behaviours, and atypical variations of structure and function, while in other contexts and for other purposes these may be considered distinguishable categories. (Wikipedia, 2009)

Some types of illness can be detected through objective medical evidence but other types may only be discernable through subjective medical evaluation or assessment. Therefore, medical evidence, documentation of treatment and medical follow up become critical elements in managing the recovery of the illness.

Similar to an injury, illness or disease can be a result of an occupational or non-occupational event. Occupational disease results out of the course of employment. Specifically, disease is defined in the Workplace Safety and Insurance Act (WSIA) as:

> ...(a) a disease resulting from exposure to a substance relating to a particular process, trade or occupation in an industry,
> (b) a disease peculiar to or characteristic of a particular industrial process, trade or occupation,
> (c) a medical condition that in the opinion of the Board requires a worker to be removed either temporarily or permanently from exposure to a substance because the condition may be a precursor to an occupational disease,
> (d) a disease mentioned in Schedule 3 or 4, or
> (e) a disease prescribed under clause 15.1 (8) (d);
> ("maladie professionnelle") (WSIA, 1997)

An example of an occupational disease is occupational asthma. Occupational asthma can develop as a result of working with or exposure to chemicals in the workplace. These chemicals damage the worker's lungs resulting in asthma or other respiratory illnesses. Such chemicals can include asbestos, mining dust, insulation dust, drywall dust, etc. Appropriate personal protective equipment can protect the worker handling these chemicals from developing such illness.

Another example of occupational illness is the person who develops lung cancer after many years of working in a smoke filled environment. Waiters and waitresses are examples of occupations which were constantly exposed to smoke filled workplaces before the smoke free workplace bylaws in Ontario were enforced in between 2003 and 2005 in south western Ontario. Since that time, many municipalities and provinces in Canada as well as states in the USA have enacted smoke free workplace policies.

The main distinction between a traumatic physical injury and a disease, especially as it relates to the workplace, is that generally the injury is an immediate result of an event whereas a disease can take many years to develop before symptoms lead medical professionals to a diagnosis. Disease typically experiences a longer latency period or a period of time that it takes for the disease to incubate or develop into any or full symptoms.

Even though it is usually disease or illness that have long latency periods, there are some traumatic physical injuries that occur over a long period of time rather than immediately. Injuries that are the result of repetitive strain can also take a long period of time before symptoms gradually develop to the point of disability. Repetitive strain These injuries arise out of the overuse of on injuries include carpal tunnel syndrome, DeQuervain's syndrome, stenosing teno-synovitis or trigger finger, gamers thumb, intersection syndrome, Golfer's elbow (medial epicondylosis), Tennis elbow (lateral epicon-dylosis), focal dystonia etc. These injuries all arise out of the over-use of one muscle or a set of muscles in repeated patterns in relative-ly short cycles of time.

Occupational disease happens out of the course of employment whereas non-occupational disease is not a result of employment ac-tivities. Non-occupational disease develops in a person's personal life. It can be a result of genetics or family history, exposure to toxic environments that are not related to work, accidents (including mo-tor vehicle, home, outside of home but not at work, etc.), etc.

The results of any accident may be the same for the person ex-periencing the injury despite the injury's link to the workplace. The injury could cause the person anything from mild discomfort to to-tally disabling challenges. The difference between occupational and non-occupational drives the difference between which insurance program or carrier will address the wage replacement and medical costs for the injury.

In Ontario, wage loss and medical expenses for occupational disease or injury is addressed through the worker's compensation program regulated by the Workplace Safety and Insurance Act. The costs of the WSIA coverage are funded by the employer.

The costs for non-occupational disease or injury is addressed by private short term or long term disability insurance programs de-pending on the severity of the disablement, the length of time of recovery, and the coverage the person may have access to. In Ontar-io, in addition to the sick and accident benefits through the employ-er's benefits program, a person has access to benefits through such government sponsored programs as Ontario Health Insurance Pro-gram (OHIP), Canada Pension Plan (CPP), Employment Insurance (Sick), etc.

The employers of some workplaces in Ontario will pay for the sick and accident benefits costs or premiums. However, not all employers pay for the premiums of such programs. Sometimes, the worker pays for the premiums for coverage of sick and accident benefits. Yet there are still other workplaces where the program premiums are shared by both the employer and the worker. The responsibility for payment of premiums for these programs is usually stipulated in the terms of the employment contract or collective agreement of the workplace.

For the coverage sponsored by the governments of Ontario and Canada, excepting the WSIA and the Employment Insurance, the costs are paid by the taxpayers. THE WSIA premiums are paid by the employer alone. The Employment Insurance premiums are paid in combination of the employer and the worker through payroll deductions.

Illness

It is common for disease and illness to be used interchangeably. The WSIA defines occupational disease, however, the Occupational Health and Safety Act of Ontario (OHSA) defines occupational illness. Similar to the definition of occupational disease, occupational illness is:

> ...a condition that results from exposure in a workplace to a physical, chemical or biological agent to the extent that the normal physiological mechanisms are affected and the health of the worker is impaired thereby and includes an occupational disease for which a worker is entitled to benefits under the Workplace Safety and Insurance Act, 1997; ("maladie professionnelle") (OHSA, 2009)

Illness like disease can be a result of exposure from either occupational risks or non-occupational risks. Similarly, the wage replacement and medical costs for the illness will depend on the origin of the illness. In Ontario, if the illness is a result of the course of employment, the costs will be addressed by the worker's compensation insurance program regulated under the WSIA.

Whereas, if the illness is a result of non-occupational exposure, the expenses will be addressed by a combination of private benefits insurance coverage like Green Shield and government sponsored programs like OHIP, etc.

There is a difference between disease and illness however, for the purposes of this discussion, illness and disease will be used interchangeably.

Disability

Disability is the umbrella that encompasses the impacts of injuries, disease, and illness both occupational and non-occupational on people, employers, and society. In general, disability is the resulting limitation(s) of any injury, disease, or illness. Wikipedia defines disability as:

> ... impairments, activity limitations, and participation restrictions. An impairment is a problem in body function or structure; an activity limitation is a difficulty encountered by an individual in executing a task or action; while a participation restriction is a problem experienced by an individual in involvement in life situations. Thus disability is a complex phenomenon, reflecting an interaction between features of a person's body and features of the society in which he or she lives... Such impairments may include physical, sensory, and cognitive or intellectual impairments. Mental disorders (also known as psychiatric or psychosocial disability) and various types of chronic disease may also be considered qualifying disabilities.
> (Wikipedia, 2009)

Disability can result in challenges in performing tasks that were easily performed prior to the injury or illness. Sometimes these challenges will be temporary and sometimes these challenges will require the injured person to make long term changes in their lifestyle including the person's career. For instance, a minor cut on the finger resulting in stitches will involve short term challenges. The person may be instructed to avoid washing dishes for a week to ten (10) days until the stitches are removed to prevent infection. This challenge is very short lived as the injury has a ten (10) day recovery period. However, a person who experiences an amputation of a hand in a stamping press accident will have to make more long term adjustments due to the greater challenges for the person.

Even when an injury heals, the person may not be able to perform tasks in the same manner that they were performed prior to the injury. In other words, the person would have to develop or find alternative ways to perform the most simple of tasks like cutting meat at dinner. In these cases, even though the healing time of the physical wound is temporary, the recovery period is extended beyond the physical healing time as the recovery period will include rehabilitation of the not only the physical but also the psychological and emotional elements. Home and workplace accommodations are included in the rehabilitation of the injured person.

CHAPTER 3
PERIODS OF TIME

In life, there is an old adage that states timing means everything. In reference to injuries, disability and recovery, timing is very critical to the outcome of the injury. It is widely believed that the longer a person takes to recover from an injury, the harder it is for the person to return to life as it was prior to the injury.

This theory would imply that a shorter recovery time, would appear to support an easier transition for the worker to return to the pre-injury way of life. Similarly, the longer the recovery or the longer term the challenges to the recovery, the more difficult for the worker to return to the pre-injury status. Therefore there is a proportional correlation between the length of time of a recovery and positive outlook and return to the pre-injury way of life.

Short term
Injuries, restrictions, and recovery have standard periods of time for each injury or illness. Commonly, there are two (2) distinct time frames of disability to review: short term and long term. Short term refers to a brief period of time. In the recovery process, short term is a transitory period of time for a person to recover from the injury. Short term implies that the circumstance or situation is temporary. In general, short term usually refers to a period of time from hours to about one (1) year. If the person does not recover within the short period of a time between a few hours and one year, then the person's recovery will be considered long term.

For injuries to be short term, not only does the physical healing have to be within fifty-two (52) weeks, the emotional and psychological healing has to be within fifty-two (52) weeks as well. A person who experiences a minor cut on the finger is likely to have a short term recovery period. If the cut only requires a band aid and anti-bacterial ointment, then the recovery period would likely be short term at a few days. If the cut required stitches, then it is still likely to be short term but the recovery would be about ten (10) days to four (4) weeks depending on the severity of the cut and the amount of stitches required to close the wound. However, if the cut results in an amputation of the finger regardless if it is due to the severity of the cut or if complications like an infection, the challenges or restrictions will likely be permanent and the recovery period known as long term.

With minor injuries like the cut healing within ten (10) days, the emotional and psychological healing time is likely proportional to the physical healing time. This means that the person scarcely is emotionally or psychologically negatively affected by the injury. Therefore, the return to the pre-injury lifestyle does not present any challenges. The person's life returns to "normal" after the injury heals.

Sometimes the aftermath of a minor injury can become disproportional to the injury. If a person experiences a cut at the same time as like witnessing the death of another person, the physical injury or cut, no matter how minor, could result into some psychological complications. These complications can lead even the most minor injuries into a long term recovery position. The recovery period is not just about healing the physical wound but also about the healing of the psychological wound from the memory of watching another person die.

Long term
In contrast to short term, long term involves a longer period of time. Long term is as it implies, a period of time that extends beyond short term and, possibly, lasting indefinitely. Generally, long term ranges from starting after six (6) months to fifty two (52) week period which is known as the short term period.

In contrast to short term, long term may not have an end date as some injuries result in permanent restrictions and impairment. For instance, an amputation of any part of the body will result in permanent impairment and permanent restrictions. Even though the actual physical healing from the amputation is short, the recovery will be long term due to the consequence of the loss of limb. The permanent impairment will change the person's life forever. In this case, the length of time of the recovery becomes dependent on the injured party as well as the medical professionals treating the injured party including doctors, therapists – physical and emotional, and network of people working with the injured party to establish a new life of productivity and fulfillment.

Rehabilitation in long term recovery periods can become very complicated depending on the injured party. If the injured party has a positive attitude and a strong will to accomplish goals accompanied by a supportive network of professionals and personal relationships, the person can achieve many things in a short period of time. Generally, the medical professional or wage replacement insurance carrier will determine the length of time appropriate for healing and rehabilitation, usually dictated by the standard recovery period and/or the objective medical evidence, both physically and psychologically.

At some point in the long term recovery period, the medical professional will determine if the consequence of the injury has resulted in any type of impairment. Short term impairment is temporary but long term impairment could become permanent.

CHAPTER 4
IMPAIRMENT

Regardless of the cause of the injury, each injury has the potential for impairment. Impairment is the degree of difficulty in performing a task, usually physically, due to the barriers or challenges resulting from an injury. In other words, a person with an impairment cannot perform a task the same way as the person was able to perform because the result of an injury has made it too difficult. The WSIA defines impairment as:

> ...a physical or functional abnormality or loss (including disfigurement) which results from an injury and any psychological damage arising from the abnormality or loss; ("déficience") (WSIA, 1997)

An impairment could result from even the most minor of injuries. For example, a worker requiring stitches from a cut to the hand could experience an impairment. The stitches to close the cut would make it difficult for the worker to move the hand in a certain manner. Certain motions may cause the stitches to reopen. Even this minor wound can have long term effects. The wound may heal but the severity of the injury might be more involved than just the cut requiring stitches. The worker may continue to experience difficulty in moving the hand or fingers because of scar tissue or some permanent damage to the tendon or ligament in the hand.

Permanent Impairment

Impairment can be of a short term or a long term duration. Short term impairment is addressed by temporary restrictions or accommodation requirements giving the worker time to recover before returning to regular duties. Long term impairment is addressed by permanent restrictions. Long term impairment results from an injury that will not fully heal or the worker will not fully recover to their pre-injury status as a result of the injury. Permanent impairment occurs when the difficulty continues to exist after the injury should have healed.

The WSIA defines permanent impairment as: *"... (an) impairment that continues to exist after the worker reaches maximum medical recovery; ("déficience permanente")"(WSIA, 1997)*. An example, a worker who experiences an amputation of the left hand in a steel stamping press will have permanent impairment. This permanent impairment will result in permanent restrictions like avoiding tasks that would involve use of the left hand or use of two hands.

Carpal tunnel syndrome (CTS) is a common injury in the manufacturing industry or fish cutting industry resulting in permanent impairment. CTS usually develops as a result of performing tasks involving repetitive bending and twisting motions with high frequency and/or force. Even though the worker elects to have CTS release surgery to improve functionality, the surgery may only produce marginal success. Consequently, the lack of function represents a level of permanent impairment. The permanent impairment will result in permanent restrictions for the worker. The company must review these permanent restrictions for accommodation.

At some point in the recovery process, the medical professional, usually the family physician or specialist will "declare" the injured worker as having permanent impairment because of the injury. In the workers compensation program in Ontario, the medical documentation supporting a permanent impairment triggers the WSIB Adjudicator to make decisions on a Non-economic Loss Assessment (NEL) award for the degree of impairment. Once a NEL award has been determined, the adjudicator will also assess the worker for eligibility for the Labour Market Re-entry Program (LMR) if the worker continues to be off work.

Usually, a permanent impairment is only declared when the worker still has restrictions that have not resolved beyond the standard recovery period. At this point, the benefits carrier may decide to assess the worker's likelihood of returning to their own occupation.

The adjudicator will need to determine if the worker can return to their pre-injury occupation or if the worker meets the criteria to participate in a retraining program.

Permanent impairment can be determined from injuries that are either of occupational or non-occupational origin. Similar to the workplace injuries, permanent impairment from non-occupationally related injuries must be determined by a medical professional after the standard recovery period has been exhausted. It is very common for medical professionals to determine a permanent impairment after the recovery of a surgical intervention to address a complication to the injury.

Regardless if the permanent impairment is a result of an occupational injury or non-occupational injury, an employer has the duty to accommodate to the point of undue hardship. The company is legally obligated to review all the jobs in the facility to assess if the work is within the restrictions of the worker. The employer is required to develop a return to work and/or a work hardening plan for long term, value added, suitable and sustainable placement for the worker. The employer's obligations under the duty to accommodate, is discussed in further detail later in this book.

Permanent impairment is important to monitor the historical injury pattern of the worker. Permanent impairment is critical to establish a link from a historical injury or pre-existing medical condition. This may allow the employer to request the benefits carrier to reopen an old claim through amalgamation.

In Ontario, the workers compensation program allows the employer to request cost relief (discounts for the claims costs) through the secondary injury enhancement fund (SIEF) if the employer can provide medical evidence that the worker had a pre-existing medical condition pre-disposing the worker to the injury. Therefore permanent impairment can be a tool to support cost strategies in claims management best practices.

For those injured parties that remain totally disabled after permanent impairment has been determined, it is unlikely the worker will be able to return to work despite the company's obligations of re-employment or duty to accommodate. The medical professionals will be key resources in determining the worker's level of capacity or total disability. Should the worker remain totally disabled, there are programs like retraining for a different career path.

Assessment for retraining will depend on the type of benefits the worker is receiving. In Ontario, if the permanent impairment is the result of a workplace injury, the WSIB claims adjudicator will review the case to determine if the worker satisfied the criteria for participating in labour market retraining. If the worker does not qualify for the labour market re-entry program, the adjudicator will assess the file for ongoing benefits to the age of 65 years old depending on the severity of the permanent impairment and the degree of total disability.

In Canada, if the injury is not related to the workplace, permanent impairment leading to ongoing total disability will likely be addressed by such long term disability programs as the Canada Pension Plan – the Disability Program (CPP). Please refer to Canadian government website www.rhdcc-hrsdc.gc.ca to review availability of various programs.

SUMMARY

Disability drives many changes in one's lifestyle and one's working life. If the disability is of a short duration then the restrictions and challenges should be temporary. If the disability is long term, then the restrictions and the challenges can be permanent. The nature of the disability and the level of impairment will determine the amount of changes, the degree of change, the length of time of change and the transition period for the injured person.

Restrictions resulting from a disability will encourage change in the way a person performs activities both in home life and in work life. For example, a person with stitches on their finger will avoid washing dishes or wear rubber gloves until the stitches are removed and the wound is healed. However, if someone has had a stroke paralyzing the right side of their body, the person may have to learn how to write with the left hand in order to write a letter.

All aspects of the healing process with an injury are important to the total recovery of the person and the injury. Early medical intervention becomes critical in returning to the pre-injury status in a timely manner. A positive outlook and continuing to be productive in life also play critical roles in the total recovery process. As such, the boundaries between perception and reality become blurred. Objective medical evidence will determine the physical extent of the injury but the mental health of the injured party will also have a significant impact on the rate of recovery as well as the quality of the recovery.

Key Terms:

Accident	Critical Injury
Disability	Disease
Illness	Impairment
Injury	Long Term
Permanent Impairment	Short Term
Total Disability	

Questions:

1. Discuss the difference between the three types of injuries.
2. Discuss the difference between short term and long term.
3. Discuss the impact of permanent impairment.
4. Discuss the significance of critical injuries.

UNDERSTANDING DIFFERENCE BETWEEN OCCUPATIONAL AND NON-OCCUPATIONAL INJURIES

Objectives:

After reviewing this chapter, the reader should be able to understand and explain the following concepts:

1. The difference between work related injuries and non-occupational injuries;
2. The differences between Short Term Disability (STD), Long Term Disability (LTD), Canadian Pension Plan (CPP), Sick leave, Sick Employment Insurance;
3. The wage replacement insurance programs such as worker's compensation;
4. Define the term "worker";
5. Define the term "employer";
6. Define the term "independent operator";
7. Compare and contrast the concepts of Independent operator vs. employer as it relates to the WSIA in Ontario; and,
8. Compare and contrast the concepts of Independent operator vs. Employee as it relates to the WSIA in Ontario.

CHAPTER 5
TYPES OF INJURIES

Not work related

Injuries, disease and illness can be separated into two categories: work related and not work related. Work related injuries, disease and illness are those that occur out of the person's course of employment. Whereas, not work related injuries, disease and illness are those that occur in one's personal life outside of work. An example of not work related injury would be the broken leg from a person falling off a ladder while retrieving a ball from the roof of the house. High cholesterol is another example of not work related disease since it is genetic in nature and related to personal choices in nutrition and lifestyle.

A work related injury would result from an injury experienced out of the course of employment. In the above example of the broken leg, the injury would be considered work related if the worker fell off the ladder while performing a work related task like changing a light bulb in the office.

Workplace injury claims have been made linking the smoke filled workplace environments. Some forms of lung cancer may be attributed to exposure to chemicals at work. A person diagnosed with lung cancer but who never smoked and has no genetic history of lung cancer could be a work related illness if the person was exposed to a smoke filled environments during work like a waitress in a restaurant (before the no smoking bylaws of Ontario were implemented).

Other workplace injury claims have included respiratory ailments like asbestos poisoning. Asbestos poisoning can result in lung cancer or emphysema. The poisoning is a result of prolonged exposure to asbestos insulation. This exposure was common in occupations in such industries as construction or deconstruction from the 1960s to the 1990s.

Regardless of the category of injury, disease or illness, each diagnosis requires a period of time for recovery. Even though each person recovers at a different pace, each injury, disease or illness follows similar patterns during recovery. These patterns have allowed medical professionals to establish standard recovery expectations as well as prescribed courses of treatment both in terms of medication and therapies for each injury.

The challenges the injured person experiences during recovery may impact the person's ability to work. Injured workers who continue to work during recovery, tend to be more productive and experience speedier recoveries. Therefore, legislation and best practices in claims management encourages employers to accommodate the workers at work during the recovery period.

Lost time from work will occur when the worker cannot be accommodated due to incompatible restrictions or the results of the injury are so severe that the worker is incapable of working. When lost time occurs, the worker will require financial support during this period of time to replace any lost wages. For lost time due to not work related injuries, disease or illness, there are benefits programs and wage replacement insurance programs. Whereas work related injuries, diseases or illnesses coverage for medical expenses or lost time replacement are handled by a workers' compensation insurance program.

Geographical locations of residence and work will dictate the legal requirements for employers in providing various benefits to workers for both work related and not work related insurance coverage. Further exploration of these types of benefits will be covered in later chapters.

Workplace Injuries
As previously stated, a workplace injury is an injury that occurs within the course of employment. There is a wage replacement insurance program for workplace injuries usually known as workers compensation benefits. In Ontario, workplace injuries are regulated by the Workplace Safety and Insurance Act (WSIA). The WSIA outlines the criteria for receiving benefits.

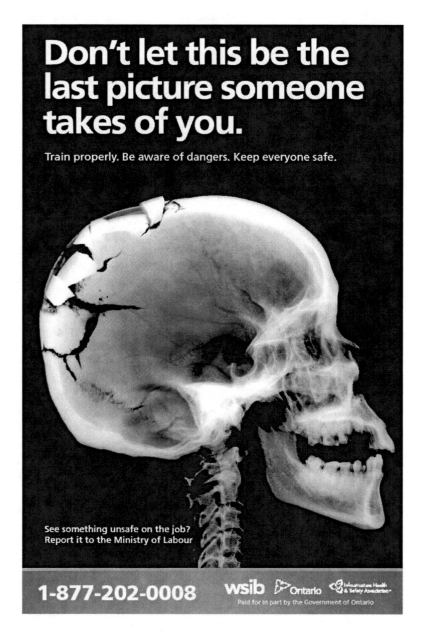

This poster was retrieved from:
http://www.labour.gov.on.ca/english/hs/sawo/pubs/poster_construction.
php

The WSIA defines a workplace injury as an injury that arises out of the course of employment. Specifically, the WSIA defines an accident as:

> ...(a) a wilful and intentional act, not being the act of the worker,
> (b) a chance event occasioned by a physical or natural cause, and
> (c) disablement arising out of and in the course of employment; ("accident") (WSIA, 1997)

In the course of employment is a task performed as assigned by a supervisor or a manager. The task is specific to work. Therefore, a workplace injury would be an injury that results from a worker performing a task as assigned by a supervisor or a manager.

Workplace injuries can be as minor as a small superficial cut to as severe as a fatality. For example, a workplace injury like a broken leg can result from a worker tripping over a box on the floor by a workstation. Another example of a work place injury would be when a worker cuts their hand on the edge of the work table and requires stitches.

More examples of workplace injuries can include a fatality from a forklift impaling a pedestrian or a gradual onset of pain such as carpal tunnel syndrome. Gradual onset of pain is produced by repetitive strain type injuries. Repetitive strain injuries are very common in workplaces where workers perform repetitive tasks with high frequency, force and repetition.

In addition to injuries arising out of sudden events or gradually occurring over time, the workplace can also be responsible and financially liable under the Workplace Safety and Insurance Act, for disease that arises out of the course of employment. Similar to the repetitive strain type injury, occupational disease usually occurs over a prolonged period of exposure to a toxic substance or chemical. The WSIA defines occupational disease as:

> ... (a) a disease resulting from exposure to a substance relating to a particular process, trade or occupation in an industry,
> (b) a disease peculiar to or characteristic of a particular industrial process, trade or occupation,

(c) a medical condition that in the opinion of
the Board requires a worker to be removed either temporarily or permanently from exposure
to a substance because the condition may be a
precursor to an occupational disease,
(d) a disease mentioned in Schedule 3 or 4, or
(e) a disease prescribed under clause 15.1 (8) (d);
("maladie professionnelle"). (WSIA, 1997)

An occupational disease is usually diagnosed long after the exposure to the toxic substance or chemical. An example of an occupational disease is occupational asthma. Occupational asthma occurs
as a result of prolonged and repeated exposure to a chemical causing
irreparable damage to the inside lining of the worker's lungs. Consequently, this damage leads to difficulty in breathing or and decreased
oxygen flow through the body. Usually the damage is permanent.

A second example of occupational diseases involves asbestos
poisoning from prolonged exposure to asbestos. Asbestos is commonly found in insulation products produced prior to the 1970s.
Usually, it is the construction or the deconstruction worker who
handled asbestos insulation without wearing the proper personal
protective equipment that is most likely to be diagnosed with asbestos poisoning. Asbestos poisoning can lead to such respiratory disease as lung cancer or emphysema.

In addition to asbestos poisoning, certain forms of lung cancer
have been determined as work related because the worker experienced prolonged exposure to cigarette smoke during work. Waitresses or waiters are typical occupations that experience this type of
workplace disease.

Exposure to chemicals as work or handling chemicals at work
without wearing the proper personal protective equipment can lead
to several different types of workplace disease. Certain forms of leu-
kemia resulting from repeated exposure to chemicals found in de-
greasers, paint, parts washing fluid, paint thinner, etc. at work have
been determined as work related injuries.

The occupationally related injuries and illnesses in Ontario are
governed by the Workplace Safety and Insurance Act (WSIA) and to
some degree by the Occupational Health and Safety Act of Ontario
(OHSA). The Workplace Safety and Insurance Board (WSIB) administer and manage claims for workplace related injuries and illnesses.

Depending on the severity of the injury at the workplace, the employer may be required to notify other government agencies such as the Ministry of Labour (MOL) for a critical injury or fatality, the police (especially for an injury as a result of an assault), the Ministry of the Environment (MOE) if the injury is the result of an environmental incident like a chemical spill, etc. Legislative requirements under OHSA, the WSIA, Environmental Protection Act (EPA), Employment Standards Act (ESA), Labour Relations Act, Human Rights Code, etc. will dictate who to notify, in the required time frame and the criteria of required notification.

Sudden or Traumatic Injuries

Sudden or traumatic injuries are those injuries that result from a sudden impact or event. For example, the broken arm caused by a slip and fall is a traumatic injury. This type of injury can occur at the workplace or outside the workplace.

Repetitive Strain Injuries (RSIs)

A repetitive strain injury is that which occurs as a result of constant wear and tear of the muscles, joints and tendons. These types of injuries usually occur over a period of time instead of instantaneous. Studies reveal that the causes of these injuries include repeating actions or motions which involve repetition, high frequency, force, weight and or awkward posturing. Carpal tunnel, tendonitis, etc. are examples of repetitive strain injuries. This type of injury can occur at the workplace or outside the workplace however, it is more common to be work related.

Awkward posturing is the joint is at any angle other than the angle of neutral posture. Bending, twisting, stooping, reaching especially if the joint is extended, etc. are all examples of awkward posturing.

Repetition is repeating the same motion over and over again. The degree of repetition will depend on the number of times the motion or activity is repeated over a specific period of time. The joint or muscle will get tired of moving the same way all the time resulting in wear on that joint or musculature if there is no rest period of time permitted between motions or activities. The risk of experiencing a repetitive strain injury is directly proportional to the amount of frequency using that motion. Essentially, the higher the frequency of repeating the pattern of movements, then the higher the risk of a repetitive strain injury. Generally, a motion is considered repetitive if a person repeats an activity or motion more than once in a 30 second time period or has to the same activity more than once more than 50% of the cycle (Silverstein et al., 1986 – Silverstein, B.A., Fine, L.J., Armstrong, T.J., 1986).

Force is the degree of effort used to complete the motion or activity. If the force required to complete the task is high, then the muscles have to bear an amount of work that the muscles may not have the strength to complete especially to repeatedly complete the tasks. For example, pinch forces used to snap clips together with resistance may start to create damage in the tissue of the fingers after a few times depending on the amount of resistance required to secure the snap and the strength of the fingers.

In addition to the risk factors listed above, there is one more risk known as vibration. Vibration is the fast subtle movement of a tool either caused by sound reverberation, energy flow through the tool, etc. The tremoring of a jack hammer or electrical drill are examples of vibration. Exposure to vibrations can damage nerve endings and tissue over time.

A person can reduce the risk of repetitive strain injuries by decreasing the amount of force, weight, number of times of completing a motion. Adding or increasing rest periods between repeating patterns of motions can also assist in the body's ability to recover from potential damage. There are also some personal protective equipment that can be used to reduce the risk of injury such as padding gloves when using vibration tools. Good ergonomic settings like adjusting work stations so that the work being performed is approximately one inch lower than the bent elbow and close to the body can also reduce the risk of injury.

PREVENT WORKPLACE PAINS & STRAINS!

Musculoskeletal Disorders (MSDs), most commonly known as pains and strains, can be serious and disabling to Ontario workers. Preventing MSDs should be a key part of every workplace.

WORK RELATED MSD HAZARDS INCLUDE:

1. Awkward postures
2. Holding any body part in one position without a rest
3. Carrying, lifting, lowering, pushing or pulling heavy or awkward loads
4. Performing repetitive actions without rest

EMPLOYERS SHOULD:

1. Train workers about MSD hazards in their job
2. Ask workers to report MSD symptoms or concerns early
3. Identify job related MSD hazards and work together to implement solutions
4. Follow up to make sure solutions are working

For more information:
www.ontario.ca/SafeAtWorkOntario

wsib ONTARIO Ontario Health & Safety ONTARIO

This poster was retrieved from:
http://www.labour.gov.on.ca/english/hs/pubs/ergonomics/poster_msd.php

44

CHAPTER 6

WAGE REPLACEMENT PROGRAMS

Regardless the category of injury, disease or illness, the results of either may and can cause the person to be away from work during recovery. When lost time occurs, the worker will seek to replace their normal wage with some sort of income in order to support their necessities of living.

In Ontario, insurance programs that address wage replacement during periods of lost time due to injury, disease or illness vary according to the category of the injury. The non-occupationally related injuries and illnesses are generally reviewed by private sector insurance companies such as short term disability, long term disability, auto insurance accident benefits, and other wage replacement protection insurance programs. On the contrary, workplace injuries are addressed by a provincial government branch called the Workplace Safety and Insurance Board (WSIB) who administers the provisions of the Workplace Safety and Insurance Act (WSIA).

Non-occupational injuries and illnesses require the same attention and procedures from employers as occupationally related injuries and illnesses in terms of duty to accommodate as well as financial management. The financial impact of any lost time claim regardless of the injury origin can become quite significant if unmanaged both in terms of premiums as well as lost productivity, morale and retraining costs.

The difference between wage replacement insurance programs and health benefits is that the wage replacement program only addresses the lost wages of the injured person whereas the health benefits will address the medical costs incurred for the injury. Workers may have to negotiate payment of the premiums for each of these coverages separately or as a package with their employer.

Not all employers will pay for the premiums of each or both of these coverages. If the employer does not offer payment for either coverage, the benefit packages can be purchased independently by the worker. It is very common for the employer to have worker compensation insurance coverage. Health care benefits can be purchased by the employer or the employee or both can share the costs depending on the employment contract.

Premiums are generally more reasonable if one purchases the insurance through a group plan rather than individually since group plans have group discounts applied to the premium based. These discounts cannot usually be accessed by each individual independently. Therefore, employers can negotiate special rates for their workers even if the employer is sharing responsibility for premium payment with the employees or if the employee is solely responsible for the payment of premiums.

Similar to other insurance programs like coverage for auto, home and life, the wage replacement insurance program is designed to replace, in whole or in part, or return the subscriber to the state prior to the loss. The biggest difference from other insurance programs to wage replacement insurance programs is that the other insurance programs try to restore the subscriber to whole state prior to the loss, for example, home insurance usually seeks to replace the house and contents after a fire at replacement costs rather than at a depreciated cost.

In contrast, unless the subscriber purchased additional personal wage replacement insurance coverage, the average wage replacement insurance program only restores the wages to a certain percentage of the pre-injury status. For example, for non-occupational injuries, the average wage replacement coverage generally pays between 50% and 66% of the pre-injury wage level depending on the benefit package purchased.

There are some wage replacement insurance plans for non-occupational injuries that pay up to 100% of the wages lost. These are not common packages and usually are privately purchased by the individual. Depending on the underwriting of the insurance policy, the additional coverage may supersede other insurance benefits or top up the other benefits to 100% of the pre-injury wage level.

Some of these wage replacement incomes are taxable benefits for the injured party while others may not be subject to taxes. This will depend on the legal requirements of the geographical area in which the insurance program covers.

Unlike non-occupational wage replacement programs, workers compensation programs have fewer options available for purchase. In Ontario, workplace injury wage replacement coverage is 85% of the net pre-injury wage level whereas in other areas of Canada and the US, this level varies. Also in Ontario, the premiums for workers compensation insurance coverage are the sole responsibility of the employer.

Regardless of the injury or illness, all insurance programs have eligibility requirements. To apply for any benefits, there are a series of specific forms required for all participants to complete. There are usually a minimum of three parties involved including the member (worker), sponsor (employer), and the medical professional(s).

Generally, all insurance programs have common requirements in order for the decision makers to review eligibility of each claim. The policies and guidelines of each program will outline the eligibility criteria by which a claim is considered for approval or denial. These policies and guidelines depend on the policy underwriting or the contract.

When the injuries and illnesses are not occupationally related, the policies and guidelines are outlined in the insurance program contract between the insurance carrier service provider and the customer (claimant). Each contract is dependent on the package purchased as each insurance policy can be custom designed according to the needs, wants and financial planning of the customer.

Wage replacement insurance programs have established criteria of eligibility which are common no matter which category of injury. Some of the most common criteria of eligibility include:

- Experience an injury, disease or illness as diagnosed by a medical professional
- Lose time from work because the medical professional supports total disability

Short Term Disability (STD)

Short term disability (STD) is a wage replacement insurance program that addresses total disability from a non-occupational injury during the acute recovery period. Generally short term covers from thirty

(30) days from the date of injury up to fifty-two (52) weeks from the date of injury. The most common available period of coverage is twenty-six (26) weeks.

Reporting an injury must be done in writing to the insurance carrier. Generally, people have up to ninety (90) days from the date of injury to file their application for benefits in writing. Once the insurance carrier receives the complete application package, including a Physician Statement, the claims adjudicator will review all the information to determine eligibility for benefits.

Benefits are not an automatic entitlement. Just as with other insurance coverage, certain injuries could be disqualified depending on the policy requirements for coverage. For example, injuries experienced as a result of a failed suicide attempt may not be covered under the policy depending on the guidelines of coverage. Therefore, eligibility to receive short term disability benefits is not an automatic one.

The medical documentation has to meet specific criteria of the policy as outlined in the policy underwriting requirements. The most common requirement is total disability. Totals disability is the condition where a person can no longer work or perform normal tasks as a result of challenges or restrictions due to a medical condition or injury.

The medical professional will provide the diagnosis on the Physician Statement. The medical professional will also include details on the injured party's prognosis or the person's course of treatment for optimal recovery. The course of treatment will include any temporary restrictions or challenges describing the person's ability or inability to work. The most important information required is the specific medical documentation outlining the diagnosis supporting the injured person's totally disabled or the person's total inability to work.

The medical professional will complete specific forms to be submitted to the insurance carrier. This medical documentation must support the total disability of the injured party. The coverage of benefits will depend on the length of time of total disability as well as the insurance policy purchased.

Most STD policies include a waiting period where benefits are not paid to the person for wage loss. However, depending on the policy, this waiting period can be waived if certain conditions are met. Some of these conditions include: the person being admitted to the hospital on the first day of lost wages; additional premiums are paid to avoid the waiting period; etc.

Long Term Disability (LTD)

Short term disability addresses temporary recovery periods and temporary restrictions whereas long term disability addresses long term recovery periods and possibly permanent impairment. Long term disability (LTD) is a wage replacement insurance program that addresses total disability beyond the short term disability period up to sixty-five (65) years old depending on the duration of the total disability as supported by objective medical evidence.

Commonly, LTD coverage begins after STD coverage ends. In a few cases, a person may apply for LTD benefits without collecting STD benefits. Therefore, it is very important for the person to complete and submit the application for LTD benefits within one (1) year to eighteen (18) months from the date of injury depending on the LTD policy guidelines regardless of collecting STD benefits. In light of this additional deadline, it is a best practice in due diligence for the employer to send a LTD application package to the worker if the worker remains off work beyond six (6) months or twelve (12) months (depending on the STD benefits program) regardless if the person is collecting STD benefits. If the employer fails to supply the LTD application to the worker within the appropriate time line, the employer may be subject to legal liability because of the omission.

In contrast to occupational injuries, employers are not legislatively mandated to report non-occupational injuries. In Ontario, employers are not mandated to report non-occupational injuries to any government branch because short and long term disability programs are optional benefits that employers may offer to their employees and the cause is non-occupational. Usually short term and long term benefits are benefits either negotiated with workers through a collective agreement in unionized workplaces or negotiated in employment contracts in non-unionized positions. A person may also purchase private insurance coverage for either or both short term and long term benefits outside of employer sponsored benefits.

Canada Pension Plan (CPP) – Disability; Sick Leave; and, Employment Insurance (EI) - Sick

In addition to the private insurance programs available, there is a federally regulated short term disability program in Canada. The

Human Resources Development Canada (HRDC) administers an employment insurance program for sick. This insurance coverage is available for any person who has legally worked in Canada for the prescribed number of weeks in the prescribed time period. Premiums are paid through automatic payroll deduction from the worker as well as a contribution from the employer. This program pays up to fifteen (15) weeks providing the worker has worked a minimum of six hundred (600) hours in the last fifty-two (52) consecutive weeks. Futhermore, there is generally a waiting period that is unpaid. For more details on this program, HRDC has a website www.servicecanada.gc.ca.

Canada also has a basic long term disability benefits program through the Canada Pension Plan (CPP) – Disability Program. This is also a federally regulated benefit with its own set of guidelines and requirements. More details can be found for this program on the Canadian Federal website www.servicecanada.gc.ca.

Workers' Compensation Program

A workers compensation program is an insurance program that replaces or supplements the lost wages and medical expenses of a worker that experiences a workplace injury. A workplace injury is an injury that occurs out of the course of employment. Workers' Compensation programs are essentially an insurance program that protects the employer from being sued and protects the injured worker for wage loss and health benefits throughout the recovery process.

Workers' Compensation insurance programs are different depending on the laws of the land. In the United States of America, each workers' compensation program is regulated by each state's respective legislative body. In Canada, workers' compensation programs are regulated by each provincial regulatory body (government). In Ontario, the workers' compensation program is governed by the Workplace Safety and Insurance Act (WSIA), managed by the Workplace Safety and Insurance Board (WSIB), and enforced by the Ministry of Labour (MOL).

In Ontario, when the claim is occupationally related, the WSIA is specific on: defining workplace injuries; eligibility criteria to receive benefits; how to report workplace juries and illnesses; circumstances of payable benefits; etc. Employer participation in this program is mandated by the provincial government in Ontario.

It is critical to remember that coverage is not automatic in all wage loss replacement programs. Eligibility of each claim depends on information provided by key participants. In the Act, each participant is required to complete specific forms as prescribed by the Act. In any type of wage loss protection insurance program, regardless of the insurance service provider or carrier, there are three (3) key participants from which information flows: the employer sponsor; the attending physician; and the claimant or worker. Each program has their own set of uniquely designed forms which each key participant has to complete and submit.

The employer sponsor will need to submit information regarding the claimant's job, wage rate, and dates losses are incurred, etc. The worker must submit information regarding the details of the series of events that lead to the injury or illness. The attending physician must submit details of the diagnosis, prognosis, and course of treatment. The most significant of the three (3) forms is the physician statement because it supports disability status of the medical condition.

Without any one of these three (s) completed statements, the claim may not be considered for payment. Each carrier has their own set of forms for completion. Essentially the forms request similar information. Some examples of forms for the workers compensation program in Ontario as required by the WSIA include but are not limited to:

- Form 6 (the injured worker's version of events)
- Form 7 (the employer's version of events),
- Form 8 (the attending physician's diagnosis, prognosis, and course of treatment)
- Functional Abilities Form (FAF) – restrictions
- Progress Reports for all 3 participants to complete and submit
- Physical Demands Analysis

The workers compensation program in Ontario is managed by a branch of the provincial government known as the Workplace Safety and Insurance Board (WSIB). Many other countries may choose to administer the program through the private sector as an insurance business or governed by a branch of the government just as Ontario.

In addition to the moral responsibility of the provincial government to protect the workers of Ontario, the WSIA is concerned with the health and safety of workers from a business perspective as well. From the business perspective, the key to reducing costs for this program is to reduce the number of workplace injuries as well as reduce the severity of those injuries. According to the WSIA, the purpose of the workers compensation program in Ontario is:

> ...to accomplish the following in a financially responsible and accountable manner:
> 1. To promote health and safety in workplaces and to prevent and reduce the occurrence of workplace injuries and occupational diseases.
> 2. To facilitate the return to work and recovery of workers who sustain personal injury arising out of and in the course of employment or who suffer from an occupational disease.
> 3. To facilitate the re-entry into the labour market of workers and spouses of deceased workers.
> 4. To provide compensation and other benefits to workers and to the survivors of deceased workers. 1997, c. 16, Sched. A, s. 1; 1999, c. 6, s. 67 (1); 2005, c. 5, s. 73 (1). (WSIA, 1997)

The WSIA is administered and enforced by both the WSIB and the Ministry of Labour (MOL) in Ontario. In order to do business in Ontario, the company has to register with the WSIB. All the employees in Ontario will be covered by this insurance program. Even people who may not be employees of the company but they are on the company's premises in Ontario may have some entitlement to lost wages under workers compensation depending on the situation and the cause of injury. In this event, the company should consult with a lawyer.

Once an injury has been reported to the company as work related, the company has an obligation to report the injury to the worker's compensation insurance program team. In Ontario, the administration team of worker's compensation insurance program is the Workplace Safety and Insurance Board (WSIB). The provincial government through the WSIA outline reporting requirements for companies who experience workplace injuries.

According to the WSIA, Section 21.1, a company has the responsibility to report an injury to the WSIB within three (3) business days of being aware of the injury. The worker has up to 6 months from the time of the injury to claim an injury under the WSIA. An injury is considered reportable to the WSIB if the injury meets the following conditions:

1. the worker seeks medical attention
2. the worker loses time after the date of injury as a result of the injury
3. the worker loses wages as a result of the injury or accommodation for the injury
4. the worker requires accommodation for more than five (5) days(WSIB website under the employer's in formation on "How Do I Report to the WSIB", 2010)

If the company does not report the injury in the prescribed time, than the company can be fined or other penalties could be levied against the company for violating the WSIA. If a company receives a high number of fines or penalties, the WSIB may have the MOL visit the company for an audit of the health and safety program, internal responsibility system and the reporting system. The WSIB may demand the company to undergo a Workwell audit which is a very detailed audit of the system. Failure to comply will result in additional and higher fines and penalties by both the WSIB and the MOL.

The WSIA dictates that the employer must and shall report all workplace injuries that satisfy the conditions discussed above. However, the employee has the option to cancel the claim via written request to the WSIB. The worker must not feel under "duress" by the company to cancel the claim nor should the worker receive any type of bonus or remuneration by the company to cancel the claim.

The company does not have the option to cancel a claim for a workplace injury. In spite of this, the company can object to the claim based on facts that support the injury occurring outside of the workplace or the injury did not occur out of the course of employment. The facts should not be emotionally based but based in evidence. The WSIB claims adjudicator will determine if the injured worker is entitlement to benefits under the worker's compensation program.

The WSIB will receive notification of a workplace injury from the employer through a completed Form 7. Sometimes the WSIB will receive the medical information through a completed Form 8 from the medical professional before receiving the Form 7. The

WSIB will send a letter to the company requesting a Form 7 to be sent immediately.

Before the claims adjudicator can review all the facts, the WSIB will send a letter to the worker requesting a statement from the worker. The worker's statement is called the Form 6. This statement will detail how the injury occurred and what the injury was according to the perspective of the injured worker. In some cases, the WSIB will allow the claim prior to receiving the Form 6 if the company does not protest or object to the claim.

Once the WSIB receives all the statements (from the employer, the medical professional and the worker), the claims adjudicator must review all the information on file to determine if the injury meets all the criteria for eligibility of the wage replacement program. The claims adjudicators consider five (5) key elements related to the eligibility requirements of the incident and the injury. These five (5) key elements are:

1. the employer must be an employer and not an independent operator (unless the independent operator is participating in this program)
2. the worker is determined as a worker and not an employer
3. the workplace is in Ontario or in a place that is covered under the WSIA
4. There is proof that the accident happened at the workplace and out of the course of employment
5. That the injury is compatible with the events that led to the injury and/or compatible with the work the worker was performing.

If any one of these elements is not met, the claims adjudicator may deny the claim. For more details on eligibility criteria under the WSIA, please refer to the WSIA (www.e-laws.gov.on. ca) or the policies of the WSIB for eligibility of claims (www.wsib.on.ca).

One way to reduce the frequency and severity of workplace injuries is to promote the health and safety of the workers in the workplaces in Ontario. The WSIB works closely with the Ministry to Labour to counsel, manage and enforce the health and safety of all workers in Ontario to set health and safety standards for workplaces through the Occupational Health and Safety Act of Ontario

(OHSA). Therefore, the health and safety of all workers are directly linked with the workers compensation program.

In order to operate a business in Ontario, the company need register the business with several branches of the provincial government. One such branch of the Ontario government is the WSIB. The WSIB classifies the business in sectors according to the nature of the business performed in Ontario. These sectors represent a collection of businesses of similar business type forming an industry sector. Industry standards are developed by compiling information from all companies in the industry sector. The WSIB then measures the health and safety performance of a company by comparing a company against the collective performance of health and safety programs of all the companies in their respective industry sector.

There are few businesses that do not have to register with the WSIB. These include but are not limited to:

- Banks, trusts and insurance companies
- Private health care practices (such as those of doctors and chiropractors)
- Trade unions
- Private day cares
- Travel agencies
- Clubs (such as health clubs)
- Photographers
- Barbers, hair salons, and shoe-shine stands
- Taxidermists
- Funeral directing and embalming

Each business operating in Ontario will have a workplace. A workplace is defined as a premise on which a company operates business activities. An employer is an owner operator of a business. In addition to ownership, the employer can be anyone who directs, authorizes, or assigns work to others. According to the WSIA, an employer is defined as:

> ... means every person having in his, her or its service under a contract of service or apprenticeship another person engaged in work in or about an industry and includes,
> (a) a trustee, receiver, liquidator, executor or administrator who carries on an industry,

(b) a person who authorizes or permits a learner to be in or about an industry for the purpose of undergoing training or probationary work, or
(c) a deemed employer; ("employeur")...
(WSIA, 1997)

Therefore, an employer includes an employer representative such as a manager, supervisor, CEO, Board of Directors, etc.

Contractors may also be deemed as employers but they can also be excluded from the definition of employer depending on the status of employees and or insurance coverage. According to the WSIA, Policy 12-02-01, a contractor can be deemed an independent operator which would mean they would not be covered under the company's the WSIB premium coverage since they are independent of the company. The contractor only provides a service for the company and the company does not direct the work of the Contractor other than the scope of the contracted work. The WSIA indicates that an independent operator is:

> ...a person who carries on an industry set out in Schedule 1 or Schedule 2 of the Act and who does not employ any workers for that purpose.
> (WSIA, 1997)

An independent operator does not have any employees. An employee is a worker who performs an assigned task or service for an hourly wage or salary. The WSIA elaborates on this definition. According to Policy 12-02-01 of the WSIB manual, a worker is defined as:

> ... a person who has entered into or is employed under a contract of service, or apprenticeship, written or oral, express or implied, whether by way of manual labour or otherwise, and includes
> a learner or student
> a member of a municipal volunteer fire brigade or a volunteer ambulance brigade
> a person deemed to be a worker of an employer by direction or order of the WSIB

a person summoned to assist in controlling or extinguishing a fire by an authority empowered to do so

a person who assists in any search and rescue operation at the request of and under the direction of a member of the Ontario Provincial Police Force

a person who assists in connection with an emergency that has been declared by the Lieutenant Governor in Council or the Premier under section 7.0.1 of the Emergency Management and Civil Protection Act or by the head of council of a municipality under section 4 of that Act

an auxiliary member of a police force

a person deemed to be a worker under Section 12, or

a pupil deemed to be a worker under the Education Act. (WSIA, 1997)

However, there are some exclusions to the classification of worker which, according to the WSIA, s.11(1), are stated as:

...an outworker (a person to whom articles or materials are given out to be made up, cleaned, washed, altered, ornamented, finished, repaired or adapted for sale in the person's own home)

an executive officer of a corporation

or a person whose employment is of a casual nature and who is employed otherwise than for the purposes of the employer's industry. (WSIA, 1997)

This broad definition of worker includes basically anyone on the premises who is employed by the company. This means that if the person is hurt on the company's premises, the company is responsible and financially liable for the injury. If the injury is related to the person's course of employment, the person would be eligible to apply for worker's compensation. Therefore it is important for company to ensure the safety of all contractors and non-employees have wage loss insurance coverage as independent operators or under their own employer's workers compensation program. Otherwise, the company will have to liability under their own WSIB coverage.

Upon registration with the WSIB, the WSIB assigns an account number and a firm number to each business. For Corporations that may have more than one business unit registered as a business with the WSIB, the WSIB may determine that the Corporation is an "Organization" rather than each being an independent business.

As the business is registered, the business is classified in the type of business that is completed during the course of the business. For example, a business that assembles car parts is classified under manufacturing of the auto industry, rate group 421 whereas a business that is in construction will be classified under a different rate group. Please see the WSIB website for the list of classifications and rate groups of the different businesses in Ontario. Premium base rates are attached to each classification/rate group. Therefore, it is very important that the business is registered under the correct classification/rate group.

Rate groups allow the WSIB to compile data on similar businesses to establish industry standards for similar businesses. These industry standards become critical in benchmarking the performance of a business against what the rest of the other companies in that industry for that type of business are performing at in regards to frequency and severity of workplace injuries. The WSIB uses frequency and severity of workplace injuries as key performance indicators for all businesses in Ontario.

In order to compare small business to larger business, the WSIB has established calculations to "normalize" each company's statistics on the frequency of injuries and the severity of injuries according to the amount of labour hours worked. "Normalizing" the statistics allows equal comparison of each company's performance regardless of the size of each company. Therefore, the small company with 50 people can be compared to another company of 500 people in the same rate group. The comparison calculations become based on the number of non-lost time injuries and lost time injuries per working hour.

The calculations are based on a percentage of the total hours worked rather than the total number of non-lost time injuries or lost time injuries. Frequency is the number of reportable non lost time workplace injuries expressed as a percentage of the total hours worked. The formula for frequency is:

of reportable (non-lost time) injuries X 200,000
total hours worked

Severity is the number of lost time workplace injuries expressed as a percentage of the total hours worked. The formula for severity is:

of lost time injuries x 200,000
Total hours worked

In both of the above calculations, the number of two hundred thousand (200,000) represents one hundred (100) workers working two thousand (2,000) hours each per year. The amount of two thousand (2,000) hours represents the number of hours each person works in one (1) year. Therefore, the calculations average the number of non-lost time injuries or lost time injuries according to the number of average hours worked.

The company pays a monthly premium to the WSIB based on a rate per $100 payroll. The premium rate is dependent on the company's rate group. As discussed the rate group is calculated based on information on the performance of all the companies in that rate group. Generally, the higher the frequency and severity of the rate group, then the premium rate for that rate group rises proportionally.

The WSIB will monitor a company's health and safety performance through the frequency and severity of injuries from that workplace. In addition to the monthly premiums, each company in Ontario can be subject to other payments. The WSIB has several prevention programs that each company can participate in to help determine the experience rating of the respective company. These prevention programs will provide incentive for the company to manage their claim costs efficiently.

The prevention programs, such as experience rating programs, allow the WSIB to further evaluate a company's performance. Each program will review the company's performance differently depending on the program the company participates in. If the company's performance is poor, meaning the frequency and/or severity rates of injuries are high, the company could be subject to additional fines, penalties and surcharges. Alternatively, if the company's performance is exceptionally good, meaning the frequency and severity rates of injuries are low, the company could receive a rebate from the WSIB. These reviews are usually done annually.

In addition to surcharges and rebates, reviewing the company's frequency and severity rates in comparison with the industry standards of the company's rate group, allows the WSIB to assess the performance of the company. If the company's rate is higher than their respective rate group's industry standard then the WSIB may target the company as high risk or identify the company as requiring a "Workwell audit". If the company's rates are lower than the industry standard, the WSIB will continue to monitor the company's performance.

The WSIB can order a company to undergo a Workwell Audit. Workwell audits involve a complete and detailed audit of the health and safety system or lack of health and safety program of the company. The WSIB will order Workwell audits when the company has a consistently poor health and safety performance record (frequency and severity performance). In addition to the company being subject to increased premiums and/or surcharges because of poor performance, the company will have to face the costs of complying with any orders written to correct the deficiencies of their health and safety program resulting from the Workwell audit.

A Workwell audit involves the WSIB performing onsite evaluations of the health and safety program. As a result of the audit findings, the inspector will make recommendations on how to improve the health and safety program. Ultimately the company's performance should improve when the deficiencies of the health and safety program are corrected.

Audits can take an average of three (3) years to work through and complete successfully. Once the company is successful in passing the audit, the company will have to maintain all the changes of the program. If the company is not successful in passing the audit, a company can continue to be evaluated, fined and penalized until the company complies to all the requirements of the Occupational Health and Safety Act.

In addition to Workwell audits, poor health and safety performers will also be highlighted by the WSIB to the Ministry of Labour. The Ministry of Labour (MOL) and the WSIB will rank the company as high risk which will precipitate increased unscheduled visits by the MOL. During these visits, the MOL will dissect in great detail the company's health and safety program. As a result of their investigations, the MOL will write orders as well as levy fines and penalties for every contravention to the Occupational Health and Safety Act. Therefore, poor health and safety performers in Ontario will be subject to close and potentially expensive scrutiny by two (2) Ontario Government Branches, the WSIB and the MOL.

The costs of the fines, penalties and any costs to complying with orders are usually unbudgeted expenses for the company. These expenses can have a significant impact on the profitability of the company in two (2) ways:

1. unexpected expenses will decrease any possible profitability directly; and,

2. potential loss of future business as poor performance ratings can deter customers from contracting new business with the company.

As discussed, a workers' compensation program is an insurance program designed to provide payments for lost wages when a worker loses time from work due to a workplace injury. In Ontario, the worker's compensation program is regulated by the Workplace Safety and Insurance Act (WSIA). The WSIA and the workers compensation program is administered by a provincial government branch known as the Workplace Safety and Insurance Board (WSIB).

A best practice for companies would be to track their frequency rate of injuries and the severity rate of injuries in order to monitor the effectiveness of their health and safety program. The WSIB and the MOL will monitor each company's health and safety performance according to their frequency and severity rates of workplace injuries, industry standards, and rate groups. By tracking these statistics, a company can review their performance regularly and develop corrective actions prior to the WSIB and the MOL involvement.

The WSIB's evaluation of the calculations of the frequency and the severity rates may produce a surcharge if the cost of injuries is higher than expected or a rebate if the cost of injuries is lower than expected. These rebates and surcharges are in addition to the monthly premiums the company pays based on the payroll expenditures.

Consequent to high rates of frequency and severity in workplace injuries, the WSIB and the MOL may require any company in Ontario to go through a Workwell audit. The Workwell audit will evaluate the company's health and safety program or assist in building of a new program through investigation of the company's compliance with the Occupational Health and Safety Act of Ontario (OHSA). Any violations of the OHSA will result in fines, penalties and written orders by the MOL to correct any deficiencies. Should the company continue to be in non-compliance, the MOL will continue to levy fines and penalties against the company until the company complies or the company ceases to operate in Ontario. The fines must be paid regardless if the company closes the business.

In summary, all government and private wage replacement insurance programs, both short term and long term, have a variety of underwriting requirements in order to outline eligibility for benefits from the program. Premiums of each program differ based on the coverage and eligibility requirements. However, all programs essentially have common requirements. One common requirement includes all decisions being based on medical documentation from medical professionals. The medical documentation must support the worker's total disability for benefits to be disbursed.

In Ontario, the company does not have the right to request details of a diagnosis but the company does have the right to medical documentation to support ongoing lost time from work. It is always important for the company to note that it is the company's right to request updated medical to support ongoing absence from work. It is up to the company's policies and procedures to determine the frequency of these requests. The legal requirement is that the requests are reasonable and that the company is not discriminating against any particular or specific worker.

Consult a reputable employment lawyer to outline all the company's legal rights in regards to requesting medical information in terms of timing and details of the medical information as well as the company's legal obligations and responsibilities for privacy and confidentiality. Other best practice tips on this subject are discussed later in this book.

CHAPTER 7

PARTIES IN DISABILITY MANAGEMENT

There are many parties in the injury and recovery process. The key parties include: workers, employers, medical professionals, the benefits carriers, etc. Each party has a set of roles and responsibilities in the recovery process and the disability management process. Defining each role is critical to understanding the legal responsibilities of each program for each party.

The Worker
Generally speaking, a person is defined as a worker when the person performs a task for another in exchange for remuneration. For example, a person agrees to perform receptionist duties for a big legal firm for a salary negotiated by the company and the worker. Salary and benefits vary from employment agreement to employment agreement; from employer to employer; from worker to worker; from union to union, etc. The details of the agreement will depend on a variety of considerations including legislation, union membership, geographical location, type of job, educational or skills requirements, company size, industry, company profit performance, demand of the skills vs. the availability of labour pool, etc.

The legal definition of a worker referenced from the Employment Standards Act (ESA) of Ontario is:

> "employee" includes,
> (a) a person, including an officer of a corporation, who performs work for an employer for wages,

(b) a person who supplies services to an employer for wages,
(c) a person who receives training from a person who is an employer, as set out in subsection (2), or
(d) a person who is a homeworker,
and includes a person who was an employee; ("employé") (ESA, 2009)

In addition, the WSIA of Ontario, Policy 12-02-01, defines a worker as:

>...includes a person who has entered into or is employed under a contract of service, or apprenticeship, written or oral, express or implied, whether by way of manual labour or otherwise, and includes:
>
>- a learner or student
>- a member of a municipal volunteer fire brigade or a volunteer ambulance brigade
>- a person deemed to be a worker of an employer by direction or order of the WSIB
>- a person summoned to assist in controlling or extinguishing a fire by an authority empowered to do so
>- a person who assists in any search and rescue operation at the request of and under the direction of a member of the Ontario Provincial Police Force
>- a person who assists in connection with an emergency that has been declared by the Lieutenant Governor in Council or the Premier under section 7.0.1 of the Emergency Management and Civil Protection Act or by the head of council of a municipality under section 4 of that Act.
>- an auxiliary member of a police force
>- a person deemed to be a worker under Section 12, or
>- a pupil deemed to be a worker under the Education Act.

...A "worker" does not include:

- an outworker (a person to whom articles or materials are given out to be made up, cleaned, washed, altered, ornamented, finished, repaired or adapted for sale in the person's own home)
- an executive officer of a corporation or a person whose employment is of a casual nature and who is employed otherwise than for the purposes of the employer's industry. (WSIA, 1997)

For the purposes of this text, the worker will be considered the same as the definition under the Employment Standards Act (ESA) and the Workplace Safety and Insurance Act (WSIA), both of Ontario.

The Employer
An employer, in general terms, is considered the person who hires, directs, delegates, anyone who supervises another worker to perform a job or task for remuneration. A representative of the employer can be deemed an employer under various pieces of legislation as well since they represent the employer or the enterprises of the employer.

The legal definition of an employer referenced from the Employment Standards Act (ESA) of Ontario includes:

> ... (a) an owner, proprietor, manager, superintendent, overseer, receiver or trustee of an activity, business, work, trade, occupation, profession, project or undertaking who has control or direction of, or is directly or indirectly responsible for, the employment of a person in it, and (b) any persons treated as one employer under section 4, and includes a person who was an employer; ("employeur")... (ESA, 2009)

Furthermore, the Occupational Health and Safety Act (OHSA) of Ontario defines an employer as:

> ... "employer" means a person who employs one or more workers or contracts for the services of one or more workers and includes a

contractor or subcontractor who performs
work or supplies services and a contractor or
subcontractor who undertakes with an owner,
constructor, contractor or subcontractor to perform work or supply services; ("employeur")...
(OHSA, 2009)

In Ontario, the Workplace Safety and Insurance Act (WSIA)
defines an employer similarly to the ESA. The definition is stated
under the WSIA as:

... "employer" means every person having in
his, her or its service under a contract of service
or apprenticeship another person engaged in
work in or about an industry and includes,
(a) a trustee, receiver, liquidator, executor or
administrator who carries on an industry,
(b) a person who authorizes or permits a learner
to be in or about an industry for the purpose of
undergoing training or probationary work, or
(c) a deemed employer; ("employeur")... (WSIA,
1997)

Moreover, the WSIA broadens the definition of an employer to
include that of independent operators under specific conditions of
work. Recently, the WSIA changed the definition of an employer
under Bill 119 to include independent operators in order to ensure
coverage under the worker's compensation program in Ontario for
all appropriate "workers" in Ontario. Under the WSIA, the definition of an employer is extended to include:

...Deemed employer
(2) When a person is deemed to be a worker
under subsection (1), the independent operator,
sole proprietor, partnership or corporation, as
the case may be, is deemed to be the employer
for the purposes of the insurance plan. 2008,
c. 20, s. 4....
...Definitions
(10) In this section,

"exempt home renovation work" means construction work that is performed,

(a) by an independent operator, a sole proprietor, a partner in a partnership or an executive officer of a corporation, and

(b) on an existing private residence that is occupied or to be occupied by the person who directly retains the independent operator, sole proprietor, partnership or corporation, or by a member of the person's family; ("travaux de rénovation domiciliaire exemptés")

"member of the person's family" means,

(a) the person's spouse,

(b) the person's child or grandchild,

(c) the person's parent, grandparent, father-in-law or mother-in-law,

(d) the person's sibling, or

(e) anyone whose relationship to the person is a "step" relationship corresponding to one mentioned in clause (b), (c) or (d); ("membre de sa famille")

"private residence" includes,

(a) a private residence that is used seasonally or for recreational purposes, and

(b) structures that are,

(i) normally incidental or subordinate to the private residence,

(ii) situated on the same site, and

(iii) used exclusively for non-commercial purposes. ("résidence privée") 2008, c. 20, s. 4.."
(WSIA, 1997)

For the purposes of this text, the definition of employer will follow that of the ESA and the WSIA.

The Independent Operator

In Ontario, every employer has to register with the WSIB. However, there are some business owners who are not considered employers. Independent Operators are business owners who do not have any employees. Traditionally, the WSIA has allowed independent operators the option to be covered by workers compensation for additional premiums. However, with the recent changes under Bill 119 to the WSIA previously discussed, there are specific conditions where independent operators are considered workers instead of the employers. This change results in specific independent operators mandated to purchase coverage under the WSIA for workers compensation benefits instead of the benefits being optional for the operator to purchase.

The Independent Operator status is for the business that has no employees and only the owner works in the business. According to the Workplace Safety and Insurance Act (WSIA), Policy 12-02-01, an Independent Operator is:

> ... is a person who carries on an industry set out in Schedule 1 or Schedule 2 of the Act and who does not employ any workers for that purpose. (WSIA, 1997)

In addition, the WSIA defines an independent operator as:

> (a) an individual who,
> (i) does not employ any workers,
> (ii) reports himself or herself as self-employed for the purposes of an Act or regulation of Ontario, Canada or another province or territory of Canada, and
> (iii) is retained as contractor or subcontractor by more than one person during the time period set out in a Board policy, or
> (b) an individual who is an executive officer of a corporation that,
> (i) does not employ any workers other than the individual, and
> (ii) is retained as contractor or subcontractor by more than one person during the time period set out in a Board policy. 2008, c. 20, s. 4.
> Compulsory insurance — construction
> Deemed workers
> 12.2 (1) The following persons are deemed to be workers to whom the insurance plan applies:
> 1. Every independent operator carrying on business in construction.

2. Every sole proprietor carrying on business in construction.
3. Except as otherwise provided by the regulations, every partner in a partnership carrying on business in construction.
4. Except as otherwise provided by the regulations, every executive officer of a corporation carrying on business in construction. 2008, c. 20, s. 4... (WSIA, 1997)

Bill 119 reached royal assent in the Ontario Parliament in November 2008. This bill changes the criteria of coverage for an independent operator under the WSIA. The changes include mandating independent operators to purchase that optional insurance for wage loss coverage especially in Construction rate groups. Details to this bill can be found on E-laws Ontario website.

Essentially, Bill 119 has changed the criteria for the optional insurance. Bill 119 which will become part of the WSIA by January 2010, has also broadened the definition of an "employer" and an "independent operator". The rules for an independent operator for the industry group for construction businesses have been most affected by the change.

The new amendment(s) to the WSIA will allow the independent operator to obtain workers compensation insurance through the WSIA. In some instances, the independent operator may be mandated to participate in the insurance program in Ontario. According to the new changes to the WSIA, purchasing this insurance coverage is compulsory when the independent operator is in the construction industry and the WSIB considers the independent operator as a worker. The WSIA specifically states:

...12.2 (1) The following persons are deemed to be workers to whom the insurance plan applies:
1. Every independent operator carrying on business in construction.
2. Every sole proprietor carrying on business in construction.
3. Except as otherwise provided by the regulations, every partner in a partnership carrying on business in construction.

4. Except as otherwise provided by the regulations, every executive officer of a corporation carrying on business in construction. 2008, c. 20, s. 4... (WSIA, 1997)

For those independent operators that are not mandated to participate in the WSIA program in Ontario under Bill 119, they may still elect to purchase optional insurance coverage under the WSIA. According to the WSIA, Policy 12-02-01, the independent operator must complete a questionnaire to apply for the workers compensation coverage. The questionnaire is located on the WSIB website as the WSIA optional insurance form. Once the form is completed and submitted to the WSIB, the WSIB Account Manager will review the application and determine if the independent operator may participate in the insurance program.

If an independent operator does not know their status for purchasing workers compensation insurance benefits, they may contact the WSIB. It would be a good practice for the independent operator is to complete the questionnaire and to have the WSIB make a determination on their status. The determination would allow the independent operator to develop policies and procedures to ensure compliance with the legislation in Ontario.

The optional insurance available for independent operators under the WSIA is limited to coverage for disability as a result of work related injuries or illness. For more complete disability insurance coverage, the independent operator should review other disability insurance packages through private carriers.

The packages of private carriers could expand the disability coverage include disability as a result of injury or illness despite the cause of the injury. However, there may still be conditions for the coverage depending on the package and the carrier. For example, it is quite common for most packages to exclude death from suicide as this is not a result of an "accidental" or unexpected injury or illness.

The Independent Operator vs. The employer
Essentially, the difference between an independent operator and an employer is that that the employer has people working for the company whereas that independent operator is an owner of the company with no employees. Another difference is that some independent operators are not required to participate in the workers compensa-

tion program under the WSIA whereas the employer is mandated to participate.

Bill 119 made some changes recently to the WSIA regarding independent operators' obligation to purchase workers compensation coverage under the WSIA. Therefore some independent operators will be mandated to purchase the insurance coverage whereas others will have the option to purchase additional disability insurance coverage from the WSIB for wage loss coverage in the event of a work related injury. This optional insurance is to replace any private wage loss insurance coverage purchased by the business owner.

As discussed previously, depending on the classification of the employer vs. the independent operator under the WSIA, the WSIA will outline the company's obligation or legal responsibility in Ontario vs. the company's optional opportunities. The chart below will illustrate in detail the difference between the independent operator and the employer. The chart is taken from the WSIB Policy 12-02-01.

Illustration 7-1: Independent Operator vs. Employee

	Workers	Independent Operators
Instructions	• Comply with instructions on what, when, where, and how work is to be done.	• Works on their own schedule. • Does the job their own way.
Training/ supervision	• Trained and supervised by an experienced employee of the payer. • Required to take correspondence or other courses. • Required to attend meetings and follow specific instructions which indicate how the payer wants the services performed.	• Use their own methods and are not required to follow instructions from the payer.
Personal service	• Must render services personally. • Must obtain payer's consent to hire others to do the work.	• Often hires others to do the work without the payer's consent.

	Workers	Independent Operators
Hours of work	• The hours and days of work are set by the payer.	• Work whatever hours they choose.
Full-time work	• Must devote full-time to the business of the payer. • Restricted from doing work for other payers.	• Free to work when and for whom they choose.
Order or sequence of work	• Performs services in the order or sequence set by the payer. • Performs work that is part of a highly coordinated series of tasks where the tasks must be performed in a well-ordered sequence.	• Performs services at their own pace. • Work on own schedule.
Method of payment	• Paid by the payer in regular amounts at stated intervals. • Payer alone decides the amount and manner of payment.	• Paid by the job on a straight commission. • Negotiates amount and method of payment with the payer.
Licenses	• Payer holds licenses required to do the work.	• Person holds licenses required to do the work.
Serving the public	• Does not make services available except on behalf, or as a representative, of the payer. • Invoices customers on employer's behalf.	• Has own office. • Listed in business directories and maintains business telephone. • Advertises in newspapers, etc. • Invoices customers on own behalf.

	Workers	Independent Operators
Status with other government agencies	• Terms of the relationship are governed by a collective agreement. • Canada Revenue Agency either makes no ruling on the person's status, or rules that the person is a worker under the Canada Pension Plan (CPP) and the Employment Insurance Act (EIA). (A ruling is made after the relevant parties complete the form "Request for a ruling as to the status of a worker under the CPP or EIA".) • Collects and pays GST and other applicable taxes on payer's behalf. • Payer deducts EI, CPP, insurance, income tax, etc. from pay.	• Terms of the relationship not governed by a collective agreement. • Canada Revenue Agency has made an official ruling that the person is not a worker under the CPP and the EIA. • Collects and pays GST and other applicable taxes on own behalf. • Takes no deductions from pay for EI, CPP, insurance, income tax, etc.
Continuing need for type of service	Payer has a continuing need for the type of service that the person provides. A payer has a continuing need for service if all persons who perform such services, collectively, spend **more** than 40 hours a month on average doing the work, or if the work continues full-time for more than 4 months.	Payer does not have a continuing need for the type of service that the person provides.
Hiring / supervising / paying assistants	Hires, supervises, and pays workers, on direction of the payer (acts as a supervisor or representative of the payer).	Hires, supervises and pays workers, on own accord and as the result of a contract under which the person agrees to provide materials and labour and is responsible for the results.

	Workers	Independent Operators
Doing work on purchaser's premises	Payer owns or controls the worksite.	Works away from payer's premises using own office space, desk, and telephone.
Oral and written reports	Required to submit regular oral or written reports to payer.	Submits no reports.
Right to sever relationship	Either the person or the payer can end the work relationship at any time without legal penalty for breach of contract.	Agrees to complete a specific job and is responsible for its satisfactory completion or is legally obligated to pay for damages or loss of income that the payer sustains because of the failure to satisfactorily complete the work.
Working for more than one firm at a time	Usually works for one payer.	Works for more than one payer at the same time.

This chart is taken from the WSIB Policy 12-02-01.

The Medical Professionals

There are many professionals that deal with health care. Conventional practice identifies medical professionals as doctors. Holistic practice identifies many other types of professionals that contribute to the medical care of any disability, illness or injury. For the purpose of this text, we will explore those medical professionals that are recognized by the worker's compensation program in Ontario known as the WSIB.

Common medical professionals include licensed general medical practitioners, specialists, physiotherapists, chiropractors, nurse practitioners, etc. There are also some medical practitioners that may not diagnose but are recognized to complete ongoing progress reports, etc. including massage therapists, acupuncture, etc. A company's health care benefits package or the workers compensation guidelines will identify which services are covered for reimbursement of costs. The list of services may also be exclusive to the list of pre-approved service providers. These details should be outlined in the benefits guidelines or by the claims adjudicators.

Medical professionals or health service providers are responsible for assessing the injuries and providing diagnoses to the injured party. The medical professional is obligated to provide medical details to the benefits insurance carrier. The medical professionals medically manage the injured parties' recovery process including diagnosis, treatment plan, medical testing, restrictions, etc.

In Ontario, the employer is not legally entitled to any diagnosis information not even for workplace injuries. Under the Privacy Act of Ontario, the employer is not allowed to ask any worker about any medical conditions. However, regardless of the insurance program, the employer is legally entitled to request restrictions and updates on restrictions when reasonable.

Workers may choose to divulge sensitive medical information to their employer if they require assistance or accommodation. The employer is then obligated under the same Privacy Act to secure this information in a safe place. The employer is responsible for maintaining strict confidentiality of this information. The information can only be shared should the worker agree to disclosure.

Many wage replacement insurance programs will have a list of preferred service providers. A preferred service provider is a medical professional that has been recognized to render medical professional services according to the knowledge of the wage replacement program. The rates are also usually pre-negotiated at preferred rates. These service providers may have professional reputations or expert knowledge that supports the mandate of the wage replacement insurance program.

Some medical professionals prefer not to deal with wage replacement insurance programs. The WSIB has a preferred service providers list for each location in Ontario. For example, in Windsor, Ontario, there is a list of health care service providers that the WSIB prefers to deal with because their reports are clear, consistent, dependable, and will be defensible in a court of law or at the WSIB tribunal hearings.

A best practice in an effective disability management program is to develop a medical network of health care service providers to assist in the recovery and the return to work processes. The list of preferred health care service professionals used by the wage replacement insurance program can be a significant influence when a company is developing a medical network. These service providers already have established credibility in their profession and with the benefits carrier. Their credibility will in turn support the credibility of the company's return to work and claims management programs. The medical documentation from these practitioners when used to develop the recovery plan will be readily accepted by the benefits carriers since the medical documentation will be credible and consistent in itself.

SUMMARY

In summary, the worker's compensation insurance program in Ontario is regulated by legislation known as the Workplace Safety and Insurance Act (WSIA). The WSIA clearly defines who and what responsibilities the employer has under the worker's compensation insurance program in Ontario as well as those of an independent operator.

In the past, independent operators were excluded from the mandatory legal obligation to participate in the worker's compensation insurance program in Ontario. The coverage for workers compensation for independent operators was optional. If the independent operator wanted to participate, they had to complete and submit a questionnaire subject to the approval of the WSIB to obtain coverage under the worker's compensation program. The independent operator would pay premiums for this coverage.

Recently, new legislation known as Bill 119 has mandated certain independent operators to participate in this insurance program just like any other employer in Ontario. Thus revising the exemption rules to participation of the insurance program as well as providing new language for the independent operator coverage. For any owner of a company that has further questions on coverage for the independent operator, they should consult with a lawyer who specializes in employment law.

Key terms:

Employer	Frequency
Health Services Provider	Independent Operator
Long Term Disability (LTD)	Medical Network
Medical Professional	RSI
Severity	Short Term Disability (STD)
Total Disability	Traumatic Injury
Wage replacement program	Worker
Worker's compensation program	

Questions:

1. Compare and contrast in detail the difference between an employer and an independent operator.
2. Describe the difference between frequency and severity. What is the significance of these items?
3. Discuss the term total disability and its significance to wage replacement programs.
4. Define and discuss the different types of wage replacement programs. What is the impact of any wage replacement program? Discuss the common criteria of the different wage replacement programs.
5. What are the roles and responsibilities of the medical professionals?

SECTION III

UNDERSTANDING RECOVERY

Objectives:

After reviewing this chapter, the reader should be able to understand and explain the following concepts:

1. Define recovery.
2. Explain standard recovery period.
3. Understand the reporting process.
4. Outline the responsibilities of each party in the recovery process and the return to work process.
5. Define the term no lost time.
6. Explain the term lost time (both occupational and non-occupational) and discuss its significance.

CHAPTER 8
RECOVERY

The recovery process involves many steps. Generally, recovery is defined as a period of time that is taken including the actions taken to return to the injured person's pre-injury health status. For those injured parties that do not return to their pre-injury health level, the recovery period becomes the period of time that reflects the healing through the acute phase of the injury. Once a permanent impairment has been determined by the medical professional for the injury, no further recovery is expected to take place.

The acute phase in the recovery period is the short term time period where the injury is experiencing it most severe symptoms. This time period is generally in the beginning of the injury. The acute recovery period can begin again at the point where medical intervention such as surgery is performed to correct the injury. Wikipedia, a website for definitions, defines the acute phase of the injury as:

> ... the period of time in between when the injury is sustained, and the beginning of the sub-acute phase. Depending on the severity of injury, and the age and health of the patient, this phase can take up to four or five days. The acute phase is characterised by some or all of the following: immediate pain, tenderness, swelling, inflammation and oedema, contour deformity, bleeding, and loss of normal function of the injured area... (Wikipedia, 2010)

The acute phase can last a little longer than an hour or two to lasting many years depending on the severity of the injury. For example, a broken leg may be a few weeks or until the cast is removed from the leg whereas a strained back may never recover fully. The acute recovery phase for an injury that never recovers fully will follow the standard recovery period for that injury.

If the recovery period goes beyond the short term acute phase, the recovery period can enter into the chronic phase. The chronic period is long term and can last a long time. If permanent impairment has been determined, then the period has passed into the chronic phase. Generally, in the chronic phase, recovery occurs very slowly if at all. In fact, the recovery can cease progressing at some point leaving the injured person in the chronic phase.

Standard Recovery
Each injury has a standard recovery period according to the American Medical Association Guide. The standard recovery period is the average period of time required for that injury to heal. A standard recovery period is the same as the maximum medical recovery period. Once the maximum medical recovery period has been reached, if the injury has not healed or the worker's functional difficulties or disfigurement have not recovered to the pre-injury health status, the medical professional can determine the functional difficulty as a permanent impairment. The permanent impairment will likely require permanent restrictions. The restrictions will be based on objective medical evidence. Appendix L: for the Standard Recovery Period Chart as outlined by the American Medical Association Guide and used by the WSIB as a tool.

When injuries involve long recovery periods, the challenge for the injured worker, the company and the medical professionals is to assist the worker through the transition of returning to regular duties or regular capabilities. At this stage, injuries with long recovery periods can lead the worker to perceive their limitations as more disabling than the objective medical evidence supports.

Perception is reality. The worker's reality will become what the worker believes to be true or believes to be their ability to perform. The worker will perform to the abilities they perceive to possess because the worker wants to prevent further injuries. Regardless if the medical evidence indicates the worker can still perform certain tasks, if the worker believes he or she cannot perform the task, then the worker will not perform the task. For example, if an injured worker believes he cannot move his leg despite all the medical tests indicating that there is no nerve damage and there is no other medical reason for the paralysis yet the worker cannot move his leg. Therefore, the permanent impairment is determined by medical professionals based on objective medical evidence rather than on the subjective opinion of the perception of the worker.

CHAPTER 9

THE REPORTING PROCESS FOR OCCUPATIONAL INJURY

Despite the best health and safety programs, workplace injuries still may occur. The Occupational Health and Safety Act requires the company to develop a reporting mechanism for workers to report injuries to the employer. The incident report will be the initial form to submit the information describing the event that occurred resulting in an injury, near miss, property damage, or risk exposure. The incident report will drive further actions including investigation(s), root cause analysis, as well as corrective action activities.

The incident reporting form should be completed by the supervisor and the person reporting the unsafe event. The supervisor completing the incident report with the worker will provide the information required to remedy the situation to prevent similar events from occurring in the future. Therefore, it is a best practice for companies to mentor their supervisors in communication skills, analytical skills, investigative skills, problem solving skills, etc. to support supervisors in making effective decisions.

A comprehensive incident report will include information that will:

- Describe the event – what happened (end result) (include times and pictures)
- Describe the event – how it happened

- Describe any injuries or property damage (if any)
- Describe first aid measures or repair activities (include any costs)
- Outline an offer for modified work if restrictions are required
- Identify the people involved in the event
- Describe the clean-up required
- Define the root cause of the event
- Identify potential corrective actions
- Identify any and all activities taken to protect the workers from further injury or from recurrences

See Appendix A for a sample comprehensive incident report.

The incident reporting form is only one part of the reporting process. Two additional components to the incident reporting process is the reactive activity as well as the proactive course of action(s) taken once the event has occurred. The reactive course of actions are actions taken in response to an event that has already occurred. Reactive actions should include the company's responsibilities and obligations under the Workplace Safety and Insurance Act (WSIA).

The proactive course of actions refers to the activities taken to prevent future recurrences. Preventive activities are also a responsibility of the employer under the OHSA. Sometimes, proactive course of actions can occur without an actual injury precluding the change. For example, developing a housekeeping program in order to prevent slip and fall type injuries even though the company does not have a history of slip and fall injuries.

According to the WSIA, an employer has to report any injuries that occur at the workplace and in the course of employment. The injury is reported to the Workplace Safety and Insurance Board. There are conditions by which the injuries should be reported to the WSIB. Policy #15-01-02 of the WSIA states that the company is obligated to report any workplace injury to the WSIB if the injury:

- requires medical attention;
- requires accommodation beyond 5 working days;
- causes a change in wages; or,

- causes lost time beyond the initial date of accident

Therefore, a company is not obligated to report any injury to the WSIB if the injury only receives first aid or only requires modified work at regular pay for less than seven calendar days, following the date of accident (but no medical attention is sought). For example, a worker cuts their hand while taking a part out of a machine. The worker goes to the first aid room to clean and dress the cut. If that is the only step the worker takes with the injury, then the employer is not required to report it to the WSIB.

However, if the same cut injury used above gets infected a few days later, the worker decides to go to the clinic for medical attention, perhaps for antibiotics. This medical attention is one of the requirements under the WSIA for an employer to report the injury to the WSIB. Therefore, the employer will report this injury to the WSIB. If the employer does not report the injury within the prescribed time period, the employer will be fined by the WSIB for a late report or non-compliance.

Only the employee has the option to cancel the workers compensation claim. The cancelation must be a written request submitted to the WSIB. The request must indicate the worker's intent not to pursue the claim. The worker must not feel under "duress" by the employer to cancel the claim nor should the worker receive any type of bonus or remuneration by the employer to cancel the claim.

On the other hand, the employer is mandated to report the claim. The employer has no authority to cancel the claim. The employer can object to the claim in writing to the WSIB. The objection must be based on facts that support the injury occurring outside of work or not in the course of employment. The objection should be free of emotional conjecture and only state the facts. Ultimately, only the WSIB claims adjudicator will determine if the injured worker is entitled to benefits under the worker's compensation program.

In addition to the WSIA, there are pieces of legislation dictating to whom and what to report for workplace events. The Occupational Health and Safety Act (OHSA) indicates that the Ministry of Labour (MOL) must be notified if there is a workplace injury that meets the criteria of a critical injury. For example, respiratory injuries requiring medical attention must be reported to the MOL in addition to reporting the injury to the WSIB. Furthermore, any critical injuries must be reported to the MOL as well as to the WSIB. The chapter on critical injuries later in this book will outline the criteria for critical injuries.

Similarly, the Environmental Protection Act states that the Ministry of Environment (MOE) also have to be notified of specific events that occur at the workplace in Ontario if the event causes or has potential to cause damage to the environment. Likewise, under the Environmental Protection Act, if an environmental event occurs causing an injury or imposes a health and safety risk of exposure to the community, the event must be reported to the Ministry of Environment.

Once an incident has been reported, the incident report becomes the driver for a series of independent courses of actions. It is imperative that the supervisor complete an incident report with the injured worker with as much detail as the worker can recall. Best practices in due diligence is to set out a procedure and train supervisors in their responsibilities under the law and company expectations in the following areas:

- how to complete an incident report
- how to respond to an injury
- how to investigate the incident
- how to complete root cause analysis
- how to develop and implement corrective action
- how to evaluate the corrective action to prevent future recurrences

During the incident reporting process, different people have different responsibilities throughout the process. It would be a best practice to incorporate each party's responsibilities under the WSIA in the company's incident reporting procedure. As with all new procedures or new changes to procedures, part of the implementation process is to ensure that all parties receive the appropriate training. Follow up with each of the parties would ensure that each party understands their role and responsibilities.

As discussed previously, once a worker seeks medical attention for a workplace injury, the worker is obligated to report the incident to the employer as well as report to the employer that medical attention was sought. Seeking the treatment of a chiropractor meets the definition of medical attention. Furthermore, the incident is reported to the employer when the worker completes an incident report with the supervisor. The Supervisor is required to submit the completed incident report to Human Resources and or to the Health and Safety Advisor. The management representative is then required to complete and submit the Form 7 to the WSIB using the completed incident report.

According to the Workplace Safety and Insurance Act (WSIA), Section 21, a company has 3 business days to report the workplace injury to the Workplace Safety and Insurance Board (WSIB) using the WSIB's Form 7. As previously discussed, in order to be able to complete the Form 7 appropriately, the company should develop and implement an incident reporting procedure which includes a comprehensive incident report form to be completed jointly by the worker who was injured and the worker's supervisor. The incident report will need to include information that will be needed to complete the Form 7.

Once the Form 7 is completed, it must be faxed to the WSIB. With some health and safety management software, the Form 7 can also be completed and sent electronically. The Form 7 can also be completed online at www.wsib.on.ca, /Employers/Forms/#0007A.

The Form 7 is the first opportunity for the company to communicate the company's version of the event causing the injury to the WSIB. Only the facts should be reported on the Form 7. Conjecture and emotional based opinions will not be considered in the decision for entitlement. This is important for a few reasons. The worker can ask for a copy of their file at any time from the WSIB at which time, the worker will be able to read everything the company has submitted or said to the adjudicator up to the time the copy of the file was requested. Opinions and conjecture instead of fact can damage employer and employee relations. To encourage and maintain good employee relations, trust, integrity, human rights code and due diligence, it is best to speak to the facts and not make accusations especially without supporting evidence.

Another reason to list facts instead of conjecture on any communication with the WSIB, is the information required for the adjudication process. Adjudication is the process of decision making used by the WSIB. The decision making must be objective and based on evidence. The adjudicator must be able to defend the decisions made. Facts are easy to defend in a court of law. Therefore, it is best to let the facts spell out the issue for the WSIB claims adjudicator in order for the adjudicator to make solid, defendable decisions.

Facts could be used to support the claim or deny the claim entitlement. Full disclosure of the facts as known at the time of completing the Form 7 should be common practice including times, witnesses, cycle times, weights, activities, etc. The WSIB will favour the worker if all facts are equal. However, if the employer is concerned about the origin of the injury as work related, then it is important to indicate the objection and follow it up with facts that support the objection.

The WSIB requires many forms to be completed by all parties of the recovery process at various times in the recovery. All forms required by the WSIB can be obtained in the following ways:

- Website download, completion, printing, faxing
- Order forms from the WSIB printing shop
- E-filing through the WSIB disability management software
- Copy to the WSIB, copy to the injured worker, and a copy in the worker's WSIB claims file

Much information will be required to be reported to the WSIB by all parties. The employer completes the Form 7. The injured worker completes the Form 6, telling the worker's version of the events leading to the injury. The medical professional details the initial diagnosis on the Form 8. Ongoing progress reports may be completed by all parties at various times in the recovery process. For example, essentially, the type of information required by the WSIB on the Form 7 includes:

- personal and contact information of the worker,
- contact information of the company contact,
- the company's WSIB account information,
- what happened to cause the injury,
- wages of the worker at the time of the injury,
- modified work available and offered,
- lost time details including four (4) weeks prior to the injury wage history,

- Any additional information material to the case/event including any disputes or concerns the company may have supporting the injury is or is not work related (based on objective evidence),
- A copy of a Form 7 from the WSIB (Ontario) is found on Appendix C

Furthermore, the company has some additional reporting requirements should the injury reach a specific level of severity. In addition to the WSIA reporting requirements for a workplace injury, the Occupational Health and Safety Act (OHSA) has requirements for reporting severe workplace injuries to the Ministry of Labour (MOL). If an injury is a critical injury, the company has to report the injury not only to the WSIB but also to the MOL as well as the MOE, police and ambulance depending on the nature of the injury.

If the injury is critical, the MOL will conduct a full investigation and depending on the negligence, the police may want to also conduct a full investigation. These investigations are in addition to the full investigation that the company should be conducting for its own corrective action process. For critical injuries while waiting for the MOL inspectors, the company is required to secure and preserve the accident scene. If the scene is not preserved, the MOL will penalize the company with fines in addition to any fines and orders the MOL will file against the company for violations of the OHSA causing the injury.

The Non-occupational Injury
The reporting process for the non-occupational injury will depend on the wage replacement program available to the injured party. Each program has a unique application package of forms to be completed. Commonly, the application package will include a form for the person applying for the benefit and a separate form for the medical professional to complete. If the program is an employer sponsored program than the application package will also include a form for the employer sponsor to complete and submit.

Generally, to avoid delay, all the forms should be completed and submitted at the same time to the benefit carrier for adjudication. Adjudication is the decision making process used by the carrier. A decision will not be made without the medical documentation. If the documentation provided does not contain all the pertinent medical information, a decision will be delayed until the appropriate medical information is submitted.

The injured party applying for the benefits is responsible for ensuring that the benefits carrier receives all the pertinent medical documentation to adjudicate the claim. In Ontario, the employer sponsor cannot be responsible for this as the employer is not entitled to communicate with the doctors of the workers unless the worker has signed a specific consent form allowing the doctor to release confidential medical information to the employer. These consent forms can be developed by the company's Human Resources Department or a lawyer.

Once all the documentation from the application package has been submitted, the benefits carrier will review the information for completeness and eligibility for initial entitlement of benefits. If any information is missing, the carrier will request additional information from the injured party. The injured party is then responsible for collecting and submitting the requested information. Additional medical information is requested at various times during the recovery progress by the carrier as well.

It is common for the carrier to request additional medical information from the injured party to collect from the medical professional. Sometimes the information received requires clarification or more details. For example, sometimes the carrier requires more details on the course of treatment the medical professional is prescribing for the injured party or the severity of the injury or diagnosis requires more details especially when lost time is prescribed.

The initial adjudication will either accept or deny the claim. If the claim is denied, the injured party always has the option to appeal the decision within a specified time period from the date of the decision. In order to appeal the decision, the injured party must submit a letter indicating their intent to appeal, the reason for their appeal, and any supporting evidence. The injured party has better chance at winning the appeal if they submit specific medical documentation supporting the injured party's total disability. Personal opinion does not influence decisions. The injured party should report the facts about capabilities and recovery details.

For employer sponsored programs, the employer may provide an objection if the employer has concerns of the claim's validity. Again, personal opinion does not influence decisions. If the employer objects to the claim, the employer must submit evidence that the injured party is not totally disabled. The evidence must be indisputable and clear. Videotaping a person performing tasks contrary to their reported level of capability can support the appeal.

However videotapes can be disputed in many ways. The video tape may only show a portion of time that does not include after the activity. One of the arguments from the worker could be that the worker had a good day that day so were able to do more things. Consequent to pushing their limits, the days that followed the videotaped activities were filled with pain and challenges even though the videotape does not illustrate the difficult days. In addition, the worker may state that the videotape itself was a violation of their privacy under the privacy act or the human rights act.

Once the claim is approved, benefits will be approved for a specified period of time according to the information on the medical documentation. Periodically, the benefits carrier will ask for additional information throughout the course to support ongoing benefits and extend benefits or continue paying benefits.

The claim will terminate when the carrier determines the injured worker is not totally disabled or when the maximum limit has been reached for the program. If the injured party has reached the maximum limit of a short term disability program, then the injured party may apply for a long term disability program. If the claim has been terminated because the medical documentation no longer supports total disability, the injured party should have recovered some capabilities to return to work. If the injured worker has not recovered, the medical documentation may not be current or may not show sufficient detail to support ongoing total disability.

In the cases where claims are terminated for insufficient medical information, the worker should discuss the situation with their medical professional. The medical professional may or may not provide the worker with additional medical that supports the current situation of recovery of the worker according to their medical opinion. This additional information should be submitted to the benefits carrier for reconsideration of ongoing benefits.

Chapter 10

The Responsibilities of Each Party

In a company's comprehensive incident reporting procedure, responsibilities and obligations of all parties should be clearly outlined. For workplace injuries in Ontario, legislation like the WSIA and the OHSA, summarize the responsibilities and obligations of workers, supervisors and the company. A best practice would be for a company to build these roles and responsibilities into their health and safety program including the incident reporting process. For example, if a worker indicates that they have had a workplace injury which requires a change in placement, an FAF package should be given to the worker after an incident report is completed and the supervisor should advise the worker to seek medical attention as soon as possible. These actions meet with compliance to legislative requirements as well as provide the necessary information to manage the claim appropriately.

In addition, it is a best practice to send the worker to the clinic upon giving the worker the functional abilities form (FAF) package. For further details on what is included in a comprehensive FAF package, please see section IV of this textbook. The worker has the right to go to their own family doctor if they choose. FAFs should be given to the worker to have medical professionals complete at different stages of recovery. These follow up FAFs are prefilled with the company's information and the worker's information. The FAF also can be pre-fill the section regarding modified work being offered to the worker.

The employer must discuss return to work with the worker before the section on the FAF regarding modified work can be pre-filled. It is important to always discuss the return to work plan with the worker each time the FAF is requested by the worker or by the employer. The supervisor will be able to use a body part chart program with the new FAF to make any necessary adjustments to the return to work plan.

The Worker

A best practice in this process would include ensuring the worker knows and understands all their responsibilities and obligations. These roles and responsibilities include but are not limited to:

- The worker and the supervisor should complete an incident report together immediately upon an injury occurring. A comprehensive incident report form includes the worker completing a detailed root cause investigation of the incident with the supervisor. The incident report should be signed by the worker, the supervisor and the Joint Health and Safety Committee (JHSC) worker representative.

- In Ontario, the worker must complete and submit a Form 6 describing the worker's version of what happened to cause the injury in the worker's own words. The Form 6 is the worker's statement of events and should be completed with facts. A copy of the Form 6 must be sent to the employer.

- At any time, the worker may have a union representative or/and a JHSC representative present during any discussions with the supervisor or management representative.

- The worker is required to take a functional abilities form (a WSIB form) (FAF) package to a medical professional to complete should the injured worker require accommodation. The chapter on "Return to Work (RTW)" will further discuss what an FAF is and the importance of this form.

- The worker should inform the doctor that the injury is work related.
- The worker should inform the medical professional that the company has a modified work program, if the company has such a program.
- The worker then returns the completed FAF to the company immediately (within 24 hours).
- The worker and the supervisor should review the FAF together to determine suitable work available.
- The worker shall keep the supervisor and the claims management advisor informed of the progress of recovery or of any (material) changes to their condition.
- The worker will actively participate in developing a specific return to work plan. The injured worker must cooperate in all therapy prescribed by the medical professionals and the WSIB.
- The worker must maintain regular contact with the supervisor and the Human Resources/ Claims Management Advisor.
- The worker must communicate to the supervisor or Claims Management Advisor and the WSIB of any difficulties or concerns regarding the duties assigned.
- The worker will notify the company and the WSIB of any material change to their condition.
- The injured worker cannot change medical practitioners unless the change is pre-approved by the WSIB and the company.
- The injured worker should be encouraged to make medical appointments before and/or after their shifts to avoid pay changes. However, the company should not deny the worker's leave request for such medical appointments.
- When a worker leaves the facility, they should be clocking out when they leave and clocking back in upon their return. The worker should

only leave the facility after the approval of the supervisor. If it is an office person leaving, they should be communicating with their supervisor before departing. Supervisors need to know who and where people are in a shift in case there is an emergency or the supervisor is required to change the schedule for any reason.

The Employer or the Employer Representative (including Supervisors and Managers)

The responsibilities and obligations for employers and employer representatives include but are not limited to:

- Any management representative should advise and allow the worker to have a union represent or/and a JHSC representative present at any time during the process.
- The supervisor should complete an incident report together with the worker.
- The supervisor should complete a detailed root cause investigation of the incident. The incident investigation should include such information as pictures, witness statements, recreation of events, potential corrective actions, etc.
- The supervisor should sign the incident report along with the worker and the JHSC representative.
- The supervisor should submit the completed incident report to human resources or the health and safety advisor within 24 hours of the incident.
- The supervisor should offer the worker accommodated work at the time the worker reports the injury. The modified work should be safe and suitable for the injured worker.
- The supervisor should distribute the FAF to the worker prior to the worker leaving the facility for medical attention. The company cannot stop nor force the worker to receive medical attention. However, medical attention is highly

recommended when the injury requires additional medical intervention above first aid. It is a best practice for the company to prepare an FAF package for the doctor to review and complete prior to injuries occurring. The FAF package should include a functional abilities form (FAF – a WSIB form), a letter to the medical professional explaining that the company has a modified work program, and instructions to the worker explaining their responsibilities and obligations.

- In Ontario, the company representative must report the injury to the WSIB within three (3) business days from the date of awareness of the injury. The reporting process to the WSIB includes completing and submitting a Form 7. The employer must send a copy of this Form 7 to the worker as well.

- Upon the worker's return to the company, the supervisor should review the FAF with the worker to determine suitable work available.

- The claims management advisor should develop and implement return to work and work hardening plan(s) based on the medical information (restrictions) from the FAF, FAE, IME, etc.

- The Supervisor must keep the HR and Claims Management Advisor informed of the progress of recovery or any (material) changes to the worker's condition as reported to the supervisor by the worker or observed by the supervisor.

- The supervisor and the claims management advisor must actively participate in developing a specific return to work plan with the worker.

- The health and safety advisor and the claims management advisor serve as consultants for the supervisors, workers, and Union Representatives, etc.

- The claims management advisor shall maintain regular contact with the worker and the WSIB.

- The claims management advisor shall communicate to the WSIB and the medical professionals any difficulties or concerns regarding the duties assigned to the worker.
- All management representatives should encourage injured workers to make medical appointments before and after their shifts to avoid pay changes. The company should be consistent in treating all medical appointments the same. The company should not deny the worker's leave for such medical appointments. There are systems that can be put in place to discourage workers from leaving work during scheduled work hours. Such systems include but are not limited to some rules like:
- The company can request the worker to submit appointment cards for each appointment. This is a reasonable request when the appointments become excessive.
- The company does not pay for the lost time. In doing this, the company must submit the lost time to the WSIB for payment consideration. The company can object to any or all lost time using the argument that the modified work plan is suitable and available. Depending on the WSIB Claims Adjudicator, some appointments will be approved for payment. However, the company can argue that the appointments can be made outside of work hours as other medical appointments are made. The WSIB may pay for the first few appointments but they may eventually deny ongoing lost time for appointments. The company must weigh the costs of this little bit of lost time against the WSIB costs when projecting rebates and surcharges. If the culture is responsible and will not take advantage of the company's good faith, then it might make more sense for the company to pay the lost time for medical appointments if these appointments are not too frequent and/or are very short in time. These are decisions that

must be made internally weighing all financial information to make the best decision for the company's culture and bottom line.

- The supervisor(s) needs to track people leaving the plant and advise the claims management advisor accordingly. Any lost time and lost wages must be reported by the company to the WSIB within three business days.

- The supervisor(s) should provide ongoing support and encouragement to all workers starting with assigning the restricted worker with safe, suitable, and sustainable work to accommodate restrictions, communicating with the worker, working with the worker regarding ongoing issues, follow up on restrictions and progress, etc.

- The supervisor will control and monitor the activities of the injured workers. It is the legal obligation of the supervisor to ensure the injured workers are working within their restrictions.

- The claims management advisor will monitor the progress of the recovery and adjust the return to work and recovery plans accordingly.

- The company has a duty to accommodate any restricted worker. Even when the restrictions are long term, the employer has a duty to accommodate the permanent impairment with a long term, suitable, sustainable, value added position.

- The company must practice due diligence in implementing corrective actions and preventing further injury both to the injured worker and to other workers. The company must develop and implement programs to prevent injuries stemming from the information on the incident reports.

- The responsibilities and obligations of the company may be carried out by a number of different people. The environmental health and safety advisor, the claims management advisor, the human resources generalist, the plant manager, the labour relations representative, etc. Working as a team, these representatives will be able to effectively address the root cause of the incident as well as maintain productive workers even when a worker may be working on a modified work program during the recovery process.

- Different positions within the company and this team of management representatives will be responsible for different roles and tasks as defined in the company's procedures. Each position will have a unique set of duties related to their role in the company.

- The environmental health and safety (EHS) advisor should track all incidents and injuries to analyze the information for trends and patterns. This may help in developing and implementing corrective actions that will prevent recurrences.

- All management representatives should assist in identifying hazards in the workplace. Once the hazards are identified, the management representatives should develop and implement appropriate corrective actions.

- The EHS advisor or HR should coordinate all health and safety training.

- Some companies may have an EHS Advisor and a claims management advisor as two separate positions. In these cases, the EHS Advisor and the claims management advisor can work as a cohesive team to support both the health and safety program and the disability management program. In conjunction with the roles and responsibilities of the EHS Advisor, the claims management advisor also is responsible for:

- Liaising between the WSIB, injured workers, medical professionals, management representatives, supervisors, etc.

- Managing claims including ensuring restrictions and other relevant medical is current, developing suitable and sustainable modified work plans, mediating between management and injured workers, arranging additional medical when required, clarifying information and questions from all parties, etc.

- Monitoring FAFs and deadlines for updating FAFs and other medical documentation
- Communicating clearly and consistently with the injured workers about rules, responsibilities, procedures, recovery process, modified work plans, claim status, etc.
- Assisting in developing and implementing programs to prevent injuries
- Developing and implementing programs to better manage injured workers
- Providing a safe work environment including identifying and communicating any risks, provide safety training, etc.
- Ensuring policies and procedures meet legislative obligations proactively
- Completing a Form 7 (based on the incident report as submitted by the supervisor and the injured worker). The Form 7 is a form from the WSIB. It is required by the WSIB to be completed if a workplace injury has occurred.

In addition to the EHS Advisor and a claims management advisor, a member of the company team could also include a certified ergonomist. A certified ergonomist can offer valuable insight into the relationship between the restrictions and the physical demands of the jobs available in the company. The matching of restrictions to physical demands of jobs ensures the company is assigning safe, suitable and sustainable tasks to restricted workers. Other roles and responsibilities of the certified ergonomists include but are not limited to:

- Developing work hardening plans to assist injured workers to continue in productive employment during the recovery process. These work hardening plans bridge the time between working with restrictions and returning to full regular duties.

- Job coaching the injured workers during the re-covery process to prevent re-aggravation and facilitate healing.
- Working with uninjured workers to prevent in-juries. Job coaching can include demonstrating movement techniques, posture awareness, pre-ventative training, stretching education, etc.
- Assisting the claims management advisor and the Supervisors in matching the restrictions of a worker to safe and suitable job placements.
- Advising management of recovery times, poten-tial risks, etc. to assist in developing preventa-tive programs or corrective actions.
- Advising management of challenges and barri-ers in the recovery process.
- Translating medical documentation to infor-mation to assist in modified work placements.
- Liaise between the company and the medical professionals for clarification on restrictions and other medical documentation to support work hardening plan and or potential cost relief or amalgamation in claims management.

Employers and employer representatives like supervisors have more responsibilities than the workers under the law. Along with the responsibilities under the WSIA and the OHSA, the Supervisors also have obligations under Bill C-45. Therefore, training and clearly defined roles for the supervisors are critical for a productive incident reporting procedure, effective return to work program and an efficient health and safety program. In addition to the obligations required under the OHSA as a competent supervisor, understanding the obligations and responsibilities of the Supervisor(s) will provide evidence of due diligence and legal compliance.

The Medical Professional
A best practice in the claims management process would be to iden-tify the responsibilities and obligations for medical professionals

within the program. These roles and responsibilities of any medical professionals include but are not limited to:

- Examine the injured party.
- Complete a Form 8 (a WSIB form) and submit the completed form to the WSIB. The form should include a diagnosis, prognosis and the course of treatment required. The employer is not entitled to a copy of this confidential information in Ontario unless the worker has signed a consent expressly giving permission to the medical professional to release this information or the worker freely submits a copy of the form to the employer.
- Complete the functional abilities form (a WSIB form) (FAF) with corresponding restrictions for the worker at different stages of the recovery period.
- Assist the worker through the modified work program development in terms of providing accurate and clear restrictions, appropriate medical intervention if required, etc.
- Advise the injured party on the course of action to be taken during the recovery including writing the appropriate prescriptions for treatments (like medications, chiropractic, physiotherapy, massage therapy, etc. whatever the medical professional deems appropriate course of action).
- Perform periodic reviews of the injured worker's condition and progress.
- Adjust the restrictions as required with new FAFs at different stages of the recovery.
- Prescribe further medical testing as required.
- Submit progress reports to the WSIB.
- Communicate any difficulties, barriers or concerns regarding the medical condition or recovery of the injured party to the WSIB. Injured workers cannot change medical practitioners unless the change is pre-approved by the WSIB and the company.
- Determine permanent impairment if required.

The (Internal) Worker Representative or Union Representative

A worker representative can assist the worker through the recovery process. A worker representative could be a member of the Joint Health and Safety Committee (JHSC) or a union representative. At any time the worker should be able to request the presence of the representative. Therefore outlining the responsibilities and obligations for the worker representative or the union representative would enable them to support the injured worker. These roles and responsibilities include but are not limited to:

- Witnessing and signing the incident report with the worker and the supervisor.
- Actively assist and participate in monitoring the workers progress in recovery and in the return to work plan.
- Communicate any difficulties, barriers or concerns regarding the assigned duties of the injured worker to the supervisor and/or the Claims Management Advisor.
- Notifying the company of any material change as they are made aware of by the injured worker.

The roles and responsibilities of each party are briefly discussed above however they are not all inclusive. For further details, please consult the Occupational Health and Safety Act (OHSA), the Workplace Safety and Insurance Act (WSIA), the workers compensation insurance program policy and guidelines, the wage replacement insurance program policy and guidelines, a reputable Employment Lawyer, etc.

In general, each party in the recovery and the return to work or the work hardening processes has a set of roles and responsibilities. The roles and responsibilities will vary at different stages of any process. At any time in the process, any breach of these roles and responsibilities may result in fines and penalties being levied, the benefits carrier may decline payments of benefits, the claim could be terminated, etc. depending on the party that violated or breached the responsibilities. The roles and responsibilities may change depending on the legislative requirements of the geographical area of the worker as well as the type of wage replacement program involved. However the roles and responsibilities discussed have covered the common duties and will help the company to establish a practice of due diligence.

CHAPTER 11

A LOST TIME INJURY VS. A NO LOST TIME INJURY

What is a no lost time injury?

A no lost time injury refers to injuries, regardless of occupational or non-occupational, which do not experience any time away from work due to any disability from the injury. These injuries may still require medical attention and further treatment. However both the physical results of the injury and the course of treatment do not support total disability leading to lost time or time away from the workplace. Lost time from work due to medical appointments regarding the injury can change the status of the injury to a lost time injury.

Traditionally, the claims with no lost time incur lower amounts of costs. Generally, these claims only incur costs as a result of medical treatment(s). These types of costs are usually called health care costs. Since the claims do not incur lost time from work, the costs associated with lost time from work including lost wages, lost productivity, etc. do not exist in a no lost time claim. The company can minimize costs of these claims by ensuring that an effective modified work program exists to mitigate the potential for lost time and related costs to lost time.

What is lost time (regarding occupational and non-occupational injuries)

Lost time claims are injury claims where the injured party is unable to work as a result of the injury during the recovery period. The lost time could occur for a variety of reasons. Minor reasons to lose time would include attending medical or therapy appointments. Whereas, a more extreme reason would be the worker is incapable of working due to the extent of the injury.

All lost time should be supported by medical documentation. If the lost time is due to medical appointments, an appointment card can be sufficient documentation to support the lost time. However, if the lost time is for longer periods of time, doctor's notes and other medical documentation should be submitted to support the ongoing absence.

Wages lost due to missing work is considered for payment through the respective wage replacement insurance program. For workplace injuries, the workers compensation program should be notified of the absence and consider the evidence to support the absence in order to determine eligibility for benefits. According to the Workplace Safety and Insurance Act (WSIA) of Ontario, any worker with a workplace injury who loses time on the initial day of injury only, the company must pay the worker for a full regular shift regardless if the worker works the entire shift. The employer is not required to pay overtime should the worker be delayed in excess of the normal shift due to seeking medical attention. Any lost time on the initial day of injury does not count as lost time. The injury will remain a no lost time claim until lost time occurs beyond the initial date of injury.

According to the WSIA, lost time begins when a worker loses time from work resulting in lost wages due to a workplace injury after the initial day of injury. If the worker requests to leave and they have reported an incident, even if the schedule is slow and the workers are going home, the worker should be sent for medical attention before being allowed to go home. If the worker insists to go home and the reason is not due to the workplace injury, have the worker complete a leave form to document and sign indicating the reason for the request to leave as not related to the injury. For non-occupational injuries, lost time is any time away from work (and without wages) from the instant of injury.

A best practice in monitoring lost time would be for the company to request medical documentation to support lost time through company policy or procedures. Benefits carriers, especially the WSIB, will request medical documentation to support lost time before considering the lost time for payment. The employer can challenge or object to any lost time payments especially if the company has an approved and effective return to work program designed to accommodate a wide variety of restrictions. Each case and each period of lost time must be evaluated on timing, return to work plans, restrictions, worker capabilities, worker cooperativeness and attitude, accommodations, etc.

Lost time claims are a large cost to any company. The costs can be mitigated with well-developed and implemented health and safety programs and disability management programs including return to work plans and modified work programs. In Ontario, the worker's compensation program, administered by the WSIB has a strategic goal to reduce the amount of workplace injuries in the province to zero. The slogan for the goal is known as the "Road to Zero".

Through legislation, the Ontario government is applying pressure on the employers of Ontario to reduce the number of all types of workplace injuries with particular emphasis on reducing the number of lost time claims and the number of lost time days as well as eliminating fatalities. The Ontario Ministry of Labour (MOL) is enforcing the OHSA requirements to ensure that employers are developing effective health and safety program in order to reduce the number of workplace injuries and reduce lost time.

In addition to legislative requirements, employers are encouraged to reduce claim costs through financial incentives. For non-occupational benefit carriers, the financial incentive to reduce claim costs may include premium adjustments. For workers compensation claims in Ontario, for every dollar the WSIB spends on a worker's claim, the WSIB charges the company approximately five (5) dollars back. The WSIB costs added to the cost of lost productivity and lower morale, the claim costs become costs that can easily become large unexpected financial burdens to the company. Therefore, in addition to the legislative pressure for Ontario employers to reduce the number of workplace injuries, it is also in the company's financial best interest to reduce injuries.

In addition to implementing return to work and return to regular duties programs, tracking lost time injuries is critical for reducing lost time days and claim costs. Each day a person loses time from work because of an injury must be reported to the respective benefits carrier. For example, if the worker experienced a workplace injury and loses time from work, the lost time must be reported to workers compensation carrier. In Ontario, that would be the WSIB. If the injury is not related to work, then the benefits carrier could be a short term disability carrier. The short term disability carrier may be a benefit that is available through the employer's health benefits plan or the carrier is from a personal disability insurance plan. Short term disability programs are also available through programs available from the federal government of Canada such as the Employment Insurance – Sick program.

Illustration 11-1: Lost time day tracking. In the example below, it shows that the amount of the lost time days decreased in 2007. It is interesting to note that the number of lost time days intersect at the same point that a new return to work program was implemented in 2007. The company could infer that the decrease in lost time days was a direct result of the implementation of an effective return to work program.

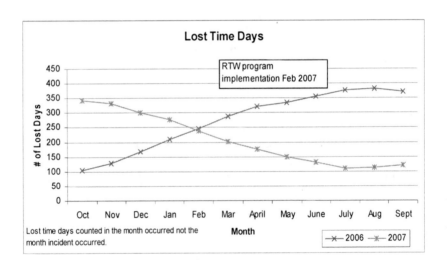

SUMMARY

In summary, every injury has a standard recovery period as determined by the American Medical Association. These standard recovery periods are supported by the Canadian medical community, the National Institute of Occupational Safety and Health (NIOSH) and disability insurance programs such as the Workplace Safety and Insurance Board (THE WSIB). Once the standard recovery has been reached, the worker should be assessed for permanent impairment by the medical professionals.

The recovery period starts after the injury occurs. The injury must be reported by the injured party to the company. The company must report the injury to either the WSIB if the injury is work related or the short term disability carrier if the injury is non-occupational.

Best practices for a company include a comprehensive reporting process as a mechanism for the injured worker to report a work related or a non-occupational injury. The cause of the injury will dictate the type of wage replacement insurance carrier and their respective forms used in the reporting process.

There are several parties involved in the reporting and recovery process. Each party is obligated to satisfy a set of roles and responsibilities throughout the program. Some of these roles and responsibilities are legal obligations, some are morale obligations, and others are best practices. The roles and responsibilities should be clearly outlined in the company's policies and procedures for the program.

The Form 7 is a form designed by the WSIB. It is a form completed by the employer to describe the event resulting in the injury as well as the details of the injury itself. The Form 7 is the employer's opportunity to describe the events leading to the injury. The Form 7 should include any facts providing evidence of the company's due diligence such as detailing any training, policies, procedures, and physical demands of the tasks causing the injury. The information should also include details of any prior history of injury to the same body part.

Managing claims and lost time becomes critical in mitigating costs for claims. Development and implementation of return to work plans is just one tool in mitigating the costs of claims. This tool is a very important tool in effective claims management practices. These plans allow the workers to return to work safely while recovering without losing wages. The plans allow the employer to satisfy any legal or moral obligations to accommodate injured workers, reduce costs in the claims, and reduce lost productivity.

A thorough understanding of these roles and responsibilities as well as understanding the standard recovery periods for each body part, is critical to implement appropriate return to work plans. This understanding is an important component of developing a comprehensive reporting process. Policies and procedures that encourage this understanding will assist the employer in developing best practices for reporting and managing claims.

Key terms:

Adjudication	Lost Time
No Lost Time	Recovery
Reporting Process	Standard Recovery

Questions:

1. Describe the recovery process and discuss the significance of standard recovery for the recovery process.
2. Discuss the common elements and the differences between occupational and non-occupational injuries including differences within the reporting process.
3. Compare and contrast the roles and responsibilities of each of the parties in the recovery process.
4. Explain the differences and the significance of no lost time and lost time for injuries.

SECTION IV

UNDERSTANDING DISABILITY MANAGEMENT

Objectives:

After reviewing this chapter, the reader should be able to understand and explain the following concepts:

1. Define claims management.
2. Define disability management.
3. Discuss the difference between claims management and disability management.
4. Develop mechanisms for communication channels.
5. Planning how to monitor recovery.
6. Explain the concept and significance of restrictions.
7. Discuss the importance of medical documentation including Functional Abilities Forms, etc.
8. Understand the concept of accommodations.
9. Understand and apply any relevant legislation.
10. Identify the roles and responsibilities of each party.

CHAPTER 12

DISABILITY MANAGEMENT

Disability management is a program or a process, not a task. A well designed disability management program will assist the company to assign appropriate work, manage costs, maintain productivity, provide support for preventive activities, etc. To accomplish these goals and more, there are a number of elements and tools that need to be developed and implemented. Those elements include policies, procedures, forms, modified work program, and a program to facilitate and encourage recovery. A combination of these elements will assist the company in managing claims effectively.

Effective management of claims will have several advantages including decreased costs. It only takes one claim to get "out of control" to have a significant negative impact on a health and safety record as well as become very costly to financial bottom line of the company. In fact, depending on the wage replacement insurance program, the negative financial impact to the company can continue over three to five years from just one claim with high costs. The negative financial impact can include surcharges, lost opportunity for rebates, premium increases, fines and penalties from government agencies such as the Ministry of Labour or the Workplace Safety and Insurance Board, loss of future contracts or business, lost productivity, decreased morale, etc.

A disability management program should apply to claims from occupationally related injuries and illnesses as well as those that are not occupationally related. To demonstrate due diligence, a company should align the practices for managing both the occupationally related and non-occupationally related injuries and illnesses. Each injury and claim should be reviewed under its own merit but best practices dictate that the company's response to the claims should be consistent and fair. In order to ensure consistent and fair treatment of claims, a company can develop methods and mechanisms to address communication, return to work programs, work hardening programs, accommodation, due diligence, etc.

An interpretation of the Human Rights Code, would dictate that companies should not treat the non-occupational injuries any differently than the occupational injuries in terms of accommodation and return to work. In treating the accommodation and return to work program issues differently between the non-occupational and occupational injuries, companies would be open to discriminatory practices resulting in fines or penalties under the Human Rights Code of Canada, the Human Rights Code of Ontario, the OHSA, the WSIA, Employment Standards Act and the Labour Relations Act. Therefore, it is important to note that an effective disability management program should align the practices for return to work and accommodation activities for occupational and for non-occupational injuries in order to avoid any inconsistencies resulting in discriminatory treatment, fines, and/or penalties.

A best practice in ensuring that both occupational and non-occupational programs are aligned, the company can start by incorporating each of the insurance carrier's forms and build the company forms and procedures around the requirements of legislation (laws of the land) as well as the provider, and the business strategies of the company. For example, the company can develop a leave report form for the workers to request time off for any type of leave from work with options for occupational or non-occupational appointments, leaves, etc.

A key procedure to align practices in managing both the occupational and non-occupational claims is the return to work and work hardening programs. One form can facilitate any person that returns to work requiring accommodation and or work hardening regardless of the cause being generated from occupationally related incident or a non-occupationally related incident.

The common elements of the return to work form include listing the restrictions required and the rotation plan for various work assignments for a designated period of time. These common elements provide the structure to treat all restricted workers in the same, fair and consistent manner without distinguishing the claims by their origin. This will cover the employer for due diligence in treating all restrictions and all workers the same reducing chances of violating human rights and or mitigating inadvertent discriminatory practices.

Disability management programs depend on forms for consistency and diligence in legal record keeping. However, there are other key elements to an effective disability management program which include but are not limited to: communication, monitoring recovery, proactive response to feedback, planning, and assisting workers to a productive level despite any long term restrictions if necessary.

CHAPTER 13
COMMUNICATION

One mechanism to foster communication between the company and the worker is the incident report. The report form requests all the information summarizing the details of the event that occurred regardless if the event included injuries, property damage or otherwise contrary to procedures of the company. The incident report should include questions that will collect the information required to complete any government forms such as the WSIA's Form 7 for a workplace injury or any Ministry of Environment forms for an environmental event.

Even though the incident report form is primarily used for workplace accidents, the form can be used for near miss events. Reporting near misses will help the company resolve potential issues before injuries happen through developing and implementing corrective actions as preventive measures. The incident report form becomes a critical element in the company's prevention activities development.

Communication is significant since it can provide valuable feedback from the worker and or the benefits carrier including the adjudicator. The feedback will help the company to adjust the return to work plans, influence decisions on claims, discovery, etc. Feedback can occur constantly throughout the various stages of the claim from open to closure. Monitoring claims provide constant opportunities for communication with the adjudicator of the benefits carrier allowing the company to understand the information influencing the claim.

Information discovered through communication can include factors influencing decisions, medical implications to restrictions, requests of the benefits carrier, monitor the status of requests by the company (including decisions on entitlement, cost relief from Secondary Injury Enhancement Fund (SIEF), amalgamation, objections to lost time or claim entitlement), etc. This information is crucial to assist the company in planning the next steps in return to work process, considering the use of independent medical evaluations, requesting cost relief through SIEF, objecting to entitlement of the claim based on facts, objecting to lost time based on modified work plans, and projecting claim costs.

Communication with the worker is essential in understanding the worker's concerns and requests during the recovery process. Activities as a result of these concerns and requests can prevent reinjury or expedite recovery. This does not mean the company should relinquish any management control because of the requests of the injured worker. The company must maintain control of business operations as well as review the worker requests for accommodation.

In other words, the injured worker should not be dictating what they should or should not do. However, the worker should participate in the planning of the return to regular duties. The worker providing constructive feedback will allow the company to understand the barriers and adjust accordingly. This is a particularly difficult line in the sand to manage. The chapter on return to work and return to regular duties will further discuss some tips on managing the delicate line between managing workers and managing accommodations.

Nevertheless, all communications with anyone in relation to the claim whether it be the worker, the medical professionals, the adjudicators of the benefit carrier, the company's executives, can be evidence of due diligence. Therefore it is critical that any communication should be documented in writing (or email) and filed into the appropriate file. Disability claims files should be separate from the employee's employment file.

The written documentation trail will provide support for any decisions made along the recovery process. It is critical to document all communications. The written note could be as simple as the casual reference to a person's body motion during an observation, to something as complex as the notes from a formal meeting with the worker. It is very important to document a worker's concern or a worker's explanation for lack of performance because it may become evidence later in the claim supporting functionality. This information could support decisions in the claim such as adjustments to the plans, closing the claim, denial of benefits, etc.

Constant communications between the company and the wage replacement benefits carrier is important for effective claims management. Sharing current information on the claim will allow the adjudicators of the claims to make appropriate and informed decisions on the claim. The information assists the company to monitor and adjust the strategies to manage the recovery of the worker.

The sharing of information with the benefits carrier will assist the company in preparing work hardening plans for the worker to mitigate lost time and lost productivity. The company will also be able to plan the release of FAFs. Furthermore, it will allow the company to determine if and when a second medical opinion would be appropriate. The company can use the results of independent medical evaluations to provide evidence to address contentious issues like capabilities, permanent restrictions, degree of total disability, status of recovery, etc.

All communications should be recorded on file. The documentation may serve as evidence in the file at any time. Each file should be treated with the same consistent and fair management style. The style should assume that any documentation filed will be used in legal proceedings either as part of an appeal process or maybe proceedings to address human rights violation complaint. Future reviews of the file or legal proceedings will rely heavily on the documentation to piece together the facts of the event. Human memories can become inconsistent over time. Consequently, memories are not as reliable in legal proceedings. Written documentation is consistent and reliable. Even though communication may take many forms such as verbal, electronic, fax, written, etc., a written record of every communication is essential for supporting appropriate decision making, efficient claims management and potential legal proceedings.

CHAPTER 14
MONITORING RECOVERY

An effective disability management program should involve activities that support the progress of recovery. Monitoring the status of claims and the recovery progress will assist the disability management program in developing a continually evolving plan for each injured worker. The activities taken to assist the worker in returning to work will demonstrate the company's activities to comply with their legal obligations under various pieces of legislation. Therefore, monitoring and facilitating the recovery process is important in assisting not only in returning the worker back to the worker's pre-injury health and levels of productivity but also to demonstrate the company's activities in due diligence and compliance.

Despite the most comprehensive and well-functioning health and safety programs, injuries may still occur ranging from very minor to fatal. Every injury has a recovery period. The time it takes injuries to heal varies depending on the severity of the injury and each injured party's personality. To further understand the recovery process starts with exploring all the possible outcomes of an injury. Every injury has one of three (3) outcomes:

1. The injury heals and the worker is able to return to their pre-injury health;
2. The injured worker dies from the injury or complications of the injury; or,
3. The injury does not heal but death does not occur, however, the results of the injury are at a

level of severity that the medical professional declares a permanent impairment and consequently, permanent restrictions.

Most companies in Ontario understand and comply to their obligations in reporting occupational injuries to the WSIB. If the company has a short term or long term disability program as part of their employee benefits program, the company will administer the paperwork accordingly for non-occupational injuries. However, effective disability management does not stop once the initial claim paperwork has been filed. There are several key strategic steps that follow the initial application for benefits that are critical in mitigating further costs, lost time, morale, lost productivity, etc. Some of these steps include but are not limited to:

- monitoring status of claim
- monitoring worker history
- monitoring status of restrictions
- monitoring employee emotional and mental status
- monitoring recovery
- monitoring return to work progress
- monitoring return to work plan
- monitoring decisions
- monitoring costs of claims
- projecting future costs of claims and budgeting
- monitoring the premiums
- monitoring lost time away from work
- monitoring days away from pre-injury or regular duties
- monitoring accommodations
- monitoring requests of workers
- monitoring requests of the benefit carrier
- monitoring requests of the employer on either the worker or the benefit carrier
- communicating with workers
- communicating with the benefits carrier
- documenting of all discussions and interactions
- managing information – electronically and manual paper

- managing files – historical, future projections and future planning
- managing and planning strategically

Monitoring the recovery and severity of each injury regardless of occupational or non-occupational origins, is very important to determine key timeframes such standard recovery, return to work, claim closure, etc. In addition to the key timeframes, monitoring claims allows for immediate claim status awareness, current decision status, current claim cost status, current projection of future WSIB costs, etc. If a company does not monitor the claim, the claim could exceed the normal recovery and have increased costs or the worker does not return to work or regular duties in a timely fashion resulting in increased costs, poor employee morale, increased (and likely preventable) amount of lost time, increased the amount of preventable lost productivity, etc.

In Ontario, companies are not permitted to request specific medical information or details on a medical diagnosis. Employees may give such information to an employer but the employee is not required to divulge any personal medical history or current conditions to the employer unless the medical condition is part of a bona fide requirement of the job.

One tool that a company can use to monitor the progress of a person's recovery or current status in the recovery period is a Functional Abilities Form (FAF). The FAF outlines the injured person's restrictions or capabilities at specific stages of recovery. This information is critical for the company to develop a suitable and appropriate return to work and or work conditioning plan for the injured person. The plan can be adjusted as the information on the FAF changes during each phase of the recovery.

The FAF is a form from the WSIB used in the workers compensation program in Ontario. However, an employer can develop an internal FAF type form to use for either occupational or non-occupational disability management since the return to work program should not be specific to only one or the other type of injury. FAFs are controlled by the employer and are given to workers upon the worker's request or the company's request for updated information. The updated information is critical for continually improving or reviewing the suitability of the return to work or the work conditioning plan.

Each time the FAF is completed by a medical professional, the medical professional charges the WSIB a fee. The cost of the fee is then charged back to the injured worker's WSIB claim. As a result, the WSIB claim costs are charged back to the employer at a ratio of $5.00 for every $1.00 the WSIB spends in the claim.

In addition to direct claim costs, the FAF may also initiate a new claim set up with the workers compensation carrier or wage replacement benefits carrier. The FAF could generate the setup of a new claim because the Form 7 has not yet been received by the WSIB from the employer. However, sometime, a new claim will be set up in error because the FAF does not have the claim number on it. This error will cause a duplication in claims and the employer must object to the WSIB based on the fact the claim already exists and this was FAF was not the result of a new incident.

An employer can avoid this potential error of duplication by only issuing a blank FAF for claims not yet established. Once a claim is established, the employer should pre-fill the portion of the FAF form that identifies the current claim number. A best practice for any employer is to tightly control the issuance of new FAFs. Any requests for subsequent FAFs should be emailed to the Claims Management Advisor to issue prefilled FAFs. The prefilled FAF will be printed and delivered to the Supervisor's Office or to the employee directly within the same or the next shift. This practice will avoid duplication in claims processing at the benefits carrier and it will allow the company to control the costs of issuing FAFs.

In addition to the FAFs, employers can monitor recovery through communication with and feedback from the injured party. The feedback from the injured worker to the supervisor, HR or the claims management advisor can provide valuable information regarding the progress of the recovery as well as the suitability of the work plan. The worker reporting difficulties or the astute observations from coworkers or supervisors can provide information to promote early intervention before the fully debilitating exacerbation can occur.

Feedback from the worker is required for the company and the medical professionals to address any barriers to the assignments or to the recovery. Feedback from the Supervisors will help the company to adjust the plans appropriately. Feedback from the medical professionals is necessary for the company to provide the worker with suitable accommodation. The feedback between the company and the medical professionals as well as the benefits carrier will assist in the effective management of the claim, ensuring suitability of the work plans, promoting the health and wellness of all workers, ensuring open communication of all the parties involved, ensuring all levels of management are aware of the worker's progress and status, etc. It is a best practice to document each communication in order to maintain a paper trail of all information related to the claim.

Furthermore, the feedback from the worker can also promote active participation in developing and adjusting specific return to work plans or work conditioning plans. This active participation will assist in greater cooperation in the plan itself as well as promote positive relationships between the employer and the worker. All feedback should be reviewed and considered when developing and implementing the return to work or work conditioning plans. With some information, a consultant may be used to review the validity of the information as well as how to incorporate the value added portions of the feedback into the plans.

As previously discussed, any form of communication with the worker and the supervisors should be documented to the worker's file. Accurate documentation should assist in the development and implementation of suitable and sustainable return to work plans or work conditioning plans. Each return to work plan or work conditioning plan starts with a written offer of accommodated work by the employer. The employer must present this offer and review the offer with the worker and the worker representative. The presence of the worker representative is a good idea because the representative is a witness to the discussions in the meeting. As a witness, the representative can assist both the worker and the employer in understanding all the concerns in the discussion.

The written offer of accommodated work is a valuable tool for the employer to monitor the effectiveness of the accommodation during the recovery of a worker. The effectiveness of a return to work or work conditioning plan depends on several factors including the written offers, the accuracy of the restrictions, the suitability of the work performed during recovery and the worker's cooperation with the treatment as prescribed by the medical professionals.

In addition to the written return to work offer, implementing methods to monitor and facilitate recovery will support the modified work program in an effective disability management program. Methods for monitoring and facilitating recovery include developing systems to:

- Track the severity (lost time) and the frequency of injuries or illnesses
- Designing ergonomic workstations
- Developing medical networks
- Using independent medical evaluations (IMEs)
- Developing and implementing policies and procedures to prevent injuries and ensure compliance to all legal requirements
- Participate in Safety Groups
- Building Positive Relationships between the company and
  - workers
  - the WSIB and other benefits carriers
  - Ministry of Labour (MOL)
  - Ministry of Environment (MOE)
  - medical professionals

The return to work program includes the offer of modified work and the work hardening plan. In order to provide the most suitable work within the worker's restrictions, the restrictions must be current and up to date. By monitoring each claim in a timely fashion, the company can request timely updates in terms of restrictions from the worker. The worker will then review the status of restrictions with their medical professional. The medical professional will complete a new FAF. The worker will return the new FAF with current restrictions to the company. Finally, the company will make the appropriate adjustments to the return to work plan or the work hardening plan.

Other methods of communication and feedback include conversations with the worker on the progress of the recovery, communication with the benefits carrier to review claim status, arranging for assessments or evaluations at strategic points in the recovery, requesting cost relief from the WSIB, etc. Essentially, the company should not just accommodate a worker at the onset of the restrictions and leave the worker there without follow up both from the worker and the benefits carrier on progress of the recovery. Monitoring the claim and facilitating the recovery can progress the return to regular duties in a more timely fashion increasing productivity and reducing costs. Therefore, as a best practice, the company should foster a supportive and cooperative recovery process with the injured worker, benefits carrier and the respective medical professionals.

There are many advantages to both the worker and the company in monitoring and facilitating the recovery process through support, cooperation and an effective return to work program. The reduction of severity of the injury reduces the recovery time of the worker and the decreases the potential of costs for the employer. The reduction of lost time will clearly reduce the costs of the employer as well as return the worker to productive life in a timely manner. The reduction of costs over the recovery period and the life of the claim will assist the company in increasing potential profit.

An effective program should improve labour relations between the company and all workers. The worker continues to perform value added work through the return to work program increases the worker's productivity and confidence during recovery. The pre-injury health and productivity are restored in a shorter period of time reducing costs for the company and restores the lifestyle of the worker. Fostering a health and safety culture that is patient and supports the recovery process can facilitate the worker's full recovery and improve morale of the workplace.

Monitoring recovery is very important to ensure that the worker returns to pre-injury health status and productivity levels. It can also to assist the worker through the recovery by offering alternatives for challenges or barriers in the recovery. For example, if the worker is not getting the therapy as prescribed by the doctor due to costs, then the company can review any assistance they may provide to allow the worker to get the necessary therapy.

Another example of the employer removing barriers for the worker can be related to timely medical intervention. If a worker does not have a family physician to follow through the recovery, the company can offer to arrange an appointment with a company sponsored physician. This medical appointment can provide the worker with follow up progression as well as provide the employer with a second opinion. The medical intervention can also assist in arranging for further medical testing, etc. to ensure appropriate diagnosis, prognosis, and courses of treatment. However, despite medical intervention being required, the employer cannot force the worker to participate in any therapy or medical procedure if the worker does not want to participate. The company should allow the benefits carrier to determine the worker's refusal as contrary to the worker's obligations. Once the carrier has determined the worker has violated their obligations by not participating in prescribed medical treatment, then the carrier will likely terminate the worker's claim.

A strategic element in the recovery process is early medical intervention. Early medical intervention can provide treatment for an injury at the early stages of an injury. Treatment at the early stages of an injury increases the chances of full recovery, reduces the chances of recurrence, reducing the chances of permanent impairment and shortens the recovery period. Sometimes the injured worker may not have access to expedient medical intervention. Therefore another best practice for a company is to establish a medical network that will assist the injured worker with receiving earlier medical intervention and provide the employer with second opinions.

The medical professionals can also provide valuable medical information to the carrier on behalf of the employer. The employer can use this information to request cost relief, claim entitlement termination, amalgamations, etc. This medical intervention could include:

- treatment such as physiotherapy or chiropractic therapy;
- Medical testing like CT scans and MRIs within a reasonable period of time without the eight to twelve (8 – 12) month waiting list; and,
- Second (medical) opinions in the face of disagreements over restrictions and safety concerns.

Recovery is dependent on the type of injury, severity of the injury and the person. Each person heals in their own time. By closely monitoring the recovery process, the company can provide guidance and assistance in progressing the worker's return to regular duties and pre-injury health in a safe work environment. One way to accomplish this is for the company to hire an ergonomist either as a consultant or as a direct employee.

An onsite program with an ergonomist can provide job coaching and job mentoring to all the workers. The job coaching and mentoring may prevent injury from occurring when working with workers who may be experiencing a little bit of pain but they have not (yet) reported an injury. Job mentoring can also correct poor body movement to prevent injury with workers who may be at risk for injury because of how they are completing a task. This practice will encourage workers to use the ergonomist's services prior to getting injured.

Ergonomists can assess all the workstations in the company for optimal body function reducing the risk for injuries. The ergonomist will complete a physical demands analysis of each work station. The physical demands analysis will identify any placement, motion, activity at the workstation which would be high risk to causing injury. The ergonomist would then work with the engineers to correct any high risk areas of the workstation to reduce the risk of injury.

The ergonomist can also work with engineers to develop standard guidelines in designing product and work stations. These standards can implement consistent low risk workstation designs. Low risk workstation designs can save the company additional costs by developing the workstation correctly before launch and before any injuries occur rather than spending additional resources to correct the issues after the launch and after injuries occur.

In addition to these services, the ergonomist can also assist the company in monitoring and facilitating the recovery of each worker by supervising the progression of recovery. The ergonomist can report to the company any recommendations for medical attention and further treatment or testing that would benefit the worker. Ergonomists can gently press the recovery forward with the worker with simple job coaching and communication.

Even the best medical care and treatment cannot guarantee quick recovery. It cannot even guarantee recovery within the standard recovery period. Even the standard recovery is considered the average time that a specific injury takes to heal. Monitoring recovery periods will enable the employer to recognize when some injuries will exceed their standard recovery period. This will allow the employer to plan for future long term suitable and sustainable placements for those injuries that do not heal to the pre-injury status.

For those injuries that do not heal within the standard recovery period, the medical professional may consider permanent impairment. In addition to long term or permanent impairment implications for injuries that do not heal within the standard recovery periods, long term injuries have a higher likelihood to experience peripheral complications such as depression, adjustment difficulties, addictions, etc.

Prolonged recoveries and prolonged restrictions can contribute to additional stress and mental health issues for injured workers not only in the worker's work life but also in their personal life. It is very important to assist the injured worker in maintaining positive attitude and remain focused on the worker's capabilities during the recovery process. By focussing on what the worker can do rather than dwell on what the worker cannot do, will assist the worker to stay positive. As a result, the worker will be able to work through the challenges during the recovery process especially during prolonged recoveries.

In the cases where prolonged recoveries are occurring, the medical professional, usually the family physician or a specialist will "declare" the injured worker to be permanently impaired. The permanent impairment is caused by the injury. The medical professional will only consider declaring permanent impairment when the worker continues to experiences challenges beyond the standard recovery period. The determination of permanent impairment and subsequent permanent restrictions will trigger a series of actions from the medical professional, the wage replacement benefit carrier and the employer regarding the future of the worker especially the future employment options for the worker.

Upon the determination of permanent impairment, the wage replacement benefits carrier will have to make some decisions on the claim. If the worker has not returned to work during the recovery process, normally, the benefits carrier will determine if the worker is eligible for retraining. Sometimes the permanent impairment is so severe that the worker will remain totally disabled until the person reaches the age of 65. Once a worker turns 65, benefits and, essentially, the claim will be terminated. At the age of 65, the worker will be eligible for Canada Pension Plan (CPP) or/and Old Age Security (OAS) for Canadian residents. If the worker is eligible for retraining, then the carrier will review the requirements for new career path and enrol the worker in the retraining program accordingly.

The workers compensation program in Ontario, bases decisions on medical documentation. The medical documentation supporting a permanent impairment triggers the WSIB Adjudicator to begin the process of assessing the file for a non-economic loss (NEL) award and for eligibility in the labour market re-entry program (LMR). Usually, a permanent impairment is only declared after the standard recovery has expired but the worker still is experiencing barriers that have not resolved.

Once the permanent impairment has been determined, the benefits carrier may decide to assess the worker's likelihood of returning to their own occupation or retraining for another career. If an employer has done an efficient job in monitoring the recovery in these types of cases, the permanent impairment should not be a surprise development in the recovery.

In Ontario, regardless of the wage replacement benefits carrier, in cases of permanent impairment, the employer has a duty to accommodate the worker if the worker is capable of working. The employer has a duty to accommodate the worker to the point of undue hardship. Undue hardship will be discussed later.

Once the worker approaches the end of the standard recovery period and is not showing continual progress in recovery, the employer should start preparing a suitable and sustainable long term placement. This preparation will provide evidence of due diligence regarding the employer's legal obligation of duty to accommodate. Developing a suitable and sustainable long term placement can be a daunting task. An employer can use the consulting services of specialists like ergonomists to assist in the developing and assigning the appropriate tasks. The duty to accommodate may mean changing the tasks up to accommodate the restrictions of the worker.

The Human Rights Code holds the employer to high standards in the legal obligation for duty to accommodate. Even when the employer finds it extremely difficult to accommodate all of the requirements, the duty to accommodate still exists regardless of the origin of the injury (occupational vs. non-occupational). The level of difficulty has to be at the point of undue hardship.

Furthermore, the employer should consult with an employment lawyer to specifically define their legal obligations especially if the accommodation requirements appear beyond the capability of the employer. The employment lawyer will assist the employer in understanding the legal definition and thresholds for undue hardship in relation to the employer's duty to accommodate.

CHAPTER 15
RESTRICTIONS

Restrictions are exactly what the word implies. The restrictions are a set of movements that the worker assigned the restrictions should refrain from performing. Should the worker continue to perform such movements, the movements will interfere with healing as well as may prohibit healing altogether. Medical professionals must balance activity and non-activity through the recovery process to avoid negative effects of both restricted movement and lack of movement such as atrophy of muscle tissue, "frozen shoulder", paralysis, etc. Only medical professionals will be able to assist the worker through this phase.

The role of the medical professional is to provide diagnosis, prognosis, and courses of treatment. The medical professional will provide restrictions to assist the employer in accommodating the worker during the recovery period. The role of the employer is to accommodate the restrictions by offering regular work or work that has been modified in order that the worker can safely perform the assigned work productively.

Restrictions will change throughout the course of recovery for every injury. It is important that return to work and return to regular duties plans adjust according to the changing restrictions in order to provide a safe environment for the worker as well as encourage the recovery process within the standard recovery period. Impasses may occur during the recovery process.

Impasses generally result from the company's return to regular duties plans conflict with the worker's perceptions of their capabilities. When impasses are reached, the employer has the right to request updated medical information. If the updated medical information is inconclusive or does not clarify the impasse, the employer also has the right under the law (the WSIA, Section 36 and the right to manage) to request an independent medical evaluation (IME). The IME should be able to provide the information required to clarify the capabilities of the worker.

In short term disability cases, restrictions are generally temporary. The restrictions will be in force until full recovery is reached. In this phase, the worker would temporarily refrain from performing activities that are outside the restrictions set out by the medical professional until the worker has fully recovered. Once the worker has fully recovered, the worker will be able to resume all activities they previously enjoyed prior to the injury.

In contrast, long term disability cases have restrictions that are long term. These long term restrictions may result in permanent impairment or permanent restriction status. These permanent restrictions will demand a long term or more permanent change in lifestyle for the worker. At this point, all parties should focus on the worker's level of function to perform tasks. This focus will enable to the worker to move forward in a productive manner.

If the focus of the worker is on their lack of function, the worker may become susceptible to depression or other complications that will prohibit or challenge the worker in moving forward with their new life. The employer can assist the worker in focusing on positive change and productivity by concentrating on capabilities of the worker continually. In doing so, the employer can provide support for both the worker's total wellbeing as well as to bolster the worker's confidence for improved productivity levels.

Regardless of the period of time required by the restrictions, the importance of the restrictions is that they give objective medical evidence of what the worker can or cannot do. It is this objective medical evidence that the employer relies on to develop and implement safe and suitable work for the worker during the recovery process. Restrictions are generally communicated to the worker and the employer by the medical professional on forms or letters. The WSIB uses the functional abilities form (FAF). Other wage replacement insurance carriers use other forms that allow the medical professional to answer the same questions or opportunity to list the restrictions of the worker.

The Functional Abilities Form (FAF)

If a worker receives medical attention for an injury which occurs at work, the company should be giving the worker a functional abilities form (FAF) for the doctor to complete. In the case where the worker requires restrictions, the medical professional will complete the FAF. An FAF is a WSIB form found on the WSIB website. Any software that supports worker compensation claims for any Ontario workplace should have the ability to print an FAF. The FAF is a tool for the doctor, the worker, the employer and the WSIB to monitor the progress of recovery through the changes in restrictions.

While the FAF should be used exclusively for occupational related injuries, the employer can develop a standard functional abilities form to be used for either occupational or non-occupational cases. However, the standard functional abilities form of the company will need the approval of all the benefits carriers involved before using the form. In additional to obtaining the approval of each of the benefits carriers, the company will have to negotiate the fee payment of the forms with each medical professional.

One of the biggest benefits of this type of form consists of the employer's ability to monitor changes in the restrictions' status in order to adjust the work plans accordingly regardless of the origin of the injury. The responsibilities in developing such a form for the employer include the following:

- The employer must get the approval of the WSIB to use the form in replacement of the existence of the WSIB's FAF.
- The employer must get the approval of the wage replacement insurance carrier for the short term and long term disability benefits.
- The employer must set up a payment system with the medical professionals to cover the fee for completing the internal FAF form. The amount of the fee can be negotiated. These fees will assist the employers in budgeting the appropriate amounts of these forms. Periodically, the employer should verify the amount being charged with those standard charges that

the WSIB or the insurance carrier would approve for payment. This comparison ensures
that the medical professional is not over charging the employer.

Supervisors and managers require sensitivity training so that they
understand how to keep medical information confidential and how
to avoid the medical information becoming the topic of discussion
with any employee. In fact, under the Privacy Act, employers are
required to physically lock up under lock and key any personal information which includes the employees' identity and medical information including employee files, worker's compensation files, as well
as short/long term files. Best practice dictates that each of these
personal records should also be filed separately and locked up separately.

The FAF will reveal important information about the worker's
capability of performing tasks. The FAF is used by disability management professionals to establish a strategic plan to assist the worker in working safely during the recovery process. The strategic plan
becomes part of the work hardening plan through the modified work
program. These strategic plans will be discussed later in this book.

The restrictions from the FAF are critical in developing and implementing a suitable work hardening or modified work plan. The
timing of receiving this information is also significant in an early and
safe return to work initiative in the health and safety program and
disability management program. To satisfy one of the responsibilities of the supervisor to offer the worker safe and suitable work
within the worker's restrictions, the FAF will allow the supervisor
some insight to the worker's capabilities. Once the supervisor understands the worker's capabilities, they are able to appropriately
schedule (offer) the worker with safe and suitable work.

FAFs should be distributed to the worker prior to the worker
leaving the facility for medical attention. It is important to understand that the company cannot stop nor force the worker to receive
medical attention. However, medical attention is highly recommended when the injury requires additional medical beyond first aid.
It is a best practice for the company to prepare an FAF package for
the doctor to review and complete, if the worker seeks medical attention.

The FAF package should include a functional abilities form (a
WSIB Form), a letter to the medical professional explaining that the

company has a modified work program, and instruction to the worker explaining their responsibilities and obligations throughout the recovery period.

Under the WSIA, only the worker or the employer can request an FAF form to be completed. Health care professionals should complete the form but they should not generate it. Any medical professional can complete the FAF. Doctors, chiropractors, physiotherapists, nurse practitioners are all considered medical professionals recognized to complete the FAF.

Each FAF has a time limit which usually correlates to the standard recovery chart. The timing of the restrictions is identified in Section 4 of the FAF. The health care professional completes this section. The new restrictions should show evidence of progression in recovery. If 14+ days section is checked, a best practice is to issue a new FAF to the worker at the second or fourth (2 or 4) week mark depending on the injury and the stage of recovery. When the time limit expires, the worker should bring another FAF to the medical professional for an update on the current restrictions.

The claims management advisor will issue a prefilled FAF at the appropriate time. If the worker requests a new FAF form, please refer them to the claims management advisor. When the timing expires, the employer should not assume that the worker can return to regular duties. Assumptions are usually incorrect and can lead to prolonged recovery. It is a best practice to continue to issue the FAFs until the medical professional releases all the restrictions or indicates that the worker can return to regular duties work without restrictions.

The FAFs, regardless of using the WSIB form, the form from the wage replacement carrier, or an internal form, are a key tool for the employer to use to develop and implement safe and suitable work plans for restricted workers. These forms outline critical information to allow the employer to understand how to accommodate the worker.

Accommodation

Accommodation is an action or series of actions to change the "normal" procedures or processes of performing a task in order for a person with restrictions to perform the task safely with reduced risk of re-injury or further aggravating the injury. For example, the employer can change the cycle time to a task from 30 seconds per part to 60 seconds per part to accommodate the restrictions to avoid repetitive work.

The word "accommodate" is a verb. Webster's Dictionary defines the word accommodate as *"...to make fit, suitable or congruous..."* Therefore, to accommodate a restricted worker is the action the employer takes to adjust a job so that it can be performed safely within a specifically defined parameter. The parameters are defined by the restrictions of the worker. The restrictions are listed on the FAF or on some other medical documentation.

A common misconception is that a restricted worker automatically requires "light duty". Generally, accommodation requires changing a normal job to a job that is lighter in physical demand since the restricted worker should be reducing the amount of physical demands placed on the injured part of the body. However, just because a worker has restrictions does not mean that a worker should "automatically" be assigned the lightest job or light duty jobs in the facility for two main reasons:

- Not all "light duty work" match the restrictions of the worker.
- In some cases, regular work may be determined as suitable within the worker's restrictions. In these cases, there would be no need to change the job at all in order for the worker to perform the tasks safely.

Accommodation requirements are based on restrictions. Restrictions should only be generated by medical professionals. There will be times that the wage replacement benefits carrier will impose restrictions for the worker. However, usually this is also based on medical documentation on their file for the worker. Just as some restrictions are short term, the corresponding accommodation will also be short term unless otherwise agreed upon. Similarly, permanent restrictions will provoke long term accommodation.

The accommodation is based on restrictions regardless if submitted directly from the medical professional to the employer or if the wage replacement benefit carrier imposes restrictions for the worker. Should the restrictions be permanent, the employer always has the option to request the worker to attend an independent medical evaluation (IME) to assess and clarify the worker's capabilities especially if the long term restrictions are vague or in contention.

This second opinion will assist the employer in providing evidence for due diligence in the duty to accommodate process when developing the long term suitable sustainable placement for a worker with permanent impairment.

Relevant legislation

There are several pieces of legislation that will influence both the claims management program as well as the health and safety program. Essentially, the common element for all pieces of relevant legislation is to prevent injury. However, if an injury does occur, there is a prescribed manner in which the injury has to be managed including return to work programs.

The relevant legislation in Ontario for a claims management program includes but is not limited to the following:

- Human Rights Code
- Occupational Health and Safety Act
- Privacy Act
- Ontario Disability Support Program Act
- Employment Standards Act
- Workplace Safety and Insurance Act
- Ontario Works Act

Each geographic area will have different legislation to account for especially when there are different countries involved. Each piece of legislation will address a specific subject or element of either program. The legislation will outline the rules, roles and responsibilities of each element.

SUMMARY

In summary, disability management is not a task. Disability management is a program that includes many vital elements to be effective. The company must develop and implement a set of policies and procedures outlining the commitment of the company and support the disability management process. The disability management program includes legislative requirements, ties to corporate business strategies, and requirements of the insurance carrier. The policies and procedures will allow for consistent and fair application of rules and treatment of all workers. Consistency will serve to diminish the risk of discriminatory practices or activities that could violate the human rights code.

The company could use the forms of the respective benefits carrier. However, the company may also develop their own forms to cover the requirements of the insurance carrier or legislative requirements to assist the company with disability management. The information from these forms will provide information critical in developing corrective actions, prevention activities and continuous improvements.

In addition to the forms, a modified work program including a written return to work offer and methods to monitor and facilitate the recovery process will be effective tools in efficient disability management. The documented historical pattern of the claim can provide valuable insight to future amendments and or future claims. Furthermore, the documented file will provide support and evidence of due diligent activity by the company. Should any disagreement in the file proceed to a hearing whether it be a WSIB Tribunal, a Human Rights Commission Tribunal, or a Labour Relations Arbitration, the documented file will provide the legal support of the position of the company. The documentation will exemplify the company's due diligence by demonstrating the company's effort(s) in providing accommodation for the worker within their available means.

Monitoring and facilitating the recovery process is a best practice in effective disability management because it supports the recovery of the worker. A worker who recovers to their pre injury level is more productive through the recovery process as well as upon full recovery. As the recovery progresses towards pre-injury health, all workers will start to understand that the return to work program is effective. The workers will support the company's programs upon seeing the results of the programs.

Workers will believe in results of a program. If the program provides evidence of the company's commitment to the return to work program and the prevention program, the workers will start to respect the programs of the company. Should the recovery not progress and the company fail to act, the workers will lose belief that the program is effective. Once workers begin to lose respect in the program, the workers may begin to become uncooperative in the process.

A worker with restrictions does not automatically justify assignment to light duty work. In some cases, regular duty type work assignments can be safe and suitable for some restrictions. Therefore duty to accommodate can be very simple with no special changes required. Duty to accommodate can also be very complicated requiring extreme amounts of special changes. The company is obligated to make changes to accommodate to the point of undue hardship.

It is important for the company to act in a timely manner when the program requires adjustment. Further medical assessments, evaluations of capabilities, communication with works, and consultations with the benefits carriers will be required to make the appropriate adjustments necessary to keep the recovery progressing. The recovery process should be a constantly evolving progression. The company must be prepared and strategically plan each step in each claim to effectively return the worker back to the pre-injury status.

Key Terms:

Accommodation	Duty to Accommodate
FAE	FAF
Human Rights Code	IME
Modified work	Recovery Period
Restrictions	Suitable
Sustainable	Undue Hardship
Work Conditioning	Work Hardening

Questions:

1. Define the recovery process.
2. Explore the purpose of restrictions.
3. Explain the employer's duty to accommodate. Compare and contrast the roles of each party.
4. Discuss the significance of communication within the recovery process.
5. Define FAF. What role does it plays in accommodating restricted workers?
6. Develop a plan to monitor recovery.

SECTION V

DISABILITY MANAGEMENT STRATEGIES

Objectives:

After reviewing this chapter, the reader should be able to understand and explain the following concepts:

1. Understand and develop an effective disability management program including managing both non-occupational and occupational related injuries.
2. Discuss the importance of a comprehensive reporting process and the role of the body part chart.
3. Explain the objection process as a strategy.
4. Applying historical patterning as a strategy to claims management.
5. Explain and apply due diligence from a reactive perspective.
6. Demonstrate an understanding of the company's obligations under duty to accommodate.
7. Explain undue hardship and its role in accommodating restricted workers.
8. Detail and develop a return to work program incorporating relevant legislation and social responsibilities for both lost time and no lost time injuries
9. Prepare modified work offers compliant with relevant legislation.
10. Define and integrate ergonomics into the development of the return to work program.
11. Develop and implement the physical demands analysis as a tool in the return to work program.
12. Differentiate work hardening and work conditioning in the return to work program.
13. Discuss the importance and legalities of networking.
14. Discuss the importance and roles of developing medical networks.

15. Recognize the role of independent medical evaluations (IMEs) and understanding the critical strategies of timing.
16. Explain the term maximum medical recovery and its role in the management of the recovery process.
17. Describe a Non-economic Loss (NEL) award and the process to have a NEL declared.
18. Discuss Labour Market Re-entry (LMR) and vocational retraining opportunities for workers with permanent impairment.
19. Understanding the legalities of frustrating contracts (anniversaries, use employment lawyers and responsibilities of benefits).

CHAPTER 16

EFFECTIVE DISABILITY MANAGEMENT

Disability Management is a process, not a task. In many companies, the disability management program will be separate and distinct from the health and safety program. While in other companies, the disability management process will be only one element of the health and safety program. Either way, both programs can only be as effective as their policies and procedures. Furthermore, the programs must include methods for monitoring and tracking effectiveness of the application as well as developing mechanisms for implementing continuous improvements.

In general a significant difference between the health and safety program and the disability management program is the focus of the program. The health and safety program focuses on the workplace only, whereas the disability management program considers both occupational and non-occupational elements. Regardless of the focus of the program, each program requires policies and procedures. Some of the policies and programs may overlap between the two programs. Similarly, the goals and objectives of each program may overlap between the programs.

Targets and objectives are critical in monitoring the effectiveness in any program. Strategic goals and objectives for both the health and safety program and the disability management program should be aligned with those of the company's strategic business goals and objectives. By linking the goals and objectives with the company's strategic business goals and objectives, the performance of the program will have a direct impact on the company's overall performance. Management will review the performance of each program as strategic partners in operational management. Therefore, the disability management program, by design, becomes another instrument management recognizes as an intricate part of doing business.

One strategic goal for the company is to reduce costs in order to increase profits. The goal for the health and safety and disability program management programs should reflect this strategic goal by incorporating the cost reduction focus on objectives like reducing the program's budget costs through continuous improvements. Therefore, it would be a best practice to align objectives of the disability management program including decreasing costs, with the corporate objective of decreasing costs to improve the company's positioning for profitability.

There are many ways to reduce costs. In disability management, one way to decrease costs is to decrease the number of lost time days since lost time days are one of the biggest cost drivers in claims management. More specific advantages of decreasing the number of lost time days include:

1. Decreasing the costs in terms of insurance premiums for the workers compensation program and the wage replacement programs.
2. Decreasing the costs of replacing the lost wages.
3. Decrease the lost productivity of injured workers during the lost time and during recovery.
4. Decrease the lost productivity of coworkers covering the regular duties of the injured worker.
5. Decrease the need for overtime to cover the injured worker's lost productivity.
6. The reduction in lost time days results in the reduction of lost productivity. If productivity increases, then the following costs are not incurred:
   a. Costs of training a replacement;
   b. costs of recruiting a replacement;
   c. costs of low morale;
   d. costs of short shipments;

    e. costs of the poor quality of a newly hired replacement; and,

    f. costs of workplace disruptions; etc.

7. The decreased costs of potential legal fees for:

    a. legal counsel and advice;

    b. tribunals for the WSIB and Labour Relations grievances;

    c. arbitrations; and,

    d. mediations.

In order to achieve the objective of reduced lost time, the company should focus on reducing the number of injuries. Similar to the health and safety program's target to reduce workplace injuries, a target of disability management would be to reduce the number of lost time days as a result of injuries (both occupational and non-occupational). It would be difficult to decrease the number of lost time days if the health and safety program was not committed to decreasing the number of workplace injuries.

Reducing the number of lost time days also extends to address the lost time for non-occupational injuries. While the company has very little control over the frequency and severity of non-occupational accidents and injuries, the employer does have control of providing health and wellness options to the employees to encourage healthy choices. These healthy choices can lead to reduced injuries and illnesses that would result in lost time and increased costs.

Consequently, a company can reduce the number of injuries by engaging in activities to prevent injuries from occurring. Corrective actions and legal compliance to the Occupational Health and Safety Act can lead to preventing injuries at the workplace. Similarly, providing health and wellness options to employees such as gym memberships, smoking cessation programs, etc., can lead to the employees making healthier choices outside the workplace. These healthier choices can lead to reduced injuries and illnesses outside the workplace. Therefore, prevention is a fundamental corner stone to a functioning health and safety program and an effective disability management program.

Disability management is not only about workplace injuries but also about managing non-occupational injuries. Best practices in disability management will include procedures in supporting the worker in the recovery and return to work process of any injury whether the injury is related to the workplace or non-occupational. The origin of the injury makes a slight difference in the paperwork but not in the process of disability management for the company.

Regardless if the injury is the result of an occupational or non-occupational event, under the Human Rights Code of Canada, the Human Rights Code of Ontario, and the WSIA, the employer has an obligation to accommodate restricted workers. The WSIA is designed specifically to address occupational injuries. In comparison, wage replacement insurance programs for non-occupational injuries are not directly regulated as closely by legislation. Even though there is no specific legislation to parallel the WSIA for the management of occupational injuries, the Human Rights Code for both Ontario and Canada protects the rights of disabled workers for dignified work and return to work without discrimination.

The alignment of management practices for occupational and non-occupational injuries can provide evidence for legal compliance under both the WSIA and the Human Rights Act. Applying strategies for return to work for both occupational and non-occupational injuries can ensure fair and consistent treatment of all injuries regardless of the origin of the injury. Despite the origin of the disability, the employer is legislatively required to evaluate the restrictions of the disabled worker in order to develop and implement a return to work plan which is safe, suitable, and sustainable.

To align the return to work strategies with the corporate strategies, monitoring all the claims become important. Monitoring claims can provide a mechanism to the company for measuring effectiveness. In addition to effectiveness, monitoring claims can result in the following advantages:

- administering timely return to work plans to reduce lost time and associated costs;
- ensuring the claim closes in a timely fashion to reduce costs;
- ensuring only appropriate costs are charged against the employer's account;
- monitoring the timing of the recovery against the standard recovery period in order to request cost relief from Secondary Injury Enhancement Fund (SIEF) (for work related injuries);

- tracking accurate severity of injuries through lost time days;
- ensuring restrictions are current and appropriate resulting in return to work plans being current and appropriate to effectively reduce the potential of complications during recovery or prolonging recovery; and,
- current restrictions and appropriate return to work (including return to regular duties) plans assist in mitigating lost productivity and increased training costs; etc.

In addition to monitoring restrictions for updates and appropriateness, monitoring other elements in the process can lead to effective claims management. Monitoring the employee's mental health and the progress of a return to work or return to regular duties plans are interlinked in effectively managing claims. If the worker has a positive attitude towards recovering and is actively participating in treatment, the more likely the worker is to participate in the return to work plan. Participating in the return to work place can lead to timely recoveries.

Effective disability management is an overall process. In order to monitor the recovery process, not only does the company need to monitor the restrictions, but the mental health of the worker is critical as part of the healing process is the attitude towards healing. In other words, if the worker has a positive attitude towards healing and returning to regular duties, then the worker is likely to return to regular duties in a timely manner. However, if the worker is exhibiting signs of depression or refusing to participate in the course of treatments or return to work plans, then the worker may likely experience delays in the recovery process.

CHAPTER 17

NETWORKING – MEDICAL AND LEGISLATION

One critical element to a successful disability management program is building professional relationships. These relationships should be based on respect, courtesy, information, fact, professional services, professionalism, business etiquette, etc. Networking is important to establish support, information network, decision making partnerships, broad range of services availability, lessons learned database, etc. There are several types of networks to set up for an effective disability management program. The networks can work independently or interdependently.

The company and the workers are not the only participants in the return to work process that have responsibilities. The medical professionals have obligations to provide the appropriate information to assist the workers in returning to safe suitable work including completed FAFs, FAEs, further medical investigations where appropriate, benefit carrier forms for disability information, etc.

The medical information is distributed in different routes. For instance, the restrictions and any information related to the worker's capabilities of performing tasks should be routed to the worker and the employer as well as the benefits carrier. Any medical information should be routed to the benefits carrier including the WSIB. Medical professionals communicating with the worker, the benefits carrier and to some extent, the company is important to ensure the return to work plan is safe, suitable and timely for all parties.

Each network system is comprised of key members providing services or information. Strategic members of a networking system for disability management for any type of claim include but are not limited to:

- Medical Networks including:
  - Occupational Physician
  - Nurse
  - Physiotherapist
  - Chiropractor
  - Specialists
  - Other medically related therapists (ie: massage therapists, orthotics, etc.)
- Ergonomists
- Employment Lawyer(s)
- Like Professionals in other companies
- HRDC
- Professional Associations
- Social Assistance
- Government of Canada – CPP
- Employee Assistance Programs (EAP)
- Social Workers
- Counselors
- CMHA (Canadian Mental Health Association)
- Legislation websites
- Health care benefit providers
- Arbitrators
- Mediators
- Benefits Insurance Providers – account managers, resources, etc.

For disability management dealing with worker compensation claims specifically, key members of this network will include but are not limited to:

- WSIB Account Manager
- WSIB Claims Adjudicators
- WSIB Nurse Case Managers
- Ergonomists

- WSIB Prevention Specialist and Services
- WSIB Return to Work Specialist
- WSIB medical consultant
- Appeals Resolution Officers (AROs)
- WSIAT
- MOL Inspectors
- Injured Worker Councils
- Employment lawyers

Networking can provide a pool of contacts and resources which will assist the company in disability management practices. These contacts and resources will provide valuable insight on current issues to correct problems or prevent recurrences. Situations and problems can be analyzed for solutions and effectiveness of solutions by using information from the collective networks.

A best practice for disability management is to send the worker for a functional abilities evaluation to determine the worker's capabilities. The employer would send the worker if the worker refuses the return to work plan or if there were some concerns about the injured workers capabilities. Another example would be to send a worker for an independent medical evaluation should there be prolonged recovery or a dispute on restrictions or treatment and no further action taken by the primary medical professional.

The medical documentation must be clear. Employers will use this medical documentation to support the company's position in order for the information to be an effective legal tool in managing claims. Other types of medical documentation that can assist in effective decision making include but are not limited to: updated restrictions, medical histories to support pre-existing medical conditions for cost relief, credibility to support objections, assessment of suitable modified work programs, mentoring and coaching for compliance and continuous improvements in the health and safety program, etc.

Functional Abilities Evaluation (FAEs)

A functional abilities evaluation (FAE) is an assessment that determines a person's capabilities in terms of physical or psychological function. The assessment is used to determine the physical capability a person can actually perform and the level the capability can be performed. The assessment will allow the medical professional to provide more accurate detail on the restrictions and limits or levels of a person's function. Typically medical professionals such as physiotherapists will conduct the physical function testing whereas a psychologist will perform the psychological function testing.

The testing is usually funded by the employer or the benefits carrier depending on who is requesting the clarification of information. The worker may also request this assessment but generally they will negotiate with the employer or carrier to fund the testing. However, if the worker is intending to use the results of the assessment to support their objection, then the employer and or the carrier may decide not to fund the assessment. This would force the worker to fund the testing to support their own objection.

If the employer has requested the FAE, the medical network of preferred service providers will allow the employer to arrange the appointment for the worker quickly. Choosing the medical professional from the predetermined medical network will assist the employer to choose a reputable and credible professional. The professional's credentials would be recognized and respected by the benefits carrier. The work of this respected professional will support the credibility of the report that the professional will produce at the end of the assessment.

The testing consists of a series of activities that are timed. The activities are designed to determine how long the person can perform the task and define the level of physical (or psychological) demand at which the task can be performed safely. It will also outline what tasks the person cannot perform at all. The tasks including lifting, carrying, walking, running, kneeling, crouching, standing, bending, fine motor finger movements, etc. These tasks will determine the tolerance levels which the person can perform each task safely. As a result, restrictions will be more accurately and better defined.

The testing generally takes about 4 hours and the worker should be advised to wear comfortable clothing including running shoes. Throughout the whole testing process, the worker will be encouraged to talk to the medical professional facilitating the testing. The communication will help the facilitator to understand what is happening to the worker as the person is performing the tasks. The worker will not be expected to perform tasks that will endanger them or will further injure them. The only way to avoid re-aggravation is for the worker to communicate pain levels and other symptoms as the tasks are performed. It is important for all the participants to understand that the worker is not being judged but rather the degree of function is being determined.

During the testing, the worker will report pain levels. Pain is subjective rather than objective evidence. The testing is designed to test the same function in different ways in order to determine if the pain or person's own interpretation of function are driving the test results. The facilitator will compile all the results of all the testing and interpret the results into a report outlining the functional abilities, restrictions as well as detailing the methods of testing.

Once the assessment and the report have been completed, the report is sent to the employer. The report should not include any personal medical information. It should only discuss the person's functional capabilities as they relate to performing tasks. The employer will use this report to adjust the return to work and work hardening plans accordingly should any changes be required. The employer should be sending a copy of this report to the benefits carrier along with a copy of the revised return to work or work hardening plans. Of course, if the worker objects to the information in the report, they will be able to express their concern through the objection process of the internal responsibility system of the company as well as through the benefits carrier.

FAEs can be requested anytime during the recovery process however they are expensive tests. It is cost efficient to request FAEs only for dispute resolution. It is very common to use this test for return to work plans that are particular difficult to determine. The testing is used to clarify the ambiguous information on file. Ambiguous information on file only results in further difficulties. FAEs will also be used after the recovery has surpassed the standard recovery period. The FAE at this point in the recovery process is used to determine the level of permanent impairment.

Independent Medical Evaluation (IMEs)
Independent medical evaluations (IMEs) can be used for a number of reasons. Classically, the employer will use the IME as a second opinion. The IME can also be used as medical intervention when the worker has not attended any medical intervention. This becomes effective to establish restrictions where the worker has continued to request accommodation but has not submitted the supporting medical documentation.

In Ontario, the workers compensation program (the WSIB), the WSIB has an established network of medical resources for the workers and the employers. Each party can tap into this medical network of resources to assist in the return to work and return to regular duties process. The resources include access to specialists, the Hand and Upper Limb Clinic (HULC), ergonomists, physiotherapists, etc. The employer can communicate with adjudicators to discuss these opportunities on a case by case basis. The employer should use these resources where it is reasonably necessary to do so. For instance, the requests should be based on facts and or conflicts in the return to work or return to regular duties process.

The main objective of an independent medical evaluation is to provide medical evidence to clarify any issues or ambiguity in the return to work plan. The IME report on restrictions and capabilities from the medical professional will need to be reviewed to amend the return to work plan accordingly. If the worker still contests the return to work plan despite the IME report, then a few things may happen:

- If the injury is work related, the WSIB may order the worker back to work if they approve the return to work plan. If the worker continues to refuse to return to work even after the WSIB has indicated that the plan is suitable, the WSIB may terminate benefits of the worker.
- If the injury is work related, the WSIB may determine that the return to work plan is not suitable. In this case, the worker will continue to remain off work and continue to receive loss of earnings benefits. The plan may not be suitable for many reasons such as:
  - The work outlined in the plan is not within the worker's restrictions; or,
  - The work is not sustainable or not a placement that will cover a long enough period of time.
- For long term work related injuries, the WSIB will determine permanent impairment, non-economic loss (NEL) award, then, review the file for eligibility for the labour market re-entry (LMR) program. In addition, at 72 months into the claim, the claims adjudicator will make

some determinations regarding permanent loss of earnings.

- If the injuries are not work related, the benefits carrier can make the same determinations as in option 1 or 2 above. In addition, a benefits carrier will consider the 24 month change of determination in a long term disability claim. At this point in the claim, the carrier will determine if the person continues to be totally disabled not only in the person's own occupation (such as is considered during short term disability and the first 24 months of long term disability) but in any occupation. If the medical on file does not support total disability from any occupation, then the benefits will be terminated. If the medical on file does support total disability from any occupation, then benefits will continue for as long as the medical supports the total disability.

The purpose of the IME should be to clarify the restrictions. This right should be exercised when it is reasonable to do so. This should not be an action the company exercises in the short term of the claim unless there is significant conflict regarding restrictions and capabilities of the injured worker. The timing is important to consider since the company does not want to appear unreasonable or the results are outdated before the conflict can be resolved. Sending the worker for too many of these appointments can be very costly and ineffective. The company would consider exercising this right because:

- The worker indicates that they cannot perform the work even though the work assigned is within their restrictions;
- Recovery is lingering beyond the normal or standard recovery period;
- The company suspects that the worker may have a pre-existing medical condition which is affecting the recovery of the current injury. From a worker's compensation perspective, this information will assist the company in obtaining

cost relief from SIEF. More importantly, regardless of the cause of the injury, this evaluation will help the company and the worker to
understand if there are further permanent restrictions. These restrictions may be new to the
company and they will affect the modified work
plan tasks and timing.

- Assist to resolve any conflict in getting the
worker back to work; and,
- Clarification of restrictions both in terms of
current restrictions as well as in terms of timing
of restrictions within the recovery process.

Independent Medical Evaluations (IMEs) can take many forms
depending on the reason for the evaluation. If the company requires
clarification on the capabilities of the worker, then a functional abilities evaluation (FAE) from a physiotherapist might be the best
course of action. FAEs evaluate how and if the worker can perform
certain tasks and the limits of these tasks as overseen by a certified
physiotherapist for example how much weight the worker can safely
lift and at the appropriate frequency.

Another type of IME can be a doctor's appointment. If the
company requires evidence of a pre-existing medical condition for
the WSIB to consider cost relief through SIEF, then an appointment
with a doctor or specialist may be more appropriate. Physicians can
review and or refer the worker for additional medical tests such as
ultrasounds, MRIs, EMGs, x-rays, etc.

In addition to determining pre-existing medical conditions, the
IME can allow the medical professional to expedite medical testing
and specialist appointments for the worker to attend. By expediting
these appointments, earlier medical intervention can prescribe more
timely therapies resulting in more timely recoveries and potentially
full recoveries.

Regardless of the reason of the evaluation, the medical service
provider is the choice of the company. The company should have a
list of medical professionals in their medical resource network to
choose from. The medical resource network should be compiled
according to need, expertise, reputable professional in the community, credibility with the WSIB or other benefits providers, certified or
licensed to practice in their area of expertise, etc. It is very important
that the service provider be reputable and credible with the benefits

carriers. Otherwise, any decisions to terminate claims or noncooperation could be jeopardized.

The company should research the medical professional prior to building the network. The research should not only verify the reputability and credibility of the professional, the cost is also a factor for the company to consider. According to the WSIA, not only is the choice of the service provider the responsibility of the company, the cost of the provider is also the responsibility of the company.

However, cost should not be the factor that justifies a less reputable or less credible provider. The return on investment for the service provided is calculated from the direct cost savings or cost avoidance the company realizes when a claim is denied, terminated, cost relief is awarded, as well as through indirect savings from activities implemented to prevent future injuries.

It is important to note that the doctor, under Ontario law, cannot provide medical details of the worker to the company despite the fact that the company paid for the services of the provider. If the worker signs a consent waiver for disclosure, then the medical professional can disclose medical information to the employer specific to the conditions of the signed agreement. Regardless of consent, the medical professional can speak on behalf of the company to the benefits carrier. The medical professional can supply medical evidence to the benefits carrier on behalf of the employer to request cost relief or other critical decisions on the claim that could influence the status or costs of the claim.

Once the worker has seen the medical professional for an IME, the medical professional should send a report to the employer. Once this IME report has been received, best practices in disability management suggests that the return to work plan should be reassessed. All the jobs available should be reassessed as well to re-examine suitability. This type of medical documentation is required to support the return the worker to a long term, suitable and sustainable position or to seek further legal advice on other options like frustration of contract.

In summary, independent medical evaluations (IMEs) are a valuable tool to assist in resolving misunderstandings between perception and actual physical capabilities or providing medical evidence to the benefits carrier for consider on matters like cost relief, amalgamation, permanent impairment, etc. The company has the right under the WSIA and the Human Rights Code to request a worker to attend an IME if it is reasonable to do so both in terms of timing and grounds.

The timing of a request for an IME is strategic. Therefore, careful consideration must be given to timing, reason, and service provider. The service provider must be reputable and credible for the results of the evaluation to have any influence in determinations in the claim and the claim status. The cost of the service provider is the sole responsibility of the company. Despite the cost of the evaluation, the potential return of investment can be significant in terms of direct cost savings, indirect cost savings and cost avoidance. The cost savings and cost avoidance result from favourable decisions from the benefits carrier such as a claim is denied or terminated, cost relief is awarded, and, future injuries are prevented. The IME is very significant in disability and return to work management. It is critical that the company establish a medical resource network of preferred service providers in order to provide medical assistance and support should any conflicts arise in the recovery process.

Maximum Medical Recovery (MMR)

Maximum Medical Recovery (MMR) is the same concept as standard recovery. Standard recovery period has been previously discussed in depth in an earlier chapter in this text. For the purposes of this text, MMR will be used interchangeably with the Standard Recovery limit.

Prolonged recoveries and prolonged restrictions can contribute to additional stress and mental health issues for injured workers not only in the worker's work life but also in their personal life. It is very important to assist the injured worker in maintaining positive attitude throughout the recovery process. It is important for all parties to remain focused on the worker's capabilities during the recovery process. By focussing on what the worker can do rather than dwell on what the worker cannot do, will assist the worker to stay positive resulting in working through the challenges during the recovery process especially during prolonged recoveries.

MMR becomes a tool in strategizing for the recovery planning process as it will allow the employer to understand the time limits in the recovery period and when to anticipate the declaration of any permanent impairment. In understanding the limits and the results of the limits, the employer can plan accordingly for return to regular duties or planning for long term suitable sustainable work plans.

Non-economic Loss (NEL) Awards

At the point in the recovery process where maximum medical recovery has been reached and the worker is still experiencing disfunction as a result of the injury, the medical professional, usually the family physician or specialist will "declare" the injured worker to have permanent impairment. Benefits carriers will have to make some decisions on the claim based on the medical documentation on file including the permanent impairment, permanent restrictions, and the possibility of return to work. The medical documentation supporting a permanent impairment triggers the WSIB Adjudicator to begin the process of assessing the injured worker for permanent impairment awards such as non-economic loss assessment (NEL) and vocational retraining such as the labour market re-entry program (LMR).

A non-economic loss (NEL) assessment is a medical assessment that determines functionality, limitations, and the effect of a permanent impairment will have on the person's whole life, personal and professional. Based on this assessment, the worker will be rewarded a financial sum depending on the degree of impairment and the level of change the impairment presents to the worker's life. For example, the worker who has experienced a broken finger injury at the workplace which did not heal properly. The finger does not bend then way it should lessen the strength of the grip and hand because of this new deformity in the finger. The severity of the deformity and the decrease of the strength will be factors that are considered to determine the NEL award. These considerations will be compared against the standard with a corresponding amount as established by the medical professional association guidelines.

In this case with the deformed finger, the NEL award would not be too large because the finger is not a critical body part to maintaining a "normal" life. However since it has created a permanent impairment that would have a negative effect on the worker's lifestyle, a NEL would be awarded. Generally, for this level of impairment the award may be as low as $500 to $5,000. In contrast, if the permanent impairment involved an amputation of the leg, the NEL award would be much greater. The NEL could be any amount including as high as over $100,000 depending on the level of change in function and lifestyle this injury has made as determined by the medical professional.

The NEL award is a sum which represents the settlement from the employer to the worker for the cause of the injury. This sum replaces the traditional court award for "pain and suffering" since the worker has waived their right to sue the employer for the injury by participating in the WSIB program in Ontario. The WSIA mandates that all employers in Ontario with workers participate in the WSIA insurance program. This is not optional for the employer or for the worker. As part of participation in the workers compensation program in Ontario, the worker gives up the right to sue the employer for the injury. The trade-off for giving up this right is the amount of money the WSIB determines for the NEL award for injuries involving permanent impairment.

The amount of the NEL award is determined by a chart used to compare the severity of the impairment with a predetermined amount according to each body part affected. The amount may be paid in a lump sum or in a series of instalments whichever is preferred by the injured worker. Of course, the injured worker or the employer has the right to appeal the amount of NEL by following the objection process as outlined in the WSIA policy and guidelines.

The NEL award will increase the costs of the claim and the employer is responsible for all the costs in the claim. If the employer participates in the NEER incentive program, then the NEL award also changes the claim type. The claim type will affect the NEER assessment of the employer. This change in claim type will have a financial impact on the employer's rebate or surcharge potential for that claim year.

Further changes to NEER include:

- the NEL award being captured in the Pension column of the NEER statement instead of the regular costs column, and,
- the NEL awards are not factored into the claim costs used to calculate the projected future costs

Labour Market Re-entry (LMR)
Usually, the determination of a permanent impairment will not only drive the NEL assessment. It will also set in motion the assessment of the injured worker's eligibility for the Labour Market Re-entry (LMR) program or vocational retraining for non-occupational injuries. After the NEL is assessed, the claims adjudicator will decide if the worker is qualified to participate in the LMR program or vocational retraining. It is rare for the WSIB to refer the claim to LMR without first assessing the person for a NEL award. To assess a worker for eligibility for participating in the LMR program, the

claims adjudicator must evaluate the worker's likelihood of returning to their pre-injury occupation based on the permanent impairment and the medical documentation on file.

Before the claims adjudicator can evaluate the injured worker for the LMR program, the employer must determine if they have a long term, suitable, sustainable placement within the permanent restrictions as determined by the permanent impairment of the worker. Should the employer not have any placement available, the employer must advise the claims adjudicator of the inability to accommodate the worker's restrictions. It is upon this advisement that the benefits carrier will begin the evaluation of the injured worker for vocational retraining.

In determining the long term, suitable, sustainable placement for the injured worker, the employer must consider other factors in addition to the permanent restrictions. It is not a decision that should be lightly considered. The decision has moral, financial and legal ramifications. These factors include but are not limited to:

- The employer's duty to accommodate under the Human Rights Code;
- The employer's duty to re-employment under Section 41 of the WSIA;
- The guidelines under any relevant collective agreement, if applicable;
- The Employment Standards Act;
- The culture of the workplace;
- Other relevant legislation; and,
- Costs of not returning the worker to work.

The WSIA, Section 41 (6) states that the employer must accommodate the worker to the point of undue hardship. If the employer cannot accommodate the worker, the WSIB has to determine if the employer has breached the WSIA, Section 41, the Obligation to Re-Employ. The employer is under the obligation to re-employ the worker, under subsection 7,

...until the earliest of:
(a) the second anniversary of the date of injury;

(b) one year after the worker is medically able to perform the essential duties of his or her pre-injury employment; and

(c) the date on which the worker reaches 65 years of age. 1997, c. 16, Sched. A, s. 41 (7); 2000, c. 26, Sched. I, s. 1 (3).... (WSIA, 1997)

Once the WSIB determines that the worker is medically fit to return to work and it is within the time period stipulated in Section 41 (7), then the employer is obligated to accommodate the worker with work within their restrictions at a comparable rate of earnings. Further in this Section of the WSIA, the employer must continue to employ the injured worker for six months or longer. If an employer terminates the employment with the worker within this six month period, the employer could be found in breach of their re-employment obligations and fined accordingly.

For non-occupational injuries, the employer still has re-employment obligations under the Human Rights Code. The employer is still obligated to accommodate the worker to undue hardship. It is a best practice to align the return to work program and its deadlines in order to avoid fines and penalties and discriminatory practices. Should the employer be accused of being in breach of the WSIA or the Human Rights Code, there will be an investigation by the respective authorities.

After an investigation, if the investigation determines that the employer breached the conditions of the Obligation of Re-employment under either the WSIA or the Human Rights Code, penalties and fines may be levied against the employer. The fines and penalties from violating either the WSIA or the Human Rights Code are not interdependent. The fines and penalties can be levied under both pieces of legislation where appropriate.

The employer must provide the burden of proof for undue hardship or that this worker was not the only person to be terminated or laid off. The employer must show that the worker was laid off due to seniority or standard past practice. Seniority is easy to defend in a court of law or at the Tribunal.

According to the WSIA, the claims adjudicator must determine if the worker can return to work, what type of barriers the worker will face when the worker returns to work, and if the worker cannot return to any type of work, the adjudicator must decide on the length of time to extend payment of benefits to the worker. If the employer cannot accommodate the worker and it is determined that the worker cannot return to any type of work because of the impairment, then the WSIB will likely decide to continue paying lost wages benefits to the worker until the worker reaches sixty-five (65) years of age. If the permanent impairment is so severe that the worker is not eligible for vocational retraining, then the WSIB will determine to pay lost wages until the worker reaches the age of 65. At sixty-five (65) years old, the benefits end according to the WSIA guidelines. At sixty-five (65) years old, the person can apply for CPP Disability, CPP Retirement, and Old Age Security.

In evaluating an injured worker for vocational retraining, the worker will be assessed for functionality, employability, marketability and transferrable skills, experience, wage earnings, etc. Generally, the claims adjudicator will outsource the task of evaluating the injured worker for job readiness and job suitability. The third party will determine the worker's aptitude for specific types of jobs and any skills or knowledge that is required for the worker to secure employment in this new career field.

The claims adjudicator will receive a report from the 3rd party facilitator outlining the career field chosen, the reasons for the choice and the course of action to obtain the necessary skills and education to secure employment in this new career. The report will also include a quote for the facilitator to continue managing the plan for the worker including the costs of the education plan. The claims adjudicator will then decide to approve the plan or deny the plan. If the plan is denied, then the worker will be reassessed or it will be determined that the worker is unemployable.

If a vocational retraining plan is approved, the claims adjudicator will not only continue to pay the worker ongoing wage replacement benefits, they will also pay for all the costs of the vocational retraining plan including that of the 3rd party facilitator, the costs of education and retraining, skills development costs, etc. In addition, the claims adjudicator will continue payment of benefits for about six weeks after completion of the vocational retraining plan in order to give the worker time to learn how to search and secure a job. All these costs in this course of action will add up very quickly.

The third party will not only make the assessment required but also manage the worker's skill development plan. Retraining and education plans can take a number of years to complete. Plans can include a university degree or college diploma after upgrading any high school credits that may have been below standard or nonexistent in the worker's profile but are necessary as pre-requisites to continue the plan for the University degree or College diploma. Therefore some plans can take years to complete and will incur large costs to the claim.

In summary, the vocational retraining program criteria include:

- The claims adjudicator refers a case to the vocational retraining program when:
  - Injury reaches MMR
  - Permanent impairment determined
  - NEL award determined (in workers compensation claims in Ontario)
- company is unable to offer long term, suitable, sustainable, value added placement to the worker
  - the benefits carrier determined if the company has breached their re-employment obligations under Section 41 of the WSIA or under the Human Rights Code
  - Layoffs with no recall dates can have the same effect as the company not accommodating the worker
- Vocational retraining costs are only applied to the claim as costs are incurred

Vocational Retraining in Non-occupational Injuries
Similar to the LMR process through the WSIB in an occupationally related injury, the benefits carriers of non-occupational injuries must make determinations on return to work and retraining if the return to work is not possible. There may be some differences in the timing of decisions however, the results are similar. The benefits carrier for non-occupationally related injuries will continue to pay benefits to the injured worker as long as the worker continues to be medically total disabled from their own occupation. After the prescribed amount of time as outlined in the carriers' policy and guidelines, if the worker cannot medically return to work, the worker will be assessed for eligibility for long term disability.

The average length of time for short term disability benefits ranges from six (6) months to twelve months depending on the policy and guidelines. In long term disability, the first 24 months will be assessed for total disability of the worker within the worker's own occupation. After 24 months of long term disability, the worker will be assessed for total disability in any occupation. At this point in the claim, the adjudicator may evaluate the worker for the potential of return to work or for retraining in other careers.

If the evaluation determines that the worker is able to return to work at the pre-injury employer, the carrier will notify the employer of the return to work option and the restrictions if any. The employer has a duty to accommodate those restrictions under the Human Rights Code to the point of undue hardship. The employer should go through the same return to work procedures as those used for the occupational related injuries as discussed above.

If the carrier has determined that the worker is unable to return to the pre-injury employer. The determination must be made regarding the worker is able to work again just not in the same occupation. The adjudicator then must have the worker assessed for retraining to a suitable new career. This process would be very similar to the process for retraining as the LMR process. Just the same as in the LMR process, the retraining program required may be as simple as taking a course like English as a second language (EASL) to as complex as a full University degree.

Regardless if the injury is caused from an occupational or non-occupational task and despite the best effort of the employer, there will be some cases that the employer cannot accommodate for a variety of reasons. For example, a company that is hired to do visual checks for quality parts would have a hard time accommodating a person who has lost their eye sight regardless of the cause of the injury (occupational or non-occupational). In these cases, the employer should consult a lawyer that specializes in employment law for consultation on frustration of contracts.

For frustration of contracts, the employer must consider the legal obligations under the Employment Standards Act, Human Rights Code, etc. The employment lawyer will ask the company for information on all the activities in the claim from start to finish. The company will have to prepare information from the file which includes evidence of the company's activities and due diligence to comply with their legal obligations. The employer should be prepared to provide this information not only to the company's lawyer but also to the worker's legal representation upon request.

Firstly, the employer should prepare information to support the frustration of the employment contract. The employer must be able to prove without a doubt that the worker has been and will continue to be absent from work for an extensive period of time. The definition of extensive period of time is interpretative. The lawyer will guide the employer through the process of determining the length of time that is appropriate to qualify as extensive.

In order to be sure that the worker will continue to be off work for an extensive period of time, the employer must be able to prove the worker's prognosis. The prognosis must support the worker's continued absence from work for the unforeseeable future. The medical documentation on file should support whether the worker will be able to return to work or not. If the prognosis from the medical professional's report indicates that the worker will never be able to return to work, this would be a good indication that the worker will continue to be absent from work for the unforeseeable future.

The employer will still have to follow all of the provisions of the Employment Standards Act for terminating a worker. A frustration of contract is terminating the employment contract with the worker. Notice of intent to terminate the employment relationship still has to be provided by the employer to the worker. The notice should be non-disciplinary in nature. The employment lawyer would be best suited to consult and advise on the whole process of frustrating the contract.

If the workplace is unionized, the employer will also have to consider all the provisions as set out in the collective agreement if a collective agreement exists. The employer is obligated to follow all the provisions of the collective agreement. If there are no specific provisions to guide the employer through this particular situation or in addition to the provisions of the collective agreement, the legislative requirements of the land where the business operates will have to be considered. If there is a written employment contract with the worker, all provisions of this contract must be met as well. The lawyer who specializes in employment law for the geographical area where the worker is working, again, will be the expert to consult with for the best advice on the matter.

Lastly, the employer must provide documented evidence supporting the company's activities. The evidence must show that the company has not violated their legal obligations for their duty to accommodate to the point of undue hardship. The lawyer will advise on what documentation is required to prove that the employer attempted to comply with their obligation under duty to accommodate but that the employer just was not able to accommodate.

The employer should not rely on the information from the carrier only regarding total disability or permanent impairment that may lead to the worker not returning to work. The employer should take additional steps such as sending the worker for an IME and FAE in order to determine accurate restrictions and capabilities to perform a thorough job match search. The company will then have documented evidence that the company took every step to accommodate the worker with restrictions.

Undue hardship is difficult to defend in a court of law. Undue hardship will have to be reviewed according to the company's market share, business status, financial status, the costs of accommodations, the costs of modifications, the costs of reconfigurations, etc.

Some other minor considerations the employer may want to review include the impact the termination will have on the rest of the workers in the workplace. The employer will have to be prepared to mitigate the risk of negative impact and any potential grievances that may result from the actions to frustrate the employment contract. The employer must anticipate all the ramifications should the employer pursue this course of action. Maintaining good employee relations is critical to successful effective business operations. Therefore it is important for the employer to protect and encourage continuously improving employee relations by anticipating and mitigating any bad public relations.

In short, when considering frustrating the employment contract of any worker due to absence from an injury, the employer should consult with a lawyer that specializes in employment law and disability law for the geographical area where the worker works prior to making any decisions or starting the process. Monitoring employee reaction to various activities of the employer will assist the employer in anticipating the further reactions of the workplace on activities such as terminating employees. The burden of proof is on the employer to support the inability of the company to accommodate workers with restrictions to the point of undue hardship. There are many factors in determining compliance with legal obligation as well as the factors to be considered for meeting the standards of undue hardship. All standards must be met before the employer can frustrate the employment contract. Employment lawyers are the best party to consult prior to frustrating the contract.

CHAPTER 18

HISTORICAL PATTERNING

History can reveal much information about a person's habits, life-style and culture. Similarly, historical patterning can establish a pattern of behaviour that will lead to estimating future behaviour. Historical patterning is the process of establishing predictions in a claim or for specific injury and recovery stages using the history of the person's claims. Patterns can be identified when a person continues to experience the same type of injury or injury to the same body part more than once. The details of each claim, the nature of each injury, the length of time for recovery, the amounts of lost time, the body parts involved in each claim, can all be statistically analyzed to predict the outcome for the future including the frequency of establishing new claims, the duration of future claims, the costs of future claims, etc.

Historical patterning will assist in prevention activities in developing and implementing corrective actions through anticipating future issues. Historical patterning can also help the employer to request specific changes to a claim which may result in cost savings. Therefore accurate and thorough record keeping in each person's file for claims is critical in effective and efficient activities in the claims management process.

Obtaining successful decisions to amalgamate a recurrence to an initial injury claim will depend on the congruency and compatibility of the previous claim to the current claim including the medical documentation on both claims, details of the injury, details of the events causing the injury, the link or continuity of medical care or treatment between the initial and the recurrence, etc. Through monitoring and thorough claims management practices, an employer can establish these links and compile all the necessary information on file through historical patterning.

The employer should monitor the history of the worker in order to determine historical injury patterns in order to request amalgamation of claims should the same injuries recur over time. This will result in appropriating costs in the proper claim year and possibly set up future claims for cost relief. The benefits of monitoring the claim include mitigating the risks of: further injury, prolonged recoveries, disproportionate costs, excessive lost time, aligning historical injury patterns to reopen claims instead of starting new claims, non-compliance with legal regulations (WSIA, OHSA, etc.), frequent or increased visits from the Ministry of Labour, employee job dissatisfaction, Workwell audits, customer dissatisfaction or non-compliance to customer requirements, increasing premium costs, surcharges and penalties, etc. Therefore, best practice would encourage companies to monitor their injury claims closely in order to: reduce costs, increase productivity, and improve recovery of injured workers.

Historical patterning will assist the employer in managing the claim and the costs of the claim. Historical patterning will allow the employer to better manage the current and future claims of a person by building a documented file with objective medical evidence to support requests by the employer to the wage replacement carrier including, but not limited to, amalgamation and cost relief or discounting. Amalgamation will back date a current claim to the original injury date instead of using the current date, merging all related claims into one claim.

Cost relief or discounting may occur when pre-existing medical conditions can predispose a person to injury or prolonging the recovery. The carrier will award a percentage of cost relief or a discount on the costs of the claim to the employer because the pre-existing medical condition was partially responsible to causing the injury. The cost relief is more prevalent in workers compensation programs rather than short or long term disability programs.

Amalgamation
The benefit for the employer for amalgamating claims is that the benefits carrier will pay benefits to the worker from the previous claim. These benefits will be calculated on past wage rates rather than on current wage rates. Depending on the age of the previous

claim will determine the past wage rate the benefits carrier will use to determine the benefits to be paid to the worker. The current income level is likely higher than the income level of the date of the original injury.

In an amalgamated claim, lower amounts of benefits will be paid out significantly reducing the claims costs. Since the claim costs are reduced, the charge back to the sponsor are reduced both in terms of premium and surcharges. Therefore, there is a potential for significant savings to be realized by the sponsor or the employer through amalgamating current claims to older claims. Despite the significant cost savings for the employer, there is only a marginal difference in the amount of benefits paid to the worker from the current level to the level that existed at the original injury date. The difference is small because benefits are paid based on a percentage of the wage. The percentage between the current wage level and the previous wage level is much smaller than the difference between the wage rates.

In addition to the cost savings from the lower benefit payouts, amalgamation will also affect the timing of transitions between short term to long term (own occupation) and or to long term (any occupation). These transitions may result in cost savings for the sponsor or employer depending on who pays the premiums for each program as well as how long the sponsor is responsible for the costs of the claims. For example, in a workers' compensation claim in Ontario, a Schedule 1 employer participating in the NEER incentive program, is responsible for claim costs for the current year plus three years (which is known as the NEER window) or until the claim is terminated whichever occurs first. The WSIB uses reserve factors to project the cost of each active claim beyond three years in order to charge the employer for costs that are expected to accumulate for the entire duration of the claim within the NEER window. Any excess charges will go into the "Unfunded Liability" amount.

Depending on the claim year the current claim is amalgamated back to, the current costs of the claim may not financially impact the employer through the WSIB assessment charge backs such as surcharges or loss of rebates. For example, if the claim is amalgamated to a previous claim dating back more than four years (beyond the NEER window), then the costs of the claim would not be considered in the surcharge or rebate assessment calculations. This cost avoidance can save the employer a significant amount of money in terms of a NEER surcharge.

In amalgamating claims to previous years outside of the NEER window, an employer can save a significant amount of money. Even if the person continues to lose a considerable amount of time from work generating increased claim costs, the old claim will not have a direct financial impact on the employer.

Employers in the CAD7 program have a charge back or assessment window of up to current year plus five years and MAPP employers also have a charge back window. If the employer is a Schedule 2 employer under the WSIA, then the costs of the claim will continue to be charged back to the employer regardless of the age of the claim for the life of the claim. In this case, amalgamation may not be as cost efficient for a cost strategy as with the other programs.

Usually the employer is more successful establishing the current claim as a recurrence at the time of the recurrence than obtaining a successful decision to amalgamate a new claim to an old claim. In the workers compensation program for Ontario, the employer should complete an RE07 form instead of a Form 7 for recurrences. For example, in a workers' compensation claim in Ontario, a workplace injury has a worker working with restrictions but lost time occurs because the restrictions change or there is a medical appointment, the RE07 should be completed in order to inform the WSIB of the recurrence rather than risk using the Form 7 and the WSIB as a result generating a new claim in error.

If there is question about whether the claim is a recurrence or a new claim, the employer should complete the regular Form 7 submitting additional information supporting the employer's position of recurrence and request amalgamation. The WSIB adjudicators will review the file and determine if the claim is a recurrence and to amalgamate the claim or if the claim is a new claim.

Sometimes, the worker has been working for some time without any problems and there has been no activity on the claim resulting in the WSIB closing the claim. However, the worker experiences a recurrence many months later. Some general tips to assist the employer when requesting the WSIB to consider recurrences and amalgamations rather than new claims include but are not limited to:

- The employer will be required to submit medical documentation supporting continuous medical treatment. Evidence of continued medical treatment from the time of the original claim to current must be submitted to the WSIB to support the request for amalgamation.

• If there is a permanent impairment determination on file, the employer will be able to use this information as evidence of a pre-existing medical condition that is likely to cause the recurrence.

• If the recurrence is within six (6) months of the last occurrence, the WSIB should allow amalgamation upon request of the employer.

Difficulties in obtaining successful amalgamation decisions will happen when the recurrence occurs after six (6) months of the claim closes. If the WSIB terminates the claim and permanent impairment has not be determined or listed on file, then the employer may experience challenges in obtaining successful decisions for amalgamating the claim.

Evidence of medical continuity in the claim from the termination date to the date of the recurrence becomes critical to the WSIB to support that the injury has not resolved. For instance, if the recurrence is after six (6) months of the last of the claim closure, the employer will have to submit to the WSIB medical evidence to support the claim is ongoing in order to have their request for amalgamation considered.

Compiling medical evidence can be difficult since the employer is not entitled to have access to a worker's medical information. If permanent impairment has been declared on file, then the chance for recurrence is significantly higher than if the worker was not previously injured. For this reason, permanent impairment on file provides the employer with the medical evidence required to support the amalgamation request.

The employer has other methods to collect medical information to support requests to the benefits carrier which are within legal constraints. The employer can request the worker to sign a form consenting to release medical information to the employer. Another method is to send the worker for an independent medical evaluation (IME) where the results are reported on behalf of the employer directly to the WSIB rather than to the employer.

The employer must establish a network of medical professionals in order to have the medical professionals provide opinions to the benefits carrier on the employer's behalf. To establish the medical network, the employer must gather a group of qualified medical professionals that will provide such services as independent medical evaluations, functional abilities evaluations, second opinions, and referrals for specialists, referrals for permanent impairment determinations, etc.

For short or long term disability benefits, employers can pursue the same historical patterning however, the timing can a bit different than with the workers compensation programs. The non-occupational wage replacement benefits for short term benefits claims usually consider two (2) weeks as a time period between claims for recurrences. For long term claims, the period between claims may be longer, sometimes up to thirty (30) days depending on the policy underwriting.

In some cases, the time allotted for recurrences between claims may even be longer depending on the return to work and work hardening plans. In cases where gradual return to work plans are longer than thirty (30) days, the time between claims may also be extended to the time period just beyond the completion date of the gradual return to work plan especially if there are long term or permanent impairments determined in the claim.

It is important to note that a recurrence of an injury is the same in this text as a re-aggravation of an injury. Technically, the new claim is an initial injury with no history of a claim or the injury has been caused by unique event. A recurrence is an injury that "flares up" despite the normal or undemanding event. Even though the difference between a new claim and a recurrence is remarkable, in this text the two terms will be interchangeable. Therefore monitoring historical patterning is important to manage claims appropriately both for efficiency and cost effectiveness.

In terms of short term and long term disability claims (non-occupational), amalgamation will impact the claims for consideration of key determination dates in the life of each claim. Depending on the time frame of eligibility for each type of claim, amalgamating claims can change the status of a claim from short term disability to long term disability (total disability from own occupation) to long term disability (total disability from any occupation).

Typically, depending on the benefits package of the employer, the employers pay the majority, if not all of the premiums for the short term disability programs. In contrast, typically, the workers pay the majority, if not all of the premiums for the long term disability programs.

The cost benefit of amalgamation for the non-occupational injury wage replacement programs is a little different than in the workers compensation program. If a claim is to be amalgamated from what would have been a current short term claim to a past claim, depending on the timing, the claim could change from a short term to a long term claim. This can result in some cost savings for the employer in premium changes or any excessive usage surcharges because the claim would change from short term to long term disability.

Usually, the employer is only responsible for the premiums of short term disability, the cost savings will be in the reduction of costs when the short term claim ends. The claim costs now become the responsibility of the long term disability program which is paid by the worker. Therefore, the cost of the long term claim would not have a direct financial impact on the short term disability program costs. However, this transfer to a long term claim may have a negative impact on the premiums for the long term disability program which are usually the responsibility of the worker.

Amalgamating claims can save costs for the employer. In Ontario's workers' compensation program, if the worker has a medical history of injury to the same body part involved in the workplace injury, then the company may argue that the workplace injury's date of accident can be back dated to the initial date of injury. In doing so, the company is requesting an amalgamation.

The request for an amalgamation must be based on medical evidence or a clear historical pattern of injury. The company may request the WSIB to consider an amalgamation based on:

- Establishing evidence of an initial injury prior to workplace injury that resulted in permanent disability and permanent restrictions. The permanent impairment will become supporting evidence that the permanent impairment was at least partially responsible for the initial injury as well as predispose the worker to future re-aggravations.

- Using the medical information on file including the permanent impairment determination(s), the company can submit the information to prove or support the request for amalgamation in that the initial injury predisposed the worker to re-aggravation in a normal activity.

- The employer must establish continuity of medical attention from the time of the initial injury to the time of the current "flare up". Evidence to support continuity can include notes or reports from the doctor, therapists, etc. This evidence can be requested by the WSIB or by the employer to have the medical professional submit to the WSIB directly.

- The employer must establish the level of significance of the workplace event believed to have been responsible for the workplace injury. If the workplace event was very insignificant but the injury and the previous injuries were significant. The severity of the injury is disproportionate to the event. This disproportion of cause and effect will support the employer's position that the previous injury has been re-aggravated rather than a new injury has occurred.

- The employer may even find success with arguing that the injury is non-occupational since the pre-existing is responsible for the injury and not the normal tasks at work. This would shift the costs of the claim from workers compensation to short or long term disability. Since the short or long term disability program costs are lower than the worker compensation claims, the employer will save money both in terms of cost savings and cost avoidance.

Historical patterning practices will not only assist the employer in amalgamation requests but also with requests for cost relief. For worker compensation claims, if the employer can provide sufficient medical evidence that a pre-existing medical condition is at least partially responsible for the injury. In addition, the permanent impairment may contribute to an underlying medical condition causing an historical pattern of injuries. The employer can request cost relief for the claim since non-occupational medical condition or the permanent impairment is at least partially responsible for the injury.

In short, the accurate and thorough record keeping in the historical patterning process will assist the employer in establishing a foundation for evidence to support the request for amalgamation and cost relief or discounting resulting in the ability to recognize some cost savings through successful decisions by the benefits carrier.

Cost Relief

The accurate and detailed information gathered during the historical patterning process will assist the employer in supporting their requests for amalgamation and cost relief in disability claims. As previously discussed, cost relief is typically related to occupational injuries claims management. The major benefit of cost relief is discounting a portion of the costs of the claim because a pre-existing medical condition was determined to be responsible at least in part, for the cause of the injury. The percentage of responsibility the pre-existing medical condition is responsible for in the injury will be the percentage of discounting in claim costs. The discounting are claim costs that are not charged back to the employer or sponsor from the benefits carrier.

In wage replacement programs for non-occupational injuries, the carrier covers medically supported lost time. The cause of the non-occupational injury is considered in eligibility decisions. If the injury was self inflicted, the lost time may not be covered depending on the underwriting of the insurance program. For example, suicide may not be eligible for life insurance coverage as it is self inflicted.

Another example would be if a person is intentionally harmed by another, like a person is beaten by another at a bar. The victim may be still eligible for benefits but there may also be some opportunity for "reimbursement" or compensation through the court system or subrogating to another insurance carrier under a liability clause. For more details on either of these options, liability insurance carriers or lawyers should be consulted.

In an occupationally related injury, the workplace may only be partially responsible for the injury. The pre-existing medical condition may also be responsible for the injury. A task at a workplace may be deemed safe and suitable for the average person to complete. However, if a person has a pre-existing medical condition, the task may have more risk for injury attached to it depending on the nature of the pre-existing medical condition.

For example, a person may have arthritis in the spine which is very common as people grow older. A simple task like picking up a pen off the floor is a task with very low risk of injury for a "healthy" person but for a person with arthritis in the spine, the task can elevate the risk for a low back injury expedientially.

In the case above, the employer can request the workers compensation claim be denied since the pre-existing medical condition was more responsible for the injury than the task of picking up a pen from the floor. The request would be based on the fact that a task of picking up the pen presented no risk of injury to a person in reasonable physical condition.

If the request for denial is not approved and the claim is approved for entitlement, then the employer should request cost relief on the claim. Cost relief should be determined based on the percentage of responsibility of the pre-existing medical condition to the cause of the injury.

The cost relief will allow a decrease in a percentage of the costs from the total claim charges to the employer. This is the cost relief is recognition of the workplace activities not being responsible either in part or in whole for the injury. Since the cost relief determines the percentage of responsibility between the workplace and the non-occupational condition, cost relief is more common in workers compensation claims.

In the workers' compensation program in Ontario, the cost relief is determined using the WSIB policy for SIEF or Secondary Injury Enhancement Fund. The adjudicator usually only considers requests for cost relief from SIEF once the injury has surpassed the standard recovery period. Only those employers who are classified as Schedule 1 NEER participants are eligible for cost relief through SIEF. A later chapter in this text will discuss the classifications of employers in more detail.

The portion of claim costs that is discounted from the employer's costs is charged to the "Unfunded Liability". The Unfunded Liability is a fund covered by the general premiums of the insurance program as well as from the projected future and overhead costs of each claim. At the beginning of this century, the Unfunded Liability exceeded several billion dollars which the insurance program did not have the reserves to cover. The WSIB hired some actuarialists to develop reserve factor tables proportional to severity and claim costs in order to ensure employers are charged back the appropriate costs. Essentially the WSIB is spreading the costs of the Unfunded Liability over all the employers in Ontario through premiums and surcharges.

In Ontario, the workers' compensation program for occupationally related injuries is governed by the Workplace Safety and Insurance Act (WSIA). Policy 14-05-03 guides adjudicators in how to apply cost relief in occupational injury claims where pre-existing medical conditions have predisposed the worker to injury and prolonged the recovery of an injury. SIEF awards range from 0 to 100% but the most common award is 50%. The chart in this policy indicates that the percentage of cost relief is proportional to the severity of the pre-existing medical condition.

Illustration 18-1: SIEF Chart, the WSIB Policy #14-05-03

Medical significance of pre-existing condition*	Severity of accident**	Percentage of cost transfer***
Minor	Minor	50%
	Moderate	25%
	Major	0%
Moderate	Minor	75%
	Moderate	50%
	Major	25%
Major	Minor	90%-100%
	Moderate	75%
	Major	50%

The WSIA, Policy 14-05-03

There are some changes happening to the application of cost relief from SIEF starting in 2010. It will become increasingly more difficult to secure a successful decision in cost relief. Therefore, it is more important than ever to insure that the request for cost relief is supported by as much medical documentation of objective medical findings.

Medical findings can be documented by sending the injured party for an independent medical evaluation (IME). The findings must support that a significant medical condition existed prior to the injury which would clearly predispose the worker to the injury and prolong the recovery from the injury. If the company does not have access to the medical information, the medical practitioner can write a letter on behalf of the company requesting the cost relief from SIEF and submitting the medical documentation directly to the WSIB. This course of action supports the importance of establishing a medical network of preferred medical service providers.

In addition to the prior history of an injured body part, the Form 7 should include any facts about any pre-existing medical conditions known to the employer that would have made the injured worker predisposed to any injury or delay the recovery of an injury. This information on the Form 7 will support the employer's position for cost relief or amalgamation.

Currently, the WSIA legislation indicates that even though worker's compensation in Ontario is based on a no fault insurance basis, the employer can request cost relief through the Secondary Injury Enhancement Fund to balance the entitlement. The WSIA Policy #14-05-03 is based on pre-existing medical conditions which enhances or prolongs the workplace injury. For example, a worker has disc degenerative disease (DDD or a form of arthritis) in the spine caused by the natural course of the aging process. Arthritis is a naturally occurring genetic disease that affects the bones. A worker with arthritis is prone to bone fractures.

Bumping into the door may cause a healthy person to bruise, however, the same action may cause a worker with arthritis or degenerative disc disease a bone fracture. The worker with arthritis may not have to even bump into anything to cause an injury. For instance, a worker can experience severe back pain or "slip a disc" by simply sneezing or bending over to pick up a small pencil from the floor. If this activity were to happen while at work, despite the pre-existing medical condition, the injury can be considered as a workplace injury.

The arthritis or DDD in these cases have predisposed the worker to more serious injuries with a longer recovery period. The same activities would have resulted in smaller or less severe injuries for a healthier person. For these types of cases, the WSIB would recognize that the company had no influence on the worker's medical condition of arthritis but could recognize the bone fracture or slipped disc as work related. To balance the non-occupational issue, the WSIB will award cost relief through SIEF to the company depending on the severity of the injury, severity of the event, and severity of the pre-existing medical condition.

In summary, the WSIB claims adjudicator will review all the information on file when determining the eligibility of the claim. Medical documentation will be considered to have more weight in the decision making than subjective interpretation or opinion. In most cases, the claims adjudicator will not render a decision regarding cost relief from SIEF until the injury has reached maximum medical recovery or surpassed the standard recovery period of the injury. The WSIB will require medical documentation to support the employer's position of the worker having a pre-existing medical condition as well as the level of severity of the pre-existing medical condition.

CHAPTER 19

DUE DILIGENCE - REACTIVE

Due diligence is a "standard of care" to which a company has a legal obligation to provide. A more formal definition of due diligence can be found on the WSIB website. According to the WSIB fact sheet on the company's internal responsibility system and due diligence found on www.wsib.on.ca, due diligence refers to:

> ... to the employer's legal responsibility to take every reasonable precaution to prevent injuries and illnesses and prove that they have done this. This is in addition to complying with the provisions of the Occupational Health and Safety Act (OHSA) and Regulations and is not limited by them. (WSIB, 2009)

In other words, due diligence refers to a standard of care that would include doing or not doing what a reasonable person would do or not do to prevent injuries or harm to others.

With due diligence, companies not only have a legal obligation but they also have a moral responsibility to their workers. In addition, the company has a social responsibility to the community to protect the workers from harm by both preventing initial harm as well as reacting appropriately once harm has already occurred.

In addition to ensuring legal compliance, due diligence also includes activities in preventing injury or harm. Preventing injury includes preventing initial injury as well as preventing further damage or recurrences when an injury or the harm has already occurred. Therefore, the company's due diligence extends beyond the point of initial injury in the company's reactive activities.

Due diligence in a reactive state would consist of completing accident investigations, completing root cause analysis, developing and implementing corrective action plans, developing safe and suitable return to work plans, protecting a worker or person from harm or further harm, etc. Furthermore, due diligence in a reactive state could also include obtaining appropriate medical attention, participating in prescribed courses of treatment, etc. because these activities will prevent the existing injury from worsening or it will promote recovery.

A general rule of thumb for due diligence is to determine if the company has corrected the root cause of the problem that caused or can cause harm. The company can demonstrate due diligence if they have done everything they could reasonably do to protect the worker from further harm should harm occur despite the company's best efforts to prevent injury or harm.

In due diligence, the term "reasonable" is defined by the court system of the land in which the harm took place. For instance if the injury occurred on private property in Ontario, then the laws the govern Ontario and Canada will determine what level of reasonable care the landowner should have taken to prevent the injury or mitigate the loss, damage or severity of the harm or injury. If the landowner is determined not to have acted according to that level, then the landowner has legal liability for the outcome of the harm or injury.

When the harm or injury occurs on public property or commercial property, the person or persons responsible for the care of the property can be deemed to be liable for any damages based on the definition of reasonable care. Depending on the type of harm or injury will determine the legal ramifications and insurance program which will address the lack of due diligence taken to prevent the initial harm or injury as well as preventing further harm or injury.

An example of due diligence in the reactive state is when a Supervisor secures the scene of an injury. The first responsibility is to tend to the injured party and ensure the injured party receives the appropriate level of medical attention. If the injury is beyond the help of simple first aid, then the competent supervisor would send the injured party to the hospital or clinic via ambulance or taxi depending on the severity of the injury. Once the injured party's injuries have been addressed and the risk of further injury to the injured party has been removed, the competent or diligent supervisor will investigate the accident. The investigation should determine the root cause of the accident enabling the company to develop and implement appropriate corrective actions to prevent further injuries.

Further in this text, due diligence is discussed in greater detail. This section is simply to point out that the company's legal responsibility does not end at the point of injury. The company has further responsibility under due diligence in the reactive state to take actions that would mitigate the loss or harm or injury through corrective action activities and encouraging a supportive environment for recovery.

CHAPTER 20

DUTY TO ACCOMMODATE

In Ontario, every person has the right to equal treatment under the law. According to the Human Rights Code of Ontario and of Canada, an employer must treat every worker equally. Section 5 of the Ontario Human Rights Code indicates that the employer must not discriminate against any worker regarding employment. The specific prohibitive grounds of discrimination include race, ancestry, religion, place of origin, colour, ethnic origin, creed, sex, age, marital status, family status, sexual orientation, record of offences for which a person has been pardoned, in receipt of public assistance, or disability. In addition, an employer is obligated under the WSIA Section 41 to re-employ an injured worker and Section 40 to cooperate in an early and safe return to work plan not to discriminate.

The interpretation of the Human Rights Codes of Ontario and of Canada as well as the WSIA conclude that it is not just enough for an employer to determine that there are no positions available for a worker with restrictions or barriers. The employer is obligated under these pieces of legislation to evaluate all positions within the company for any "reasonable" accommodation requirements to the point of undue hardship. Consequently, by integrating evaluation processes, job assignment reviews based on medical documentation, physical demands analysis, and bona fide requirements of each position into the company's health and safety program and the disability management program will provide guidelines for the company to meet their due diligence responsibilities.

The duty to accommodate as outlined in the WSIA and the Human Rights Code indicates that the company is legally obligated to accommodate a worker with restrictions to the point of undue hardship. The company's health and safety program and the disability management program should be designed to facilitate the necessary activities by the company to practice due diligence. The company must have documented evidence of an understanding of the barriers of the worker, demands of each job in the company, and evaluations to determine appropriate job match will demonstrate the company's due diligence in trying to accommodate restricted workers.

Duty to accommodate is a complex concept. Essentially the company has the obligation to accommodate a restricted worker by eliminating any barriers where reasonable to enable the worker to work. The reasonable test is to the point of undue hardship. Professor Michael Lynk, who teaches Labour, Human Rights and Constitutional Law at the Faculty of Law at the University of Western Ontario, in London, Ontario in his paper, *"Disability and the Duty to Accommodate in the Canadian Workplace"* (original paper 1999, updated 2002) defines duty to accommodate as:

> ...employers and unions in Canada are required to make every reasonable effort, short of undue hardship, to accommodate an employee who comes under a protected ground of discrimination within human rights legislation. (M. Lynk, 2002)

Furthermore, Professor Lynk expands this definition to not only include considering the physical demands of jobs when reviewing job availability but also to also consider "reasonable" accommodation changes to jobs so the jobs become suitable within the person's restrictions. Specifically, Professor Lynk states:

> ...the duty requires more from the employer than simply investigating whether any existing job might be suitable for a disabled employee. Rather, the law requires an employer to determine whether existing positions can be adjusted, adapted or modified for the employee, or whether there are other positions in the workplace that might be suitable for the employee.

This responsibility requires the employer to look at all other reasonable alternatives. (M. Lynk, 2002)

Regardless of the origin of the restrictions, the employer has a legal duty to provide safe, suitable and sustainable work under the Human Rights Code of Ontario and the Human Rights Code of Canada. If the restrictions are a result of a workplace injury, Section 41 of the WSIA will also corroborate the legal obligations under the Human Rights Code. The legal duty to provide safe, suitable and sustainable work is the employer's duty to accommodate.

The duty to accommodate applies no matter if the restrictions are temporary or permanent. For this reason, the company needs to align the early and safe return to work activities for any injury claim whether it is occupational or non-occupational, or whether the restrictions are short term or long term or permanent. A well designed disability management program will provide due diligence in the consistent application of early and safe return to work activities within the program.

In order to satisfy the duty to accommodate, the employer must provide safe, suitable and sustainable work within the injured worker's restrictions. This practice must follow the same steps in every case in order to avoid discrimination and harassment. One of the first steps to offering an injured worker safe and suitable work is to understand the worker's restrictions. To understand the restrictions, the employer must also comprehend what the restrictions mean in terms of the worker's capabilities within the restrictions. Medical documentation such as functional abilities forms (FAF) (a WSIB form) or functional abilities evaluation report (FAE) will allow the company to understand the type and duration of tasks that can be performed safely within the worker's restrictions.

Once the company has identified what tasks can be performed safely based on medical documentation, then a modified work plan can be developed. This plan should be supported by the "law" since the plan is based on the type and duration of tasks as identified in the FAF or FAE or medical documentation provided by the health care professional. Upon the development of the plan, the plan needs to be communicated and accepted by the worker. Refer to the chapter on return to work (RTW) program and modified work offer later in this book.

The offer of modified work is not the end of the employer's duty to accommodate. The return to work plan has to be implemented and successful in terms of the worker being assigned safe, suitable and sustainable tasks. The term "sustainable" implies that the plan should be long term in nature especially if the restrictions become permanent. The employer's duty to accommodate is a legal duty for as long as the worker for minimum, the life of the employment relationship and maximum to undue hardship according to the Human Rights Code. Similar to the Human Rights Code, the WSIA has a duty to accommodate. However, the WSIA defines the employer's obligation time frame a bit differently under the section for obligation for re-employment.

According to the WSIA, Section 41 (7), the:

> ...The employer is obligated under this section until the earliest of, ...(a) the second anniversary of the date of injury;
> (b) one year after the worker is medically able to perform the essential duties of his or her pre-injury employment; and
> (c) the date on which the worker reaches 65 years of age. 1997, c. 16, Sched. A, s. 41 (7); 2000, c. 26, Sched. I, s. 1 (3). (the WSIA, 1997)

If the WSIB suspects that this re-employment obligation has been breached, the adjudicator will investigate the matter. If the investigation proves this obligation has been violated, then penalties and fines can be levied against the employer by the WSIB, the Ministry of Labour (MOL), and the Human Rights Commission. If the obligation has not been breached under the WSIA, then the duty to accommodate does not necessarily end under the Human Rights Code. Even though the WSIA limits the employer's re-employment obligation, under the Human Rights Code, the duty to accommodate does not end.

Subsequent to Professor Lynk's definition of duty to accommodate, to implement fair and consistent health and safety as well as disability management programs to practice due diligence with the duty to accommodate. Practicing due diligence with the duty to accommodate will necessitate the employer to comply with the Employment Standards Act (ESA), the Workplace Safety and Insurance Act (WSIA), the Human Rights Code of Canada and the Human

Rights Code of Ontario. In order to comply, management must first understand the legal definition or legal requirements of "reasonable", "reasonable accommodation" and "undue hardship".

According to the Webster's Dictionary, "reasonable" is defined as moderate or rational. In the courts of Ontario and Canada, the legal application of "reasonable" is the "average" or normal response of a person. In other words, "reasonable" is the expected response that would be within the average person's capabilities. A "reasonable person" would be the standard of measurement used to determine a person's response against the response of an average person with the average education level and average capabilities. The standard measurement in its elemental form is simply, *"to think and act as a normal person of normal education and capacity for reason would think or act where normal usually means average according to educational standards of the land". (Retrieved from: Webster's Dictionary, 2009).*

There is a degree of subjectivity in interpretation with the definition resulting in variations in court decisions depending on the judge's interpretation of the definition and the series of events. "Reasonable" becomes an interpretation based on the psycho-social framework of the life experience of the person making the decision. Despite the degree of subjectiveness, "reasonable" is a scale of measurement used by the courts of Canada and Ontario to gauge what would be expected of the average person.

Further to the legal definition of the word "reasonable", "reasonable accommodation" is viewed as the accommodation activities that would be expected of the company. When determining reasonable accommodation, the company has to review the "bona fide" requirements of the job. The "bona fide" requirements of the job are the essential tasks of the job that must be completed. These essential tasks are called core responsibilities.

In changing any one or any series of the bona fide requirements would change the nature of the position. For example, some bona fide requirements of a firefighter are to fight fire, rescue victims from a burning building, and wear specifically prescribed personal protection equipment. If a person, due to a pre-existing medical condition, could not wear the prescribed personal protective equipment, then the person would be violating the OHSA and the company safety procedures.

Furthermore, the person how could not fulfill their bona fide requirements would be placing many people at high risk for serious injury including him/herself, other fire fighters, and any victims of

BEST PRACTICES IN HEALTH & SAFETY

the fire. However, if the tasks changed to accommodate the re-striction(s) of the pre-existing medical condition, then the fire fighter could not be involved in any fire fighting activities on the scene of a fire. Therefore, the job would be substantially changed to the point that the person is no longer fighting fires. Perhaps the accommoda-tion would be that the person becomes a dispatcher or another ad-ministrative role.

Another example is if a police officer could not use a knife or fire a weapon because of religious beliefs. The accommodation to not use any form of defence that would injury the aggressor would place the officer's life as well as the lives of the officer's partner and any victim requiring protection life in grave jeopardy. The use of a weapon is a bona fide requirement for a police officer. To avoid using a weapon would change the essential nature of the job and the costs of no defence would be much higher than the cost of accom-modating the officer in another type position that does not require the use of a weapon. Again, the accommodation may include some administrative role where a knife or other weapon is not part of the bona fide requirement.

Accommodation is an obligation of the employer. The courts of Canada and Ontario have expanded the definition of the employer obligation from basic "reasonable accommodation" to "accommoda-tion to undue hardship". Accommodation to undue hardship is a high standard for the employer to attain. According to Professor Lynk of the University of Western Ontario, in his article *"Disability and the Duty to Accommodate in the Canadian Workplace"*, "undue hard-ship" has no single formal legal definition. However, the employer must be able to provide documented evidence to show the company demonstrated its "best efforts" to accommodate.

Common interpretation of undue hardship which may not al-ways be accurate tends to follow the path just short of bankruptcy. This interpretation may exceed "reasonable" expectations however, it can assist in building a case for due diligence. It will also assist in developing practices and policies in the health and safety program as well as the disability management program.

As a result of the lack of a well defined term, inconsistent appli-cation of undue hardship occurs frequently. Professor Lynk discuss-es the Central Alberta Diary Pool Supreme Court decision which outlines some factors to consider when attempting to determine if the threshold of undue hardship has been met. This list of factors is not exhaustive but it is a starting point. Professor Lynk lists the factors as:

...Financial cost;
- Impact on a collective agreement;
- Problems of employee morale;
- Interchangeability of the work force and facilities;
- Size of the employer's operations; and,
- Safety

(M. Lynk, 2002)

In addition, Professor Lynk expands the list to include "the legitimate operational requirements of the workplace" even though, as Professor Lynk states, the courts have not yet formalized this factor.

In developing accommodation options, the employer will need to consider the *financial costs* of the accommodation requirements. An employer may choose options for accommodation requirements according to the costs. Cost efficiency does not always mean the cheapest option.

The cost(s) that will render the largest return on investment or the largest amount of benefits for the lowest percentage of dollar spent are the options better explored. When considering cost efficiency, employers need to factor the cost savings of the restricted worker working instead of incurring costs while on short term disability benefits (STD), long term disability benefits (LTD), or worker's compensation benefits as well as the lost productivity.

The threshold under undue hardship for financial cost is very high in Canada and in Ontario. The Human Rights Code of Canada and Ontario both indicate the financial cost threshold is to the point of undue hardship. However, the threshold of "undue hardship" is not consistent.

As previously discussed, a common interpretation of the undue hardship threshold is to the point where the company will likely go into bankruptcy due to the costs of the accommodations. This perception of the threshold is extreme. However, the financial hardship has to be substantial before the courts will likely allow any exemption from the company's duty to accommodate. In his article, "*Disability and the Duty to Accommodate in the Canadian Workplace*", Professor Lynk summarizes some factors, based on recent court decisions, to consider when determining the threshold for financial hardship:

> ...- (the cost has to be) related to accommodation
> Provable, and not based on surmise or speculation; and
> So substantial that they would either change the essential nature of the operation, or substantially impact upon its financial viability...
> (M. Lynk, 2002)

In other words, the costs have to be supported by documented quotes and have to be so significant that the company will withstand heavy financial losses perhaps unrecoverable losses. These significant financial losses must be to a point where the company may be in peril of irreparable damage both in terms of financial loss and market share. The exact threshold is subjective to the judge's or tribunal's interpretation of the company's financial position. Usually, bigger companies are perceived to be able to absorb higher costs than smaller companies without reaching the threshold. A corporate lawyer or an employment lawyer would be able to counsel a company regarding their position and the threshold limits unique to their position.

There are two parties involved in the duty to accommodate. In a unionized environment, a third party is added to the group. The employer has the duty to accommodate a restricted worker. The union has the duty to cooperate in the accommodation process. The union is not permitted to purposely sabotage nor create more barriers in the process unless the health and safety of the worker is at risk. The worker has the duty to participate in the accommodation process. The worker cannot refuse a reasonable accommodation plan without documented proof that their health and safety is at risk should the worker participate in the return to work plan.

In addition, there is a fourth party having a role in the accommodation process that has not yet been discussed. This fourth party is the role of the medical professional. The medical professional must provide the restrictions to the worker and the employer for the employer to evaluate and accommodate.

For example, the policies and procedures at Queen's University in Ontario support these obligations of each party involved in the workplace accommodation process. In fact, they outline a few more responsibilities of each party which assists in improving the accommodation process because each party knows and understands both their own responsibilities as well as the responsibilities of the other parties. Table 20-1 below summarizes the responsibilities under the Queen's Human Rights Office from their website (www.queensu.ca/humanrights/accommodationbrochure):

Table 20-1: Queen's University summary of responsibilities of each party

Restricted Worker	Employer	Union	Co-workers
To communicate, through the appropriate channels, and at the earliest possible opportunity, the need for accommodation	To take prompt action to meet the duty to accommodate	To educate its members about accommodation	To co-operate and participate, with an open mind, in the accommodation process
To provide necessary and appropriate documentation as required	To communicate with the employee and initiate the accommodation planning process	To encourage its members to identify and communicate their need for accommodation	
To co-operate and participate in finding and implementing a solution/plan	To identify the essential and non-essential duties of the job	To work with all parties to find and implement accommodations	
To identify and communicate any problems with the proposed accommodation	To consider the possibility of rebundling duties	To make a reasonable effort to be flexible when exceptions to the collective agreement will facilitate accommodations	
To perform the essential duties of the position within the parameters of the plan	To identify and communicate any problems with the accommodation		
	To be prepared to resolve any workplace resentment that might arise as a result of the accommodation		

By developing and implementing policies and procedures that outline each party's rights and obligations assists in each party understanding their role in the accommodation process. It also becomes good best practice for a company to develop and implement policies and procedures or negotiate in the collective agreement the process(es) to assist the restricted worker.

The policies and procedures will assist the company to address restrictions, process for accommodation, the process for managing the accommodation process. The accommodation process should include an avenue the worker can use to address discrepancies or burdens requiring corrective actions. For example, many companies have a process for:

- Dispute resolution
- Communication
- Ergonomic adjustment committees
- Assigning work to workers with restrictions
- Outlining seniority rights vs. accommodation regarding temporary postings, long term postings, etc.
- Independent medical examinations
- Requests for updated restrictions in reasonable time frames

The list above is not exhaustive. It represents a brief list of potential policies, procedures or articles in a collective agreement that may assist in guiding all the parties into successful accommodation positions for restricted workers.

Another factor to consider when determining appropriate accommodation is the risk assessment for the safety of all the workers including the restricted worker. In the example used above regarding the police officer, the safety of the worker, coworkers and community are significantly jeopardized if the bona fide requirement for using a weapon is changed to accommodate the respective restrictions. If a police officer is not able to use a weapon, the safety of the people will be jeopardized. In this case, the employer would have to consider other positions within the company within the person's restrictions that would not jeopardize the health and safety of the worker, other workers or the public in order to accommodate the worker.

According to Professor Lynk, some guidelines outlined by the Human Rights Commission in 2000 to consider in the area of health and safety risk include (but are not limited to):

> ... The willingness of a person with a disability to assume the risk in circumstances where the risk is to his or her own health or safety;
> Whether the modification or waiving of the requirement is reasonably likely to result in a serious risk to the health or safety or others;
> The other types of risk legally tolerated at the place of work; and,
> The types of risks tolerated within society as a whole... (M. Lynk, 2002)

Another example would be a worker that requires a workstation to be set at a specific height. If the company were to adjust the height of the work bench for this specific worker, this might put another worker working beside them at risk of an injury due to the set height. The company would have to review alternative options such as having smaller work benches for each station that are all height adjustable so that each worker can adjust the height of the table according to their independent and specific height. Height adjustability would necessitate the employer to change the conveyor belt into independent work stations. This would be difficult to do on a running conveyor system in a manufacturing environment where there are robots attached. However, the change might be very easy to do in a mail sorting room. Engineering becomes a vital part of planning and implementing any type of accommodations.

The *size of the operation* needs to be considered when determining an accommodation plan. In his article, *"Disability and the Duty to Accommodate in the Canadian Workplace"*, Professor Lynk explains that as a general rule, the courts in Canada and Ontario seem to have higher expectations of threshold with larger companies. The threshold appears to be proportionate to the size in terms of the number of employees as well as the profitability of the company. A larger company or profitable company will have more means and more resources in terms of affording the costs and talent to develop the solutions required. Therefore, it would be affordable for the company to accommodate the restrictions necessary.

To consider the next factor, the *interchangeability of the workforce and facilities*, the company must determine the flexibility of their operations. Professor Lynk explains that depending on the flexibility and/or the complexity of the operation(s), the company could be expected to make adjustments in practices and policies including scheduling, "rebundling" work assignments, rotation, etc. This consideration must also review core essential duties of the position including bona fide requirements. However, the weight of the decision will rest with the company's ability to rearrange and reassign tasks according to capabilities providing the reassignment does not put any (other) worker at additional risk of harm. Consequently, the size of the company can have a significant impact on flexibility of reassignment activities.

For the next factor, p*rovisions of the collective agreement* factor, in unionized environments, collective agreements are the fundamental guidelines to managing any personnel in the bargaining unit. Collective agreements are legally binding contracts negotiated between representatives of management and representatives of the workers in the bargaining unit known as the bargaining committee. These guidelines list and/or explain the rules that both members of management and the workers of the bargaining unit will work within.

A key element of collective agreements is decision making based on the seniority of the worker. For example, workers who are the last to be hired will be the first to be laid off should layoffs be executed. The workers who have worked for the company for the longest period of time will be the last to be laid off in the event that the company has a total shutdown.

In his article, *"Disability and the Duty to Accommodate in the Canadian Workplace"*, Professor Lynk states:

> ...collective agreements are important, and accommodation proposals that do not interfere with bargained entitlements must be exhaustively explored first.
> Significant job rights – such as an incumbent's job position – are not to be interfered with by an accommodation. This would amount to an undue hardship.
> Less important job entitlements, where no actual loss of a position is involved, would be eligible candidates for an accommodation. An ex-

ample would be a posted vacancy. Here, the in-
terference with collective agreement rights,
while real, would not be seen as significant, because no incumbent would be displaced from
his or her actual job... (M. Lynk, 2002)

Generally, as long as the clauses of the collective agreement do
not violate the right(s) of the worker(s) under the law, the Human
Rights Commission, the WSIAT and the courts will honour the
terms of the collective agreement. However, clauses like seniority
rights can interfere with accommodating restricted workers. For
example, if the collective agreement states that in order to assign a
job to a worker on a long term basis (or permanently), the job must
follow the posting procedures. The posting procedures dictate that
the job must be posted. If the collective agreement dictates that the
applicant with the highest seniority gets the job, then the company
may have some conflict with the union in assigning the restricted
worker to the new job posting because the job posting is within their
restrictions.

Barring the low seniority displacing a senior worker to layoff status because of this type of accommodation, the courts tend to allow
the breach in the collective agreement. There must be documented
evidence that the worker would not be able to work any other position including medical and ergonomic assessment documentation.
Consulting with an employment lawyer specializing in disability programs is a good practice to ensure the company is not breaching any
legally binding agreement. A best practice in labour relations is to
develop a good rapport with the union committee. The good relationship will foster or support constant communication and detailed
discussions between management and the union. These communications and discussions are necessary to address delicate political matters.

Using the same example as above, if the more senior worker is
displaced to layoff over the lower seniority restricted worker because
of the accommodated placement, then seniority would dictate that
the higher seniority worker assigned the work placement and the
lower seniority restricted worker be laid off. This would not generally breach the employer's duty to accommodate as the layoff is a result of seniority not a result of the restrictions. A best practice for
the company would be to document the worker's file, clearly outlining that the layoff was a result of seniority only. If a company has

any doubts when laying off workers' with restrictions, consulting legal counsel will assist in determining if any breach to the company's duty to accommodate exists.

The last factor to consider when attempting to determine the threshold for undue hardship is the *legitimate operational requirements of a workplace*. Professor Lynk notes that the legitimate operational requirements of a workplace is not well defined but has some weight in the decision making for thresholds of undue hardship. Professor Lynk believes that although this actor is not quite persuasive enough on its own merit, when combining it with any other of the factors, this factor can lend strength to the argument either by supporting or not supporting the position to accommodate or not accommodate a worker with restrictions. Professor Lynk discusses three (3) examples where accommodation is very difficult and the company could experience undue hardship:

> ...1.A person who has substance abuse problems who repeatedly does not succeed in accommodation despite several attempts with rehabilitation and future additional rehabilitation would have no promise of success.
> 2. The employee request for a "significant" number of paid religious holidays which exceed the number of paid Christian holidays negotiated in the collective agreement.
> 3. As a result of an Employee suffering from depression, the Employee is frequently and unpredictably absent. (M. Lynk, 2002)

Caution must be exercised when considering absences with documented medical conditions and terminating employment status. Consulting with an employment lawyer before terminating an employee would assist the employer in taking the appropriate steps to avoid non-compliance of the law.

In addition to Professor Lynk's opinion on duty to accommodate, in June 2008, the Supreme Court of Canada set precedent by further clarifying the employer's obligation as well as their rights in the accommodation process in the Honda vs. Keays decision. The HRPA's article, *"HRPA PLEASED WITH SUPREME COURT'S DECISION IN KEAYS VS. HONDA CANADA INC."* (2008), summarizes the court's decision in this case. The decision clearly outlined that the employer has the right to manage employee attendance as a bona fide requirement in relation to the employment contract and managing the workforce. In the process of managing employee attendance, the employer has the right to request doctor's notes to support absences even those absences related to their disability.

The other findings of this decision, according to the HRPA article, *"HRPA PLEASED WITH SUPREME COURT'S DECISION IN KEAYS VS. HONDA CANADA INC."* *(2008)* include the following:

> ... 1. Confirming that the threshold the Court uses for awarding punitive damages is high and only exceptional cases will justify such an award.
> 2. Clarifying the types of damages that can be awarded and prevent "double-dipping" by confusing the concepts underpinning punitive and Wallace damages.
> 3. Rejecting the "Wallace bump-up" and stating that Wallace damages should reflect actual damages for mental distress and not an arbitrary extension of the notice period.
> 4. Rejecting the notion that breaches of human rights legislation can constitute an "independent actionable wrong" that could result in punitive damages.... (HRPA, 2008)

Honda vs Keays is significant to human resources practices because it clarifies the duty to accommodate in the law and it allows the employer the right to manage the workforce. These are critical to good management practices in any business. In addition to the Honda vs Keays decision, the Hydro – Quebec vs. Syndicat des Employees Supreme Court decision of July 2008 also supported the employer's right to manage attendance and the workforce. Even though the case was initially from Quebec, the appeals decision from the Supreme Court of Canada will support business practices for duty to accommodate and right to terminate employment due to absenteeism anywhere in Canada under the Canadian Charter of Rights and Freedom.

According to Christopher Bird's article, "Hydro-Québec *Makes employers A Bit Less Nervous About Employee Accommodation*" (July 22nd,

2008), the Hydro-Quebec vs Syndicat des Employees Supreme Court of Canada's decision outlined that the duty to accommodate does not include changing the fundamental (bona fide) requirements of the job but instead to change the workplace around the worker as well as to be flexible with the time or schedule of the worker. More specifically, the Christopher Bird article highlights:

> ...The Supreme Court reversed the Quebec Court of Appeal's decision, finding for Hydro-Québec. Justice Deschamps noted that the issue at hand comes from the SCC's previous use of the word "impossible" in crafting the *Meiorin* test, pointing out that the purpose of the test is not to rewrite the employee/employer relationship entirely, but to prevent discrimination:
>
>> The test is not whether it was impossible for the employer to accommodate the employee's characteristics. The employer does not have a duty to change working conditions in a fundamental way, but does have a duty, if it can do so without undue hardship, to arrange the employee's workplace or duties to enable the employee to do his or her work...
>
> (C. Bird, 2008)

To assist in understanding the above decision, Christopher Bird in "Hydro-Québec *Makes employers A Bit Less Nervous About Employee Accommodation*" (July 22nd, 2008), briefly explains what the Meirin test is:

> ... the test laid out in *British Columbia (Public Service Employee Relations Commission) v. BCGSEU*, [1999] 3 S.C.R. 3 (the "*Meiorin*" case). That test reads as follows:
>
>> An employer may justify the impugned standard by establishing on the balance of probabilities:
>>
>> (1) that the employer adopted the standard for a purpose rationally connected to the performance of the job;

(2) that the employer adopted the particular standard in an honest and good faith belief that it was necessary to the fulfilment of that legitimate work-related purpose; and

(3) that the standard is reasonably necessary to the accomplishment of that legitimate work-related purpose. To show that the standard is reasonably necessary, it must be demonstrated that it is impossible to accommodate individual employees sharing the characteristics of the claimant without imposing undue hardship upon the employer... (C. Bird, 2008)

In summary, the duty to accommodate is required of any employer in Ontario under the Human Rights Code of Ontario, the Human Rights Code of Canada, the Canadian Charter of Rights and Freedoms, the Occupational Health and Safety Act, the Employment Standards Act and the Labour Relations Act. The WSIA will also have some requirements for employers under the re-employment obligation for workers who have experienced workplace injuries.

The duty to accommodate becomes a process involving several parties including the restricted worker, the employer, the union (if applicable), the co-workers, the medical professionals and to some degree, the disability insurance carrier (WSIB, STD or LTD, CPP, Employment Insurance, etc.). Each party has a set of roles and responsibilities in the accommodation process.

Employers have a legal obligation to accommodate restricted workers to the point of undue hardship. To determine undue hardship, the employer must consider factors such as the costs of accommodations, terms of the collective agreement, any problems of employee morale, the interchangeability of the work force and facilities, the size of the employer's operations, and, the safety of all workers.

In the past, courts and tribunals have been very inconsistent in determining undue hardship. However, recent Supreme Court of Canada decisions in the Honda vs. Keays (June 2008) and Hydro – Quebec vs. Syndicat des Employees (July 2008) have clarified the employer's right to manage absenteeism and in effect the workforce. These recent Supreme Court of Canada decisions will give some framework to court decisions and appeals in the matter of duty to accommodate and undue hardship.

In addition, these court decisions clarify the employer's right to request doctor's notes to support absences even those related to disability. Furthermore, the employer has the right to terminate for absenteeism providing all legal requirements to terminate have been satisfied. Finally, before any termination is considered, legal counsel should be sought to ensure legal compliance to all laws of the land in which the business operates.

CHAPTER 21

RETURN TO WORK (RTW)

RTW – Legislation, Prevention of Lost Time Strategy

The difference between occupational and non-occupationally related injuries is primarily the location in which the injury occurs. Prevention activities are essential to mitigating any risk of injury no matter where the injury occurs. Accidents can happen anywhere. To prevent accidents from occurring at home, a person can develop and implement prevention activities to make the home safer for those that live there as well as those that are temporarily on the property. For example, the home owner will remove snow from the walk ways in the winter to avoid or minimize the risk of slip and falls.

The homeowner is obligated by due diligence to ensure any person is not hurt while on the property. In addition to this legal obligation, the employer is also obligated to ensure that any worker, visitor, or contractor is not hurt while in the course of employment at the workplace. To mitigate the risk of injury, the employer will develop and implement prevention activities in the workplace. For example, lockout procedures are work instructions implemented to repair and or de-energize equipment and machinery safely.

The employer has significant responsibility for preventing initial injuries as well as to avoid recurrences. The first step in developing policies, procedures, preventive actions and corrective actions is to understand the risks that may cause injuries. The employer can perform a workplace risk assessment to identify the risks that are present. Once the risks are identified, the employer will develop policies and procedures to work safely around or with these risks. These policies and procedures will construct the company's health and safety program. The health and safety program will be the first line of defence in preventing injuries from occurring. Despite the best health and safety program, injuries may still occur. Therefore, corrective actions become critical in preventing future injuries or recurrences.

An important tool in the corrective action process is a comprehensive incident reporting method. The employer should incorporate a method for identifying the root causes of the incidents. Once the root cause is identified, the employer can initiate the development and implementing of corrective or preventive actions. One element of a prevention strategy the employer can develop and implement is an effective return to work program. This program will not only mitigate further injury during the recovery process, it will provide evidence of due diligence for legal compliance to the various pieces of legislation including the WSIA, the OHSA, and other return to work legislation.

In Ontario, the provincial government has mandated employers to develop and implement an early and safe return to work program under the WSIA. The Workplace Safety and Insurance Act (WSIA) is the legislation enforcing the early and safe return to work program (ESRTW or RTW). In addition to the WSIA, the Human Rights Code also refers to the employer's duty to accommodate. The Human Rights Code dictates that the employer shall not discriminate against any worker who has a disability (regardless if the injury is work related or not work related).

Due diligence for the employer would be to comply with legal obligations regardless of the origin of the injury. The employer should develop and implement an early and safe return to work program that incorporates the elements of non-discriminating practices for workers with a disability regardless of the origin of the injury. A best practice would be that all employers develop and implement an early and safe return to work program for all workers who are off work due to a disability, regardless of the origin of the disability (occupational or non-occupational) not only to mitigate cost of claims but also to satisfy legal obligations to re-employ or continue to employ an injured worker with restrictions.

The Workplace Safety and Insurance Act (WSIA), Section 41 states that an employer has a legal responsibility to re-employ a worker who has been injured at the workplace. The WSIB Policy

#19-02-02 outlines the goal of the ESRTW as well as the roles and responsibilities of each of the parties of the return to work process.

According to the WSIB Policy #19-02-02, the *"...goal of the early and safe return to work (ESRTW) process is to return the worker to employment that is suitable and available, and if possible, restores the worker's earnings..."* Each party has a duty to cooperate within the return to work process. For example, the employer has a duty to offer a return to work plan within the worker's restrictions. The injured worker has a duty to accept and/or attempt the return to work plan as well as help the employer find work within the injured worker's restrictions.

The union has a duty to assist in the return to work process and the union has a duty not to create additional barriers in the process. The medical professionals have a duty to provide the employer and the employee with restrictions, the worker with viable treatment, and, provide the WSIB or other disability benefits carrier with medical documentation on the progression of the employee's recovery. The WSIB team or any other benefits carrier has the duty to assist all parties in the recovery process by providing ergonomic assessments where necessary, supporting the process, providing the employee with encouragement, providing decisions on suitability of the offers, providing decisions on the loss of earnings, etc.

The employer has the obligation to make a viable return to work offer to any injured worker. Once the employer has received the worker's restrictions, the employer is able to develop a return to work offer. The return to work offer should only include tasks that are within the worker's restrictions.

Obtaining restrictions is the first step in the return to work process. The return to work offer is the second step in return to work process. A best practice would be to document each return to work offer and each time the offer is presented to the worker. Furthermore, the worker's response should also be documented for each offer presented. Documenting each encounter would be a best practice because the documentation will provide evidence of the process and the due diligence of the company.

The modified work program must include a written return to work offer. The return to work plan supports the company's commitment to their early and safe return to work legal obligation. In order to support the early and safe return to work program and provide evidence of legal compliance, the return to work offer should be made in writing and signed off by both the worker and the company representative. The written offer will provide documented evidence of the offer for consistent reference and any support of legal action if required.

By documenting the return to work offer, the employer is providing evidence of the details of the offer to the worker and to the WSIB or benefits carrier. Once the return to work offer is prepared by the employer, it should be reviewed with the worker (and the union). Before the offer is made to the worker, however, the employer should send the wage loss insurance benefit carrier a copy of the offer. The benefits carrier will want to review the offer for suitability.

The significance of these details on the return to work offer provides evidence of the due diligence of the employer. For example, dating the offer demonstrates the timing of the offer as well establishes an historical pattern for future offers as it relates to the recovery process. Listing the relevant and current restrictions of the worker sets the parameters of capabilities of the worker which is required to determine suitability of the tasks assigned at that time in the recovery.

In addition to the restrictions, the worker may have other special accommodation requirements such as a steady shift, steady break to take medications, a taxi to transport the worker to and from work, etc. The ergonomic assessment details will outline the physical demands of the tasks proposed in the offer and will detail any "assistive" equipment required to accommodate the worker including lift assists, (specific) chairs, special writing tools, etc. The physical demands of the task are important because it outlines the physical output requirements of the task proposed. In understanding the physical demands required to perform the task, the employer can match the task with the person's restrictions.

Furthermore, the timeframe of the schedule on the restrictions outlines the timeline of the expected recovery. This is especially important in the short term recovery period or what is also known as the acute recovery stage. As time progresses, naturally the recovery process is also expected to progress towards the person's pre-injury state of health.

Each injury has a standard period of recovery in which therapy and restrictions will assist the person through the acute phase of recovery. The person's restrictions will change at each stage of recovery. Therefore current and updated restrictions are constantly required during the recovery process to ensure the assigned tasks change to include the increasing abilities of the worker when suitable to progress.

The timeframe of the schedule of restrictions will assist when to update the restrictions, when to increase the physical demands of the tasks for the worker, increase the number of tasks for the worker, outline when the worker should be capable to return to regular duties or pre-injury duties, etc. Should the worker continue to require restrictions exceeding the timeframe of the schedule, the timeframe will need to be adjusted accordingly as well as the recovery process will require review for additional claim management strategies such as requesting additional medical testing (for occupational and non-occupational injury claims), request cost relief through SIEF for worker's compensation claims, etc.

It is a best practice to continue to follow up with injured workers during their recovery process for several reasons including mediating any ongoing concerns such as difficulties performing tasks assigned, reviewing progress and restrictions, reviewing expectations at different stages in the recovery process, coaching on improved ergonomics of performing normal or expected tasks, etc. Constant open dialogue with the worker maintains good labour relations. Any planned follow up meetings should be documented on the modified return to work plan so all parties are aware of the timing and expectations.

Lastly, a comprehensive written modified work offer and plan must include a comments area and a signature line. The comments area will allow each party to express any concerns or questions regarding the offer. Feedback from any and all of the parties is critical in adjusting the modified work plan until the plan works for all the parties.

Signatures of the worker and the employer will make the written modified work offer a legally binding contract of employment for a temporary placement. As a legally binding contract, the WSIB will review and respect the implementation as long as the contract does not contravene the worker's restrictions or accommodation requirements. In fact, neither the disability benefit carriers nor the Ministry of Labour will interfere with the contract unless the elements of the contract contravene the worker's restrictions or accommodation requirements.

There is a delicate balance in managing the return to work plan, the worker requirements, the worker requests and managing the business operations effectively and efficiently (from a production standard). However, any changes made to the modified offer or plan should depend on objective medical documentation rather than emotional requests. Should the worker have difficulties with the tasks assigned within the restrictions as outlined in the modified work offer, the employer should review and compare the physical demands of the tasks with the worker's restrictions.

If there is a discrepancy in the assignment of tasks where the tasks are outside the worker's restrictions, then the modified plan must be adjusted accordingly. If the tasks outlined in the offer are within the restrictions, then the worker may need to be re-assessed by a medical professional such as a doctor, therapist, specialist, etc. to determine the current restrictions more accurately.

Should any conflict continue between the worker's abilities and the restrictions, the employer may elect to send the worker for a functional abilities evaluation (FAE) to determine the worker's functional capabilities. The difference between determining restrictions and functional capabilities is that restrictions focus on what the worker cannot perform whereas the functional capabilities evaluation focuses on the tasks that the worker can perform. Once the functional capabilities are determined, the employer can adjust the modified work plan accordingly.

In the event that the disagreement has not been resolved, the employer may elect to send the worker for an independent medical evaluation with a doctor of the employer's choosing. The employer would pay the doctor directly for this assessment. The employer would send the doctor information on the worker's restrictions, the FAE report, any comments from an ergonomist and any notes from the employer that would assist the doctor in assessing the abilities of the worker prior to the worker attending the appointment with the doctor.

Depending on the evaluation, the doctor may order further medical tests to determine any complication to the recovery, pre-existing medical condition prolonging the recovery, or medical evidence to support the recovery is completed. The medical reports may support and the worker's continued belief of restrictions or pain may be a result of something other than physical objective evidence.

Sometimes, the worker's perception of their restrictions may not match the company's perception of the worker's restrictions. Perception is reality. When the worker perceives the modified plan is not within their restrictions, the worker may need to be educated on the meaning of the assigned restrictions. The medical professional or ergonomist may have to discuss with the worker how the tasks do comply with the restrictions should all the assessments support compliance.

The concept of return to work is a vital part of the disability management program. Effective return to work plans may involve many professionals and many activities. The plans are essential in an employer's best practice for due diligence. For work related injuries, the Workplace Safety and Insurance Act (WSIA) dictates that the employer is obligated to return the injured worker to work. The WSIA, Section 41 (7) specifically states that the employer is obligated to re-employ the worker in the following timelines:

> ... The employer is obligated under this section until the earliest of,
> (a) the second anniversary of the date of injury;
> (b) one year after the worker is medically able to perform the essential duties of his or her pre-injury employment; and
> (c) the date on which the worker reaches 65 years of age. 1997, c. 16, Sched. A, s. 41 (7); 2000, c. 26, Sched. I, s. 1 (3)... (WSIA, 1997)

Even if the WSIA puts a time limit on the obligation of the employer to return an injured worker to work, the Human Rights Codes does not have a time limit on the duty to accommodate. In other words, the employer continues to have the obligation to offer the injured worker a return to work plan. The obligation does have some conditions. The duty to accommodate does not mean the employer has to "create" a position for the injured worker. However, it does mean the employer should be offering work that is available and is reasonable to modify to the worker's restrictions.

The Human Rights Code outlines the employer's duty to accommodate. This duty does not mandate that the employer promote the worker to a classification higher than the pre-injury job because that is the only position that is within the person's restrictions. Moreover, the code does not force the company to change the core responsibilities of the pre-injury position to accommodate the worker.

The code does expect the company to make all reasonable changes to the job in order to accommodate the worker safely.

Therefore any modified work offer must meet the reasonable accommodation test under the duty to accommodate legal obligation. If the offer meets the reasonable accommodation test then the offer will provide support for the employer's due diligence in satisfying their legal obligations.

The duty to accommodate is not the only responsibility of the company. Each party of the return to work process has specific responsibilities and obligations to satisfy throughout the recovery process. There are other legal obligations for each party which are outlined in both the WSIA and the Human Rights Code. According to the WSIA, Section 40, the employer has the obligation to co-operate in the whole return to work process.

> ...The employer of an injured worker shall co-operate in the early and safe return to work of the worker by,
> (a) contacting the worker as soon as possible after the injury occurs and maintaining communication throughout the period of the worker's recovery and impairment;
> (b) attempting to provide suitable employment that is available and consistent with the worker's functional abilities and that, when possible, restores the worker's pre-injury earnings;
> (c) giving the Board such information as the Board may request concerning the worker's return to work; and
> (d) doing such other things as may be prescribed. 1997, c. 16, Sched. A, s. 40 (1). (WSIA, 1997)

Likewise, the injured worker also has a duty to co-operate in the return to work process under the WSIA. According to the WSIA, Section 40, the injured worker...

> ...(2) The worker shall co-operate in his or her early and safe return to work by,
> (a) contacting his or her employer as soon as possible after the injury occurs and maintaining communication throughout the pe-

riod of the worker's recovery and impairment;

(b) assisting the employer, as may be required
or requested, to identify suitable employment that is available and consistent with
the worker's functional abilities and that,
when possible, restores his or her pre-injury
earnings;

(c) giving the Board such information as the
Board may request concerning the worker's
return to work; and

(d) doing such other things as may be prescribed. 1997, c. 16, Sched. A, s. 40 (2)...
(WSIA, 1997)

The company and the workers are not the only participants in
the return to work process that have responsibilities. The medical
professionals have obligations to provide the appropriate information to assist the workers in returning to safe and suitable work
including completed FAFs, FAEs, further medical investigations
where appropriate, benefit carrier forms for disability information,
etc.

The medical information is distributed in different routes. For
instance, the restrictions and any information related to the worker's
capabilities of performing tasks should be routed to the worker and
the employer. Any medical information should be routed to the
benefits carrier including the WSIB. Communication with the worker, the benefits carrier and to some extent, the company is important
to ensure the return to work plan is safe, suitable and timely for all
parties.

Lastly, the benefits carriers also have responsibilities in the return to work process. The benefits carrier supports the process by
communicating with all parties, gathering appropriate information,
making decisions about suitability of offers, timing of offers, appropriateness of offers, etc. The benefits carrier must make decisions
on the claim. The benefits carrier can become a mediator of the
whole process should conflicts arise.

All parties in the return to work process must support the process. In supporting the process, communication, feedback, attempting plans and assisting in identifying suitable tasks are all essential
elements for the success of the plan. The plan itself is an evolving

agreement as it continuously changes to the needs of the parties to support the worker's return to pre-injury status.

The WSIA is not the only piece of legislation that guides the employer in the return to work process. The Human Rights Code also outlines the roles and responsibilities in the return to work process. There are other pieces of legislation that indirectly impact the return to work process including the Employment Standards Act, the Labour Relations Act, the Privacy Act, etc. Even though all the relevant legislation summarizes the roles and responsibilities of each party of the return to work process, the two common and most important requirements to start the return to work process are restrictions and the written offer of modified work.

RTW Modified Work Offer, PDAs, Ergonomics

A key element to disability management is the effective management of lost time regardless if the injury happened at work or outside of work. Lost time is very costly to any company in terms of lost productivity, training costs, claim costs, premium costs, morale, etc. Lost time is difficult for the injured worker in terms of returning to their "normal" life. One way to mitigate lost time is to develop a modified work program. A modified work plan that is consistently applied to both occupationally or non-occupationally related injuries or illnesses will assist in mitigating the risk of violating the right to equal treatment or any contraventions to the human rights code. Essential tools to develop a solid modified work program include but are not limited to:

- Physical demands analysis (PDAs) of all jobs available in the company
- Ergonomic assessments
- Completed functional abilities forms (FAFs)
- Functional abilities evaluations (FAEs)
- Understanding of Ergonomics in the workplace
- Medical network
- Independent medical evaluations (IMEs)

In Ontario, employers are obligated under legislation to offer modified work or accommodating restricted workers. Offering suitable, sustainable and long term placements within the workers' restrictions satisfies the employer's legal re-employment obligation under the WSIA and under the Human Rights Code. Effective return to work or return to regular duties plans depend on accurate restrictions.

Further to monitoring the claim, monitoring restrictions for updates and appropriateness is essential to effective return to work or return to regular duties plans. If the restrictions are no longer appropriate for the injured worker, then the worker can be exposed to additional risk of re-injury or new injury as well as prolonged recovery due to lack of work conditioning.

Tracking lost time is an essential activity in monitoring the effectiveness of the prevention strategies and legal compliance. To effectively reduce lost time, a company will need to develop and implement a return to work plan. Below, Illustration 21-1 shows the effectiveness of the return to work program through the clear reduction in lost time for one company.

Illustration 21-1: Lost time day tracking. In this example it shows that the amount of the lost time days decreased in 2007. It is interesting to note that the number of lost time days intersect at the same point that the return to work program was implemented in 2007. The company could infer that the decrease in lost time was a direct impact of the implementation of an effective return to work program.

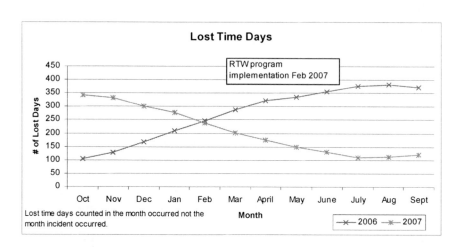

Lost time days counted in the month occurred not the month incident occurred.

Despite any employer's best effort, injuries may still occur in the work place. Employers do not have any control over the worker's personal life to prevent injuries outside the workplace. Once an injury occurs or a near miss occurs, the company's procedure should outline the incident reporting process including the form representing the incident report. In cases where the event is work related, the incident report should be completed by the worker and the worker's supervisor at the time the injury is reported to the supervisor to ensure accurate details are recorded. In addition, the benefits carrier may have each their own forms to complete. However, the employer's incident report will initiate corrective and preventive actions under the control of the employer.

Various branches of the provincial government in Ontario including the Ministry of Labour, the Workplace Safety and Insurance Board, the Premier of Ontario, etc., are applying pressure on all employers operating a business in Ontario to return injured workers to work. The employer is legally obligated to offer a modified work plan to any worker requiring accommodation due to medical reasons regardless if the injury is occupationally related or non-occupationally related. For any injuries, the employer will need to get the restrictions or accommodation requirements from the benefits carrier or the worker's medical professional.

The workplace culture should strongly encourage the reporting of all injuries at the workplace as well as any near misses that would have caused an injury at the workplace immediately. Everyone in the workplace needs to understand that verbally reporting the incident is just one small part of the reporting process. Best practice prescribes the worker and the supervisor to be trained to complete an incident report (written) each time the worker reports any event that deviates from the safe operation of a business. In turn, the completed report initiates the corrective and preventive action process as well as initiates any paperwork required for the workers compensation benefits carrier (if required). This comprehensive incident reporting practice will comply with the employer's due diligence and their legal obligations.

Completing an incident report and completing the benefits carrier's paperwork when required is just the start of the due diligence in the areas of health and safety as well as disability management. In Ontario, the employer has additional obligations under the WSIA and the Human Rights Code to offer the injured worker an early and safe return to work plan. For the company to provide evidence that the early and safe return to work plan has been offered, the offer should be made in writing.

A comprehensive return to work offer should outline several critical pieces of information for all the parties. In addition to naming the employer and the worker, the offer should detail the following:

- Date of the offer
- Any relevant and current restrictions of the worker,
- Any special accommodation requirements as prescribed the medical professional or the benefits carrier,
- Ergonomic assessment details including the physical demands of the tasks proposed in the offer
- The timeframe of the schedule,
- A list of the suitable tasks or workstations,
- Schedule of follow up meetings,
- Area for comments,
- Area for the signature of the employer representative and the worker.

In a unionized environment, the offer should be presented and explained to the worker with a union representative present. In a non-unionized environment, the worker should still have a worker representative present in order to avoid, or, at least minimize miscommunication issues. The worker should respond to the offer in writing. The written offer of suitable and sustainable work within the worker's restrictions satisfies the company's responsibility to offer the worker an early and safe return to work plan.

The written offer provides evidence of the return to work offer. It also supports the return to work program. The offer can be used for reference materials and lessons learned. The trail of written offers is evidence of progression in recovery. More importantly, the written offer is evidence of the company practicing due diligence and provides evidence of legal compliance.

In addition to the company having obligations under the WSIA and the Human Rights Codes, the worker also has responsibilities. The worker is obligated to cooperate in the process. This obligation means the worker has to attempt the tasks outlined in the plan as long as the tasks are within the restrictions and provide appropriate accommodations for the worker's successful completion of the plan.

The objective of the return to work program is to successfully reintegrate the worker into the workplace. The company and the worker working through the return to work process together, both parties increase the rate of success of the plan as well as comply with their legal obligations. Constant communication and feedback throughout the process will also assist in the successful reintegration of the worker. Successful reintegration will validate the return to work program as well as help motivate the workers and improve morale in general. The most evident result of a successful return to work program is the reduction in the number of lost time days.

Even though the early and safe return to work (ESRTW) in its written form satisfies the employer's legal obligations and responsibilities under both the WSIA and the Human Rights Codes, a key cost efficient result of the early and safe return to work is to reduce the number of lost time days. In reducing the number of lost time days, the employer can mitigate the costs of the claim regardless of the injury being occupational or non-occupational.

The expectation of the WSIB is for the employer to make a return to work offer as soon as it is medically safe to do so. The employer would also like to mitigate the number of lost time days as well as the number of lost time claims. The employer would also need to offer a modified work plan to the injured worker before lost time even occurs. To avoid lost time claims, the employer must offer a return to work plan or modified work plan before the lost time occurs. However, for an effective return to work offer, the employer must base the return to work plan on medical documentation beginning with the restrictions of the worker.

It appears to be paradoxical to offer a return to work plan based on medical documentation such as the restrictions listed on the functional abilities form (FAF from the WSIB) before the worker even seeks medical attention. The solution to this paradox, is to offer the return to work plan prior to the worker even leaving the facility (to seek medical attention) using the standard restrictions. By offering modified work at the point of initial reporting of the injury and having the worker initial acknowledgement that the offer has been made will provide the proof of written offer of modified work as required by the WSIB and or benefits carrier. Therefore, the offer occurs prior to the lost time resulting in avoiding the lost time before it even starts.

To offer modified work, the employer needs the restrictions. If the employer does not have the restrictions then the employer can use standard restrictions to develop a return to work offer until medical information is received. The WSIB uses standard restrictions guide as outlined by the American Medical Association (AMA) or the National Institute of Occupational Safety and Health (NIOSH) to confirm appropriate restrictions or permanent restrictions especially in the absence of any current medical documentation.

A strategy to avoid lost time is for the employer to offer modified work prior to the worker leaving the facility. The employer should embed the modified work plan into the incident reporting process. In order to assimilate the modified work offer into the reporting process, the employer must understand the "standard" restrictions that the WSIB uses. The employer should list the standard restrictions from the AMA or NIOSH for each body part in a chart. The chart should be integrated into the incident report.

In integrating the body part chart into the incident report, the incident report can increase in size quickly. To reduce the size of the body part chart, the company will need to focus on the body parts that are most at risk for injury at the workplace. The company's injury statistics could also reveal the body parts producing the highest number of injuries. These statistics could assist the company in focusing the modified work plan specific to the type of injuries for that specific site.

Once the list of body parts with corresponding restrictions is established, the company can compare those restrictions against the physical demands of all the tasks available in the pre-injury classification of the injured worker to determine the appropriate tasks for each body part (and restrictions). An ergonomist can assist in assessing all the tasks in the worker's classification to match with the standard restrictions for each body part in the chart. The correlation between the restrictions, each body part, and each tasks or job in the workplace is the critical link to offering modified work to an injured worker prior to the worker leaving the facility. See Appendix A attached for an example of a body part chart tool integrated into an incident report embedding the return to work offer into the incident reporting process.

The body part chart will assist the front line supervisors to confidently assign appropriate tasks to specific restrictions or and injured body parts. Once the supervisor offers the corresponding modified work plan with the injured body part, the injured worker should initial the acknowledgement of the offer. There should also be a section on the list allowing the worker to make comments on the offer of modified work. The worker should date and sign all the comments. This will all serve to document the return to work offer.

Once the worker returns from the doctors with a completed FAF, the supervisor can than compare the body part chart offer to the completed FAF to make any necessary adjustments accordingly. The FAF and the incident report must be forwarded within twenty four (24) hours to the Disability Management Advisor or Human Resources or Health and Safety Advisor (depending on your incident reporting procedure) to review the report, the FAF and the offer of modified work to confirm suitability.

The only lost time that should be incurred would be that dictated by the doctor and supported by medical documentation. For example, the FAF states something to the effect of "off for the rest of the shift" or "off work until re-evaluated again next week", etc. Benefits carriers especially the WSIB will only pay for lost wages when the lost time is supported by medical documentation. A best practice for the employer is to request medical documentation each time the worker loses time as a result of the injury.

The body part chart tool will not only assist the supervisors to assign appropriate tasks but it will also assure consistent application of the modified work program according to the standards of any benefits carrier especially the WSIB. Since the tool is based on the AMA or NIOSH guidelines, the same guidelines the WSIB uses to make determinations on claims, the employer will usually cover all the restrictions that will be or could be listed on the functional abilities form (FAF) completed by the doctor. The WSIB is more likely to accept the modified work plan as appropriate because it is based on the NIOSH guidelines.

Once the benefits carrier determines the modified work plan is appropriate, any lost time days could be denied because suitable and sustainable modified work is available for the worker to avoid lost wages. Therefore, the standard restrictions listing the corresponding appropriate assignments will serve to minimize lost time days and provide written evidence of due diligence complying with the employer's duty to accommodate.

An effective return to work plan will reduce the number of lost time days. In reducing the number of lost time days, the worker will remain productive throughout the recovery process. Not only does returning an injured worker back to work restore the worker's productivity and sense of purpose but the return to work plan will establish a culture of recovery and precedence for the practice of providing early and safe return to work for any injured workers.

In addition to assisting the worker in recovery, the return to work plan reduces the costs of the claim by restoring the worker's pre-injury wages. The return to work plan decreases costs for the employer because the worker's earnings are restored by the employer instead of the benefits carrier paying loss of earnings. Therefore, the return to work plan is a key strategy in reducing the cost of claims as the costs will decrease once the worker's earnings has been restored by the employer.

At any time in the return to work program, if the worker refuses the tasks assigned in the return to work offer, there are a number of expectations that should be considered. Just as the return to work offer is presented in writing by the employer, the refusal of performing such tasks should also be in writing from the worker. A best practice in the incident reporting process would be to include the reasons for the refusal, signing and dating the reasons, any comments relevant to the process or restrictions, etc. in the written refusal.

Upon receiving the notice of refusal, the employer should review the refusal. The employer should ensure that the tasks in the modified offer are within the current restrictions. If the employer believes the tasks assigned are within the restrictions, the report should be sent to the benefits carrier with the original offer of modified work for their review. The benefits carrier will review all the material to make a determination on the suitability of the offer as well as the credibility of the details in the refusal. If the determination is in favour of the modified work offer, the worker will be asked by the carrier to return to work. If the worker continues to refuse to return to work, the benefits carrier may terminate payment of benefits.

If the determination is in favour of the refusal, the employer will be asked by the benefits carrier to redraft the return to work plan. The employer should consider reviewing the plan with an ergonomist and other medical professionals to ensure suitability. The benefits carrier may offer the employer the services of an ergonomist, doctors, specialists, functional abilities evaluations, etc. If the benefits carrier has these resources, the company should not delay in requesting these services to continue the recovery process forward. However, if the benefits carrier does not have access to these services, the medical network of the employer should be accessed.

The employer's medical network will provide professional and a credible medical service base to draw from when disputes in interpretation of documentation or opinion exist in the return to work or recovery processes. When such conflicts arise, the employer has a legal right under the WSIA and indeed indirectly by the Human Rights Codes to request independent medical evaluations (IME) funded by the employer. The IME should only be used as a tool for clarifying medical documentation on file or to collect medical documentation to address any disputes between the worker and the employer during the recovery and the return to work processes.

Once the worker has been sent for an IME and the IME report has been completed, the medical professional will then send the employer a report of the findings with respect to the worker's restrictions and capabilities. This report will allow the employer to adjust the return to work and recovery plans accordingly.

Should the worker continue to have concerns regarding the medical documentation or the adjusted modified plans, the worker and the employer should seek to address the concerns according to the terms of the collective agreement if the workplace is unionized or according to appropriate means of the internal responsibility system. If the concerns continue, there are specific legislative courses of actions that can be pursued by either the worker or the employer through the wage replacement benefits carrier, the government or legislative regulations, etc. See the following section on conflict resolution for further details.

In Ontario, according to the Privacy Act, the employer does not have the right to know the worker's personal medical information regardless if the employer paid for the doctor's evaluation. However, the medical practitioner may speak to or send medical information to the benefits carrier on behalf of the employer. For example, the doctor will forward a copy of a detailed medical report to the WSIB (if the injury is work related) or the benefits carrier (for non-occupational injuries) at which point the claims adjudicator will review the report and make determinations on:

- length of time to continue or discontinue benefits
- permanent impairment (PI)

- non-economic loss (NEL)
- labour market re-entry (LMR)
- cost relief from SIEF
- permanent restrictions
- return to work plans
- therapy plans
- further medical treatment plans
- any other decisions related to the claim based on medical information

The decisions of the benefits carrier(s) regardless of the origin of the injury can be disputed by either party. Any decision of the benefits carrier can be appealed through an objection process. Any objections should be done in writing with details to support the objection. Medical documentation is generally the most effective evidence to support the objection. Each carrier will have their own process of dealing with the objections but usually if the highest level of objection is generally in the court room of some type including that of the court system of the land, arbitration (labour relations act/union grievances), or tribunal hearing (the WSIAT for occupationally related injuries in Ontario).

The medical network is beneficial in providing valuable medical opinions, current restrictions, functional capabilities, etc. to assist in providing the most suitable offer of modified work. In essence, if the worker refuses the return to work offer for valid reasons, the process of medical evaluations and revisions to the plans begins again.

Each party in the return to work process has roles and responsibilities specific to their position. In addition to the roles and responsibilities outlined in Chapter 10, the company or the company's representative has a few more responsibilities that establish best practices in the return to work process:

- The company or the designated representative, usually the supervisor should offer the worker accommodated work at the time of the injury if the worker requires a change in work assignment due to the injury. The accommodated work should be safe and suitable for the worker according to standard restrictions for the injury.

- The supervisor is required to provide ongoing support and encouragement to all workers starting with assigning the restricted worker with suitable and sustainable work, listening to the worker, working with the worker regarding ongoing issues, follow up on restrictions and progress, etc.

- Injured workers should be encouraged to make medical appointments related to their workplace injury before and after their shifts to avoid wage loss. However, the company cannot deny the worker's request for leave for such medical appointments. There are systems that can be implemented to discourage workers from leaving work. Such systems include but are not limited to some rules like:

  - The company can request the worker to submit appointment cards for each appointment. This is only a reasonable request when the appointments become excessive.

  - The company does not pay for the lost time. In doing this, the company must submit the lost time to the benefits carrier including the WSIB for payment consideration. The company can object to all lost time using the modified work plan. Depending on the WSIB claims adjudicator, some appointments will be approved for payment. However, the company can argue in the objection for the appointments to be made outside of work. The WSIB may pay for the first few appointments but will eventually deny ongoing lost time for appointments. The company must weigh the costs of this little bit of lost time against the WSIB costs in projecting rebates and surcharges.

  - If the culture of the workers is responsible and will not take advantage of the compa-

ny's good faith, then it might make more
financial sense for the company to pay for
the time for medical appointments that are
not frequent and are very short in time.
These are decisions that must be made internally weighing all financial information
to make the best decision for the company's culture and bottom line.

- When a person must leave the facility, they
should be clocking out when they leave and
clocking back in upon return. The worker
should only leave the facility after the approval
of the supervisor and advising the supervisor at
the time of leaving the facility. If it is an office
person leaving, they should be communicating
with their supervisor before departing. Supervisors need to know who and where people are
in a shift in case there is an emergency or the
supervisor is required to change the schedule
for any reason.

In summary, the return to work process is very important to
supporting the recovery process, ensuring legal compliance, reducing
lost time, reducing claim costs, increasing productivity, etc. All parties of the return to work process have roles and responsibilities in
the process. Medical documentation is critical in supporting requests
of either party as well as to assist claim adjudicators in making appropriate decisions in the claim at the appropriate times during the
recovery. If either party has concerns with any of the decisions
made by the claims adjudicators, the decisions can be appealed. The
objections must be made in writing. Each benefits carrier will have
their own appeal process according to their own guidelines. The
majority of objections that cannot be resolved through the appeals
process will be bound by final decisions of the courts of the land like
the Supreme Court of Canada, final arbitration hearings through Labour Relations Act and union grievances, or final tribunal hearings
like that of the WSIB's the WSIAT. Regardless of the route of the
final decision, once the final decision of the final appeal has been
rendered, all parties must comply and proceed accordingly. These
objection processes are expensive as the parties will usually elect to

be represented by qualified professionals such as labour law or employment law lawyers.

CHAPTER 22

WORK HARDENING

In an effective and efficient disability management program, the return to work program is important in returning an injured worker back to productive work. The return to work program is only one step in returning the worker back to their pre-injury status in terms of health, wages, and productivity. The offer of modified work is a step forward to reinstating the worker's pre-injury wage level. The worker cooperating with treatment during recovery is a step towards the worker returning to their pre-injury health status. Lastly, the worker can return to their pre-injury productivity levels by returning to regular duties or an equivalent level of regular duties within the accommodations.

It is important to develop and implement a return to work program. The written offer of modified duties provides evidence of due diligence for legal compliance. The plan should restore the worker's pre-injury wages resulting in reduced claim costs. A best practice in returning the worker back to their pre-injury productivity level, would be for the company to develop a work hardening program. This chapter will discuss the dynamics of an effective work hardening program focusing on returning the worker to regular duties and or long term suitable and sustainable placements within their permanent restrictions.

Any return to work program should include a written offer of modified work. The program should concentrate on the return to work plan. Once the worker agrees to return to work or if the worker has not lost time but still requires modified duties, the company has to consider the physical demands of the modified duties as well as the physical demands of time or duration of the modified work for the most appropriate or suitable accommodation for the worker. Depending on the restrictions and the amount of time the worker was absent from work or how aggressive the treatment plan for recovery is, will determine the timing of the return to regular duties and the timing of the schedule of the return plan.

Work hardening plans consider both these timing aspects and infuses gradual increase in physical demands in order for the worker to slowly regain the strength required to return to the worker's pre-injury health, strength and productivity levels. Work hardening plans can be as simple as gradually increasing hours during the return to work over a specified number of weeks. For example, the worker had a broken leg and was absent from work for 6 weeks allowing the leg to fully heal. Since the worker not only had been absent from work for a six (6) week period but was likely immobile for that time period. If the worker was immobile for a long period of time, the worker's muscles would have significantly lost muscle tone and strength. Each case is different. Each person heals differently and each recovery has its own timing. Therefore, each plan is tailored to each case, each person's needs, and each person's recovery timing within reasonable range (standard recovery).

An effective plan will reflect a gradual increase for endurance in time, in the number of tasks, or/and in the physical demands with respect to strength required to perform the tasks. Factors like the length of time the person is absent from work, level of inactivity, standard recovery for the injury, the severity of the injury, nature or demands of the pre-injury work, the status and length of restrictions, etc., will have a considerable impact on the details of the incremental steps of the graduated return to work plan and the graduated return to regular duties plan. A simple cut to the finger requiring a few stitches may only need to be accommodated by assigning the worker with tasks that do not require lifting for two (2) weeks while the cut heals. After the 2 weeks is completed, the worker can resume the regular duties with no further accommodation requirements. Since the worker did not lose any time nor did they stop being active despite their injury, the worker would likely not require a graduated return to work plan involving gradual increase in physical demands for strength and certainly not graduated increase in hours.

In contrast, a person with a severe repetitive strain injury like carpal tunnel syndrome may incur months of lost time, months or years of treatment, possible surgical intervention, permanent restrictions, etc. This type of recovery, depending on the nature of the pre-injury work/industry, may be more difficult to accommodate especially if the work requires prolonged awkward positioning of the wrists.

A return to work plan may involve ten (10) weeks of gradually increasing hours just to build the worker's tolerance to work eight (8) hours per day again. In addition, the gradual increase in physical demands for strength may be prolonged over a (very) long period of time due to the long term restrictions. Should permanent restrictions be determined, the worker may have to be retrained if the essential duties of the pre-injury work are outside the worker's permanent restrictions.

To develop the most appropriate work hardening plan, opinions and assistance from medical professionals are important in determining current and appropriate restrictions, functional capabilities, ergonomic assessments, appropriate incremental stages for increasing strength, and suitability of assigned tasks. The company would benefit from developing a network of medical professionals to support the company's activities in developing effective return to work plans and work hardening plans. The network of medical professionals should include ergonomists, physiotherapists, medical experts of various disciplines (for example: general practitioner, psychology experts, specialists, clinics, etc.).

In addition to recommending the appropriate gradual increase in hours and physical demands for strength, ergonomists can be of great assistance in job coaching and job mentoring. In a work hardening plan, job coaching and job mentoring activities include: education and awareness of proper posturing; alternative ways to complete the same task that would minimize recurrence of the injury or improve strength; alternating a variety of motions to allow for rest breaks of different muscle groups; understanding the meaning of repetitive and how to mitigate the risk of repetition based injuries; etc.

Job coaching and job mentoring activities can also happen with any of the other medical professionals. In order for the medical professional to provide competent opinions about return to work plans and work hardening plans, the medical professionals will request information about the work place and the work assigned through physical demands analysis details. The physical demands details would include information like cycle times, weights of objects lifted, frequency of lifts, heights of lifts, etc. Generally, the medical professionals will defer such opinions to physiotherapists or ergonomists for more accurate details.

It is very common for this type of activity to come from ergonomists and or physiotherapists as doctors may not have the time to dedicate to this aspect of the recovery process. Regardless of the type of medical professional hired to perform such activities, it would be prudent for the company to request evidence of the professional's credentials like a copy of certification or diploma, etc.

The more the medical professional understands the nature of the work at the workplace, the better quality work plans can be developed and better chances for successful completion of the plans. Visiting workplaces can prompt the medical professionals to have a full picture appreciation of the work environment for the worker. Therefore, it is a best practice for the medical professional to get to know and understand the workplace activities both pre-injury and the modified work program assigned by having the medical professional visit the workplace.

Along with timing schedules, similar to the modified duties offer, the work hardening plan should list the jobs that are appropriate as each phase of the incremental step increases. Actually the modified work plan and the work hardening plan should be similar in design and structure. The difference between the two is just the wording on return to work versus work hardening. Once the worker has returned to work, then the plan focuses on work hardening.

The work hardening plan will assist the supervisor to assign tasks suitable for the worker's development and recovery, balancing productivity with capabilities or restrictions. The medical professional(s) will assist in developing the timeline with the activities based on the restrictions and physical demands of the job. Not all injuries and plans will require this type of medical intervention but for those injuries that do, a tool the medical professional will be required to assess the situation using a physical demands analysis.

The physical demands analysis is a report outlining all the physical requirements of performing a particular task or duty. The physical demands analysis report is used by companies or benefits carriers to determine the compatibility of the modified work offer to the worker's restrictions. In order to create the report, a person has to evaluate or assess each task in the series of steps to each job. The evaluation of the job starts with defining each task at each work station to each and every job. The definition of each task includes listing each physical movement and other requirements to complete each job.

Planning to complete physical demands for each job in the facility will take time and effort to compile. The physical demands analysis is a critical part of the return to work plan, the work hardening plan. It is also very crucial for the WSIB or benefits carrier to determine or assess if an injury is a result of work. This is a very important tool because the employer can use this tool to object to the injury as being work related. Reverse is also possible for the worker to use the physical demands analysis to support their position that the injury is related to the tasks performed at work.

To get an ergonomist to complete the physical demands analysis is well worth the investment. The more accurate and detailed the analysis is, the more credible and indisputable the information becomes for appeals. The physical demands analysis can be the key piece of information that denies the claim potentially saving the employer a large amount of money.

To understand the physical demands analysis process more clearly, the following example will break down each step. For the purposes of this example, the process will be greatly oversimplified and in no way represents the total detailed process. In assessing the job of assembling cell phones, broadly speaking, a worker would have to take the back case, attach several electronic components, input the speaker, add the sound amplifier, insert each of the buttons, and lastly, the worker would clip on the face cover. Once the phone is assembled, the worker wraps the phone in a bubble wrap and packs the phone is a box with an operator's manual. The box then gets put in a larger bin with other boxes and readied for shipment.

In each step in the series of tasks, each body movement needs to be documented and timed. The assessment will need to include such body movements (but not limited to):

- as each reach for each of the components both in terms of number of times of reaching as well as the height of reach and distance of the reach;

Illustration 22-1

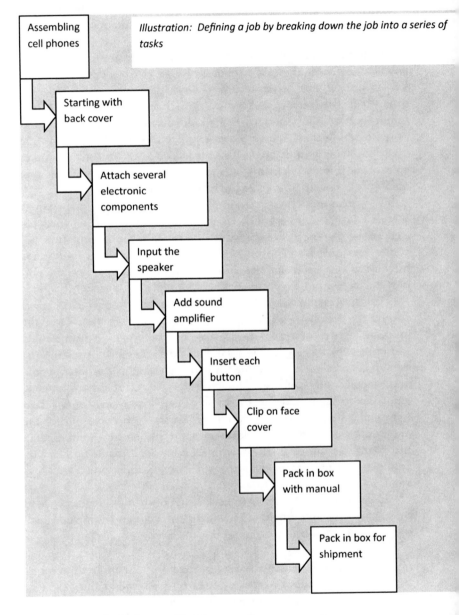

Assembling cell phones

Illustration: Defining a job by breaking down the job into a series of tasks

Starting with back cover

Attach several electronic components

Input the speaker

Add sound amplifier

Insert each button

Clip on face cover

Pack in box with manual

Pack in box for shipment

- pinch force of holding small components;
- carrying the components in terms of weight and distance;

- weights of each component at each phase of assembly; and,
- the number of times the worker bends each body part.

The movements will repeat until each body motion is recorded in terms of definition and how many times each body motion occurs at each step. The frequency of each motion, the duration of each motion, and the repetition of each motion are all key elements to record for each step in the physical demands analysis. The report will assist the company to understand if there are any ergonomic risks in the series of tasks to complete the job.

The purpose of the physical demands analysis report is to understand the ergonomic dynamics of risk of injury as it relates to the human body performing the tasks assigned at work. According to Silverstein et al., 1986, the definition of the term "repetitive" as it relates to work is repeating a task with similar motions "<30 seconds or >50% of work cycle" (*Silverstein et al., 1986 – Silverstein, B.A., Fine, L.J., Armstrong, T.J., 1986, Hand wrist cumulative trauma disorders in industry. British Journal of Industrial Medicine*). Basically, in order to design an effective workstation and mitigate risk of repetitive strain injury, the engineer will need to understand and integrate Silverstein et al.'s definition of repetitive into the design.

Essentially, the higher the frequency or the higher the repetition of the movement or body motion within a small amount of time, then the higher the risk for repetitive strain injury. Furthermore, when bending or twisting a body part while lifting will also increase the risk of injury. The risk of injury increases proportional to the amount of weight of the part and the amount of times of the bending or twisting. The company can mitigate the risk of repetitive strain injuries by allowing sufficient rest time for each body part when setting the cycle time for the task. An efficient way to consider this is to move one body part while another has a rest period.

The time that it takes to perform the entire job will also have an impact on the risk of injury. If the timing to perform the series of tasks does not allow appropriate rest time between motions, then the risk for repetitive strain type injuries increases significantly. The duration of the assigned tasks therefore must be reviewed. Similarly, if one body part continues to perform the same motion repeatedly in a short period of time, the worker will experience an increased risk of repetitive strain type injuries.

For instance, the task of packing parts requires bending at the waist, so the engineer can design the task to include activity with walking a few steps within the same cycle to allow for rest of the back. It would also reduce the risk if the bending at the waist was only occurring once in less than 30 seconds or once in 50% of the whole task in the cycle time. The walking of a few steps will stretch the back muscles and allow the rest from bending or twisting of the back within the repetitive definition. It will assist the worker to design the workstation so that the worker is directly facing the bin to pack the part to avoid twisting the trunk of the body then bending at the waist to pack. Human nature is to bend and twist if that is the "most convenient" way to complete the task. Therefore if the engineer designed the temptation of bending and twisting out of the work flow, then the worker is more likely to face the bin squarely and avoid the high risk activity of bending and twisting.

Tables 22-2 and 22-3 below will illustrate the correlation between injured body parts, repetitive motion by body part, and injury diagnosis so that this information can be matched with the work that corresponds to or complies with the restrictions. This information is vital to setting up a body part chart tool for the supervisors to assign appropriate work reassignment until medical documentation is received.

In understanding this information, it will also allow the employer to review prevention programs for corrective actions to be developed and implemented in order to mitigate further risk of injury. Understanding the correlation between physical demands of tasks or assignments and injuries to the various body parts and the results of the wrong correlation will provide the employer or company will valuable insight. This insight will translate in more effective prevention activities as well as accommodation activities. Therefore, the insight will provide evidence of due diligence and legal compliance in best practices for disability management.

Understanding the root cause of an injury enables the company to develop and implement effective corrective actions to prevent recurrence or repeat of the injury. Another preventative activity includes redesigning the workstation to reduce the repetition, duration, frequency, and force required for each body part. The physical demands analysis will help the engineer to recognize the location of the high risk components of the task.

Table 22-2: Body Movement

Table 1	
Body Movement	**Areas of Pain**
repetitive, horizontal or vertical movements of the wrist to the extreme ranges (Fig. 1A)	wrist and palm
moving fingers while the wrist is in an extreme position (Fig. 1B,1C)	
repetitive bending or straightening of the elbow from its neutral position (at a right angle)	elbow
twisting the wrist and forearm (Fig. 2)	
reaching above shoulder level (Fig. 3B)	neck and shoulder
reaching behind the trunk (Fig. 3C)	
reaching far out in front of the body (Fig. 3A)	
twisting the arm (Fig. 3C)	

Canadian Centre for Occupational Health and Safety CCOHS,
http://www.ccohs.ca/oshanswers/diseases/rmirsi.html

The corrective or preventive action of high risk areas of injury does not always mean automation. Sometimes, this is as simple as rearranging the series of tasks in the job or changing the angle to which the body is working. However, the engineer can only design or redesign an effective and efficient work station if the physical demands analysis is accurate and thorough.

It is important for a comprehensive physical demands form to be developed and implemented to compile the information required by the engineer. Only if the report compiles useful information for the engineer will the effective preventive and corrective actions be developed and implemented. Therefore careful consideration must be put into the design of the physical demands analysis report for it to become the effective tool to the engineer.

Table 22-3: Disorders and Risks

Table 2
Identified disorders, occupational risk factors and symptoms

Disorders	Occupational risk factors	Symptoms
Tendonitis/tenosynovitis	Repetitive wrist motions Repetitive shoulder motions Sustained hyper extension of arms Prolonged load on shoulders	Pain, weakness, swelling, burning sensation or dull ache over affected area
Epicondylitis (elbow tendonitis)	Repeated or forceful rotation of the fore-arm and bending of the wrist at the same time	Same symptoms as tendonitis
Carpal tunnel syndrome	Repetitive wrist motions	Pain, numbness, tingling, burning sensations, wasting of muscles at base of thumb, dry palm
DeQuervain's disease	Repetitive hand twisting and forceful gripping	Pain at the base of thumb
Thoracic outlet syndrome	Prolonged shoulder flexion Extending arms above shoulder height Carrying loads on the shoulder	Pain, numbness, swelling of the hands
Tension neck syndrome	Prolonged restricted posture	Pain

Canadian Centre for Occupational Health and Safety CCOHS,
http://www.ccohs.ca/oshanswers/diseases/rmirsi.html

In addition to the physical demands analysis assisting with corrective and preventive actions, the physical demands analysis will also assist ergonomists to recommend the most appropriate tasks that are within the worker's restrictions. The physical demands analysis outlines the demands of the job whereas the FAFs and FAEs explain the capabilities of the worker. In order to match the restricted worker with the appropriate job, both the demands and capabilities must be considered. Along with the FAF and the FAE, the physical demands analyst will allow the worker, the worker representative (if applicable), the company, medical professionals and the benefits carriers to work together as a team to determine the most suitable and appropriate modified work offer and plan for the restricted worker.

A partnership in a medical network will assist the company in developing a suitable modified work plan. The medical network will provide information to the company in a timely manner so the company can customize the work hardening plan. Therefore the medical network must consist of a wide variety of medical experts to meet the unique requirements of each case.

When a company builds the medical network, the company should consider the specialities of each of the practitioners. The company should ensure that each specialty is well represented with credible and qualified practitioners.

In the building phase of the network, the company should negotiate the special rates for each service. The company will benefit from the preferred services at preferred service rates for guaranteed service in the practitioner's office and perhaps for services at the company's facility.

Some of the medical professionals may offer services to the company to be performed at the workplace. For example, a physiotherapy clinic may offer to send an ergonomist or therapist to the workplace for specific evaluations of workplaces or to review modified work plans with the restricted worker. This customized service can prove to be invaluable resource of information and assistance in providing the most suitable and appropriate accommodated work.

Another example of a practitioner performing a service at the workplace is the services of an ergonomist. The ergonomist must complete a physical demands analysis after evaluating the workstations at the workplace. The evaluation for the analysis must be completed onsite as the workstations are set up at the workplace and not at the practitioner's office.

An advanced disability management program may include an on-site (therapy) program where the medical professionals will administer limited services to injured workers. This may seem elaborate and costly however, for those companies that are experiencing considerable amounts of lost time due to therapy appointments may save money. Depending on the cost efficiency of the program, the return on investment for the costs of therapy on site compared to the savings or cost avoidance of the lost time saved by the workers not missing work due to attending therapy onsite may be well worth the costs of the onsite therapy program.

To consider an onsite program, there would have to be a substantial amount of workers requiring therapy at one time. In preparing a cost analysis, the company should consider the costs of lost time in terms of wages and lost productivity. Sometimes, the company can negotiate with the benefits carriers to allow the company to pay the regular wages of the workers for any lost time for medical appointments. However, the company should consider the indirect costs of paying the workers their regular wages for time away from work. Paying the lost wages for time away from work due to medical appointments may set a very costly precedent to pay all workers for lost time due to medical appointments whether the worker is restricted or not. The company may be subject to scrutiny for discriminatory practices.

Generally, the Claims Management or Health and Safety Advisor will coordinate the activity for the onsite therapy program. Activities include scheduling the workers with the therapist, scheduling the evaluations, planning the physical demands assessments, etc. Not all injuries regardless of occupational or non-occupational, requires this degree of assistance. Some of the simple injuries with standard quick recoveries may not require this type of service so the Claims Management or Health and Safety Advisor will determine which injuries or workers require these services and will initiate the services as required.

To prepare the service providers for the needs of the workers, the Advisor should communicate such information for each worker including restrictions, FAFs, FAEs, as well as any other information necessary to the treatment or suitability of the modified work plan prior to the practitioner meeting with the worker. In some instances, once the service provider knows the workplace and workstations well, the service provider may be able to develop the modified work plans prior to meeting with the worker. This will assist the Supervisors with temporary work plan until the meeting occurs.

Further to the providing therapeutic services, the service provider while onsite may also participate in prevention activities. Ergonomists may review job tasks prior to the occurrence of injuries to recommend improvements in design or the arrangement of tasks to reduce the risk of injuries. The ergonomists may also help other workers who are not hurt or have only experienced minor discomfort, to perform their tasks in a different way in order to reduce the risk for injuries or reduce the risk of more permanent injuries.

In this manner, the ergonomist can provide valuable job coaching and job mentoring to all workers. For example, the ergonomist can educate material handlers on proper lifting techniques to prevent low back strain or rotator cuff strain. Ergonomists can also provide constructive education and training on designing ergonomic friendly workstations both for production workers as well as for the office workers.

In addition to the Environmental Health and Safety Advisor and a Claims Management Advisor, a management representative could also include a certified ergonomist. A certified ergonomist can offer valuable insight into the relationship between the restrictions and the physical demands analysis of the jobs available in the company to ensure suitable and safe match for modified work placement. The ergonomist can also help to coach and mentor uninjured workers to prevent future injuries. Other roles and responsibilities of the certified ergonomists include but are not limited to:

- Developing work hardening plans to assist injured workers to continue in productive employment while in the recovery process. These work hardening plans define the transition between working with restrictions and returning to full regular duties.
- Job coaching during the recovery process to prevent re-aggravation and facilitate healing as well as working with uninjured workers to prevent future injuries. Job coaching can include demonstrating movement techniques, posture awareness, preventative training, stretching education, etc.

- Assisting the Claims Management Advisor and supervisors in matching the restrictions of a worker. Therefore assisting in assigning safe and suitable job placements within those restrictions.
- Advising management of recovery times, potential risks, etc. to assist in developing preventative programs or corrective actions.
- Translating medical documentation to information that will assist in modified work placements.
- Liaise between the company and the medical professionals for clarification on restrictions and other medical documentation to support work hardening planning and or potential cost relief or amalgamation in claims management.

In summary, an effective disability management program will include a return to work program. The return to work program will provide evidence of due diligence in complying with legal responsibilities under the OHSA, the WSIA, the Human Rights Codes of Ontario and Canada, etc. It will also prevent and manage the amount of lost time due to injuries regardless of the origin of the injuries. A comprehensive return to work program involves both an offer of modified work as well as a work hardening plan.

The difference between the return to work plan and the work hardening plan is that the work hardening strategy focuses on gradual work conditioning to perform value added work whereas the return to work course of action focuses on returning the worker to the workforce. The return to work plan must occur before the work hardening plan because the worker must return to the workplace then the worker can begin work conditioning.

The return to work program includes both the return to work plan and the work conditioning plan. These two types of plans are interdependent. Both plans serve to avoid or mitigate lost time. The two (2) methods should be coordinated and integrated to provide the optimal benefits to all parties during the recovery process.

Costs may be incurred in order to prepare the most appropriate return to work and work hardening plans for each worker. These costs may be derived from access to medical resources to determine restrictions, evaluations, ergonomics, etc. However, the costs incurred with the preferred medical service providers are generally much lower than the costs incurred due to lost time and prolonged recoveries. Eventually, the return on investment for an effective disability management program including the return to work program, offer of modified work and the work conditioning plans are significant in saving costs due to avoiding lost time, lost productivity, fines and penalties as well as improving morale, labour relations, and legal compliance.

CHAPTER 23
OBJECTION PROCESS

In all claims for wage replacement benefits, the parties may not agree with all the decisions made by the benefits carrier. Each party has an ability to appeal any decision made on the claim from initial entitlement to termination of benefits except the final decision of the appeals process. The party objecting to a decision must submit their request for appeal in form of a written letter. Objections should be based on fact that is supported by evidence rather than feelings or opinions. Facts are supported, verified, and consistent with evidence. Objections must be submitted within a specific time frame of the decision. Each carrier may have different time frames for appealing decisions. The time frame is specified in the policy. Sometimes the time frame is stated as a reminder in the bottom of the decision letter.

A successful objection will include information that can be confirmed with objective, consistent and reliable evidence. Medical evidence is the best supporting evidence as it is objective and can be confirmed by an impartial third party, the medical professional. Medical evidence is critical in proving any pre-existing medical condition(s) that may predispose a worker to an injury or prolong the recovery past the standard recovery period of the injury. It is critical to use medical evidence to support your request for denial of claim, cost relief on approved claims, claim closure, amalgamation of the claim to previous claims or back dating the claim to a previous year because the evidence is reliable, valid, credible and measurable. Arguments built on subjective feelings and opinions have no measurable or reliable basis.

A fundamental element in reducing costs of claims is to reduce the potential for lost time. Lost time increases the costs of claims very quickly. One of the key elements in reducing lost time is getting the injured party back to work as soon as it is safe to medically do so. In order to return an injured party back to work, the company is required to develop a return to work plan. By monitoring claims and injury patterns of the company, the company can develop a return to work and work hardening program prior to the occurrence of injuries in order to minimize lost time for any injury.

The return to work and work hardening programs should be recognized as suitable in accommodating restrictions by the company's benefits carriers. Ergonomists and medical professionals such as doctors and physiotherapists can assist the company in developing a suitable program together that would meet the criteria of the benefits carriers. The involvement of the medical professionals will lend credibility to the programs.

It is important for the wage replacement benefits carrier to recognize and respect the company's return to work and work hardening programs. If the return to work and work hardening programs are credible and effective, then the injured party should not be losing time from work. In some cases, returning an injured party to work can be challenging for a number of reasons. If the employer offers a suitable return to work plan but the worker refuses to comply, the employer may have grounds to appeal or object to continuing payments of benefits for lost time based on the carrier's recognition of the employer's return to work program, the credibility and suitability of the return to work plan itself. The benefits carrier will consider such evidence for the objection very seriously and the information will be weighted very carefully when the decision to continue benefits is made.

In all cases of lost time claims, the employer should be offering return to work plans as soon as possible. For more complicated recoveries, the employer will need to determine the timing of the modified work offer. Monitoring the claim progression will allow the employer to determine the timing more effectively. In managing a wage replacement benefits claim, the employer can carefully monitor the requirement of lost time through requesting updated medical documentation. The medical documentation should support the initial lost time and the ongoing lost time. During this monitoring, the updated medical documentation will reveal the timing for the employer to offer a suitable return to work plan.

The benefits carrier, especially the WSIB, will request medical documentation to support lost time before the carrier will approve the payment of lost wages. If the medical documentation does not support ongoing lost time then it is likely the benefits carrier will deny the payment of benefits for lost wages even in an approved claim.

In some cases the injured worker may not be able to return to the same work as the pre-injury work however the worker is not totally disabled. The employer is obligated under duty to accommodate to assess all the jobs in the workplace to determine if the employer has safe, suitable and sustainable work outside the worker's pre-injury job. As long as the company can offer the worker suitable work within the worker's restrictions, the employer can support their objection for payment of ongoing lost time benefits should the worker refuse to return to work.

Employers can challenge or object to any lost time especially if the company has an approved and effective return to work program. The most effective return to work programs should consist of a wide variety of accommodations to accommodate a wide variety of restrictions. Each case and each lost time event must be evaluated on timing, return to work plan, restrictions, worker, workplace, accommodations, etc.

The objection process itself usually has different levels of appeals. Depending on the carrier for the wage replacement benefits, the levels of appeal may vary. In Ontario, the worker's compensation program involves three general levels: the initial objection at the adjudicator level, the next level is with the Appeals Resolution Officer, then if the objection is still not resolved, to the tribunal level. Likewise, three general levels is quite common in most wage replacement program guidelines; the first level at the original decision maker to reconsider; the second review of the file and decision at the manager level; then, if still not agreeable decision has been reached, the file elevates to a level similar to binding arbitration.

Preparing the arguments for the first level can be handled internally by the Claims Management Advisor. Depending on the skill and expertise of the Claims Management Advisor and the level of complication of the claim or objection, all levels of the objection may be handled by the Claims Management Advisor. In some cases, the company may consider seeking legal counsel from an employment lawyer to increase their chance of success in the outcome of the appeal.

In Ontario, if the employer cannot afford a lawyer, the worker's compensation program has the Office of the Employer Advisor through the WSIB. A member of this office will be able to assist the employer through a difficult case. Similarly, the worker who cannot afford a lawyer can request the services of the Office of the Employee or Worker Advisor.

Payment for lost time is not the only reason employers or injured parties can decide to object or appeal a decision. Decisions on entitlement, medical care, benefits, etc. may also be subject to objections. Basically any and all decisions may be appealed. Employers may request cost relief or amalgamation to previous claims. If such requests are denied, then the employer can choose to object to the decision. These types of decisions rarely affect the injured party. If there is an impact to the injured party it is very minimal.

In most cases, the decisions regarding amalgamation and cost relief may not necessarily delay or alter the conditions of the claim benefits from the worker's perspective however they can change the charge back structure or claim costs of the claim to the employer. For example, a cost relief decision in a worker's compensation claim in Ontario will allow the WSIB to hold the employer financially accountable for only a certain percentage of the claim costs instead of the entire amount of the claim costs. The claim costs for the employer may be reduced if the worker has a pre-existing medical condition that predisposed the worker to the injury and prolongs the recovery beyond the standard recovery period for that specific injury. This cost relief would have no impact on the amount of benefits the worker receives even though it has significant financial impacts for the employer.

Other than a denial of benefits or payments of benefits, the decision that could have an impact on the injured party would be if the claim was amalgamated back to a previous similar claim as a recurrence. Generally, the worker would be paid benefits in the amount of the previous claim rather than at current claim levels. In most cases, this would have a negative financial impact to the worker because the benefits would be based on the earnings prior to the previous injury rather than the current earnings. Inflation, raises, etc. may have changed the rate of earnings between the time of the previous injury and the time of the recurrence. These changes are usually nominal or small in proportion to the savings that the employer may realize as a result of the decision to amalgamate.

CHAPTER 24

DISPUTE RESOLUTION

During the recovery process, the worker may experience a plateau in healing both physically and psychologically. A plateau is a level in healing where the recovery stalls for a long period of time. Sometimes, the plateau will become the final recovery level. Most times though the plateau is only for a period of time then recovery will continue. It is common for any person to experience one or more plateaus during recovery depending on the severity of the injury.

The plateaus will cause delays in the recovery. As a result of these delays, the return to work processes will be delayed as well. Sometimes, the return to work plan or work hardening plan will regress as a result of the plateaus. Regression will occur when the restrictions and medical documentation supports changes in the restrictions likely increase the amount of restrictions.

In a plateau, the worker may dispute their restrictions or work plan. The company should adhere to the restrictions on file from the medical professionals. Only the medical professionals should change the restrictions on file. If the worker continues to have concerns regarding their restrictions, they should consult with their medical professionals. Furthermore, the worker may also object to their restrictions or return to work plans through their carrier (the WSIB or STD/LTD carrier). It is the role of the claims adjudicator to review all the medical documentation on file to approve the restrictions, the timing of the restrictions, and the return to work plan itself.

Should the worker have concerns about the restrictions or the return to work plan, the company can try to resolve the conflict internally by encouraging the worker to seek medical attention to obtain additional medical documentation to support their concerns. However, even the new restrictions from the worker's medical professional may not change the current work plan or the medical that is submitted totally contradicts all the progress in recovery that has been accomplished. The company must determine whether they want to exercise their rights under the Human Rights Act or the WSIA to arrange for a second opinion through an independent medical evaluation.

If the workplace is unionized, the company may also have to consult the collective agreement for the negotiated dispute resolution process. The collective agreement should not override the company's legal right to pursue a second opinion through an IME or FAE. In addition to the worker expressing concerns about their restrictions, recovery, the return to work plan, the worker in a unionized workplace also has other avenues to express their concerns. Unique to unionized workplaces, the collective agreement will outline the steps the worker may take to object to the requests or actions of the company through a formal grievance procedure. Even the grievance procedure should outline the company's right to request a second opinion.

Generally, medical professionals determine the worker's diagnosis and the appropriate course of treatment. The medical professionals will closely monitor the health and recovery of the worker from a medical perspective. Should the worker not progress in recovery as expected, the medical professional will indicate that the worker has reached a plateau. The plateau does not necessary mean that the worker will not recover totally. However, the worker may experience some temporary delays, the worker may have to work harder or the worker may have to undergo a combination of various types of treatment to recover fully. These plateaus may stagnate the return to work progress. In some cases, the plateau may cause the previous progression to regress.

In some situations, the stagnation of the worker's progress may not be explained medically. In other words, there would be no medical reason for the worker's progress to experience a plateau. The recovery process does not only involve the actual physical recovery from the physical injury, it also includes perception and mental health plays in the whole healing process. The person's perception of what is reality becomes actual reality to the person. No matter what the situation is or what the objective medical evidence confirms, whatever the worker thinks and feels will influence the general progress of the recovery. Subjective complaints from the worker can interfere with the worker's return to their pre-injury health.

Subjective complaints are beliefs or concerns that the worker has regarding their physical condition or capabilities which are not supported objectively with medical evidence. For example, pain is a subjective complaint because pain is an emotional response that can manifest physically. There are no physical medical tests like x-rays and such that can "measure" or demonstrate the degree of pain. The psychological influence can only be measured through the worker's feedback, thoughts, emotions, and perception of what is real and legitimate standard psychological testing techniques.

Healing must occur on the physical level and the psychological level. The physical healing is monitored by the medical professionals. The psychological healing is at the control of the worker. The psychology of healing is all about the worker's belief or perspective of their capabilities and pain levels. Problems will occur with the return to work program when the worker perceives their capabilities will not allow them to safely perform the tasks of the return to work plan. However, benefits carriers including the WSIB do not consider subjective complaints in their determination of "totally disability" or a sufficient reason to prolong lost time. Total disability is determined based on physical limitations as dictated from objective medical evidence not subjective complaints.

Some problems that can occur when a worker believes that their restrictions prevent them from safely performing the tasks of the return to work plan include:

- The worker refuses to perform the assigned tasks from the return to work plan;
- Conflicts may occur between the worker and the supervisors or the company;
- There is increased potential of lost time;
- There may be a decreased potential of complete recovery; and,
- The morale for all workers in the workplace may decrease.

There are a number of steps for the company to take to resolve the conflict when a worker refuses to return to work because they do not believe the return to work plan is outside their restrictions. To resolve the conflict, the company can use the work refusal process as outlined by the Occupational Health and Safety Act of Ontario under the right to refuse unsafe work. See Illustration 24-1 for details.

A best practice in conflict resolution indicates that the company will use the expertise of one or more third party consultant types to review the return to work plans. The third party consultants should be members of the medical network. The medical network includes ergonomists, doctors, benefits carrier adjudicator, etc.

The Ministry of Labour (MOL) may also be instrumental in resolving the conflict. The company should try every means possible to resolve the conflict before inviting the MOL inspector to review the concern. However, the worker can invite the MOL to participate at any time. In fact, the benefits carriers are usually experts that will mediate the return to work issues so that the MOL inspector is almost not required.

The benefits carrier will determine if the return to work plan is appropriate for the worker. The company would be prudent to supply the benefits carrier with all the details of the return to work plan prior to the start date for the following reasons:

- To obtain the benefits carrier approval of the plan.
- To obtain the support of the benefits carrier to return the worker to work.
- To obtain the use of any mediation services the benefits carrier may offer in the return to work process.
- To obtain an opinion on the return to work plan for any necessary adjustments.
- To review any worker concerns with the return to work plan or the applicable restrictions.
- To obtain functional evaluation results.

In providing the benefits carrier a copy of the return to work plan prior to offering the plan to the worker, the company can request the benefits carrier to review the plan for approval. The approval of the

Illustration 24-1: Right to Refuse Unsafe Work

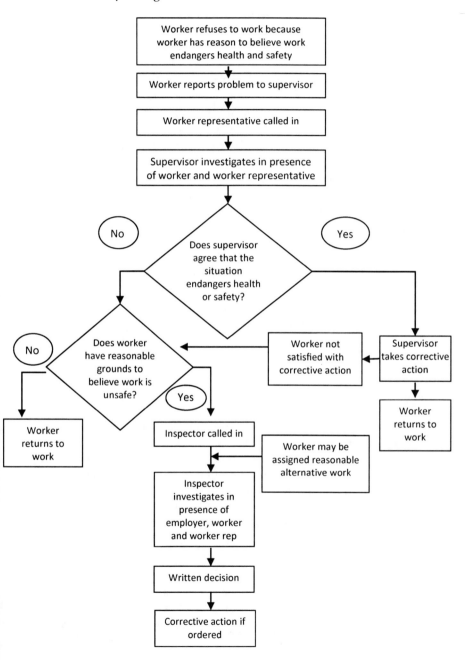

benefits carrier will lend credibility to the plan itself as well as the due diligence of the company in complying with their legal obligations under the Human Rights Code and or the WSIA to offer safe, suitable, sustainable, and appropriate return to work program to injured workers.

In addition to the approval, the support of the benefits carrier will provide the worker with encouragement to at least attempt the return to work plan. Depending on the degree of support from the benefits carrier, the worker will have a vested interest in not only participating in the return to work program but also be motivated to succeed. In many cases, the approval of the benefits carrier will inevitably mean that if the worker refuses to return to work without appropriate medical documentation to support the worker's concerns, the benefits carrier may terminate the worker's claim for non-cooperation.

Many benefits carrier programs will have specific services available to the worker or and the company during the return to work process including access to restrictions, functional abilities evaluations, mediation services, return to work consultation, vocational rehabilitation, retraining, etc. During conflicts between the worker concerns and the return to work plan, the services of the benefits carrier can provide insight or clarification of the restrictions or address the concerns of each party adjusting the return to work plan accordingly.

If the benefits carrier does not have these services accessible to either the worker or the company, the company can rely on the medical network for expert opinions in clarification. If the company is unionized, there may be some provisions in the collective agreement to address these types of conflicts. Generally, it involves the company sending the worker for a second opinion. If the worker does not agree with the results of the second opinion, then the worker may be sent for a third opinion from an expert that is mutually agreed upon by both the union and the company. Usually, the company and the union agree that this third opinion is binding.

Expert opinions carry significant weight in credibility and will influence the decision of not only the benefits carrier but also a MOL Inspector, Human Rights Mediator/Arbitrator, Labour Relations Mediator/Arbitrator, Tribunal Board, etc. In some disputes regarding restrictions and the return to work plan, the MOL Inspector may allow other decision makers such as the WSIB Adjudicator, Human Rights Mediator/ Arbitrator, Labour Relations Mediator/Arbitrator, Tribunal Board, etc. to make the final decision on suitability for safety. Therefore, the disability management theory of the refusal process would resemble Illustration 24-2 which is a slight modification of the previous flow for right to refuse unsafe work. See the Illustration 24-2 (next page):

As outlined in Illustration 24-2, if conflict exists between the worker and the company over capabilities, the first step is for the company to meet with the worker to discuss the concerns. The initial meeting should be with the Claims Management Advisor and the worker to review the restrictions, the return to work plan and the worker's concerns. Open communication at this level can assist in resolving any misunderstanding or, at the very least, establishing an understanding of the other party's position.

The collective agreement of a unionized workplace should have provisions that outline the grievance procedures the worker will take for disputes with the company. The grievance procedure is a form of conflict resolution the workers can use during the return to work or the work hardening process regardless of the benefits carrier. The grievance procedure exists to resolve conflicts internally. Therefore, the grievance procedure may not have the access or authority to resolve the conflicts with the carriers' decisions.

Most grievance procedures have common elements as well as with the processes that have already been discussed. In general, most procedures start with encouraging communication with the supervisor. The collective agreement will identify the role of the union representative for the worker in all stages of the grievance procedure as well as what happens to the grievance once it has been submitted.

Employers may not have the direct influence on the decision making of benefits carriers. The grievance procedure may not have any influence on the carrier's decisions. The worker must go through the benefits carriers appeal process. The grievance procedure does not normally extend its influence into the third party carriers. However, unions recognizing this shortfall have other means to help support their members address the workers' concerns with third party decision makers such as representing the worker in the appeal process. Unions train their representatives to have the skills and experience to represent the workers in the appeal process or they will provide the legal advice as required.

Despite the open communication between the parties, sometimes resolutions cannot be reached for various reasons. If conflict exists because the worker's perception of their capabilities does not

Illustration 24-2: Refusing Return to Work

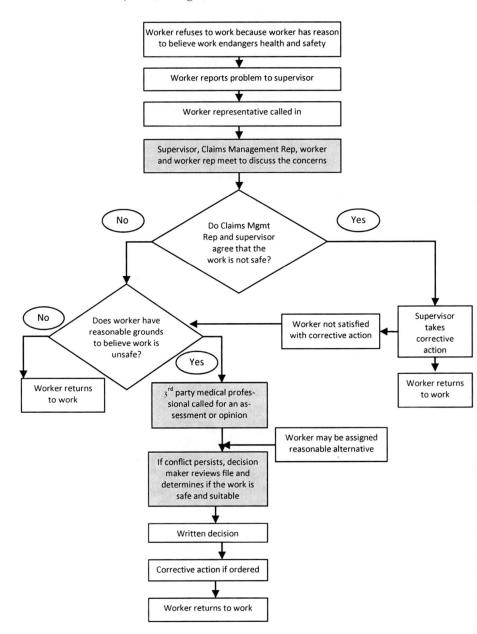

match the restrictions or the modified work plan, then the company has a choice to exercise an option to send the worker for a second medical opinion. Under the WSIA, Section 36, the company has the right to request the worker to be sent for an independent medical evaluation (IME) with a service provider of the company's choice. The Human Rights Code supports this option as well.

The worker may object to the decisions of the adjudicators. Both the worker and the company have the right to object to any decisions of the adjudicators. There are various ways to object to these decisions depending on the carrier and the workplace. Regardless of the path of objection, the weight of the arguments for an objection is based on objective medical evidence not subjective complaints or opinions.

Monitoring the activity of the medical documentation, will allow the company or the claims adjudicator to monitor restrictions, progress and may also recognize if the worker is "doctor shopping". "Doctor shopping" happens when a person moves from doctor to doctor to find a doctor to document what the worker dictates rather than challenging the worker's subjective complaints with additional objective medical evidence. In these cases, exercising the company's legal right to a second opinion through an IME or the carrier's request for a medical evaluation may assist the adjudicator in obtaining all relevant objective medical evidence to render informed decisions.

Each benefits carrier has resources to assist the return to work process. The benefits carrier will subcontract or hire a person as a Return to Work Coordinator to assist all the parties in facilitating a safe and appropriate return to work. These coordinators will meet with all the parties to review the restrictions and the physical demands of the jobs listed in the return to work plan for appropriateness. They have the ability to consult with ergonomists and other medical professionals to help clarify any questions or concerns. These coordinators will write reports to go back to the claims adjudicator of the findings during the process to help the adjudicator make informed decisions on return to work plan approvals, restriction changes, return to work plan changes, etc.

If the disputes cannot be resolved internally or with the assistance of a Return to Work Coordinator from the carrier, each carrier has a formal process of appeal that either party can elect to follow. The objection processes of most benefits carriers have common elements. The objection process begins with a decision from the benefits carrier which generates disagreement. The party who disagrees with the adjudicator's decision must formally object to the decision. The objection must be submitted in writing. The objection should clearly outline which decision is in contention a well as outline the reasons for the objection. This is the party's opportunity to explain the facts and reasons for the objection to a specific decision. Most carriers will send written letters of each of their decisions on file. Therefore, the objection should indentify the decision in contention by the date of the respective decision letter.

In addition to identifying the reasons for the objection, the objection letter should include copies of the medical evidence that support the reasons for the objection. Medical evidence will always carry more weight in the decision process than those opinions without supporting medical evidence. Medical evidence is generally objective, measurable and unbiased. Therefore it is credible, reliable, and the information can be easily defended in the appeal process.

The adjudicator will review all the information submitted carefully to determine if the decision in contention should be changed. Should the adjudicator change the decision because of the information submitted in the objection, then the party has succeeded. If the decision is not changed, then the objection will be denied. The decision on the objection request will be communicated to both the company and the worker in writing.

Each party will have an opportunity to object at the next level. The objection again is in writing and submitted to the carrier referencing the decision in contention and the date of the decision letter. Again the objection should include additional evidence that may not have been considered in the previous decisions or to review further supporting arguments not yet introduced by either party. Once all the material has been received, the claims adjudicator's manager will review the entire file to make a determination. The decision will be communicated to both parties in writing.

The objections will continue to the next level until the final level of objection is reached such as arbitration or the tribunal. Once the objections reach this level, the decision rendered at this level becomes the final decision. The final decision is binding and indisputable.

In order to prepare an argument for an appeal, the worker or the employer may request a copy of the claim file. If the employer requests the copy of the file, the carrier will request consent from the worker to release the copy of the file to the employer. If the worker refuses to release the documents, the benefit carrier will review the file and release to the employer only those documents relevant to the claim and objection. Much of the medical that is not relevant to the claim will be omitted or blacked out so the employer cannot read the information. This information is protected under the Privacy Act.

The information on the file is critical in understanding all the facts of the case and may or may not help the employer or the worker to prepare their arguments or provide evidence to support their arguments.

This flowchart of the objection process illustrates the first level of objections with the claims adjudicator at the benefits carrier.

Below is Illustration 24-3: Early Resolution Process outlining the overview. The chart was taken from the WSIB website (WSIB, 2010).

EARLY RESOLUTION PROCESS

THE HANDLING OF DISPUTES BY THE BUSINESS UNIT

OVERVIEW

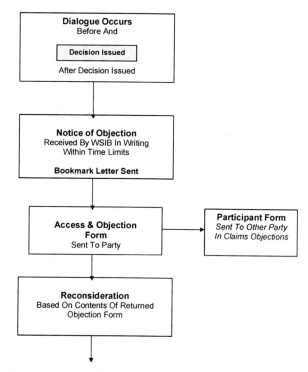

In the workers compensation program in Ontario, if either party still objects to the decision, an appeal can be requested by either party. The objection will then be elevated to the Appeals Board where an Appeals Resolution Officer (ARO for the WSIB) will review the entire file including all arguments from all parties involved. The parties can elect a 60 day expedited decision process where the ARO reviews the file and renders a decision based on what is on the file.

Otherwise, the parties can elect to have a formal appeals hearing where the parties will each have a chance to state their arguments. At this level, in addition to the medical information supporting the parties' argument, the parties should also be submitting past Appeals decisions that are similar to the case at hand which support the decision the party is requesting. Every Appeals decision and Tribunal decision is recorded and filed publicly. Past appeals and tribunal cases can be reviewed www.canlii.org.

At any level of appeal, either party can elect to have some professional representation such as a lawyer that specializes in all the relevant legislation such as WSIA, OHSA, Human Rights Codes, etc. If either party cannot afford a lawyer, then the WSIB have resources available to each the employer and the employee. Their website is www.workeradviser.ca. The resources for the employee can be obtained through the Office of the Worker Adviser. The resources for the employer can be obtained through the Office of the Employer Adviser. Their website is www.employeradviser.ca.

Formal appeals hearings will also allow each party to have witnesses speak to support the party's position. The company should have medical experts as witnesses as well as a document trail of all restrictions, return to work plans, discussions, meetings with workers, ergonomist reports, FAEs, IMEs, etc. These experts and documentation will serve as evidence of the company's due diligence. After all the evidence from each party is presented to the ARO, then the ARO will review all the evidence and make a decision on whether to approve or deny the appeal.

Once the decision on the appeal has been made, the written decision will be mailed to each of the parties involved. Upon receiving the decision, either party has the right to object to the decision. The objection will be elevated to the tribunal level, the WSIAT.

In order to elevate the objection, the intent must be submitted in writing. In addition to all the previous arguments, the objection should include reference(s) to any relevant previous WSIAT decisions which can be found at www.wsiat.on.ca.

Below is a flowchart, Illustration 24-4, of the appeals process at the WSIB. The chart was taken from the WSIB website (WSIB, 2010).

APPEALS BRANCH

THE HANDLING OF APPEALS BY THE APPEALS BRANCH

OVERVIEW

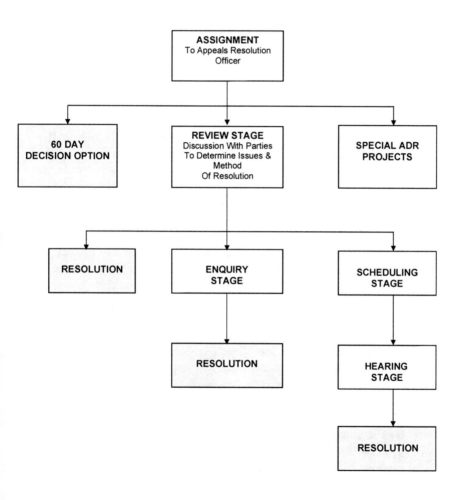

At this level of appeal, the arguments, material, and file will be reviewed by a panel of independent and separate adjudicative group of people known as the Order-In-Counsel (OIC). According to the WSIB, the OIC is:

> ...An Order-in-Council (OIC) is an order from the provincial cabinet, and is effective on the date signed by the Lieutenant Governor. Each Vice-Chair, Member and the Chair is named to his or her position through an Order-in-Council appointment. The WSIA confers authority to hear and decide Tribunal appeals to individuals appointed by OIC... (http://www.wsiat.on.ca/english/appeal/oic.htm, 2009)

At all levels of appeals, there is a time deadline to file the objection for each party. The deadline for first level of objection at the local claims adjudicator level is generally six (6) months for workers. Employers have thirty (30) days from the date of the decision letter for LMR decisions. Otherwise, the employers have six (6) months to object to the decisions from the date of the decision letter. The objection must always be submitted to the WSIB in writing.

Similar to the WSIB appeal process, the appeal process for short or long term disability, the objection must be submitted to the carrier in writing within a specific time frame which varies from carrier to carrier. Also similar to the WSIB, the objection should be based in fact and supported by objective medical evidence.

While the highest level of objection, the WSIAT is unique to the worker's compensation program in Ontario, other carriers have generally three levels of objection. These levels are 1) the local or initial adjudicator; 2) the adjudication team's manager; and, 3) a special objection adjudicator or team of claims managers to review the file for final decisions.

There may be other avenues for the parties to pursue. Depending on the geographical location of the claim, the party may pursue any options through the legal court system. To explore this option, the party should seek the counsel of an employment lawyer specializing in disability.

Another avenue is unique to a unionized environment. In a unionized environment, workers may choose to grieve decisions through the grievance procedure as outlined in the collective agreement. The grievance procedure will not address many decisions of the WSIB. In contrast, the grievance procedure may grieve decisions in the short and long term disability benefits programs. However the problem with the worker using the grievance procedure for objecting to decisions is that the collective agreement does not have any influence of third parties outside of the collective agreement. The employer usually does not have control or influence over the decisions in the short or long term benefits program.

The grievance procedure is generally an internal mechanism to resolve conflict or problems between the employer and the worker. If a third party is responsible for the decision the worker is grieving, then the employer may not have any control or influence to change the decision in question. However, if the grievance elevates to mediation or arbitration, the arbitrator may order the employer to pay the worker to replace denied wage loss benefits. The liability for the lost wages may now become the responsibility of the employer instead of the benefits carrier. The employer would be responsible for the payment even though the third party carrier is responsible for the decisions because the arbitrator will levy the judgement against the employer despite lack of control, influence or responsibility over the decision of the benefits carrier. Employment lawyers would be able to counsel the employer through this type of process.

SUMMARY

To summarize, an effective disability management program requires many elements. Each element is a process within the disability management program. Incident reporting, recovery, return to work and the work hardening processes are only a few processes in the disability management program. The employer has several avenues to develop and implement tools that will assist them through each of the processes. The following are summaries of some of the most common programs to assist the employer to manage disability in the workplace.

The employer should develop and implement a comprehensive incident reporting process to facilitate communication of injuries, difficulties, safety issues, correct action process, accommodation process, provide information for further legislative or carrier reporting. Establishing and embedding a body part chart system within the incident reporting process can give the supervisors a tool to reassign a worker prior to receiving medical information on the restrictions. This tool will help minimize lost time for injuries and establish due diligence in the company's attempt to accommodate restricted workers.

The employer should develop and implement a functional return to work and return to regular duties (or work hardening/ conditioning) plan to accommodate restricted workers. Incorporate ergonomic workstation design and personal ergonomic awareness and training to facilitate recovery, accommodation, and coaching on injury prevention both within the return to work or regular duties plan as well as to avoid injury prior to injury.

In addition, using tools such as physical demands analysis will also assist the supervisors and the company to determine suitable work assignments for restricted workers. A functioning program will establish the employer's legal compliance for the employer's obligation for re-employment and duty to accommodate. A well designed program will also assist in reducing lost time, reducing costs of claims directly and indirectly, increasing productivity and increasing morale. All return to work offers should be written and signed off by all parties to ensure compliance and understanding.

Each party in the recovery process has a unique set of roles and responsibilities. Should any of these parties violate or breach these roles or responsibilities during the recovery process, there may be legal repercussions including fines, penalties, claim benefits termination, claim closure, etc.

Understanding the recovery process will help the employer understand the different accommodate needs of the injured worker. Standard recovery or maximum medical recovery periods will assist the employer in planning the return to work and work hardening schedules as well as allow the employer to monitor the costs of the claims. The employer will also understand strategies to navigate through recovery plateaus or conflicts in interpreting restrictions by using tools like IMEs, FAEs, etc.

Exceeding the standard recovery will trigger a series of decisions from the benefits carrier including declaring permanent impairment and permanent restrictions, oblige the employer to make decisions on the accommodation to a long term, suitable, sustainable placement within the permanent restrictions to the point of undue hardship. The employer will need to consider all legal obligations to duty to accommodate as well as understand the financial impact associated with not accommodating the worker. If the employer cannot accommodate the worker, the carrier will proceed with making decisions on the claim regarding Labour Market Re-entry or vocational retraining for the worker.

By monitoring claims from beginning to end, the employer will be able to encourage timely claims decisions, develop return to work activities, reduce claims costs, consolidate historical trends, request cost relief where appropriate, plan medical intervention if required, and, strategically plan the targets and objectives of the program to address corporate goals and objectives. In understanding the employer's rights and obligations under legislation such as the WSIA, the OHSA, the Human Rights Codes, etc. and the standard recovery periods, the employer can strategically plan medical intervention when required, as well as request amalgamation of claims and cost relief through SIEF where appropriate.

Medical networks can assist in supplying medical information at all stages of the recovery process. They can provide valuable service and information at crucial stages of the recovery in order for benefits carriers to make accurate and clear decisions in the claim. The medical documentation is critical in the objection process for either party as the objections are only as strong as the medical documentation supporting the objection.

A best practice in employee relations is to develop a mechanism for communication between the workers and the company. Within this communication method, each workplace should have a process for the company to address concerns from the worker including objections to company decisions. The employer should also develop a rapport with each of the benefits carrier to encourage open communication. An open flow of information may assist in timely decisions.

Each carrier will have their own appeal process as outlined in their policies and procedures. Both the employer and the worker have the right to appeal decisions from any the benefits carriers. Again, medical documentation is critical in supporting the objection.

If the employer is considering frustrating the employment contract with a worker, the employer should consult with a lawyer specializing in employment law and disability law for the geographical area where the worker works. There are several legal considerations to review and a lawyer will navigate the employer through the various pieces of legislation including but not limited to the Employment Standards Act, the Privacy Act, the Disability Act, the Human Rights Codes, the WSIA, the OHSA, etc.

It is important to note that every decision from the benefits carrier can be appealed up to a specific point. Generally there are three levels of appeals. Only the last level cannot be appealed as it is the final decision regardless if the parties agree. Every objection is required to be submitted in writing to the carrier at each level of the appeals. Each objection should be supported with objective medical evidence and previous appeal decisions relevant to the issue. When the arguments between the parties are equal, the judgement will often favour the worker.

In unionized environments, the worker may choose to grieve a decision made by the employer or the wage replacement carrier despite the fact that the employer has no control or responsibility in the decision making process. The final decision in the grievance procedure by an arbitrator may find the employer liable for wage replacement depending on the case regardless of the employer's lack of influence over the decision making process of the benefits carrier.

Key Terms:

Amalgamation	Appeal
Claim Costs	Cost Relief
Disability Management	Dispute Resolution
Due Diligence	Duty to Accommodate
Ergonomics	FAE
Grievance procedure	Historical patterning
IME	LMR
Medical Network	Objection process
Return to Work	Roles and Responsibilities
SIEF	Undue Hardship
Vocational Retraining	Work Hardening

Questions:

1. Explain the elements of an effective disability management including both non-occupational and occupational related injuries.
2. Discuss the importance of a comprehensive reporting process and the body part chart.
3. Illustrate the objection process as a strategy.
4. Describe the effects of using historical patterning as a strategy in claims management.
5. Apply due diligence from a reactive perspective.
6. Demonstrate the impact of the employer's duty to accommodate.
7. Explain the concept of undue hardship.
8. Explore the importance of the return to work plan by detailing important elements of the program.
9. Define and discuss the impact of integrating ergonomics into the return to work program.
10. List and discuss the uses for a physical demands analysis including the advantages of using the tool.
11. Discuss the steps involved in preparing the physical demands analysis.
12. Differentiate between the return to work plan and the work hardening or work conditioning plan.
13. Discuss the importance and legalities of networking and developing a medical network.

14. Compare and contrast the role of the independent medical evaluations (IMEs) and FAEs in a disability management program.
15. Discuss maximum medical recovery as a strategy.
16. Define and explain the roles that non-economic loss (NEL) awards and labour market re-entry (LMR) or vocational re-training play in the disability management program.
17. Discuss the implications and steps of frustrating contracts when disability is involved.

SECTION VI

UNDERSTANDING PREVENTION AND PREVENTION STRATEGIES

Objectives:

After reviewing this chapter, the reader should be able to understand and explain the following concepts:

1. Prevention
2. Relevant legislation - MOL and the WSIB
3. Due diligence – preventive perspective
4. Prevention techniques
5. Safety Group
6. EHS program including OHSAs18001
   - Ergonomics – prevention
   - PDA – prevention
   - Repetitive
   - Rotation
7. Internal reporting system (IRS)
8. SCAR process
9. Monitoring Injuries including stats from both occupational and non-occupational injury carriers
10. Evaluation/audit process

CHAPTER 25

PREVENTION

A best practice strategy in a disability management program is prevention. Prevention starts with a functioning health and safety program. An effective health and safety program will not only meet compliance for legislative requirements but it will also help workers understand what everyone's responsibility is in keeping the workplace safe and preventing workplace injuries. The health and safety program will include procedures to address legislative compliance requirements, accident prevention, accident investigation and corrective action, risk assessment, and due diligence.

One of the critical elements common to both the health and safety program and the disability management program is due diligence. Due diligence must be understood and threaded through every policy, procedure, practice, training, and activity of the company for all employees, both salaried staff and workers alike. Due diligence will be explored in a separate chapter.

An effective health and safety program will consist of many policies and procedures outlining how to complete tasks safely. Due diligence dictates that these policies and procedures be communicated constantly to the workforce as well as reviewed at least annually to ensure continued effectiveness. To provide evidence of due diligence, the company should have all policies and procedures documented and an historical record of training. However, before training and communication can occur, the policies and procedures have to be developed and implemented.

The first step in implementing an effective health and safety program is to develop a health and safety policy. The health and safety policy must clearly state the company's commitment to the health and safety of all the workers. It should be written and communicated to the entire company as well as any and all visitors.

The next stage in developing and implementing the health and safety program is assessing the risks and hazards of the workplace in order to understand what procedures, policies and training are required to address legislative requirements and injury prevention specific to the company's workplace. For example, if the company requires the use of forklift operation than the company will have to assess the certification and training requirements for forklift operators. The employer then must develop a procedure for the operators to safely operate the forklift and meet the strategic goals to make timely deliveries.

Developing and implementing an effective health and safety program as well as disability management program is a lengthy constantly evolving process. It may take years for the effectiveness and advantages of the program to be recognized through productivity and financial gains. Both programs must evolve and adapt as the local economy, global economy, company's operations, strategic goals, and legislation change. Linking these programs with the company's strategic goals will be discussed near the end of this text in the chapter discussing strategic planning.

CHAPTER 26

RELEVANT LEGISLATION

Prevention is one of the most effective tools in health and safety and disability management programs. If the injury is prevented, then there will be no need for a disability management program. Despite the best efforts of workers and employers, injuries still may occur in and outside the workplace.

Different geographical areas will have different legal requirements for people to follow including employers, workers, landowners, visitors, etc. Legislation will have different names in different geographical areas but the subject matter is relatively the same. Some pieces of legislation that relate to disability management include but are not limited to: the Occupational Health and Safety (OHSA), the Disability Act, any legislation relative to workers compensation insurance programs (WSIA in Ontario), legislation relative to short term and long term disability, Canada Pension Plan – Disability, Human Rights Code (of both Ontario and Canada), Equal Rights, Employment Standards Act, Privacy Act, etc. Usually every level of government will have some piece of legislation that will influence the company's health and safety program.

Although legislation varies across different geographical locations, the commonality with health and safety or disability management types of legislation is that it only sets out the minimum standards. It is the responsibility of every company to develop an effective health and safety program to ensure compliance to all relevant legislation. The purpose of the program is preventing injuries as well as providing a foundation for legal compliance.

A functioning health and safety program mitigates the risk of injuries. An effective program will be designed to exceed the legislative requirements. In addition, by incorporating health and safety best practices into core strategic business objectives from planning to design to development to output to sales will assist in mitigating the risk of injury. However, injuries can happen despite an effective health and safety program.

In Ontario, each company has to meet the minimum standards of the Occupational Health and Safety Act of Ontario (OHSA). Other areas will have similar legislative requirements depending on their laws and culture including most of the countries in Europe, Mexico, etc. The United States of America will have very similar legislation which may vary in technical language from state to state.

Outlined below are some pieces of legislation discussing the legal obligations and responsibilities of each party in a workplace in Ontario. Furthermore, prevention or disability management will also be discussed. Other geographical areas in Canada and the USA will have similar or common pieces of legislation.

The Occupational Health and Safety Act of Ontario (OHSA)

The Occupational Health and Safety Act of Ontario is a piece of legislation that outlines minimum standards for promoting the health and safety of all workers. This piece of legislation is critical in assisting the employer in Ontario to develop a health and safety program for preventing workplace injuries. The legislation just outlines the minimum requirements. To demonstrate the company's commitment to health and safety of its workers as well as practice due diligence, the company should build these minimum standards through all policies and procedures of the daily operation of the business.

To comply with the legislation, the employer must implement policies and procedures to address each requirement of the act. However, compliance may not be enough to prevent injuries in the workplace as well as the act only represents minimum requirements. The company should endeavor to establish a health and safety program which will address the legal requirements of the act as well as detail how to safely perform any and all tasks. The focus of the policies and procedures should be to address any and all hazards present in a specific workplace. The policies and procedures will assist the employer in providing documented evidence of due diligence in the activities of the prevention of injuries.

The OHSA covers a variety of workplace practices including the Joint Health and Safety Committee to material handling to confined space, etc. The Act's essential focus is to mandate employers to develop and implement a health and safety program that will provide a mechanism for workers to perform their assigned tasks safely and without injury. The program will require rules, procedures, and training to comply with their legal obligations under this Act.

The OHSA is a piece of provincial legislation and it is regulated by the Ontario Government. It is enforced by the Ministry of Labour (MOL). The MOL has an investigative branch of occupational inspectors who deal specifically with ensuring employers in Ontario are complying with this legislation. These inspectors have the right to enter any workplace in Ontario unannounced to inspect the premises for violations of the act.

Generally the inspectors will visit a workplace for one of a few reasons:

- A worker calls the Ministry of Labour to report an unsafe condition. The inspector will review the documented concern with the employer and the Certified JHSC Co-chair worker representative. The review will include the actual "alleged" unsafe condition, requests for training records, certifications, etc.
- The company has a poor health and safety performance record with the WSIB in terms of high frequency and/or high severity of workplace injuries.
- Random visit
- Workwell audit
- Critical injury investigation

At any time the MOL inspector can inspect a workplace. Fines and penalties can be levied for violations of the OHSA. These fines and penalties can be monetary or represented by incarceration. The fines and penalties can be levied against the employer, a supervisor or a worker depending on the circumstances and the situation. It is unusual for the MOL inspector to visit a workplace and not issue a fine or work order.

A work order may be levied for something as simple as a forklift operator not wearing a seat belt. More serious violations that may cause a fatality may generate a greater number of written orders, fines or penalties. Generally the work orders, fines and penalties are levied against the employer. However if the employer can prove that the worker has received appropriate training, the worker was aware of the work instruction to safely perform a task, and, the company issued progressive discipline to enforce the procedure, then the fine or penalty may be levied against the worker. The worker can receive fines and penalties for not complying with their roles and responsibilities under the Act by applying the skills and knowledge from training to the task.

Each province in Canada has its own Occupational Health and Safety Act as well as each state in the United States of America. All of them have the same focus but vary in topics covered and their respective legal requirements. Other countries have similar pieces of legislation which vary according to the rules of the land.

A full copy of this act can be found at www.e-laws.gov.on.ca, under O for Occupational Health and Safety Act.

Ministry of Labour (MOL) Guidelines
In addition to the OHSA in Ontario, the MOL has set out additional guidelines as an extension of the OHSA. These guidelines assist the employer in developing policies and procedures that will address any reasonable precautions to protect the health of the worker. For example, in addition to the OHSA section on material handling, the Guideline for Safe Operation of Powered Lift Trucks outlines more minimum requirements that would shape the related procedures to reasonably protect the health and safety of the workers that interact with forklifts in the workplace.

The guidelines specify one minimum requirement as mandating the certification of all operators of the powered lift trucks. Part of the certification process involves training and licensing recertification of a minimum of every three (3) years. A practical evaluation must be completed at the eighteen (18) month mark of the licensing timeline.

The OHSA itself does not specify licensing requirements for the operation of powered lift trucks. The MOL determined that the majority of accidents involving powered lift trucks, especially accidents with fatalities, were due to a lack of "certified" training. The MOL developed these guidelines to address the lack of training and provide a mechanism for minimum standards to "authorize" the appropriate personnel who were competent to safely operate the equipment.

The Guideline for Safe Operation of Powered Lift Trucks is just one example of a guideline launched by the MOL. The MOL has established several guidelines throughout the years to address various gaps in legislation to assist the employer in implementing policies and procedures to protect the worker at work. There are more guidelines instituted by the MOL. In order to ensure compliance, each employer in Ontario should review related guidelines when preparing policies and procedures. To find these guidelines, please visit the MOL website at www.labour.gov.on.ca.

The Workers Compensation - Workplace Safety and Insurance Act (WSIA)

In Ontario, the workers' compensation program is regulated by the Workplace Safety and Insurance Act of Ontario. This act outlines each party's roles and responsibilities in the process of handling workplace injuries, recovery and return to work. It also outlines the criteria of eligibility for wage replacement benefits for workers who have experienced a workplace injury. The Act also describes criteria for employers' eligibility to participate in the program.

The Provincial Government regulates this piece of legislation. The Workplace Safety and Insurance Board (WSIB) administers the provisions of the Act. Similar to the Ministry of Labour, the WSIB has authority to levy fines and penalties for breaching the requirements of this act.

The WSIB and the MOL will collaborate in some initiatives to motivate the employers in Ontario to reduce the number of workplace injuries. For example, the WSIB will monitor the frequency and severity rates of each employer in Ontario. The WSIB will provide a list of poor performing employers as identified through high frequency and severity rates to the MOL. The MOL will randomly inspect these workplaces to evaluate the compliance of their health and safety program.

The WSIA is critical in establishing an effective disability management program in the workplace for several reasons. The act outlines the process to report injuries, the employer's obligation to re-employ an injured worker, the duty to accommodate an injured worker and vocational retraining if required. The act includes more details however the key ones to preparing the disability program that will address compliance and due diligence.

Each province will have its own workers compensation act to address the loss of wages due to workplace injuries. Each will vary in process however they will share the common elements of describing the criteria for benefits eligibility and claims management. Similar to the OHSA, these common elements are just the minimum requirements. To provide evidence of due diligence and effective claim management, the employer must establish policies and procedures. These policies and procedures will provide evidence for the fair and consistent treatment of all workers and the consistent management of injuries, recovery, return to work, and long term accommodation.

For review of the whole act, please visit at www.e-laws.gov.on.ca, under W for Workplace Safety and Insurance Act.

The Regulation 1101 First Aid,

In addition to addressing wage replacement for workplace injuries, the WSIA's Regulation 1101 (First Aid) outlines the specific first aid supplies and their respective quantities required in each workplace in Ontario. Consistent with the pieces of legislation reviewed above, this regulation only outlines the minimum requirement for employer. Due diligence would dictate that employers should exceed the minimum requirements to provide evidence of their commitment to the health and safety of their workers. Therefore compliance to this legislation will only strengthen the health and safety program in the workplace by providing the employer with the tools and supplies to treat workplace injuries in a timely manner.

As with all legislation, any employer found to be in violation of these requirements will be subject to fines and penalties. Violations of this regulation will be addressed by the MOL in Ontario.

The Workwell Audit

Under the WSIA, Policy #13.01.02, the WSIB will track and monitor the health and safety performance of each employer in Ontario. Should an employer perform poorly, the employer may be subject to an audit of their health and safety program. The poor performer is an employer who has a high frequency and or high severity rate of injuries. In addition, the employers who have a history of non-compliance to the OHSA may also be labeled as a poor performer.

The WSIB will notify the poor performing employer that they will be subject to a Workwell audit. The program is designed to assist the employer in reducing the number and severity of the workplace injuries and force the employer to comply with the Occupational Health and Safety Act of Ontario.

Once the employer is notified that they must undergo a Workwell audit, the employer will have a specified period of time to prepare for the audit. The WSIB will send third party auditors to the employer to evaluate the compliance of the health and safety program to the law. The auditors will also evaluate the injury statistics of the employer for a mechanism of root cause analysis and corrective action implementation.

The auditors will report on the discrepancies between the health and safety program and the legal requirements. The auditors will also recommend changes for improvement to the program and the prevention activities of the employer. These changes should assist the employer in making the changes necessary to comply with legislation and reduce their frequency and severity rates of injuries. Those employers that fail the audit will be subject to penalties and fines as well as deadlines to implement corrective actions to comply with legislative requirements.

According to Policy 13-01-02, the WSIA explains the Workwell program as:

> ...Workwell identifies employers with particularly poor accident records and/or high accident costs compared to their rate group and/or rate groups, or who have a history of non-compliance with the Occupational Health and Safety Act and encourages them to improve their prevention programs.
>
> Workwell requires these employers to participate in a workplace health and safety evaluation. employers that fail the evaluation are given a specified time frame to make improvements. If improvement does not occur within the given time the WSIB issues an additional premium charge...
>
> ...The WSIB determines whether an employer is a candidate for a Workwell evaluation by considering any of the following:

- the number and rate of Ministry of Labour workplace orders that have been issued and the degree of compliance with those orders,
- the type of order and the severity of the contravention of the Occupational Health and Safety Act,
- prosecutions initiated for failure to comply with Ministry of Labour orders,
- injury frequency information,
- injury cost information,
- severity of injury information,
- compliance with first aid regulations,
- complaints or referrals from workers or other parties, or
- any information concerning deficiencies or mitigating activities related to an employer's health and safety measures.

The information received from these various sources is reviewed and assessed by the WSIB's Workwell Program. When reviewing and assessing injury frequency and/or injury cost information, the WSIB adopts a comparative approach by evaluating an employer's record relative to the record of other employers of a similar size and industry. This comparative approach is applicable to any and/or all of an employer's rate groups; all of an employer's business activities are subject to evaluation.

Following identification, employers are notified in writing that there is going to be a Workwell health and safety evaluation of their workplace...

...The Workwell evaluation verifies the existence, the consistent application, the implementation and the enforcement of an employer's health and safety program.

Evaluation consists of an initial phase and a follow-up phase. Each evaluation receives a score, weighted to the risk posed...

...Employers are informed in writing of the [initial] results of the evaluation. Those that do not achieve a score of seventy five percent (75%) or better compliance with the evaluation criteria fail the initial evaluation and are eligible for a Workwell additional premium charge. employers have 6 months to improve their compliance with the evaluation criteria.

...employers that fail the initial evaluation are required to work with a health and safety program provider (e.g. a Health and Safety Association) to improve their compliance with the evaluation criteria. Failure to do so results in the immediate levying of the additional premium charge, based on the initial evaluation score...

...The WSIB staff re-visit the employer at the conclusion of the 6 months to re-evaluate the workplace and calculate the additional premium charge if indicated...

...The amount of the Workwell additional premium charge is dependent on the degree of the employer's non-compliance with the evaluation criteria at the second evaluation. If the score at second evaluation is 75% or better there is no additional premium charge.

Employers with a score less than 75% at second evaluation receive an additional premium charge ranging from 10% to 75% of their annual premium. The maximum additional premium charge is $500,000.
(WSIA, 1997; www.wsib.on.ca, 2010)

The Workwell Program is one tool the WSIB has to assist employers in developing an effective health and safety program. In addition to complying with legislative requirements, the purpose of developing the effective health and safety program is to prevent injuries. By preventing injuries, the employer will reduce the number of injuries and the severity of the injuries in the workplace. This is a unique section of the Workplace Safety and Insurance Act of Ontario. Other provinces and countries may have similar legislation but it would be reflective of the laws of the land by which it is governed.

Human Rights Code

There are two Human Rights Codes that affect people in Ontario. These codes are: the Human Rights Code of Canada and the Human Rights Code of Ontario. The Human Rights Code of Canada outlines the minimum requirements for the equal and fair treatment of all people in Canada. The Human Rights Code of Ontario does not supersede the Human Rights Code of Canada but rather compliments it. The Human Rights Code of Ontario adds to the minimum requirements of the Human Rights Code of Canada.

Both codes have a Commission to regulate and enforce the code in their respective jurisdictions. The Human Rights Code of Canada is regulated and enforced by the Canadian Human Rights Commission. It is enforced throughout Canada for all workers and employers in Canada. The purpose of this act is to prohibit the discriminatory activities of employers and workers in Canada. According to the Act, the purpose is:

> ...to extend the laws in Canada to give effect, within the purview of matters coming within the legislative authority of Parliament, to the principle that all individuals should have an opportunity equal with other individuals to make for themselves the lives that they are able and wish to have and to have their needs accommodated, consistent with their duties and obligations as members of society, without being hindered in or prevented from doing so by discriminatory practices based on race, national or ethnic origin, colour, religion, age, sex, sexual orientation, marital status, family status, disability or conviction for an offence for which a pardon has been granted... (Canadian Human Rights Act, 2010; www.chrc-ccdp.ca, 2010)

In addition to the Human Rights Code of Canada, each province or territory has implemented their own Human Rights Code that builds on the Canadian code. These provincially established codes will be enforced by provincial enforcement bodies. The Human Rights Code of Ontario is regulated and enforced by the Ontario Human Rights Commission. This code is applicable for the employers and workers of Ontario. The purpose of this act is also to prohibit and discourage the discrimination of workers in Ontario. The Act specifies:

> ...Whereas recognition of the inherent dignity and the equal and inalienable rights of all members of the human family is the foundation of freedom, justice and peace in the world and is in accord with the Universal Declaration of Human Rights as proclaimed by the United Nations;
>
> And Whereas it is public policy in Ontario to recognize the dignity and worth of every person and to provide for equal rights and opportunities without discrimination that is contrary to law, and having as its aim the creation of a climate of understanding and mutual respect for the dignity and worth of each person so that each person feels a part of the community and able to contribute fully to the development and well-being of the community and the Province... (Ontario Human Rights Act, 2010; www.ohrc.on.ca, 2010)

Employers have to develop policies and procedures that will prevent the discrimination or harassment of any worker (or potential worker). Discrimination is any action or lack of action based on any one of the prohibitive grounds. The prohibitive grounds include: race, ancestry, colour, gender, marital status, ethnic origin, family status, age, disability or handicap, place of origin, citizenship, creed, or sexual orientation.

Policies and procedures should dictate the appropriate behavior and provide the mechanism for decision making resulting in fair, consistent and equal policy enforcement. Practices, behaviours, words, the culture of the workplace will all be affected by fair, consistent and equal decisions for all workers. Practices and policies can address anything from hiring, disciplining, terminating, training, promoting, demoting, accommodating, etc. Basically any decision made in the general operation of the business in relation to managing workers should be fair and consistent.

Essentially both Human Rights Codes outline the minimum requirements for employers to treat all workers equally, consistently and fairly. Any decisions made based on any prohibited grounds will expose the employer to discriminatory practices. In addition to these decisions resembling poor management practices, the employer could be subject to penalties and fines by the Human Rights Commission. Therefore the importance of this Act is to assist the employer in developing a health and safety program and a disability management program free of discrimination.

There are similar codes in other countries especially industrialized nations. There may be countries that do not have laws for human rights. However, there are organizations that monitor the activities in such countries and promote human rights for everyone such as Amnesty International.

The Privacy and Confidentiality Acts - Release Consents

Every employee in Ontario and in Canada has the right to privacy. Both Ontario and Canada have specific legislation known as the Privacy Act to address the privacy and confidentiality requirements for sensitive information. This sensitive information about workers include social insurance numbers, addresses, phone numbers, personal information, information on their family, personal medical conditions, etc. These Acts outline what information is considered confidential and subject to the Privacy Act and how the employer is required to handle or treat such information.

These pieces of legislation will outline the acceptable information the employer is allowed to ask or collect and what information that the employer is not allowed to request of the worker. For example, in Ontario, the employer is not allowed to ask questions about the worker or potential worker's medical history. However if the worker volunteers the information, under the rules of confidentiality, the employer must lock the information up under lock and key. The employer is not allowed to share this information with any other person unless the worker has given full and knowing consent to do so.

Confidentiality presents challenges in developing an effective disability management program. Medical history is instrumental in obtaining cost relief, amalgamation, permanent impairment, judging if the person is physically capable of performing the essential duties of the job, accommodation requirements, medical emergency requirements, etc. However, if the employer is not permitted under the Privacy Act to request such information, the employer must develop other means of providing the information to the benefits carrier.

Even though the employer is not allowed to request personal medical history from the worker as well as the worker is not required to advise the employer of any of such information under confidentiality and privacy, the worker is required to inform the employer of any restrictions. Any worker with restrictions should advise the employer because the employer is obligated to accommodate the worker. Under the duty to accommodate the employer is legally required to accommodate the worker to the point of undue hardship. However the employer can only accommodate restrictions that are known to the employer.

As with other pieces of legislation, the provincially regulated Privacy Act will vary from province to province but the essential core purpose of the Act will be comparable. Similarly, other industrialized nations may have legislation that would outline the legal responsibilities of the employer with regard to sensitive information. The legislation will vary from country to country so it is important to understand the laws of the land in which the employer is operating business including satellite operations in other countries. One rule for one business operation in one country may not be suitable for a business operation in another country. This may be true for both the health and safety and disability management programs of a corporate office and all their satellite operations throughout the world.

Employment Standards

There are employment standards in Canada and the Employment Standards Act of Ontario, are structured so that the provincial legislation builds on the federal legislation in defining the roles and responsibilities of each the employer and the worker in the employment relationship. These roles and responsibilities will outline requirements for such things as vacation pay, statutory holidays, minimum wage, hours of work, overtime, etc.

The Ministry of Labour is the government branch in Ontario who enforces the Employment Standards Act. Any worker who perceives their "entitlements" as defined under the Employment Standards Act were violated may contact the Ministry of Labour. The MOL will investigate the allegations. If the employer had violated the worker's right, then the employer would be subject to fines and penalties. The amounts of such fines and penalties would depend on the right violated, the severity of the violation, the size of the company, etc.

The Employment Standards Act forms the foundation in defining the responsibilities of each party in the working relationship; the worker and the employer. This act is critical in understanding the legal requirements of the employer to operate a business in Ontario with respect to managing workers.

As with other pieces of legislation, each province, each country, each geographical locations have their own version of the employment standards legislation dependent on the culture, economy, norms, values, and government agenda.

The Canada Labour Code

The Canadian Labour Code is regulated by the Federal Canadian government. Each province has their own labour act however there are some business operations in each province that are not necessarily subject to provincial law including federal government offices, crown corporations, banking, international and interprovincial transportation and communications, broadcasting, grain production, fisheries, mining and uranium processing. These types of operations are regulated by federal regulations.

The Canada Labour Code is similar to the Ontario Labour Relations Act. This act helps define the union-labour-employer roles, responsibilities and interrelationships including the collective bargaining process only for federally regulated business operations.

The Pension Act

There is both a federal and provincial pension act. The Pension Act outlines the responsibilities of the employer in managing a pension fund. The rules define the manner in which the employer participates in any pension fund including type of fund or program/subscription, reserves required, investment, contributions, deposits, transactions, vestment, etc. The act will also dictate how the worker contributes if possible, withdrawal, age of retirement, investment planning, etc.

The Labour Relations Act

The Labour Relations Act is an act that defines the union-labour-employer roles, responsibilities, and interrelationships. This act outlines the certification process to which a company becomes unionized and regulates the collective bargaining process.

This Act is regulated by the Ontario Labour Relations Board (OLRB) and enforced by the Ministry of Labour. The OLRB regulates the union certification process and the collective agreement process. It adjudicates over the union-employer relations. According to the Ontario Labour Relations Board, there function and mandate include:

> ...The Board is an independent, adjudicative tribunal issuing decisions based upon the evidence presented and submissions made to it by the parties, and upon its interpretation and determination of the relevant legislation and jurisprudence. It plays a fundamental role on the labour relations regime in Ontario and encourages harmonious relations between employers, employees and trade unions by dealing with matters before it as expeditiously and as fairly as reasonably possible.
> The OLRB's mandate is to provide, as an independent tribunal, excellence in administrative justice through the effective resolution of labour and employment disputes. (Labour Relations Act, 2010)

For more information on the OLRB, please refer to their website at www.olrb.gov.on.ca.

The Bill C-45 (EHS negligence under the criminal code)

Bill C-45 expands the ability of law enforcement in Ontario to charge supervisors, executives, or managers with a criminal offence for safety violations including gross negligence causing bodily injury, or, regretfully, fatality. In Ontario, if the Ministry of Labour investigates a workplace injury usually a critical injury. The MOL will determine if the injury was a result of negligence of a supervisor, manager or executive. If the MOL determines there is negligence, they will involve the local law enforcement to charge the supervisor, manager or executive with a criminal offence. The criminal offence can be anything from a misdemeanor to a felony depending on the severity of the injury, severity of the negligence, and the violation itself.

For example, a forklift is driven off a receiving dock. As a result, the driver is pinned between the ground and the mast of the forklift.

Unfortunately, despite the many efforts of the first responders, ambulance attendants, and medical professionals, the driver does not survive the injuries. Once the ambulance takes the injured worker away from the workplace, the MOL is called to the scene of the workplace accident since this accident meets the criteria of a critical injury. Upon investigation, the MOL uncovered that the driver of the forklift was not licensed to drive the forklift. Not only was the driver not licensed, the employer could not provide any evidence that the driver was actually trained to operate the forklift, much less operate the machinery safely.

Under the Occupational Health and Safety Act of Ontario, the employer has the responsibility to take every reasonable precaution to protect the worker. Every reasonable precaution includes training the worker to perform assigned tasks safely. Training is the only way to ensure that the worker has been "properly" instructed to operate or perform the task safely.

The act also has a section that outlines the requirements for material handling. Even though this section does not describe the licensing requirements for operating powered lift trucks, the Ministry of Labour has adopted a set of guidelines, the Guidelines for Safely Operating Powered Lift Trucks, as every reasonable activity to protect the workers. Within these guidelines, the employer is required to be able to provide documented evidence that each forklift operator is licensed. Licensing involves in class training for the operator every three (3) years with a practical evaluation at the eighteen (18) month mark (between the trainings dates). By following these requirements, the employer can demonstrate due diligence in training and providing the appropriate instruction to the operator of the powered lift truck in order for the worker to operate the lift truck safely.

In our example above, the employer could not provide the evidence of the training or fulfilling the licensing requirements according to the Guidelines of Safely Operating the Powered Lift Trucks. Therefore, the MOL will likely fine the employer under Section 25 of the OSHA for not taking every reasonable precaution to protect the worker. In addition to the MOL charging the employer with fines and penalties, the local law enforcement will charge the employer with gross negligence causing death under Bill C-45.

Depending on the level of authority which takes responsibility for the decision to assign the operation of the forklift to that worker will determine who is charged with the gross negligence. If the Supervisor assigned the worker to operate the forklift knowing that the worker was unlicensed or untrained, then it is likely the Supervisor will be charged under Bill C-45. If the mandate from the top was that no operator will be licensed to operate a lift truck, then the executives can be charged either in addition to the supervisor or instead of the any member of any lower level of management.

The Bill 168 (Violence in the Workplace), Amendment to OHSA 2010

Bill 168 outlines the employer's responsibilities in developing and implementing a program to assess and reduce the risk of violence or harassment in the workplace. This Bill is an amendment to the Occupational Health and Safety Act of Ontario effective as of June 15, 2010. This act is a direct result of some fatalities at the workplace in Ontario caused by violence. An example, is the violent death of Lori Dupont's at the hands of a coworker/ex-boyfriend while at the workplace at Hotel Dieu Grace Hospital in Windsor, Ontario. Another death considered included the death of a subordinate at the hands of her manager at Sears in Chatham, Ontario. These cases were significant in demonstrating that violence in the workplace occurs. The inquiry in these cases determined that management did little to protect the worker which formed the foundation of Bill 168 changes.

Bill 168 expands the responsibilities of the employer to develop and implement a program that will assess and reduce the risk of injuries at the workplace as a result of violence and harassment. The Ministry of Labour in Ontario will enforce this legislation.

Bill 118 – Prohibiting the use of handheld electronic equipment while driving a vehicle

Bill 118 is a new piece of legislation in Ontario (2009) that prohibits the use of handheld electronic equipment while driving a vehicle. This affects any employer in Ontario in two main ways: the law would prohibit the worker from working on a personal digital assistant (pda) while driving a company vehicle or prohibit the worker from conducting business on the cell phone while driving a personal car.

It is the responsibility of the employer to develop and implement a policy and procedure to ensure compliance to this bill. The local law enforcement will be the enforcement agency for this bill.

The Canada Pension Plan (CPP)

All workers over the age of 18 years in Canada will contribute to the federal pension plan known as CPP. It is normally a payroll deduction. Upon the age of 65 or retirement, whichever is later, the worker can apply for this benefit to the Federal government of Canada as an income source during retirement based on the percentage of contribution throughout the worker's working life.

According to the Federal Government of Canada website, www.servicecanada.gc.ca, the CPP is:

> ...is a contributory, earnings-related social insurance program. It ensures a measure of protection to a contributor and his or her family against the loss of income due to retirement, disability and death.
>
> There are three kinds of Canada Pension Plan benefits:
>
> Disability benefits (which include benefits for disabled contributors and benefits for their dependent children);
>
> Retirement pension; and
>
> Survivor benefits (which include the death benefits, the survivor's pension and the children's benefits).
>
> The Canada Pension Plan operates throughout Canada, although the province of Quebec has its own similar program, the Quebec Pension Plan. The Canada Pension Plan and the Quebec Pension Plan work together to ensure that all contributors are protected.
>
> (www.servicecanada.gc.ca, 2010)

This social program is designed to supplement the income of people in their retirement regardless of the person's retirement savings. The idea was to help those people who may not have had a retirement or pension plan through their work benefits. It was also to financially assist those people who worked and are not able to work due to age or disability.

Canada Pension Plan (CPP) – Disability
This branch of the CPP specifically reviews files where a worker can no longer work due to disability and permanent impairment. Entitlement to this benefit is not automatic. The disabled worker would have to meet the criteria of the program for eligibility of the benefits.

Similarly, disability or permanent impairment does not automatically mean the worker cannot work any longer. Sometimes workers, after retraining, the worker can re-enter the workplace to work within their restrictions. This type of disability program applies for people who are medically declared unfit to work ever again in any type of occupation.

The Disability Acts
As with other acts, there is a provincial and federal Disability act. These acts assist employers in understanding their responsibilities in accommodating workers (and customers) with disabilities. This can range from structural changes to the building such as installing elevators and larger bathroom stalls for wheelchair accessibility to ensuring the workplace is not discriminating against any worker due to their disability.

For more information on either the provincial or the federal Disability act, please refer to:
Provincial: www.ontario.ca/en/communities/disabilities
Federal: www.ccdonline.ca/en/socialpolicy/fda

The Employment Insurance (EI) – Sick
The Federal Canadian government administers a social employment insurance program for workers in Canada to assist workers financially should they lose their job due to layoff. There is a branch the Employment Insurance program that reviews cases where the worker is not working temporarily due to medically supported illness. This element of the insurance program is referred as Sick EI.

Sick EI is very similar to the short term disability benefit that some employers offer. Sick EI is typically used by those workers who do not have access to a short term disability program through work or private insurance coverage or they have been denied short term disability benefits from the employer's carrier.

The Pay Equity Act
In Ontario, the Pay Equity Act outlines the rights of workers to have equal pay for work of equal value. The employer has to develop and

implement a policy regarding the company's commitment to treating all workers fairly regardless of their race, gender, ethnicity, etc. This act requires employers to develop an assessment program that will evaluate or assess the value of each job in a workplace. Once each job has been assessed, jobs will be grouped together based on their value even though the jobs may belong to different departments or have vastly different tasks. An appropriate wage range will be assigned to each group of jobs that have equal value.

There is a Pay Equity Commission in Ontario that regulates and enforces the Pay Equity Act of Ontario. Employers in Ontario found to be in violation of this act will be fined and given deadlines for compliance. The members of the commission can unexpectedly visit the workplace for an audit of the company's Pay Equity Plan and assessment process.

Pay Equity will assist the employer in their practice of due diligence with regard to discrimination. This will also give some structure for the employer to follow during the return to work process and wage payment.

The Canada Standards Association (CSA)/ANSI Guidelines

The Canadian Standards Association is a not-for-profit organization that regulates the safety standards and certification of import product to ensure that Canadians are not injured while using imported product. The safety standards developed and enforced through the CSA are recognized internationally as the standards that exporters must comply with to sell product in Canada. The CSA standards are similar to the ANSI Guidelines of the USA.

In Ontario, the Ministry of Labour uses the CSA standards to compliment the OHSA. These standards provide any employer in Ontario or Canada with additional responsibilities in their health and safety programs. The employer should incorporate procedures to address CSA standards to ensure due diligence in taking every reasonable precautions to protect the safety of all workers.

To review the standards and learn more about the CSA, please refer to the following websites:
CSA - www.csa-international.org; and
CSA Standards - www.csa.ca/cm/ca/en/home

The Building Code

The Building Code of Ontario sets out the standards to which a building is constructed and certified after final inspection. These standards include regulatory requirements for accommodation under the Disability Act, Human Rights, etc. such as elevators and disability accommodation in bathrooms, etc. The Ministry of Labour may use this code to evaluate the workplace for compliance to supplement the OHSA for safety practices.

To learn more about the Building Code of Ontario, please refer to the following website: www.obc.mah.gov.on.ca.

The Electrical Safety Code
Similar to the Building Code, the Electrical Code of Ontario includes outlining the safety requirements of wiring buildings and using electricity in Ontario safely including how to handle electricity safely. The Electrical Safety Authority (ESA) is the authoritative body to regulate electrical safety in Ontario. However, just like the Building Code, the Ministry of Labour can use this code to evaluate the workplace for compliance to compliment the OSHA for safety practices.

For more information on the ESA or the Electrical Safety Code itself, please refer to the following website: www.esainspection.net.

CHAPTER 27

DUE DILIGENCE - PREVENTIVE

Each company is legally obligated to provide a safe work environment including identifying and communicating any risks to everyone at the workplace, the workers, any visitors or contractors, etc. In preventing injuries or harm to workers and to avert legal repercussions, a company must develop a systemic best practices program in health and safety. The program should include practicing due diligence in all the company's decisions and business activities as well as providing training on working safely.

Due diligence is critical when establishing a comprehensive and effective health and safety program. By building due diligence into a health and safety program, the company not only ensures compliance to the minimum legal requirements under the Occupational Health and Safety Act but also allows the company to provide documented evidence of taking every reasonable precaution to protect the health and safety of the workers.

Due diligence is a "standard of care" to which a company has a legal obligation to provide. A more formal definition of due diligence can be found on the WSIB website. According to the WSIB, fact sheet on Internal Responsibility System and Due Diligence found on www.wsib.on.ca, "due diligence refers to the employer's legal responsibility to take *every reasonable precaution* to prevent injuries and illnesses and prove that they have done this. This is in addition to complying with the provisions of the *Occupational Health and Safety*

Act (OHSA) and Regulations and is not limited by them." In other words, due diligence refers to a standard of care that would include doing or not doing what a reasonable person would do or not do to prevent injuries or harm to others.

According to the Occupational Health and Safety Act (OHSA) of Ontario, part of the duties of an employer under Sec 25.2(h) is to take every precaution reasonable in the circumstances for the protection of a worker. Furthermore, the OHSA indicates that the duties of the supervisor under Sec. 27.2(c) include but are not limited to taking every precaution reasonable in the circumstances for the protection of a worker. (OHSA, Sec 25.2(h) and Sec 27.2(c), R.S.O. 1990, c. O.1).

In this reference, every "reasonable precaution" translates to an effective and efficient health and safety program that is exceeds minimum requirements. A systemic health and safety program should not only cover the minimum standards as outlined by any and all legislation for the land on which the business is operating, but also include policies and procedures to address prevention of injuries and harm to workers, visitors, contractors, etc. which may not be specifically addressed in any specific legislation. Failure to meet the legal obligation of due diligence will result in negligence. Negligence is a legal liability which may result in injuries, penalties, fines, and in some cases, jail time. Among many circles of health and safety, due diligence has become a key phrase in developing a program not only to prevent injuries to workers but also to "keep the executives out of jail".

Evidence of due diligence is the written policies and procedures instructing workers on the proper methods to conduct business. These policies and procedures identify methods to perform a task safely. These should also outline the requirements of performing the task safely to eliminate the risk of injury or harm. In addition to the policies and procedures, there should also be hard copy records on file supporting the training for each worker. The training should not only include the knowledge of the policies and procedures but the worker should also be able to demonstrate their understanding of their roles and responsibilities.

One way to understand what reasonable precautions are required for the safe operation of a business, is to complete a comprehensive risk assessment of every section of the operation of the business. The risk assessment should outline what risks will need to be addressed with policy, procedure, work instruction, or instruction.

This exercise must be documented. The documentation of this exercise will serve as evidence to support company activities to comply with the OHSA requirements.

The risk assessment will also help the company to understand what activities are required to protect the workers injury. The risk assessment will determine recommendations to assist the worker to perform the work safely. For example, the recommendations can include but are not limited to: identify training needs, proper storage, proper handling, certification requirements, and personal protective equipment, etc. The due diligence part of this exercise is to understand the risks in the workplace, prepare to instructions to work safely with the risks, develop and implement corrective and preventative measures, etc. The exercise provides evidence to support the company's commitment to the good health and safety of all the workers. The Ministry of Labour (MOL) will request to see this evidence to measure the company's compliance to OHSA.

The WSIB recommends that a best practice in an effective health and safety program is keeping records. According to the WSIB's fact sheet on Internal Responsibility System and Due Diligence, the WSIB recommends:

> the health and safety program to include:
> - A policy that outlines the firm's health and safety objective, listing management's commitment and all employee responsibilities for maintaining a safe workplace
> - Injury and illness prevention activities to achieve objectives of the policy and to ensure regulatory compliance
> - Details specifying when the prevention activities would be done, by whom, and how the activity should be recorded. Some examples include but are not limited to:
>   - emergency response program
>   - maintenance schedules
>   - joint health and safety committee: role, size, interval of meetings
>   - lock-out procedure
>   - inspections
>   - accident investigation and reporting

- new worker or new job orientation
- first aid
- return to work program

(WSIB, www.WSIB.on.ca, 2010)

Subsequently, policies and procedures are important tools to help the company outline their expectations and the workers understand what is expected of them. The policies and procedures also provide documented evidence of compliance and other activities demonstrating the company's commitment to the health and safety of all workers. To this end, the policies and procedures as well as the training records for each worker for each policy and procedure become documented evidence of due diligence for the company.

In addition to policies and procedures assisting in the safe business operations, this documented evidence can be used as a legal defence for violations in legal compliance to OHSA, Human Rights Act, Employment Standards Act, WSIA, Bill C45, etc. The Ministry of Labour can levy penalties, fines, jail terms, etc. for violations of the OHSA to executives, managers, supervisors, and or workers. Under Bill C45, criminal charges can be levied against executives, managers or and supervisors in the event that gross negligence has caused injury to the worker.

Some steps that an employer can take to ensure that proper documentation is being recorded is to incorporate due diligence into the health and safety program. Essentially due diligence is the taking of precautions to protect the health and safety of the workers. By establishing a program that not only meets the minimum standards of the Occupational Health and Safety Act and other legislative guidelines, but surpasses these legal expectations, an employer has built in due diligence into the health and safety program.

To summarize an information pamphlet from the Canadian Centre for Occupational Health and Safety (CCOHS), building due diligence into the health and safety program requires integrating some critical areas into the health and safety program. According to CCOHS, the conditions include but are not limited to:

> ...written occupational health and safety policies, practices, and procedures
> - demonstrating and documenting safety activities such as workplace safety audits, identified hazardous practices and hazard-

ous conditions and made necessary changes to correct these conditions, and provided employees with information to enable them to work safely.

- provide training and education to the employees
  - employees need to understand and carry out their work according to the established policies, practices, and procedures.
  - All training must be documented and recorded
- Provide training to supervisors to ensure they are competent persons, as defined in legislation.
  - All training must be documented and recorded
- monitor the workplace and ensure that employees are following the policies, practices and procedures.
  - Records of written documentation demonstrating actions of progressive disciplining for breaches of safety rules
  - Reinforcing workers' responsibilities in their duty to take reasonable care to ensure the safety of themselves and their coworkers including following safe work practices and complying with regulations.
- Establish an accident investigation and reporting system
  - Encourage employees to report all incidents including "near misses"
  - All incidents should be investigated
  - Information from investigations used to develop and implement preventative and corrective actions preventing future occurrences and recurrences (CCOHS)

In review, written records and documentation of all safety activities including the above actions will provide a history of the company's activities as well as demonstrate the company's commitment to the health and safety of its workers. This history will document progress and provide current rationale for the activities. This history will form the foundation for the due diligence defence. In order for these conditions to be effective for a due diligence defence, these elements must be implemented and operating prior to the occurrence of any injury or incident. The CCOHS succinctly indicates, *"...due diligence is demonstrated by your actions before an event occurs, not after."*

Due diligence in accordance to OHSA, would strongly recommend that short term corrective actions should be reasonable and timely. Short term corrective actions should be an immediate response to the report of an injury. Both the short term and the long term corrective actions should be designed to prevent the injury and the event from recurring. In reducing the likelihood of recurrence, the company can effectively reduce the number of injuries and the number of lost time days. Corrective action activities are only one part of the due diligence equation and effective health and safety program. The other part is prevention activities.

Prevention activities will assist in compliance to legislation such as OHSA and they will also assist in providing evidence of due diligence. Prevention activities such as procedures to operate forklifts safely in accordance to the CSA Standard B335-94 which the MOL considers the same as legislative requirements are activities that are implemented to prevent injuries before they occur.

In conclusion, according to the Canadian Centre for Occupational Health and Safety (CCOHS), due diligence can be used for a legal defence for violations of health and safety legislation. However, in order for due diligence to be an effective defence, specific documentation must be compiled to support the decisions made leading to the alleged violations for which the fines and penalties were imposed. Due diligence can be used as a legal defence but it is rarely successful because the supporting documentation is nonexistent or insufficient or completely irrelevant. As previously indicated, the supporting documentation must include proof that all precautions were taken to protect the health and safety of the workers. In order to prepare the best defence using due diligence as the defence, or for any legal defence, consult legal counsel.

CHAPTER 28

PREVENTION TECHNIQUES

An effective disability management program will include best practices in health and safety as well as practices that assist the worker through recovery and through the return to work process. The health and safety program should be focused on preventing workplace injuries and enabling worker wellness whereas disability management should be focused on response to workplace injuries and improving the worker wellness through the recovery and return to work processes. Both programs are concerned about worker wellness. However, health and safety is focused on pre-injury and disability management is post-injury. Most companies blend the two programs because they are interdependent.

There are several prevention techniques in any health and safety program. Some techniques are more effective than others depending on the hazards and risks of the workplace. To demonstrate due diligence, a company should consider all techniques relevant to their workplace. The following are just some of the prevention techniques available to companies operating in Ontario but by no means is the list a comprehensive or exhaustive list.

Safety Group

Safety Groups are an excellent example of networking. Safety Groups is an incentive program in Ontario sponsored by the WSIB. This program coaches health and safety representatives of companies who are participating in the program on how to develop the foundation for a basic but effective health and safety program. The incentive for the company to participate in this program is the "rebate" the WSIB grants to the participating companies who complete all the criteria of the program each year.

In this incentive program, the participants need to set five (5) targets for a health and safety program and complete an action plan to accomplish each of these targets. The participants have one year to accomplish these targets. The incentive part of the program is in the monetary reward for completion. If the group achieves all of their targets and objectives, they will receive a percentage of their WSIB premiums as a rebate. The rebates are calculated based on the percentage of accomplishment of the group of participants' yearly individual targets. At the end of each year, the WSIB randomly selects 10% of the participants to be audited to ensure that the accomplishments reported have been completed as reported.

The WSIB auditor calculates the percentage of completion through the results of the randomly selected participants. The percentage is then applied up to 5% of the group's total WSIB premiums. For example, if the group earned 85% completion of their targets, then each member of the group will get 85% of 5% of their WSIB premiums back from the WSIB as a rebate for their accomplishment in safety group. Depending on the size of the company, this rebate can add up to a sizable amount. The return on investment becomes a sizable amount of cost savings for developing and implementing a health and safety program which is already a legal obligation under the Occupational Health and Safety Act (OHSA), the Workplace Safety and Insurance Act (WSIA), etc.

Despite the fact that the concept of Safety Group is embedded in the WSIB incentive program, it is also an essential network building opportunity. As part of the criteria for completing their obligations, the participants of the safety group have to meet a minimum of three (3) times per year to discuss topics including but not limited to: the group element, how to set and accomplish your five targets, discuss any problems as well as share any lessons learned.

The opportunity for sharing of knowledge will not only allow each of the participants to learn what is expected to complete the program but also what has worked for other companies with similar situations, what has not worked, how to develop policies and procedures, and tips on implementation. The sharing of knowledge provides for the group to network with each other outside the setting of the safety group for other matters in business operations as appropriate. Learning from each other instead of re-inventing the wheel, will help each of the participants to successfully develop and implement an effective and efficient health and safety and or disability management programs.

Another advantage to participating in a Safety Group will also help representatives to understand the legislative requirements especially as outlined in the Workplace Safety and Insurance Act (WSIA) as well as Occupational Health and Safety Act (OHSA). In covering these acts in the health and safety program and the disability management program will assist in covering the company's obligation for demonstrating and practicing due diligence.

EHS Certification Programs including OHSAS 18001

As mentioned before, an effective health and safety program will assist in identifying and reducing risk of injury at work. Even the most effective health and safety program may not eliminate all injuries. An operational health and safety program may not eliminate all lost time claims as a result of injuries, however, an efficient health and safety program will assist in identifying and reducing any risks of occupational injuries. Despite a strong functioning health and safety program, workplace injuries may still occur and these injuries may generate lost time. As a result, all companies should develop and implement an early and safe return to work program, modified work program, commitment to early medical intervention, short term and preventative corrective actions, and written modified offers as key initiatives to reduce lost time and reduce costs.

Management's commitment to health and safety as well as return to work programs are an essential fundamental building block to the success of developing, implementing and maintaining each program. Verbal commitments are evident through speeches, dialogues with employees, and daily verbal instructions. In addition to the verbal commitment, it is best practice for the commitment to not only be communicated verbally but to be documented and signed by executive management. The signed document should be posted for all the employees to read as a daily reminder of management's commitment. Documentation of the commitment will provide evidence of the commitment for enquiries from the MOL, the WSIB, unions, customers, OHSAS 18001 auditors, etc.

The most important best practice in illustrating management's commitment to health and safety as well as return to work programs is for management to lead by example. Demonstrating executive management's commitment through activities such as regular reviews and monitoring of each incident. Management should also monitor trends, address health and safety issues through corrective actions in a timely manner, address return to work issues through corrective actions and communication in a timely manner, regular communication meetings with all employees reviewing trends and solutions, ensure all employees receive the same messages on the seriousness of each program and any serious consequences of non-compliance, mandate training, etc. The daily consistent and fair application of each program includes application of consequences for non-compliance. The application of consequences will provide evidence to demonstrate a clear commitment of zero tolerance for violations and due diligence.

In the absence of the executive management's commitment, both programs will tend to be less effective because:

- Corrective action investigations are not taken seriously or are not completed;
- Solutions are not implemented because resources and talent are not committed to the continuous improvement;
- Costs are not allocated for solutions;
- Costs are not allocated for proper training;
- Unsafe practices are tolerated and thereby condoned since the behaviour is not corrected through retraining or progressive discipline;
- Resources are not allocated for development and implementation of preventative activities including lessons learned for future projects;
- Unsafe conditions, behaviours, or attitudes lead to continued or recurrence of injuries;
- The number of injuries rise;
- The number of lost time days increase;
- The risk of non-compliance to legislation (OHSA and WSIA) rises;
- The MOL visits the workplace more frequently resulting in more written orders and possibly an increase in fines and violations including potential of jail time under Bill C-45;

- Increase in potential fines and penalties by the WSIB;
- Increasing the risk of fatalities;
- Decreasing morale of the workers;
- Decreasing quality;
- Decreasing customer satisfaction;
- Decreasing employee satisfaction; and,
- Decreasing the company's positioning for profitability.

Once a company has documented their commitment to each the health and safety program as well as the return to work program, the programs must be developed and implemented. A well designed program will consider:

- compliance to all relevant legislation;
- conformance to OHSAS 18001, ISO14001, WSIB Accreditation or Safety Group requirements; and,
- requirements unique to each specific worksite and culture.

Legislative requirements are just minimum standards. For more effective programs, a company should set their standards to exceed the minimum standards. Therefore, a company should develop and implement policies and procedures that exceed the expectations of legislative requirements not only to cover legal compliance but also to demonstrate due diligence in attempting to establish and maintain a safe workplace.

A strong health and safety program will assist in developing and implementing a strong disability management program. The health and safety program will assist in decreasing the number of injuries. In reducing the injuries, the program should aim at reducing the severity of the injuries by implementing procedures to prevent injuries or recurrence of injuries and mitigate the risk of incidents with severe injuries.

Internal Reporting Process – prevention
A functional element of a health and safety program that also serves as an effective tool in the disability management program is the inci-

dent reporting process. Once an incident occurs in the workplace, the incident report should be completed by the injured worker and the supervisor.

A comprehensive incident report form will include descriptive details of the event leading to the injury. In these details, once analyzed, corrective actions can be developed and implemented to prevent recurrences. The details provided in the incident report will also supply the information required to complete the worker's compensation paperwork if required.

Additionally, the incident reporting process must include a comprehensive incident investigation process. Once the worker has been taken care of and all workers have been relocated to a safe location if required, the supervisor should investigate the incident. The results of the investigation will lead to short and long term corrective action activities. Best practices would indicate that the supervisor should have developed and implemented a short term corrective action at the time the incident was reported.

For best practices and consistency, link the internal incident reporting process with the SCAR process so that the investigational results will be entered into the SCAR process for numbering, development, implementation, follow up, evaluation, continuous improvements, etc.

System Corrective Action Report (SCAR) Process
Even the most comprehensive health and safety program may still experience injuries. Despite the best efforts of practicing due diligence through appropriate hazard assessment activities and training activities, events still occur. Therefore an effective health and safety program will continue to evolve for the life of the business operation.

In the event that an incident occurs, it should be made mandatory to report any incident no matter how minor to management. The process to report the event includes completing a detailed incident reporting form with a supervisor. The incident report is an essential tool to obtain a preliminary idea of what occurred to cause the event. If properly developed, the incident reporting process will incorporate due diligence by including processes to obtain pertinent information to facilitate:

- aid the investigation;
- assist in completing worker compensation claim forms;

- understanding of the risk;
- development and implementation of short term corrective actions;
- development and implementation of long term preventative actions;
- initiation of the monitoring the recovery process;
- establishment of statistical tracking and monitoring trends; and,
- a historical pattern of activities demonstrating commitment to due diligence and continuous improvement in the health and safety program.

Built into a comprehensive incident reporting process is a detailed investigation process. The incident investigation process should include but not be limited to: pictures, witness statements, recreation of events, potential corrective actions, etc.

Short term corrective action plans can be developed and implemented at the point of completing the incident report providing the incident report has a root cause analysis section built into the report. Once the supervisor and the worker have determined the root cause of the incident, then a short term corrective action can be developed and implemented relatively without much delay.

In some instances, the short term corrective action plans can become the long term corrective action plan if the situation is remedied through the short term corrective plan. For the short term corrective action plans that are only implemented to ensure the safety of the workers in the immediate situation. This type of short term corrective action plan is like a band-aid until the whole problem can be addressed in a more long term manner. For example, a short term corrective action to a slip and fall may be to put pylons or post signs saying "caution...slippery surface" around the hazard.

Where short term corrective actions are meant to address the immediate situation, a long term corrective action is meant to address mitigating the risk from recurring. A long term corrective action must be developed and implemented in a timely manner to protect the safety of the worker. In the example above regarding the slip and fall, a long term corrective action would be to fix the floor. Mopping up the water on the floor to remove the immediate threat of being slippery is short term but fixing the leaky roof would eliminate the hazard and therefore be the long term corrective action.

The next level to an evolving health and safety program and disability management program would include monitoring the effectiveness of all corrective actions implemented. The implementation of any corrective action does not ensure the success of the corrective actions. Monitoring the effect of the corrective action will allowing the company to determine if the corrective action was successful as well as adjust the plan if the actions did not achieve the desired results.

In addition to monitoring corrective actions for success, monitoring the corrective actions can also allow the company to recognize trends. If the company remains singularly focused on the corrective actions without assessing the whole picture, the company can miss the opportunity to analyze trends and patterns revealing more intrinsic problems that are occurring. For example, five (5) separate incident reports for various injuries but all the injuries occurred at the same workstation or line over a specific period of time. Each incident was remedied effectively for that injury type evident through no further occurrences for that specific injury. However, by examining the trend of the five (5) separate incident reports from the one area, the company noticed that the design of the work area had an inherent flaw exposing the workers indirectly to the risk of an assortment of different injuries. A classic example of this would be to consider the space or layout of a workstation that is too tight resulting in the workers bumping into the equipment and hurting various areas of their body.

Other Components of an Effective Health and Safety Programs
In addition to OHSA18001, other components of an effective health and safety program regardless if the workplace is certified as OHSA18001 or not, should include programs such as:

- A New Hire Health and Safety Orientation which review all the health and safety rules of the workplace with each worker as they are hired at the workplace. This program should be executed within the first day of employment of each worker to ensure the worker is aware and understands all the health and safety rules and procedures prior to starting work. This should reduce injuries due to errors from lack of awareness or lack of knowledge of the work-place health and safety rules.

- A condensed Health and Safety Orientation provide review and refresher training to remind workers who have a high frequency of work-place incidents. The purpose of reminding workers with high frequency of incidents, would be to ensure understanding of the rules and provide a foundation of progressive discipline if the worker continues to violate the health and safety rules.

- A further condensed orientation may serve as a reminder for all active workers to continue to work safely. The reminder will help the workers remember the rules and safety procedures that will assist them to perform the tasks assigned to them at work. The objective is to reduce injuries from lack of awareness or lack of knowledge.

- Reintegration after long absence from work which includes a refresher Health and Safety Orientation to remind those workers who have been away from the workplace for a prolonged period of time. Procedures can be forgotten with time away from the workplace or there could have been many changes to the work-place since the last time the worker was at work.

- An ergonomics program for awareness and training the workers to work using proper body mechanics and motions to perform a task safely and reduce the risk of repetitive strain injuries. Ergonomics is also effective in designing the workstations at the beginning of the design phase. Engineering ergonomics into designing the product as well as designing the workstation will decrease the risk of repetitive strain injuries as well as support the any objection the employer may have that an injury is work related. NIOSH has standards for ergonomics like heights and reaching measurements that will as-

sist engineers and employers to designing ergonomics into the workplace.

- A physical demands analysis (PDA) breaks
down each motion of a task and rates the risk
of each motion for injury. The goal of the employer is to reduce the risk of each motion to a
level where the risk is low enough not to contribute to an injury. The risk is not just on each
motion independently but also should be evaluated based on the cumulative effect of all body
motions within a cycle time. The risk is based
on the time it takes to perform a task, the force
required to perform the task, duration and repetition of the motion to complete the task of
each body part. The WSIB and short or long
term benefits carriers will request copies of these PDAs to determine if the injury is work related. The PDAs will also be used to determine
if there is a safe, suitable, long term position
available within the worker's restrictions.

- Rotation schedules for the workers. The rotation can be within the same line by rotating
through the different work cells as well as department wide through all lines over a longer
period of time like a week or a month. The rotation schedule will depend on the variety of
body motions on each workstation, line and
plant wide. The object is to rotate through different tasks in order to work with different
body parts. This will afford appropriate rest periods for each body part while another body
part works during each cycle. In this way, an
effective rotation schedule will reduce the risk
of injury especially repetitive strain injury for
each body part.

- A stretching program prior to each shift or
throughout the shift will assist the worker in
properly conditioning their muscles for the demands of the tasks while working. The stretching will allow the workers' muscles to be limber
enough to withstand the endurance and

strength required to complete the tasks assigned throughout the shift. The purpose of the stretching program is to mitigate the chance of injury.

- Evaluating the culture of the workplace will allow the company to understand if injuries are resulting from complacency or other behaviour based reasons. There are some safety training programs on the market that will help the company address habits based in behaviour that may cause injuries including complacency, not paying attention on the task at hand or lack of focus, etc. A well rounded safety culture will include training to address awareness and empowerment to injury within the worker's control.

- Develop and implement a program for preventing violence and harassment in the workplace. Companies should be enforcing a zero tolerance culture in the workplace. In Ontario, Bill 168 (2010) amends the Occupational Health and Safety Act (OHSA) to include legislative requirements for establishing policies and procedures for preventing both violence and harassment in the workplaces of Ontario. Employers will have to incorporate elements of risk to evaluate during workplace inspections to assess risk of violence or harassment as well as provide employees with mechanisms of communication to file concerns. Investigations must occur in a consistent method and corrective actions must be implemented as a result of each investigation as required. Bill 168 also allows workers the right to refuse work should they feel at risk of violence or harassment. There are more requirements under this Bill which can be reviewed under the Ministry of Labour website: www.labour.gov.on.ca/english or www.e-laws.gov.on.ca .

CHAPTER 29

MONITORING INJURIES

Monitoring injuries can help evaluate the effectiveness of the health and safety program. In addition, monitoring and evaluating the effectiveness of the corrective actions developed and implemented will foster continuous improvements. The company should develop mechanisms to monitor injuries include tracking statistics of both occupational and non-occupational injuries, analyze historical patterns and trends to forecast or predict injury spikes, supply management with supporting documentation for evaluating key performance indicators or strategic goals and objectives, etc.

In order to identify trends and patterns, a method for monitoring incident reports must be created. One tool to monitor incident reports is to record each and every incident report into charts by plotting points of reference of different sections of information from the incident reports. For example, a specific body part can be tracked regarding how many times this body part is injured, the workstation(s) where this body part was injured, the cause of injury, etc.

These charts are part of the visual factory concept to easily identify problem areas at a glance by looking at a graph or chart. Injury statistics also serve to prove due diligence in continuous improvements since the charts and graphs provide a trail of written documentation of activities. In addition, injury statistics assist to monitor the efficiency and effectiveness of the company's health and safety program. Accordingly, injury statistics become a very valuable mechanism to drive continuous improvements and prevention activities.

Injury statistics are the report card of a company's health and safety program and disability management program. In analyzing the injury statistics, management can determine:

- where the problem areas are in terms of work-stations as well as processes;
- short term corrective actions through root cause analysis;
- long term preventive corrective actions through root cause analysis;
- effectiveness of processes and previous corrective actions;
- efficiency of the existing systems;
- projecting future claim costs; and,
- providing a record of the historical pattern(s) of activities demonstrating commitment to due diligence and continuous improvement in the health and safety program.

Monitoring injury statistics is a very valuable method to evaluating the effectiveness and efficiency of the company's health and safety program. It is instrumental in developing and implementing corrective short term and preventive long term actions. The statistics establish a set of historical records of lessons learned for due diligence. Therefore, determining what statistics to monitor requires careful consideration.

To determine what statistics to monitor, management must decide the intended purpose and use of the information derived from the statistics as well what actions they will commit to as a result of that same information. There is a wide range of statistics that can be tracked. Each statistic can reveal unique data open to interpretation according to the company's intention of understanding and planning. For example, if the company wanted to evaluate the trends of the body parts are most reported as injured, the company should track injuries by body part. By analyzing the trends and patterns of each body part, a root cause analysis can be completed to determine the underlying cause(s) of the injury and assist in developing and implementing the corrective action (both short term and long term) to prevent future injuries.

In above example, the compiled data will reveal the body part with the highest number of injuries was the wrists. In addition to identifying the wrists as the most commonly injured body part, the data also revealed that the cause of the injuries was carpal tunnel. Carpal tunnel is a medical condition caused by repetitive strain. Repetitive strain injuries are caused by repetitive, frequent and rapid movements. The company can review the workstations and processes to evaluate the movements of the wrist. Even though the injuries occurred on a variety of lines or processes, the common thread in these processes will be frequent, rapid and repetitive twisting at the wrists. Carpal tunnel can occur for different body parts however, the wrists are the most common body part afflicted.

After analyzing the trend(s) of incidents, the company can investigate the root causes collectively. The company can address these intrinsic problems by implementing additional long term solutions. Once the intrinsic problems have been corrected, the trend will change. In fact, the injuries should stop in that area if the long term solution was effective or if the root cause analysis was completed proficiently. If injuries continue to occur in that same area, then the root cause analysis must be revisited. However, if the solutions are effective and the injuries decline, the productivity should increase and employee morale should improve.

The practice of root cause analysis allows engineers to understand what changes are required for prevention of recurrence or future injuries. The engineers can then redesign the layout of the process or workstation to reduce or eliminate the high risk motion of the body part. By reducing the amount of high risk movements of the body part per cycle or eliminating the motion altogether will prevent future injuries to that body part.

In cases of carpal tunnel of the wrist, some ways to reduce the twisting motion of the wrist would be to have the parts fall onto the conveyor at a certain angle. The angle will prevent the operator's arm from twisting to retrieve the part. Another preventative action would be to install an end of arm tooling like a robot. The robot can turn the part all about at different angles instead of the human arm during repetitive sections of the process. By having the robot performing the twisting motion instead of the worker, mitigates the risk of repetitive strain injuries to the worker.

Both solutions reduce the number of times the wrist turns therefore reducing the risk of another repetitive strain type injury to the wrist. The golden rule in any occupational health and safety program is to eliminate the risk. If elimination of the risk is not possible then the actions will have significantly reduced the risk. Risks can be mitigated through engineering controls, administration controls, or personal protective equipment. Hazard assessment, risk assessment and training are also critical tools to significantly reduce the risk of injuries.

Of course the above example is greatly oversimplified. However the example clearly illustrates the use and purpose of specific statistics. Some other common statistics that can be monitored include but are not limited to:

- Incidents by cause;
- Incidents by body part;
- Skeleton showing all the body parts and the number of injuries at each body part;
- Incidents by line, workstation, process;
- Pyramid, recording the amount of near misses, first aids, medical, lost time under 5 days, lost time over 5 days, fatalities, property damage only (no injury);
- Incidents per capita as a whole and per position or job title;
- Incidents by occupation or position;
- Top 5 issues of each statistic;
- Log of decisions from all benefits carriers;
- Severity and frequency;
- Costs for claim mgmt (additional sales to cover costs);
- Lost time days; and,
- Lost time claims.

Upon compiling and analyzing the data that has been determined to be noteworthy to the business objectives, the company can develop strategies for prevention and management of the problems that occur. To support the visual factory and allow management to analyze the data quickly at a glance, graphs and charts are supporting aids in illustrating problems and driving recommended solutions for change. Below are some descriptive examples of charts and graphs that could be practical in analyzing problems.

Illustration 29-1: Injury by Body Part Summary and Comparison of Previous Year

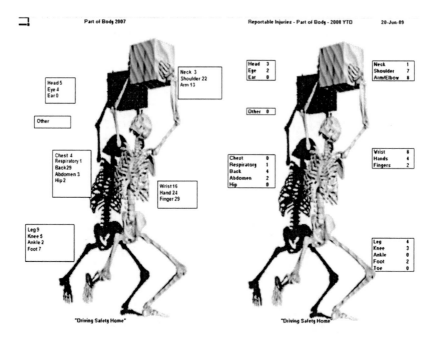

Illustrations 29-1 and 29-2 compare the number of injuries by body part from the previous year(s) to the current year. At a glance, the chart and the graph will assist in evaluating the effectiveness of the previous corrective actions through the reduction of the number of injuries of the same body part from the previous year to the current year. In the above example, the number of wrist injuries in 2007 was 16 and in 2008 the wrist injuries were 8. Therefore, the significant decrease in injuries from one year to the other may suggest that the corrective actions applied in 2007 have been effective in reducing the number of injuries even though the corrective actions were not effective in eliminating the injuries totally.

For this assumption to be true, there are other situations that require consideration such as production volume changes from one year to the next, population changes from one year to the next, etc. The only way the assumption can be true, is if the environment remains relatively the same or stable from one year to the current year. If any element of the environment changes, then the company will have to adjust the charts and graphs to track the injuries per capita to monitor changes and effectiveness.

The graph below illustrates the same point only graphically rather than pictorially given that the years being compared experienced stable environments.

Illustration 29-2: Comparison of Injured Body Parts

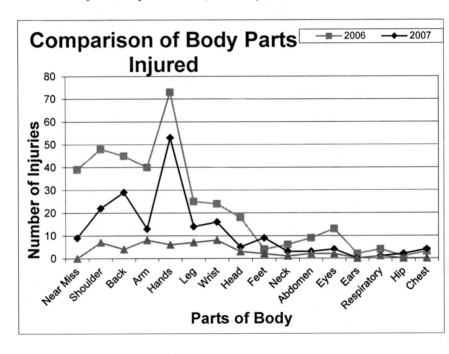

Illustrations 29-3 and 29-4: Both the pyramid chart and the graph break down the injuries from the previous year and the current year to date into categories including Near Miss, First Aid, Medical Aid, Lost Time under 5 days, Lost Time over 5 days, and Fatalities. These categories will assist in comparing the previous year to the current year to date. The higher the number of claims in the medical aid level and higher lost time areas will mean higher claim costs.

A best practice goal would be to have less injuries than near misses however ideally (but unrealistically) the company's goal would

Illustration 29-3: Pyramid of Incident breakdown

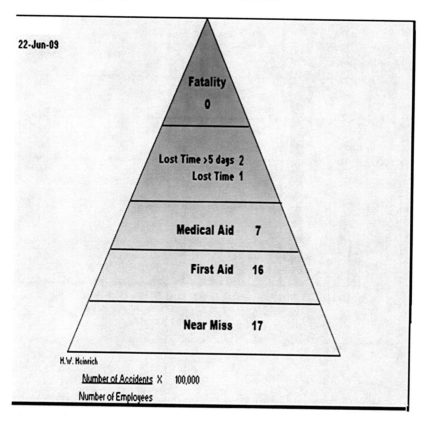

be to have no injuries and no near misses. Even though near misses do not result in injury, it will only be a matter of time until the near miss would become an injury if it is not remedied through a corrective action. Therefore, it is important to evaluate even the near misses for prevention activities in order to avoid future injuries.

Illustration 29-4: Incident Breakdown by severity of injury

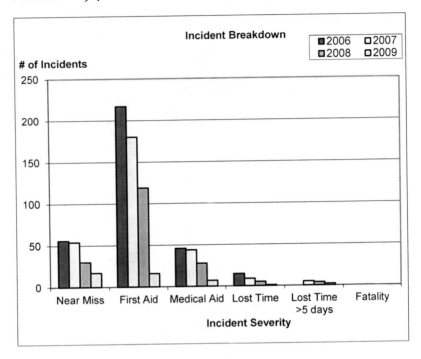

Illustrations 29-5 and 29-6: Top 5 issues in injury stats – by cause, by line, injury type, by shift, by time of injury, etc. Depending on the mandate of what to monitor, these graphs can illustrate trends that will be able to drive corrective action plans for prevention. These graphs can reveal at a glance where the problems are located and they can be ranked from highest to lowest. Incidents by cause will identify trends on the biggest cause of the incidents occurring in the facility. Once the top 5 causes have been identified, then the company can start brain storming to determine appropriate corrective actions. These corrective actions can include engineering controls, administrative controls or personal protection equipment.

Similarly, identifying the top 5 types of injuries as well as the top 5 cells or lines where the incidents are occurring in the facility will assist in identifying processes that require improvement in design or work instruction.

Illustration 29-5: Incidents by Cause

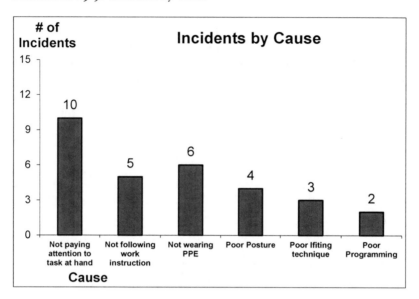

Illustration 29-6: Type of Injury

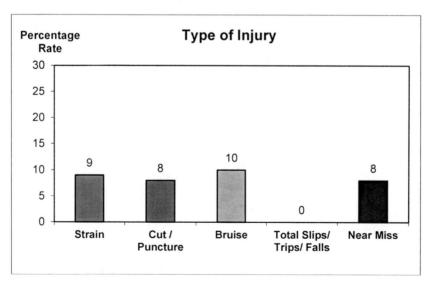

Illustrations 29-7, 29- 8 and 29-9: Graphs that include incident rates per month, per capita number by occupation, and per capita to overall population changes can monitor the performance of the health and safety program despite economic fluctuations. This can identify "seasonal" or time sensitive trends that may be related to temperature or seasonal elements that are not an intrinsic part of operational processes. For example, high rate of injuries in late July (after a shut-down) may signify that operators need to be reconditioned physically upon returning to work after an absence from work.

Illustration 29-7: Incidents by Month per Year

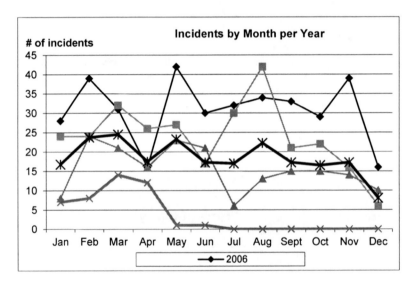

Per capita graphs can monitor the effectiveness of the health and safety program despite the number of people working. If spikes occur despite labour reductions, then the company must evaluate operator work load or the cultural effects of layoffs or right sizing to determine underlying problems causing the spike in incidents when the population decreases.

Incident rates per position will allow the company to evaluate risk level to position level to determine if additional procedures are required to mitigate the risks. If the incident rate is disproportional to the population rate than there may be some underlying risk that have not been properly evaluated.

Illustration 29-8: Incidents by Month per Year per Capita
(of # of Employees)

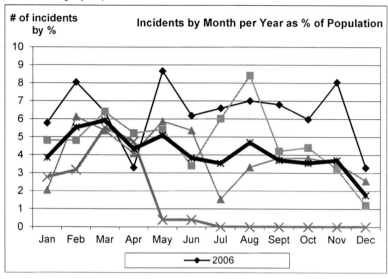

Illustration 29-9: Incident Rate per Position or Job

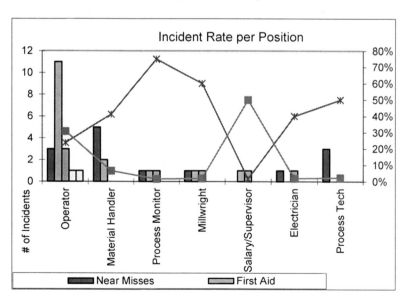

Psychological elements may contribute to the underlying risk of injuries. Evaluating the culture and current events that affect the workplace directly and indirectly can also assist in developing and implementing corrective actions to mitigate the risk of injuries.

Illustration 29-10 (below): demonstrates lost time day tracking. In this example it shows that the amount of the lost time days decreased in 2007. It is interesting to note that the number of lost time days intersect at the same point that the return to work program was implemented in 2007. The company could infer that the decrease in injuries was a direct impact of the implementation of an effective return to work program.

Illustration 29-10

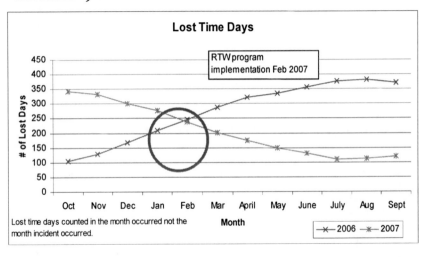

CHAPTER 30

EVALUATION/AUDIT PROCESS

In addition to injury statistics to initiate corrective actions and preventive activities, injury statistics can help determine the effectiveness of the return to work and modified work programs. By graphing out the amount of lost time injuries and lost time days over time, then charting when the programs take effect as well as any continuous improvements, a company can analyze the results of the programs and changes. For example, the graphs below illustrate how implementing a return to work and modified work programs significantly decrease the number of lost time days hence showing the effectiveness of the programs.

Illustration 30-1: Lost Time Days Tracking

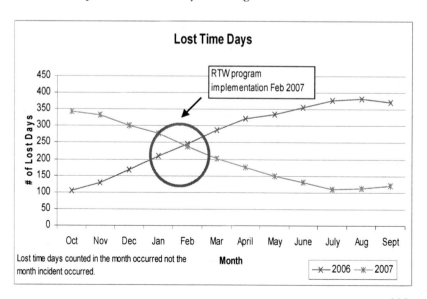

Illustration 30-2: Lost Time Days

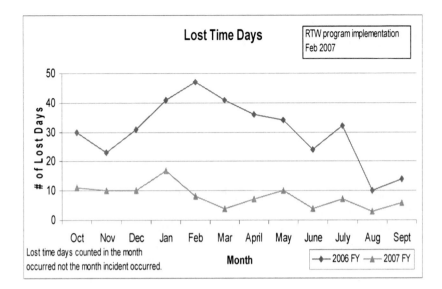

As the preceding graphs demonstrate, the effectiveness of the modified work and return to work programs from the point of implementation (top graph) as well as from the significant differential of lost time from one year to the next (bottom graph).

A well-developed return to work program and modified work program will not only reduce the amount of lost time days, the programs will also provide the due diligence to satisfy the company's obligation to re-employ under the WSIA, and the company's responsibilities under the duty to accommodate in the Human Rights Codes.

Once analysis of the statistics has been completed, reports should be prepared to express the findings and discuss the proposed corrective actions if required. Each system of statistical tracking will allow the company to assess the effectiveness of any related program or corrective action that has been implemented. Even if the stats do not reveal that the program or the corrective action implemented is not effective does not mean the program or the corrective action is completely unsuccessful.

A careful review of the program or corrective action in correlation to the statistics may reveal that a number of elements used in the compilation may be flawed. Each method in collecting or depicting the statistics should be evaluated to assess the method of compilation or measurement, the way the data is measured, or further improvements are required to make the corrective action more effective.

While statistics are essential in identifying gaps and trends, audits are a mechanism for management to examine their programs for the level of legal compliance and identify any gaps or breakdowns in any system including the health and safety program, the disability management program, etc. Audits can be performed by third party auditors, including the conformance auditors in the OHSAS 18001 program, inspectors like police or Ministry of Labour inspectors, internal auditors including managers or specifically trained workers to be auditors of a program, quality inspectors, etc.

Any audit performed should have a paper trail of the details of the location or program being audited, the auditor, the findings, and any corrective actions taken as a result of the audit findings. The audit findings will describe any gaps, systemic breakdowns, inefficiencies, non-conformances, non-compliances, or opportunities for continuous improvements specific to the program being audited. Generally, these findings will require responses in the form of corrective actions or changes in order to address these inefficiencies or potential problems.

SUMMARY

In summary, the foundation to a strong disability management program is an effective health and safety program. Both programs will focus on legal compliance. However, disability management programs focus on post injuries whereas health and safety programs focus on prevention of injuries. Even with the most effective health and safety program, injuries may still occur. Each company should develop and implement both a health and safety management program and a disability management program including documenting all policies, procedures, and training to provide evidence of the company's due diligence.

In order to demonstrate due diligence, the company has to develop and implement policies and procedures that address all the legal requirements in the geographical location of the workplace. There are several pieces of legislation that are relevant including but are not limited to: OHSA, WSIA, Human Rights, Canada Labour Code, Labour Relations Act, etc.

In addition to legal compliance, prevention techniques such as safety group participation, OHSAS 18001 certification, internal reporting process, the SCAR process and other techniques will allow the company to develop and implement many elements of a strong health and safety prevention program as well as address prevention within the disability management program.

Evaluating each element of both the health and safety program and the disability management program will allow the company to determine the effectiveness of each program. Monitoring statistics like the frequency and severity of injuries, location of injuries, time of injuries, etc., the company will be able to pinpoint the problems. Analysis of these statistics will allow the company to perform root cause analysis, develop and implement corrective actions, and document the company's continuous improvements activities. All of these activities will contribute to cost savings and cost avoidance as well as reduce the number and severity of injuries.

In addition to statistics, the company should develop a mechanism that will assist them in auditing their policies, practices, and procedures in order to ensure legal compliance as well as effectiveness of the system. Audits can uncover gaps in the system or systemic breakdown which require the attention of the company to fix or implement continuous improvements. Audits can assist the employer in providing proof of due diligence of the systems the company uses to protect the worker.

Key Terms:

Due Diligence
OHSAS 18001
Prevention Techniques
SCAR Process

Internal Reporting Process
Prevention
Safety Group
Strategy

Questions:

1. Compare and contrast the health and safety program with the disability management program.
2. Discuss the term and significance of prevention.
3. List and explain the significance of 10 relevant pieces of legislation to prevention.
4. Define due diligence and discuss its role in both programs.
5. List and discuss 5 prevention techniques that would assist the company in developing an effective health and safety program.
6. Describe the importance of the evaluation process to the disability and health and safety programs.
7. Discuss the methods of measuring effectiveness.

Understanding Costs

Objectives:

After reviewing this section, the reader should be able to:

1. Discuss the importance of monitoring costs
2. develop a mechanism for tracking costs
3. Understand premiums from the insurance carriers
4. Explain accident cost statements of all carriers
5. Outline the dynamics of incentive programs both legally and strategically
6. Develop and implement non-occupational incentive programs – wellness programs, health care benefits, EAP, cessation program, etc.
7. Understand occupational incentive programs – EHS, WSIB – NEER, MAP, CAD7
8. Explain and apply penalties, rebates, surcharges

CHAPTER 31

MONITORING COSTS

All claims cost the company money both directly and indirectly. Costs are not limited to the workers' compensation claims. Non-occupational claims costs will have similar direct and indirect costs to any company. Under the Human Rights Codes, the outcomes of the occupational and non-occupational injuries must be considered in similar fashion. Therefore it is important to treat non-occupational and occupational lost time claims the same in the disability management program activities.

The indirect costs of claims are comprised of lost productivity, replacement costs, retraining costs, etc. Direct costs of the workers compensation claims include the costs of the claim, health care, medical tests, medications, therapy, wage replacement for any lost time, non-economic loss (NEL) award, retirement pension, labour market retraining (LMR), premiums, etc.

Direct costs of non-occupational claims will depend on the benefits structure of the company. If the company has short term and long term benefits available for their workers, then the costs will include premiums and premium adjustments. If the company does not have short term and long term benefits available then the direct costs will include medical documentation to facilitate return to work activities. Regardless of the origin of the injury, one direct cost that accumulates very quickly is wage replacement for lost time.

Lost time is a very expensive and most common cause of high claim costs. It is also one of the costs that can be mitigated or controlled through a strong return to work program. As a result, an essential strategic company objective becomes to reduce costs by eliminating or controlling the amount of claims especially lost time claims. Lost time can be avoided through effective health and safety programs or at least mitigated with functional return to work and work hardening programs.

Illustrations 31-1 and 31-2 (below): the WSIB Cost Tracking. By tracking the claim costs from year to year, a company can detect trends that may be seasonal or linked to a specific event in a year like an economic downturn, catastrophic event in the community, etc.

Illustration 31-1: THE WSIB Claim Costs Comparison

WSIB Claim Costs Comparison

			Costs
			$1,000,000
			$800,000
			$600,000
			$400,000
			$200,000
2007	2008	2009	$0

Claim Year

▭ Actual Costs ▬ NEER Costs ▲ Capped Costs ━ Breakeven line

Illustration 31-2: THE WSIB Overall Costs Comparison

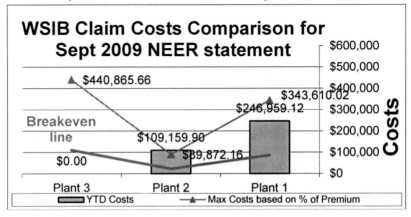

WSIB Claim Costs Comparison for Sept 2009 NEER statement

▲ $440,865.66

Breakeven line

$109,159.90

$0.00   ✕ $89,872.16

$246,959.12

$343,610.02

$600,000
$500,000
$400,000
$300,000
$200,000
$100,000
$0

Costs

Plant 3	Plant 2	Plant 1

▭ YTD Costs ▲ Max Costs based on % of Premium

Illustration 31-3 (below) illustrates the amount of additional parts that must be produced in sales and in production in order to cover the cost of claims. The concept of this graph is to help everyone in the company to understand that the burden of claim costs is on everyone in the company. Workers start to understand that if their co-worker is injured, each worker has to work a little harder to make up for the lost productivity. This supports the company strategy that health and safety is everyone's responsibility and commitment not only for themselves but also for each other. The message this graph provides to every worker at every level in the company clarifies the impact that injuries have on all areas of business.

Illustration 31-3: Cost per parts

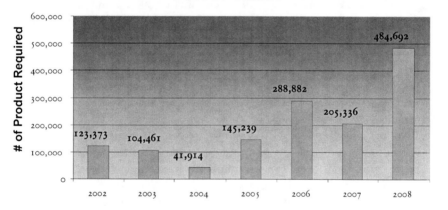

of Parts in Additional Production Required to Cover Cost of Claims

Premiums

Premiums for the workers compensation insurance program in Ontario are determined by actuarialists. These actuarialists use frequency and severity of the claims submitted by all the employers in the same rate group to determine the premiums per rate group. By grouping like employers into the same rates groups, the risk of injury should be similar due to the similar activities of the businesses. Therefore the same premium should apply to each employer within the same rate group. The premiums of each rate group are reviewed annually against the performance of the members within the group based on frequency and severity of the claims of each member of the group.

The premium of the rate group is directly proportional to the rate group's frequency and severity rates. If the rate group has a high number of frequency and severity, then the rate group will have a higher premium rate. Adversely, if the rate group has a low number of frequency and severity, then the rate group will have a lower premium rate. Premiums are paid monthly. The premium for the rate group is based on a rate per $100 of payroll. Please see the premium rate chart on the WSIB website.

For those employers who are not independent operators, they are expected to pay insurance premiums based on the premium rate for their rate group. Each employer upon registration with the WSIB is assigned a rate group according to the nature of the business. Different rate groups have different premium rates according to the performance of all the companies in that rate group.

The WSIB website posts the premiums for all the rate groups on their website for each year. Please refer to www.WSIB.on.ca under the section for employers under the section for premiums. The employer will need to know the rate group the WSIB has assigned to the business in order to retrieve the appropriate premium for that business. Illustration 31-4 is a sample of the 2008 premiums for a small portion of rate groups only to show an example of the premium chart.

The chart will also allow the employer to compare their rate group's premium with the premiums of other rate groups. It is also a best practice to review the definition of other rate groups similar to the company's business operations to ensure that the WSIB has the company classified in the most appropriate rate group especially if the nature of the business operation has changed.

To change the company's rate group, the company must submit the request to the WSIB in writing as well as complete a questionnaire detailing the business operations and the reasons for the change. The reasons have to be based on fact and related to the nature of the operation of the business. The WSIB will then determine if the reasons are valid and decide on the either granting the request to change the rate group or deny the request to change the rate group. The WSIB may elect to audit the business before a decision is made in order to clarify any information submitted or answer any questions still outstanding to assist them in making the most appropriate decision in the matter.

Illustration 31-4: The WSIB Premium Table Rates for 2008

2008 Premium Rates Table Sample

Rate Group	Description	2008 Premium Rate ($)	2007 Premium Rate ($)	Percent Change
30	Logging	10.99	10.81	1.70%
33	Mill products and forestry services	7.53	7.77	-3.10%
36	Veneers, plywood and wood preservation	4.04	4.15	-2.70%
39	Pulp, newsprint and specialty papers	2.3	2.22	3.60%
41	Corrugated boxes	2.89	2.89	0.00%
110	Gold mines	7.9	8.27	-4.50%
113	Nickel mines	5.08	5.31	-4.30%
119	Other mines	6.14	6.4	-4.10%
134	Aggregates	5.98	6.36	-6.00%
159	Livestock farms	6.78	7.1	-4.50%
167	Field crop, fruit and vegetable farms	2.72	2.72	0.00%

Similar to the workers' compensation insurance program, premiums for private sector wage compensation insurance programs such as short term disability or long term disability benefits are calculated based on usage and level of risk. For those people or groups that have a higher risk of injury will be subject to much higher premiums then perhaps a program for persons that do not partake in such high risk activity.

In addition to the risk level, the frequency of claims, the age of the claims, and the costs of the claims are considered in determining the premium of short and long term disability insurance programs. The change in premium is directly proportional to the change in frequency, length and age of claims. The higher frequency, the longer claims, and the older the people covered under the program will increase the premium rate. While lowering any one of these areas through effective healthy choices and low risk decisions will lower the premiums for coverage.

Companies should review the premiums paid for each program just to ensure that the premium is appropriate for the coverage required and to reflect the risk. Monitoring these types of costs will ensure the company is paying the most appropriate premiums.

Accident Cost Statements – All Carriers

In addition to sending companies invoices for premiums, most insurance program carriers for wage replacement will send the subscriber a statement of costs. These costs reflect the costs that are reimbursed through the program. The costs could include medical care, wage replacement, etc.

These statements would support the renewal fees for the program based on frequency of use (the number of claims) and the amount of benefits paid. For workers compensation, short term and long term disability benefits, the subscriber should receive statements from the carrier to outline costs of claims. Statements may be sent annually or as frequently as monthly. These statements are a tool the company can use to monitor costs of claims and project future costs.

It is quite common for the short term and long term benefits carriers to only send statements annually and only show grand totals of all costs rather than costs breakdown per claim. In Ontario, the workers compensation program, administered by the WSIB, issues statements monthly. The accident costs statement breaks down the costs by claim for each company. Illustration 31-5 is an example of an accident cost statement issued by the WSIB monthly.

As previously mentioned, every company in Ontario that participates in the workers compensation program receives an accident cost statement every month. The statement breaks down all the costs reimbursed by the WSIB per claim. This can assist the company to monitor the overall costs in the program, project future costs for the program allowing more accurate budgeting and manage the claims individually to reduce claim costs.

The accident cost statement includes all the costs for each claim registered to that company paid out in that month only. The company will have to develop and implement a tracking system in order to monitor all the claims continuously regardless if costs were incurred in any particular month. The tracking system should allow

Illustration 31-5: Accident Cost Statement

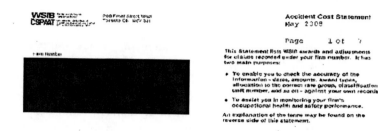

the company the ability to look at all the claims in each year and be able to determine the current status of the overall costs as well as allow the company to project costs based on understanding the claims, the costs of the claims, the system of claim expenditures and cost evaluation from the carrier, the behaviour and nature of the injury or claim to forecast the costs at different time periods in the progression of the claim, etc.

The WSIB system for evaluating a company's performance in managing claims and claims costs involves more than just the monthly accident cost statement depending on the company, the nature of the business, and the incentive program in which the company participates. Forecasting future costs will require more than the information from the monthly accident costs statements. The calculation of surcharges or rebates depends on the incentive program in which the company may participate.

It is important to review each statement. There are errors that can be made by the benefits carrier. For example, a claimant may be assigned to the wrong company firm or account number or costs are not discounted properly. Each claimant should be reviewed to ensure that those listed on the statement are actually employees of the company. If this has happened, the company will have to request in writing for the WSIB to change the claimant's claim to the appropriate company firm or account number as well as request that the amount be credited to the company's account.

In addition, the company should monitor the costs of each of the claims. By monitoring the activity of a claim and understanding the progression and the nature of the injury and recovery, the company should be able to identify the all costs expenditures incurred on each claim. If there are any unidentifiable spikes in costs or unusual costs incurred in any claim, the company should contact the claims adjudicator to understand the source of the costs. Sometimes costs are assigned to a claim number in error and the company will have to request in writing the WSIB to credit the claim for the error.

Administrative errors could cost the company large amounts of costs inadvertently. It is important for the company to monitor cost statements in order to identify these mistakes and take actions to correct these errors before the errors have negative financial impacts on the company's bottom line. Best practices in the disability management requires a program to monitor and scrutinize all claim costs, analyzing the causes off all the costs, as well as develop and implement actions or programs to reduce the costs such as return to work plans to manage lost time, assistance in medical management to insure early medical intervention to avoid long term damage, etc.

CHAPTER 32

PREVENTION AND MITIGATING COSTS FOR NON-OCCUPATIONAL INJURY INCENTIVE PROGRAMS

As reviewed previously, non-occupational injuries are those injuries that occur outside the workplace and not in the course of employment. Injuries can be prevented. Employers can develop and implement plans to prevent injuries in the workplace. However, outside the workplace or not in the course of employment, the employer has little authority in prevention activities. Despite having little authority, the employer can still implement programs to assist people in preventing injuries outside the workplace and not in the course of employment.

Similar to the workers compensation program, there are measures that a company can take to prevent or limit the severity of non-occupational injuries. At the very least, knowledge is power and the more information a person has on making healthy choices and preventing injuries, the more knowledgeable decisions a person can make regardless where the person is or what the person is doing.

With information and knowledge, people can make better decisions and healthier choices. The employer can provide information and other programs that would assist the workers in learning or acquiring the knowledge required. For example, such programs as healthy benefits, extended health benefits, EAP, wellness programs, cessation programs, nutritional awareness, exercising programs, substance abuse programs, promote medical regular examinations and early medical intervention, etc. These programs will offer people knowledge, training, awareness, and opportunity to access services and information that will provide the foundation of good health.

Good mental, physical and emotional health is a few of the best prevention programs available to any person at work and outside of work.

Health Care Benefits
Most employers offer a health care benefit package to their employees. The most common benefits packages include a combination of coverages for prescriptions, dental, vision, and extended health care. All these benefits will provide people with financial assistance in medical requirements should as the costs of medical appointments, therapies, good dental hygiene, medications, annual medical evaluations, vision correction, etc. However, these benefits programs will not cover the lost time from work for any appointment. All these services and benefits will assist the person in improving health and maintaining good health.

While prescriptions, dental and vision are fairly obvious benefits, extended health care benefits may not be as well known. Depending on the health care benefits package the employer subscribes to, extended health care benefits can cover a variety of medical expenses from both scientific and holistic paths to support the good health of the person.

The most common extended health care benefits packages can include physiotherapy, chiropractic, massage therapy, naturopathy, etc. These benefits can contribute to a person's good health through mostly reaction to problems. However, benefits like massage therapy, dental, regular annual medical physical examinations, etc. can provide preventive activities or, at the very least, early detection and early medical intervention techniques to decrease the severity of the illness.

Most workers are not aware of the extent of the benefits coverage available. As a result, workers do not utilize these benefits to the full potential. A common perception is that the benefits are only for a time when a person is already sick. In fact, these benefits can be instrumental in providing prevention of illness and maintenance of good health before the person even becomes ill. For instance, good dental hygiene practices can provide early detection of potential health risks that could lead to heart disease or cancer.

Another example is that the extended health care benefits could assist the person in reducing the amount of medication the person requires for managing a medical condition. Some of the extended health care benefits cover holistic ways to good health, pain management, and prevention to further injury.

To assist workers in optimizing usage of the benefits, employers can promote awareness of the coverage available to them. In the promotion and awareness of benefits, the employer can provide details of all the coverages, encourage usage as well as explain how accessing these benefits can result in the maintenance of good health, prevent disease and illness, or at the very least, provide early detection and early medical intervention methods.

Wellness Programs

In addition to providing a comprehensive health benefits package for employees, employers can develop a program to provide information, promote good health and encourage healthy choices. These programs can include a wide variety of advantages like posting information on a community bulletin board, providing discounted external fitness services, providing wellness services in house like stretching programs, flu clinics, yoga, tai chi, massage therapy, exercise rooms, etc. Employers can also review the wellness value of arranging discounts for external health and wellness services such as gym memberships, sponsored stretching programs, martial arts programs, nutrition counselling, etc.

Wellness programs can include stretching programs both at the work place and outside the workplace to better condition working muscles. Stretching programs can range from light stretches to stretches for specific body parts to increased amount of stretches to stretches for a variety of body parts. Stretching will prepare the muscles for work or any activity. The preparation will reduce the risk of injury while performing a task since the muscles will be conditioned to support the body during the motions of the task(s).

Another option to include in a wellness program is for an employer to ensure that there are healthy nutritional choices in the food vending machines at work. Snack foods and sodas can be sources of high levels of fat, sugar, artificial stimulants, caffeine and empty carbohydrates which can contribute to illness and disease. Healthy nutritional choices in the vending machines like raisins, whole grain snacks, water, vitamin drinks, fruit snacks etc. can promote healthier food with reduced amounts of sugars, caffeine, artificial sweeteners, preservatives, empty carbohydrates and fat.

Providing an exercise room at the workplace for workers to work out would be convenient and may entice more workers to exercise. If an employer considers providing exercise rooms in the workplace, the employer should also consider their legal liability in providing or sponsoring such a service. The employer should consult with a lawyer on due diligence and legal liability of providing such a service. The employ should discuss in detail the use and content of liability disclaimers with lawyers before such a service is offered.

Should an employer proceed with providing an exercise room after careful review and in-depth discussions with lawyers, there are several things to consider from types of equipment to make available to type of services to offer including non-violent or non-evasive programs like yoga, tai chi, meditation, fitness trainers, etc. Fitness experts should be consulted to secure the most appropriate equipment for the objectives of the service.

Information is a valuable source of wellness that all people of all cultures and body types can choose to use at any time. Communication can be instrumental in promoting information. Community bulletin boards, TVs, communication meetings, meeting minutes, newsletters, posters, messages on paycheques, letters to employees, news releases, memos, etc. are excellent and cost effective methods of providing information to a large group of people at one time. The information provided must not violate any legislation. Understanding the company's diverse workforce is critical to not offend or inadvertently violate any person's legal rights.

Public Health Units or Community Services can provide any company with volumes of information on health and wellness for free or at minimal costs. These external resources can also assist in delivering the services for free or at discounted rates such as nutritional seminars to teach the workers about important food groups and their appropriate portions, flu shot clinics, etc.

Employee Assistance Program (EAP)

In addition to health care benefits and wellness programs, other programs such as an employee assistance program (EAP) can include services from registered professionals dedicated to the health and well-being of people. These services would pay partial costs of the services for naturopaths, dieticians, legal counsel, psychiatric counselling, financial counselling, etc. that is not covered under the employee benefits package. These services can assist workers to address personal issues that can negatively affect good health. These services can assist the worker(s) in learning and applying healthy choices to avoid physical, emotional, financial and mental health problems.

EAP programs can offer a wide range of services which are designed to assist a person through problems that may arise in life. Depending on the package the employer negotiates, the program can offer a large amount of services or a narrow scope of services. The most common packages will include legal services, counselling services designed to address anger management, family issues, divorce, substance dependency issues, bereavement, coping with stress, financial management and budgeting, credit counselling, etc.

The EAP is a group program offered to many employers in the same community. Since it is a group membership, the premium to participate in the program is cheaper than if the employer sought to provide this program independently. The benefit of this program to the workers is that the costs of these services are deeply discounted to the individual user compared to the cost if the individual was to seek these services on their own.

In Ontario, these services are confidential in nature. The worker can use the program and the employer would not be entitled to know who used which service and how much money was spent for each worker. The employer will receive a statement indicating the overall costs and usage of the plan as well as a breakdown of the services used in the form of percentages to maintain confidentiality. The company can monitor the usage and costs of the plan.

Similar to the health benefits, workers are not fully aware of the existence of this type of plan nor are they aware of the benefits of this type of plan. Employers who participate in this program should promote awareness of the benefits available under this program to all the workers. In promoting the services of this plan, the employer promotes good mental, physical, financial and emotional health or at the very least, the access to services that will assist any person in their pursuit for good health. Good health in turn will support a happier and healthier worker. Healthy workers are more productive, experience less injury, and experience less absences.

Cessation Programs

Cessation programs are programs that assist the participant to quit smoking. Some health care benefit packages reimburse the participant for prescription medications to assist in their attempts to quit smoking like the patch, Nicorette, etc. For those health care benefit packages that do not reimburse for smoking cessation products, the cessation program would cover such costs.

In addition to prescription medications, cessation programs can also address the psychological and emotional components of the addiction to nicotine. Addressing these issues increases the chances for success in remaining smoke free for prolonged periods of time.

Substance Abuse Programs

Depending on the package, some cessation programs may also address other addictions. To address these other addictions more appropriately, a person should seek medical intervention to determine the most appropriate medical treatment plan for each individual according to their needs.

There are many substance abuse programs available to the general public depending on the community. Most communities will have rehabilitation centres that offer a variety of treatment plans to assist an individual in need from an outpatient weekly meetings basis to long term commitment plans.

While some very comprehensive benefit plans may include coverage for this service, the majority of plans do not offer this coverage. Even if the health care benefits package does not cover this program, the employer can model a program specific to the needs of the workers. The employer can recognize the benefits to assisting the worker in obtaining help for such an illness both morally and in productivity. Those workers granted leaves of absence to seek treatment will become more productive workers when they return clean and sober.

The employer's program can range from granting the leave of absence without punishment to granting paid leave for the absence to fully funding the leave and the course of treatment. Short term disability programs can assist the employer in funding the wage loss for the absence. The worker would still have to provide medical documentation according to the requirements of the policy guidelines to be eligible for the short term disability benefits. Those who require the benefits of the substance abuse program should not have many problems with getting the medical documentation completed by their treating medical profession or by the treatment centre's medical professional.

Most short term disability programs will cover the wages lost for the absence to seek treatment. Most health care benefits packages will not cover the expense of the treatment itself especially those treatments that require commitment. Most workers cannot afford the cost of this treatment either. Therefore, if the employer mandates the worker to seek treatment because the worker has attendance or quality problems due to this illness, then the employer should consider assisting the worker by partially or fully funding the treatment. Even if the worker seeks this treatment on their own before they are being considered or reviewed for discipline, the employer may benefit intrinsically, morally, socially and in productivity to assist the worker in funding the treatment.

Even if the company funds the worker's pursuit of a clean and sober lifestyle, it does not mean the first attempt or any other attempt will be successful for the duration of the worker's career with the employer. The employer must carefully balance the cost of funding, the frequency of funding, and monitor the success of the treatment in order to determine how many times the employer will fund this type of treatment especially for the same worker.

While the first attempt may not be successful for a prolonged period of time, the worker may find more long term success in the second or third course of treatment. However, with each attempt, success decreases significantly. At some point, the employer will have to determine in each case when to draw the line in funding this course of action. Each case must be considered on its own merit and legal counsel may assist the employer.

CHAPTER 33

MITIGATING COSTS FOR OCCUPATIONAL INJURY INCENTIVE PROGRAMS

While registered to participate in the workers compensation program in Ontario, employers can participate in one of the incentive programs. Some programs are voluntary and some are not voluntary. All incentive programs consider the performance rating of the company participating in the program. The performance rating of the company has a direct impact on assessments for premiums, rebates and surcharges. Some of the more common programs are MAP, CAD7, and NEER.

MAP

MAP is a program for small businesses in Ontario. To be eligible for this program, the company has to pay the WSIB premiums up to $25,000 per year. The closer the company is to $25,000 in premiums, the company can consider moving to the NEER or CAD7 programs depending on the nature of the business. The company would consider the changing incentive programs if the new program has more advantages for the company.

Essentially, MAP considers the company's performance in health and safety through their reported injuries to determine the company's premiums. The premiums are based on payroll but if the company has a good health and safety performance rating, then the company can have their premiums reduced. Conversely, if the company has a poor health and safety performance record, their premiums could be increased.

In considering the health and safety performance of a company, the WSIB will look at the number of injuries reported (frequency) and the severity of the injuries reported of a three (3) year review period prior to the assessment year. For example, for the year 2008 premium calculations, the WSIB will assess the number and severity of injuries in the review period of 2004, 2005 and 2006. Only claims that have claim costs higher than $500 will affect the company's rating.

A company's premium may increase if there are a sufficient number of claims or the severity of the claims is high. However, decreases in premiums will not be considered until the company has been in continuous operation for at least three (3) years. The first assessment will occur at thee (3) years.

All increases or decreases will be a percentage of the company's basic premium rate. There is a MAP cost tool and worksheet on the WSIB website that will be of assistance if a company would like to try to project any increases or decreases in their premium. For more information please visit the WSIB website at www.WSIB.on.ca, click on the Prevention tab then click on the Programs tab. Under the Programs tab, scroll down to and click on the MAP section.

CAD7

Unlike MAP, CAD 7 applies to companies in the Construction sector only. CAD7 includes companies who have average annual WSIB premiums of more than $25,000. Another difference in this program is that the premiums remain proportional according to the company's payroll. The WSIB considers the health and safety record of the company for rebates or surcharges separate from the payment of premiums.

Essentially, the company will pay the respective premiums according to their payroll. Once a year, the WSIB will assess the health and safety performance record of the company in the review period to determine any rebate or a surcharge to charge the employer. The company may receive a rebate if the company's health and safety performance record is good. However, if the company's health and safety performance record is poor, the company may receive a surcharge.

One of the biggest differences between MAP and the CAD7 is the CAD7 is not as straightforward in the calculations for rebates and surcharges. CAD7 is currently under review for program changes. Currently, the program compares the number and cost of claims of a company to the average of the company's rate group in the Construction sector.

According to the WSIB website, if the company's frequency and claims costs are lower than would be expected for a company of certain type and size. As a result, the company will receive a rebate. However if the company's frequency and claims costs are higher, then the company will likely receive a surcharge. The size of the company is directly proportional to the adjustment to the premium.

The review period of the assessment considers claims up to five (5) years old. The claim costs are considered in the year the costs occur rather than in the claim year. Claims that involve long term illnesses, such as long term hearing loss and cancers which are diagnosed years and years after the exposure, are not considered in this assessment. Only the costs incurred of the previous two (2) years (providing the claim age is less than 5 years).

For more information please visit the WSIB website at www.WSIB.on.ca, click on the Prevention tab then click on the Programs tab. Under the Programs tab, scroll down to and click on the CAD7 section.

NEER

The New Experimental Experience Rating Program, known as NEER is another incentive program. Similar to the CAD7 program, NEER is an incentive program for company's whose WSIB premiums are greater than $25,000 per year. However, NEER is for companies in sectors other than the Construction sector. Companies are evaluated against other companies in the same rate group comprising the industry standard in order to compare similar risk exposure.

Additionally, companies participating in either NEER or CAD7 are subject to either rebates or surcharges based on the frequency and severity of the claims of similarly sized companies. Accordingly, companies with a good health and safety performance record may be assessed with a rebate. On the contrary, those companies with a poor health and safety performance record may be assessed with a surcharge.

A company, depending on size and type, with claim costs lower than expected, may receive a rebate. Consequently, a company, depending on size and type, with claim costs higher than expected, may receive a surcharge. Similar to CAD7, long term illnesses such as cancers and hearing loss are not included in the assessment.

The key differences between CAD7 and NEER are the review periods. NEER has a review period of three (3) years previous to the assessment year. Another difference is that the claims costs in NEER are assigned to the year of the accident date rather than in the year the costs were incurred.

Another critical difference between NEER and all other incentive programs are the maximum limits imposed on individual claims as well as on the company as an overall total. NEER is assessed considering the company claims costs as a whole total based on individual totals.

There is a NEER cost tool and worksheet called the NEER Cost Calculator on the WSIB website that will be of assistance if a company would like to try to project any rebates and surcharges.

Currently the NEER program is under review by the WSIB for program changes. For more information please visit the WSIB website at www.wsib.on.ca, click on the Prevention tab then click on the Programs tab. Under the Programs tab, scroll down to and click on the NEER section. This section also has a NEER User Guide to help understand the details of the incentive program.

Penalties, Rebates, Surcharges

Most carriers of wage replacement programs will review the performance of each company annually. The company's performance is based on the frequency of claims and the amount of benefits paid out in total (severity). A high frequency of use and or a high amount of benefits paid will produce increases in premiums for the next year or the carrier may charge penalties or fines. The carrier will compare the company's performance in frequency and severity is rated against the cumulative performance of other companies in the same industry or community or risk level.

In Ontario, the workers compensation program under the WSIB has a complex system of calculations for each company depending on the incentive program in which the company participates. In the NEER program, the premium is based on the performance of the industry rate group. However, the company's performance is individually assessed as well for rebates or surcharges.

Depending on the incentive program, the company could be charged with additional surcharges if the total of their claim costs for any given year exceeds the expected costs for that respective year.

The company could also receive a rebate if the total of their claim costs for any given year is below the expected for that respective year.

The calculations of such surcharges or rebates are determined by the WSIB financial analysts. The Illustration below shows an example of a NEER statement to show the assessment of a surcharge.

Illustration 33-1: NEER Statement

200 Front St. West
Toronto ON M5V 3J1

NEER Firm Summary Statement

Page No.   1

company name

Address

Accident Year	Premium ($)	Expected Cost Factor (%)	Expected Costs ($)	NEER Costs ($)	Rating Factor (%)	Performance Index
2006	55,960.20	35.82	20,044.94	547.67	82.12	0.03
2005	109,018.44	38.47	41,939.39	316,717.24	82.85	7.55*
2004	111,411.03	38.37	42,748.41	13,229.26	83.60	0.31
2003	82,874.84	46.40	38,453.93	24,874.81	67.16	0.65

Refund/Surcharge Calculation			
Accident Year	Primary Adjustment ($)	Previous Adjustment ($)	Current NEER Adjustment ($)
2005	227,653.45	.00	227,653.45
2004	24,678.01CR	22,585.79CR	2,092.22CR
2003	9,119.74CR	3,802.76CR	5,316.98CR
TOTAL SURCHARGE			220,244.25

* SUBJECT TO MAXIMUM SURCHARGE

This is your firm's NEER Quarterly statement for September 30, 2006.

***** PLEASE NOTE IMPORTANT MESSAGE ON THE BACK OF THIS PAGE *****
RE REBATES AND SURCHARGES

Penalties can also arise out of poor performance such as increased written orders or fines from the Ministry of Labour. The WSIB flags and reports a company as a poor performer in health and safety to the MOL in Ontario. As a result, the MOL will increase the visits to the company. Increased visits from the MOL will increase the potential for written orders and or fines and penalties for non-compliance.

Furthermore, the company who has been flagged as a poor performer in health and safety may be ordered to undergo a work well audit. As previously discussed, a Workwell audit can prove to be very expensive for a company in terms of time, labour, penalties, etc.

SUMMARY

In summary, the workers compensation program in Ontario has incentive programs for employers. The chart below will summarize the incentive programs.

Chart 33-2: Incentive Programs Comparison Summary

Criteria	MAP	CAD₇	NEER
Premiums	<$25,000	>$25,000	>$25,000
Sector	any	Construction only	Any except Construction
Good Health and Safety Record	Premium decrease	Potential rebate	Potential rebate
Poor Health and Safety Record	Premium increase	Potential surcharge	Potential surcharge
Review Period	3 years previous to assessment year	2 years previous to assessment year	3 years previous to assessment year
Claims considered	3 years previous to assessment year	Under 5 years old	3 years previous to assessment year
Maximum claim limits	None	none	Depending on premiums
Maximum total costs limits	None	None	Depending on premiums

As previously discussed, premiums, penalties, and surcharges are all examples of the direct costs of the claims for injuries. When monitoring the costs of claims, the company should also consider the indirect costs of lost productivity, down time, manpower changes, increased training, etc. All these costs should be monitored by the company in order to understand the full financial impact of the workplace injuries for the company.

Furthermore, monitoring the costs of the worker compensation claims as well as the short term and long term claims, will also contribute to the full financial impact of the company. The next section will discuss the importance of all these costs in order to budget, project, and forecast costs for accurate accrual and setting reasonable targets and objectives to achieve.

Key Terms:

Accident Cost Statement	CAD7
Cessation	EAP
Health Care Benefits	Incentive Programs
MAP	NEER
Penalties	Premiums
Rebates	Substance Abuse Program
Surcharges	Wellness Programs

Questions:

1. Compare and contrast the incentive programs available through Ontario's workers compensation program (WSIA). Explain the differences of each program and use examples.
2. List and explain five (5) non-occupational injury incentive programs employers may use. Include the reason these programs are used and the significance of each program.
3. Discuss the reasons employers should monitor costs.
4. Explain penalties, rebates and surcharges and how they would impact strategic targets and objectives.

LINKING BUSINESS STRATEGIES WITH DISABILITY MANAGEMENT, PREVENTION PROGRAMS AND COST STRATEGIES

Objectives:

After reviewing this section, the reader should be able to understand and explain the following concepts:

1. Determine a method to set targets and objectives for effective disability management and occupational health and safety programs which are linked to corporate strategic goals
2. Discuss how the use of incentive programs can assist the employer in achieving targets and objectives
3. Explain how cost reductions and cost strategies are important to achieving targets and objectives
4. Describe how budgeting, projecting and forecasting costs can assist the employer in strategizing to achieve targets and objectives
5. Learn the importance of linking performance with targets and objectives with cost strategies

CHAPTER 34

DEFINING BUSINESS STRATEGIES

Setting Targets and Objectives for Disability Management and Prevention

To evaluate the performance of any system, management will review the outputs of the system or the results of the actions taken. Results are quantifiable, if they are measured in terms of numbers or percentages. Each program should evaluate their effectiveness through monitoring costs, injuries, and other outputs determined to be important by management. Management will use these outputs to identify the targets and objectives that will assist the company in striving for specific outcomes for continuous improvements within the programs. For example, the company may decide to reduce the number of lost time days as a strategic goal for the following year. The company would have to track the number of lost time days from the year previous and the current year. To see if the company achieved their objective, the company will have to company the number of lost days from the previous year to that of the current year.

Targets and objectives can be set for short term achievement or for long term realization. Best practices would indicate to have a combination of both short term and long term goals for the company. This will assist the company in evaluating their immediate performance as well as their performance for long range growth and improvement.

Generally, management will communicate to the rest of the company the position or changes that are required to happen for the coming year. This mandate will challenge each department in the company to set targets and objectives that will assist the department in reaching the corporate mandate. Once targets and objectives have been set for the year, the department will have to develop and implement strategies to achieve the goals.

Targets and objectives may be set by each individual. Each individual's goal(s) will assist the department to achieve the department goals which will in turn contribute to achieving the corporate goals. Therefore, the targets and objectives of the individual are tied to the corporate business strategies.

Setting targets is an effective method of evaluating performance of any program. The targets should be quantifiable, measurable and reasonable to achieve. Targets set for programs that are in an infancy phase, should reflect program building objectives. The targets should be reasonable to achieve within reasonable time frames. The goals should be within the skill and talent of the management team to complete. It is a common mistake to set goals that are lofty or unreasonable to achieve in the specified period of time. Unrealistic expectations may predispose the program for poor performance or lack of output.

As the company's programs are successful in achieving their targets and objectives, management can begin to set the goals to a higher level or standard to promote evolution and growth through continuous improvement. The targets and objectives of previous years become stepping stones for those goals of the future years. Therefore the success or disappointments of the performance in achieving the goals of previous years also become lessons learned for plans for the future years. Lessons learned can be valuable insight in developing and implementing the strategies for future goals and future growth in the evolution process.

If a program has no target nor objective to strive towards or no level of standard to measure against, the performance of the program cannot be measured. If the performance is not measured, then the company will not realize any continuous improvements. Without continuous improvements, the program will not evolve. Goals can be as "simple" as writing a commitment statement to as complicated as developing and implementing an entire program for legal compliance. The company must be sure not overreach their resources by setting targets that are not reasonable. Setting targets that are beyond the resources of the company will undermine the progress of the program.

The targets and objectives for the health and safety program and the disability management program may be intertwined since the programs have a mutual interdependence. For example, the target of reducing the number of lost time incidents for the health and safety program will assist in the target of reducing the number of lost time days for the disability management program. Even though each program may have unique strategies to achieve each of their targets, by achieving the goal in one of the programs, may assist in achieving the target in the other program. For this reason, a best practice is to align the objectives of both of the programs, health and safety with disability management.

In addition to aligning the goals of both programs, the targets should also be synchronized with the corporate goals. By aligning the objectives of the programs with the strategic corporate goals, the program becomes a partner in the strategic business plan. The partnership between the program objectives and the corporate goals lends credibility and weight to the program from all levels of management.

It is best practice to align objectives of the disability management program including decreasing benefits or claims costs, with corporate objectives such as decreasing overall costs to improve the company's positioning for profitability. One way to decrease claims costs is to decrease the number of lost time days. In addition to the decrease of costs, the advantages of decreasing the number of lost time days include:

- Decreasing costs in terms of premiums for the WSIB, STD, LTD as well as in terms of penalties and fines (surcharges) and optimize potential for any rebates available;
- Decreasing costs of lost wages replacement in terms of claims costs;
- Decreasing lost productivity of injured workers;
- Decreasing lost productivity of coworkers covering the regular duties of the injured worker;
- Decreasing the need for overtime to cover injured worker's lost productivity;
- Decreasing the costs of lost productivity as the following activities are not required:
  - retraining a replacement;

- costs of recruiting a replacement;
- improving morale;
- short shipments;
- poor quality of a newly hired replacement;
- workplace disruptions; etc.;
- decreasing the potential legal fees for:
  - counsel;
  - tribunals for the WSIB and Labour Relations grievances;
  - arbitrations; and,
  - mediations.

The advantages listed above illustrate how the reduction of the number of lost time days results in the reduction of costs and increase the company's positioning for profitability. Some strategies to reduce the number of lost time days include but are not limited to:

- Management's demonstrated commitment to the health and safety and the return to work programs;
- Compliance to health and safety legislation (OHSA) and worker's compensation legislation (WSIA);
- An effective and functioning health and safety program;
- An effective and functioning disability management program;
- A functioning return to work program;
- Prevention activities and methods;
- Continuous improvements commitment and mechanism to identify and address continuous improvements; and,
- A practicing health and safety culture which includes safety based behaviour.

Consequently, the effectiveness of each the health and safety program and the return to work program depend significantly on the commitment of the executive management. In fact, the health and safety and the return to work programs become important strategies for management to manage efficiently in order to increase their positioning for profitability on many different levels from employee satisfaction to customer satisfaction to legislative compliance. Leading by example will allow management to demonstrate their commitment to each program.

Monitoring claims is critical in file management and strategic planning for disability management. In addition to the initial paperwork of the claims and any documentation throughout the course of the recovery, accurate file management can clearly outline the history of the worker (and injuries), assist in claim costs projections, and, future planning of the recovery process.

History of the worker (and injuries) will support the company's request for amalgamation where appropriate or request cost relief through SIEF. By documenting all interactions throughout the course of recovery, the company has the proof required to support requests such as denial of lost time, denial of entitlement, cost relief and amalgamation. Tracking the lost time will assist in claim cost projections and planning the recovery process as well as strategic planning of future activities in disability management as a program.

Setting targets and objectives are just the first step in strategic planning. However, it is not enough to set the targets and objectives. The company has to develop and implement plans to achieve the goals over a specified period of time usually within a year. Some projects take longer than a year depending on the complexity and magnitude of the project. Regardless the project or the timing requirements, the company should plan to achieve the goals.

Where a goal is not achieved than the company should be completing a root cause analysis to determine the reasons the plan did not achieve the goal. Once the root cause analysis is completed, a lessons learned report should be developed to understand the reason(s) the goal was not achieved as well as how to revise the plan to achieve the goal or change the goal if the goal has become unrealistic. A log of the lessons learned will assist in developing more effective courses of actions presently and in the future.

In addition to root cause analysis, the activities developed and implemented to achieve the targets and objectives must be reviewed and evaluated at the end of the project or minimally annually for effectiveness. Some evaluation techniques include expected outputs realized, other outcomes realized that were not expected, the level the plan was successful, the costs incurred, the return on investments, etc. The tracking and monitoring of specific measurables will assist in the evaluation of activities and their effectiveness towards achieving a specific outcome like reducing lost time (severity) or reducing the number of injuries (frequency).

Using Incentive Programs to Achieve Targets and Objectives

Setting targets and objectives are an effective tool in not only creating efficient health and safety and disability management programs but encouraging continuous improvements of both programs as well. In order to evaluate each program, the company must monitor and track the outputs of the program. Part of best practices in either program includes:

- Statistics tracking;
- Trend analysis;
- Short term corrective actions;
- Long term preventative actions;
- Projections in claims costs vs. projections in health and safety program costs;
- Due diligence; and,
- Effective Cost of claims.

By tracking and monitoring these outputs, the company can understand which areas require the most attention for continuous improvements. It is these areas that should become the focus when setting the targets and objectives. The areas of poor performance or under performance should become priority when setting goals for continuous improvements. Obviously, the highest priority goals will address legal compliance and avoiding potential fatalities.

The workers compensation program in Ontario has incentive programs for participating employers to evaluate their performance in the program. The company can use these incentive programs to determine their targets and objectives for continuous improvements of their management programs as well as to reduce costs. Monitoring the costs of the incentive program and understanding calculation process of premiums, surcharges or rebates will allow the company to project future costs, manage current costs and budget appropriately. Furthermore, an understanding of the methods of the benefits carrier for determining poor performance, the company can set targets to reduce costs by developing and implementing actions to control the costs such as an early and safe return to work program or an effective prevention element to the health and safety program.

Illustrations 34-1 and 34-2: By tracking the claim costs from year to year, a company can detect trends that may be seasonal or linked to a specific event in a year like an economic downturn, catastrophic event in the community, etc. In determining the cause of the trends, the company can use the information to set the objectives for the following year. The objectives will become the mechanism for initiating corrective actions and ultimately reducing claims and claims costs.

Illustration 34-1

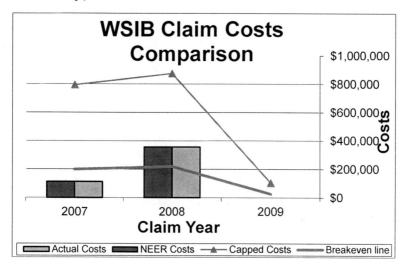

These graphical examples above and below demonstrate monitoring WSIB claim costs and NEER costs using the performance index. In comparing claim costs over a number of years, a company can evaluate claim costs against economic changes, process changes, and cultural changes to reveal trends identifying underlying problems or monitoring the effectiveness and efficiency of implemented corrective actions. A company can evaluate the claim performance using the performance index to monitor the company's performance against the health and safety performance against the industry standard performance index for the same industry rate group. This comparison allows the company to determine the performance of their health and safety program to the same of another company in the same rate group. If the company's performance index is higher than the industry standard, then the company should evaluate their programs and culture for root cause analysis of problems to be remedied.

Illustration 34-2

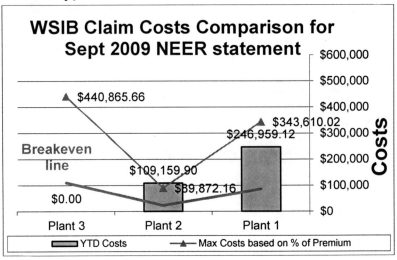

WSIB Claim Costs Comparison for Sept 2009 NEER statement

Legend: YTD Costs | Max Costs based on % of Premium

Illustration 34-3: Performance Index Comparison (NEER)

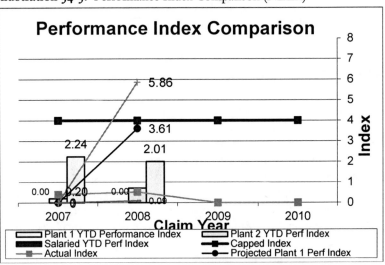

Performance Index Comparison

Legend: Plant 1 YTD Performance Index | Plant 2 YTD Perf Index | Salaried YTD Perf Index | Capped Index | Actual Index | Projected Plant 1 Perf Index

Each employer participating in the WSIB workers compensation program receives a monthly statement known as the accident cost statement. This statement details the costs for each claim which incurs costs in that month. For those employers in Ontario participating the WSIB incentive program known as NEER, in addition to the monthly cost statements costs can be monitored monthly, quarterly and annually through the NEER statements.

In addition to tracking and monitoring costs through metrics, using the monthly, quarterly and annual statements, employers can develop financial or mathematical spreadsheets that will allow them to predict the NEER annual assessment. The prediction of the NEER outcome can help management realize the financial impact of some difficult decisions regarding return to work, accommodation, accruing sufficient amounts of money for budgeting for potential NEER surcharge, expenditures, etc. Difficult decisions can include workstation redesign, creative thinking for developing new manufacturing or production methods, assimilating ergonomics in production methods, developing strategic prevention programs, adapting to legislative changes, return on investment, etc.

CHAPTER 35

FORECASTING/PROJECTING AND BUDGETING STRATEGIES

Cost Reductions

Cost reductions become a high priority goal of any company especially when facing difficult economic cycles. Regardless of tough economic times, efficient cost management of any company will contribute to the profitability of the company. Disability management can be instrumental in contributing to the bottom line by reducing costs through implementing programs that will reduce injuries both in frequency and severity as well as manage costs during recovery.

There are several options to reduce costs in effective disability management and health and safety programs. Such programs can include but are not limited to:

- Prevention methods to reduce both the number of injuries and the severity of injuries. In addition to legal compliance, these programs will include all procedures and policies to promote activities in prevention like forklift licensing, personal protective equipment, return to work, etc.
- Early and safe return to work (ESRTW) programs will help injured workers (regardless of occupational or non-occupational injuries) return to appropriate and suitable work within their restrictions in a more timely manner. This

program will reduce lost time and lost productivity costs.

- Training in awareness and safety behaviour will
reduce injuries in both the occupational and
non-occupational arenas.
- Ergonomic strategies into workstation designs
and work instructions will reduce the risk for
repetitive strain injuries. Implementing ergonomic FEMAs at the design phase instead of at
the user end will challenge engineers to engineer as much risk of strain injuries out of the
tasks as possible.

Some other methods to reduce costs that may be less popular
but still legal professionals may require the company to consider in
terms of ethical, moral, or cultural practices in the workplace. These
methods can include but are not limited to:

- According to the WSIA, Section 25(1), for occupationally related injuries, the company can
reduce or terminate the employee's medical
benefits (health care benefits such as prescription, vision, dental) after one year from the date
of injury should the worker go off work because of the injury. This can only happen if the
employer was making the premium payments
for the benefits at the time the injury occurred.
- For non-occupational injuries, the company can
consider reducing or terminating employee
health care benefits at different phases of absence of work. For example, the employer may
gradually reduce the benefits over time. The
employer may choose to reduce the employee's
medical benefits once the employee is absent
for work for a specific period of time such as
one year (or whatever time period the company
determines as appropriate at minimum of one
year). Some companies align this time period
with that of the long term disability eligibility
window.

- As previously discussed, best practices should align the treatment of occupational and non-occupational injuries. However, in practice, the company can treat these differently especially if the workplace is unionized. If the workplace is unionized, the collective agreement or negotiated benefits may differ between the two programs.

- Encourage employees to make their medical appointments outside of work to avoid lost time.

- If at any time beyond the time period of legal compliance, the employer considers terminating the employment status, the employer should consult an employment lawyer prior to proceeding.

- Early retirement options can be considered. However the employer again should consult with an employment lawyer prior to proceeding to ensure legal compliance.

There are several cost reduction methods that any company can consider to implement. The above methods discussed are only a few strategies and they are not interdependent. The list above is not all inclusive and each company will have to explore the option or options are that are correct for their business operations, work culture, etc.

SUMMARY

Setting targets and objectives are an important step towards growth, evolvement, and continuous improvements of any program. Tracking and monitoring the progress of the goals are important for evaluating the program for success. Monitoring the progress of the goals will allow the company to change the plans if the activities are not providing the expected outcomes. The goals and the outcomes of the strategies should be evaluated minimally annually to determine the effectiveness of the activities and the outcomes.

An objective for both the disability management program and the health and safety program of any company should include activities focused on mitigating the risk of injuries by combining corrective action activities with prevention activities as well as activities focused on assisting workers through recovery and safe return to work plans. Monitoring costs, lost time, program implementation activities, etc. will assist in evaluating the activities which are critical in determining the effectiveness of the plan, activities and outcomes.

An effective way to monitor claims would be to track those elements that tie to the strategic targets and objectives including injury types, injury causes, claim decisions, claim costs, cost savings or cost avoidance, corrective actions, etc. Part of some strategic planning, especially if the return to work program is not successful, includes the benefits carriers' decision making on long term claim eligibility, permanent impairment, and career retraining. These types of decisions will influence the company's planning on potential return to work and employment status. It is critical to consult with an employment lawyer before proceeding with any plan to change the person's core essential duties or employment status for any reason.

Key Terms:

Budgeting	Business Strategy
Cost Reduction	Cost Strategy
Forecasting	Goals
Lessons learned	Metrics
NEER	Objectives
Projecting	Root Cause Analysis
Strategic Planning	Targets

Questions:

1. Explain the correlation between setting targets and objectives of the health and safety program and the disability management program to corporate business strategies.
2. List and explain some targets for the disability management program.
3. Compare and contrast some business strategies as they relate to effective claims management.
4. Describe the correlation between prevention and each of the following:
   a. Targets and objectives
   b. Business strategies
   c. Cost management
5. Compare and contrast budgeting, forecasting, and projecting
6. Demonstrate the importance of metrics to business strategies.

SECTION IX

SUMMARY OF BEST PRACTICES

Several topics have been discussed related to injuries, recovery and return to work planning in this textbook. This section of the book will review and summarize the many best practices examined throughout this text book. These best practices can be incorporated into a company's health and safety and disability management programs promote continuous improvement. These best practices will assist the company in developing and implementing mechanisms to measure the effectiveness and efficiency of both programs as well as ensure legal compliance.

Recent trends of globalization will add demands to all management programs notwithstanding the health and safety and disability management programs. Although legislation varies in each geographical location of the world, many of these best practices are broadly designed to exceed the minimum standards of areas with the most demanding requirements such as Canada, the United States of America and most of Europe.

Any good sports coach will advise a team that the best defence is a good offence and vice versa. This is also true with health and safety and disability management programs. One of the ways to measure the effectiveness of the health and safety program's prevention strategies is to track the reduction of frequency of injuries as well as the severity of injuries.

Just as in sports, occasionally a goal can slip through the best defensive line, even the best health and safety programs will occasionally experience injuries. An effective disability management program is required just as a good offensive or defensive line. In sports, the offensive line and the defensive line are interdependent to succeed. Similarly, the health and safety program and the disability management program are mutually dependent.

Disability management is the program designed to manage injuries, recovery and return to work activities. Plans for managing the aftermath of incidents or reactions to developing prevention strategies is a best practice. A critical best practice is to align the treatment or programs to manage occupational and non-occupational injuries.

Aligning the programs will reduce any risk of non-compliance, discrimination or violations of human rights.

In addition to due diligence, the company has a legal responsibility to provide early and safe return to work as well as not discriminating against any workers with a disability. A best practice would dictate that all employers develop and implement an early and safe return to work program for all workers who are absent from work due to a disability, regardless of the origin of the disability (occupational or non-occupational). The return to work plan will mitigate the cost of claims as well as ensure legal compliance to re-employ or continue to employ an injured worker with restrictions.

A best practice in ensuring that both occupational and non-occupational programs are aligned, the company can incorporate each of the benefits carrier's forms and build the company form requirements and procedures around the legal requirements. Furthermore, the company will need to develop and implement forms, policies and procedures that align the objectives with the business strategies of the company. For example, the company can develop a leave report form for the workers to request time off for any type of leave from work with options for occupational or non-occupational appointments, leaves, etc.

Regardless of program alignment, the company can reduce confusion, costs, and promote continuous improvements by implementing a comprehensive incident reporting process. A comprehensive reporting process is a means for the injured worker to report a work related or a non-occupational injury to the employer.

Best practice equates a comprehensive incident report as one effective tool in identifying root causes of incidents and initiating the development and implementing of corrective or preventive actions. Part of the prevention activities the employer can develop and implement is an effective return to work program. This program will not only mitigate further injury during the recovery process, it will provide evidence of due diligence for legal compliance to the various pieces of legislation including WSIA, OHSA, and other return to work legislation.

The worker and the supervisor should be trained to complete an incident report (written) each time the worker reports any event that deviates from the safe operation of a business. In turn, the completed report initiates the corrective and preventive action process as well as initiates any paperwork required for the workers compensation benefits carrier (if required). This comprehensive practice in the incident report process will satisfy the employer's due diligence for their legal obligations.

There are several parties involved in the reporting and recovery process. Each party is obligated to comply with a set of roles and responsibilities throughout the processes. Some of these roles and responsibilities are legal obligations, some are morale obligations, yet others are best practices.

Most companies in Ontario understand and perform their obligations in reporting occupational injuries to the WSIB. If the company has a short term or long term disability program as part of their benefits program for employees, the company will also administer the paperwork accordingly for non-occupational injuries. However, effective disability management does not stop once the initial claim paperwork has been filed. There are several key strategic steps that follow the initial application for benefits that are critical in mitigating further costs, lost time, morale, lost productivity, etc. Some of these steps include but are not limited to:

- monitoring status of claim;
- monitoring worker history;
- monitoring status of restrictions;
- monitoring employee emotional and psychological status;
- monitoring recovery;
- monitoring return to work progress;
- monitoring return to work plan;
- monitoring decisions;
- monitoring costs of claims;
- projecting future costs of claims and budgeting;
- monitoring the premiums;
- monitoring lost time away from work;
- monitoring days away from pre-injury or regular duties;
- monitoring accommodations;
- monitoring requests of workers;
- monitoring requests of the benefit carrier;
- monitoring requests of the employer on either the worker or the benefit carrier;
- communicating with workers;
- communicating with the benefits carrier;
- documenting of all discussions and interactions;

- managing the file (information) – electronically
  and manual paper;
- managing the file – historical, future projections
  and future planning; and,
- managing and planning strategically.

The advantages listed above illustrate how the reduction of the number of lost time days results in the reduction of costs and increase in positioning for profitability. Some strategies to reduce the number of lost time days include but are not limited to:

- Management's demonstrated commitment to
  health and safety and a return to work program;
- Compliance to health and safety legislation
  (OHSA) and worker's compensation legislation
  (WSIA);
- An effective and functioning health and safety
  program;
- An effective and functioning disability man-
  agement program;
- A functioning return to work program;
- Prevention activities and methods;
- Continuous improvements commitment and
  mechanism to identify and address continuous
  improvements; and,
- A practicing health and safety culture.

Managing claims and lost time becomes critical in mitigating costs of claims. Development and implementation of return to work plans is just one tool but a very important tool for employers to use to assist them in effective claims management. These plans allow the workers to return to work without losing wages and they allow the employer to comply with any legal or moral obligations to accommodate injured workers, reduce costs in the claims, and reduce lost productivity.

A thorough understanding of the roles and responsibilities of each party in the recovery process as well as the standard recovery periods, importance of implementing appropriate return to work plans and the importance of a comprehensive reporting process will assist the employer to develop best practices in the policies and procedures for reporting and managing claims. Communicating the responsibilities and obligations for workers, those of the employer and all employer representatives, medical professionals and union representatives (if any) would promote awareness of the process and each party's role within the process.

As proof of due diligence, a procedure should be developed and the company should train all employees of all the roles and responsibilities, legal obligations, etc. of both the health and safety program and the disability management program. The employer must ensure that all managing staff including supervisors understand the concept of competence, legal compliance and due diligence. Therefore, it is very important to train all managing and supervising staff in their responsibilities with respect to the law and the company expectations in the following areas:

- completing an incident report;
- responding to an injury;
- investigating the incident;
- completing root cause analysis;
- developing and implementing corrective actions; and,
- evaluating the effectiveness of the corrective actions to prevent future recurrences.

Supervisors and managers require sensitivity training so that they understand the requirement to keep medical information confidential and learning tactics used to avoid the medical information from becoming the topic of discussion with any employee. In fact, under the Privacy Act, employers are required to physically lock up under lock and key any personal information. Personal information includes the employees' identity and medical information. Files such as the employee files, the worker's compensation files, and the short term and long term files all must be protected under the Privacy Act. A best practice would be to file and secure each of these personal files separately.

In the incident reporting process, each party has roles and responsibilities. These roles and responsibilities should be built into their health and safety program and the disability management program. For example, if a worker indicates that they have had a workplace injury which requires a change in placement, an FAF package should be given to the worker after an incident report is completed.

After the incident report is completed, the supervisor should advise the worker to seek medical attention as soon as possible.

Developing and implementing policies and procedures outlining each party's rights and obligations assists each party in understanding their role in the accommodation process. It also becomes a best practice for a company to develop and implement policies and procedures or negotiate in the collective agreement the process(es) to assist the restricted worker and the company to address restrictions, process for accommodation, the process for managing the accommodation process including an avenue the worker can use to address discrepancies or burdens requiring corrective actions.

Further to the roles and responsibilities in the disability management program, there are many elements to an effective program. One strategic element regarding the recovery process is early medical intervention. Early medical intervention provides treatment for an injury at the early stages of an injury. Treatment at the early stages of an injury increases the chances of full recovery, reduces the chances of recurrence, reducing the chances of permanent impairment and shortens the recovery period.

Sometimes the injured worker may not have access to expedient medical intervention. Therefore a best practice for a company is to establish a medical network that will assist the injured worker with receiving earlier medical intervention. A medical network of health services providers will assist in the recovery and return to work process.

It is important to understand that the company cannot stop nor force the worker to receive medical attention. However, medical attention is highly recommended when the injury requires medical beyond first aid. It is a best practice for the company to prepare and give the injured worker an FAF package for the doctor to review and complete before leaving the facility, if the worker seeks medical attention.

The FAFs must be tightly controlled as they represent an expense to the company as well reporting obligations. Any requests for repeated FAFs should be fulfilled by the claims management advisor. The advisor will issue prefilled FAFs to the requestor in a timely manner. This practice will avoid duplication in claims processing at the benefits carrier and it will allow the company to control the costs of issuing FAFs.

Each FAF has a time limit which usually correlates to the standard recovery chart. The timing of the restrictions is identified in Section 4 of the FAF by the health care professional. The new restrictions should show evidence of progression in recovery. If 14+ days section is checked, the company should issue a new FAF to the worker at the 2 or 4 week mark depending on the injury and the stage of recovery. When the time limit expires, the worker should bring another FAF to the medical professional to update the restrictions.

The company should continue to issue FAFs until the medical professional releases all the restrictions by indicating that the worker can return to regular duties work without restrictions. Sometimes the worker will not recover and will require permanent restrictions. In these cases, the company must build a long term, suitable and sustainable plan for the worker with permanent restrictions.

In monitoring lost time, a company should request medical documentation to support any lost time. This should be clearly communicated through company policy or procedures. Benefits carriers, especially the WSIB in Ontario, will request medical documentation to support lost time before the carrier will approve the payment of lost wages. Sometimes, the employer can challenge or object to the lost time especially if the company has an approved and effective return to work program. Each case and each lost time event must be evaluated on timing, medical documentation, return to work plan, restrictions, worker, accommodations, etc. in order to determine if lost time is medically supported or if the company should proceed with an objection.

Monitoring the claim is very important to determine key timeframes such standard recovery, return to work, claim closure, etc. In addition to the key timeframes, monitoring claims allows for immediate claim status awareness, current decision status, current claim cost status, current projection of future benefits costs, etc. If an employer does not monitor the claim and its costs, the claim could exceed the normal recovery and have increased costs or the worker does not return to work or regular duties in a timely fashion resulting in increased costs, poor employee morale, increased (and likely unnecessary) lost time, etc.

When monitoring a claim, an employer can:

- effectively administer timely return to work plans;
- ensure the claim closes in a timely fashion;

- ensure only appropriate costs are charged against the employer account;
- monitor timing of the standard recovery period in order to request cost relief from Secondary Injury Enhancement Fund (SIEF);
- track accurate severity of injuries through lost time days;
- ensuring restrictions are current and appropriate resulting in return to work plans being current and appropriate and effectively reducing complications to recovery and prolonged recovery periods; and,
- current restrictions and appropriate return to work (including return to regular duties) plans assist in mitigating lost productivity and increased training costs; etc.

Monitoring and facilitating the recovery process is a best practice in effective disability management because it supports the recovery of the worker. A worker who recovers is more productive. As the recovery progresses towards pre-injury health, all workers will start to understand the effectiveness of the return to work program. Once the workers believe in the program, they will have no other recourse but support the company's efforts. Should the recovery not progress and the company fail to act, the workers will not support the program becoming uncooperative in the process.

It is important for the company to act when the program requires adjustment. Further medical assessments, evaluations of capabilities, and consultations with the benefits carriers will be required to make the appropriate adjustments necessary to keep the recovery progressing. The recovery process should be a constantly evolving progression. The company must be prepared and strategically plan each step in each claim to effectively return the worker back to the pre-injury status.

In addition to monitoring restrictions for updates and appropriateness, monitoring the recovery process, the employee's psychological health and the progress of a return to work or return to regular duties plans are all interlinked. Effective disability management is an overall process. Monitoring the recovery process includes monitoring the mental health of the worker and the worker's attitude towards recovery is critical as part of the healing process. In other words, if the worker has a positive attitude towards healing and returning to regular duties, then the worker is more likely to return to regular duties in a timely manner. However, if the worker is exhibiting signs of depression or refusing to cooperate in the course of treatments or return to work plans, then the worker may be more likely to experience delays and extended plateaus in the recovery process.

The company should foster a supportive and cooperative recovery process with the injured worker, benefits carrier and the respective medical professionals. Independent medical evaluations (IMEs) are a valuable tool to assist in resolving misunderstandings or conflicts between perception and actual physical capabilities or providing medical evidence to the WSIB to consider cost relief through SIEF.

Once this IME report has been received, the report should be compared to the jobs available within the worker's capabilities. This will determine if there is work available within the worker's restrictions and capabilities that is suitable, sustainable and long term. This type of medical documentation is required to support the decision to return the worker to a long term, suitable and sustainable position or to seek further legal advice on other options like retraining or and frustration of contract.

The employer has the obligation to make a viable return to work offer to any injured worker based on restrictions. All return to work offers should be documented. Written return to work offers is an effective method of documenting the evidence. Written offers clarify misconceptions and provide evidence in legal proceedings should it be required.

In addition to the work offer plan, the company should allow some time for the worker to gradually recondition to the physical demands of the plan. Reconditioning the worker will provide the worker with the strength and endurance to perform the tasks successful as well as provide the employer with higher productivity levels throughout the process. The work hardening program will provide the worker with a strong foundation to progress through recovery while continuing to work with reduced chance of re-aggravation.

It is a best practice to continue to follow up with injured workers during their recovery process for several reasons including mediating any ongoing concerns such as difficulties performing tasks assigned, reviewing progress and restrictions, reviewing expectations at different stages in the recovery process, coaching on improved ergonomics of performing normal or expected tasks, constant open dialogue with the worker maintains good labour relations, etc. These follow up meetings should be documented on the return to work so all parties are aware of the timing and expectations.

The concept of return to work is a vital part of the disability management program. Effective return to work plans may involve many professionals and many activities. The plans are essential in an employer's best practice for due diligence.

At any time in the return to work program, if the worker refuses the tasks assigned in the return to work offer, there are a number of expectations that should be considered. Just as the return to work offer is presented in writing by the employer, the refusal of performing such tasks should also be in writing from the worker. Best practices in the incident reporting process recommends the written refusal to include the reasons for the refusal, signing and dating the reasons, any comments relevant to the process or restrictions, etc.

Either party can submit an objection to the return to work plan or the other party's concerns to the other party and the benefits carrier. If the determination of the benefits carrier is in favour of the employer's return to work plan, then the worker will be advised to return to work or risk their claim or benefits being terminated. If the determination of the benefits carrier is in favour of the worker's refusal, the employer will be asked by the benefits carrier to redraft the return to work plan. The employer should consider reviewing the plan with an ergonomist and other medical professionals.

The benefits carrier may offer the employer the services of an ergonomist, doctors, specialists, functional abilities evaluations, mediators, etc. If the benefits carrier has these services at their disposal, the company should not delay in requesting these services to continue the process forward. However, if the benefits carrier does not have access to these services, the company should use the resources from their medical network to clarify the concerns.

Perception is reality and the worker's perception of their restrictions can have a significant impact on the worker's perception to complete the tasks in the return to work plan. The company can also choose to send the worker for a functional abilities evaluation to determine the worker's capabilities. An FAE or an IME will assess the actual capabilities of the worker. These evaluations may also explain any prolonged recovery or dispute any restrictions or treatment and no further action taken by the primary medical professional.

A best practice will prescribe that the company will also use the expertise of one of more third party consultant types to review the return to work plans when conflicts arise including Ergonomists, doctors, benefits carrier adjudicator, etc., prior to the inspector being called in to review the concern.

The medical professionals in the medical network should understand the workplace activities both pre-injury and the modified work program. Visiting the workplace and getting to know the company and the worker's capabilities are a couple of ways the medical professional can understand the workplace. It is very common for this type of activity to come from ergonomists and or physiotherapists as doctors may not have the time to dedicate to this aspect of the recovery process.

Understanding the correlation between physical demands of the tasks or assignments and injuries to the various body parts will provide the employer or company will valuable insight in prevention activities as well as accommodation activities. This understanding will allow employers to adjust work plans, redesign workstations to prevent future injuries, etc. Ergonomics and understanding the correlation between task and injury will provide the employer with the opportunities in preventive and corrective actions. Consequently, these activities will provide a course of due diligence and legal compliance in best practices in a disability management program.

It is a best practice to document each communication in order to maintain a paper trail of all information related to the claim. A best practice in employee relations is to develop mechanism for communication between the workers and the company. Within this mechanism of communication, each workplace should have a method for the company to address concerns from the worker including objections to any company decisions. Each carrier will have their own appeal process as outlined in their policies and procedures. Both the employer and the worker have the right to appeal decisions from the benefits carriers. Again, medical documentation is a key element in supporting the objection.

Communication with the worker is essential in understanding the worker's concerns and requests during the recovery process to avoid re-injury or to assist in the recovery. The accommodation process does not mean the company relinquishes any management control to the requests of the injured worker. The company must maintain control of business operations and review the worker requests under accommodation.

In other words, the injured worker should not be dictating what they should or should not do. However, the worker should be participating in the planning the return to regular duties or work in terms of providing constructive feedback to the company about their abilities within their restrictions. The line between accommodating and relinquishing control is a particularly difficult line in the sand to manage.

Furthermore, communication is significant as constant communication with the worker and or the claims adjudicator will provide valuable feedback that will help to adjust the return to work plans, and information regarding decisions on the claim, etc. Monitoring claims in combination with communicating with the adjudicator will allow the company to understand information on the claim. This information would include the decisions in the claim by the benefits carrier and medical professionals, the requests of the benefits carrier, monitor the requests of the employer with regard to the worker or the benefit carrier or the claim (including requests for cost relief from SIEF, amalgamation, objections to lost time or claim entitlement), etc. Therefore, the information is crucial to assist the company in planning the next steps in terms of return to work plans, independent medical evaluations, to request cost relief through SIEF, object to entitlement of the claim based on facts, object to lost time based on modified work plans, and projecting claim costs, etc.

Nevertheless, all communications with anyone in relation to the recovery process whether it be the worker, medical professionals, adjudicators, company executives, the communications should be documented in writing (or email) and filed into the appropriate file (separate from the employee's employment file). Written documentation is a trail that will provide support for any decisions made along the recovery process.

Even if the communication is a worker's concern or a worker's explanation for their inability to perform the tasks listed on their return to work or return to regular duties plans, it is very important that these be documented in the worker's own words as well as dated and signed by the worker. This documentation should also be copied to the benefits carrier to keep their files current and accurate at all times.

Employment status changes due to restrictions or medical condition can lead to breaches in the collective agreement, WSIA's re-employment obligation or the general employment contract. There must be documented evidence that the worker would not be able to work any other position including medical and ergonomic documentation supporting these assessments. Please consult with an employment lawyer before breaching any legally binding agreement.

Generally, changes in employment status are not considered a breach in legal obligations when there is sufficient evidence to support the layoff was due to seniority and not restrictions. Economic changes do precipitate changes in staffing. Restricted or disabled workers are not exempted from economic changes. In best practices of labour relations, constant communication and detailed discussions with the union representatives are very necessary when addressing these delicate management practices.

When the company faces right sizing the headcount, seniority would dictate that the higher seniority worker assigned the work placement and the lower seniority restricted worker be laid off. This would not generally breach the employer's duty to accommodate as the layoff is a result of seniority not a result of the restrictions. In best practices, the company should file documented evidence in the worker's file clearly outlining that the layoff was a result of seniority only. If a company has any doubts when laying off workers' with restrictions, consulting legal counsel will assist in determining if any breach to the company's duty to accommodate or duty to re-employment exists.

In addition to the company's layoff practice, the company must be careful when changing the employment status of a restricted or disabled worker due to poor attendance. Caution must be exercised when considering not approving absences for documented medical conditions. When considering terminating the employment relationship of a disabled or restricted worker, it would be diligent for the company to consult with an expert in employment law prior to taking such measures.

SUMMARY

Although legislation varies across different geographical locations, the commonality of legislation is that it only sets out the minimum standards. It is the responsibility of every company in Ontario to develop an effective health and safety program to ensure compliance to all relevant legislation including preventing workplace injuries. A thriving health and safety program mitigates the risk of injuries occurring at the workplace by exceeding the legislative requirements and by incorporating health and safety best practices into core strategic business objectives from planning to design to development to output to sales. However, workplace injuries can happen despite an effective health and safety program.

Each company is legally obligated to provide a safe work environment including identifying and communicating any risks to everyone at the workplace, the workers, any visitors or contractors, etc. In preventing injuries or harm to workers and to avert legal repercussions, a company must develop a systemic best practices program in health and safety which includes practicing due diligence in all their decisions and business activities as well as providing training on how to work safely. Due diligence is critical when establishing a comprehensive and effective health and safety program. By building due diligence into a health and safety program, the company not only ensures compliance to the minimum legal requirements under the Occupational Health and Safety Act but also allows the company to provide documented evidence of taking every reasonable precaution to protect the health and safety of the workers.

It is best practice to align objectives of the disability management program including decreasing costs, with corporate objectives such as decreasing costs will improve the company's positioning for profitability. An effective disability management will contribute to the reduction in costs by including procedures to support the worker in the recovery and return to work process of any injury whether occupationally related or non-occupational.

An effective disability management program will include best practices in health and safety as well as practices that assist the worker through recovery and through the return to work process. The health and safety program should be focused on preventing workplace injuries and enabling worker wellness whereas disability management should be focused on response to workplace injuries and improving the worker wellness through the recovery and return to work processes.

Management's commitment to the health and safety and the return to work programs is a fundamental building block to the success of developing, implementing and maintaining each program. Verbal commitments are evident through speeches, dialogues with employees, and daily verbal instructions. In addition to the verbal commitment, it is best practice for the commitment to be documented, signed by the members of the executive management and posted for all the employees to read as a daily reminder of management's commitment.

Documentation of the commitment will provide evidence of the commitment for enquiries from the MOL, WSIB, unions, customers, ISO14001/OHSAS 18001 certification auditors, etc. Keeping accurate records of all practices, policies, activities, etc. of each program is a best practice. Detail becomes important should there be disputes in any claim, restrictions, return to work, etc.

An important best practice in demonstrating management's commitment to the health and safety and the return to work programs is for management to lead by example. Demonstrating executive management's commitment through their own activities such as regularly reviewing and monitoring each incident as well as trends, addressing health and safety issues through corrective actions in a timely manner, addressing return to work issues through corrective actions and communication in a timely manner, regular communication meetings with all employees reviewing trends and solutions, ensuring all employees receive the same messages on the seriousness of each program and any serious consequences of non-compliance, mandating training, etc. The daily fair and consistent application of each program including the application of consequences of non-compliance will provide evidence to demonstrate a clear commitment of zero tolerance for violations.

Additionally, the incident reporting process must include a comprehensive incident investigation process. Once the worker's medical needs have been attended and all workers are in a safe location, the supervisor should investigate the incident and review the incident report to develop a long term corrective action. The supervisor should have developed and implemented a short term corrective action at the time the incident report was completed with the injured worker to take every reasonable precaution to protect workers.

Linking the internal incident reporting process with the SCAR process will support the corrective action process. Any investigational results will be entered into the SCAR process for numbering, development, implementation, follow up, evaluation, continuous improvements, etc.

For the management of the workers compensation claims in Ontario, the rate group of the company is a critical element in determining claim costs, surcharges or rebates, and industry standards. Therefore, it is a best practice to review the definition of other rate groups similar to the company's business operations to ensure that the WSIB has classified the company in the appropriate rate group. A review of the rate group especially if the nature of the business operation has changed would ensure the rate group is still appropriate.

Administrative errors could cost the company large costs. Monitoring the cost statements will allow the company to identify any errors. The company can then take actions to correct any errors discovered before the errors have a negative financial impact on the company's bottom line. The program should include mechanisms to monitor and scrutinize all claim costs, analyzing the causes off all the costs, as well as develop and implement actions or programs to reduce the costs such as return to work plans to manage lost time, assistance in medical management to insure early medical intervention to avoid long term damage, etc.

In Ontario, those employers participating in the WSIB NEER incentive program can use NEER as an effective tool in managing any costs. The calculations of rebates or surcharges can motivate and support management decisions to promote best practices in health and safety programs.

The employer has authority over the activity in the workplace regarding health and safety. Outside of work, the employer has very little authority over the worker's activities. However, there are some avenues the employer can explore to motivate workers to make good life choices. For example, such programs as healthy benefits, extended health benefits, EAP, Wellness Programs, cessation programs, nutritional awareness, exercising programs, substance abuse programs, promote medical regular examinations and early medical intervention, etc.

Information and knowledge can provide people with the skills to make better decisions and healthier choices. These other programs will offer people knowledge, training, awareness, and opportunity to access services and information that will provide the foundation of good health. Good psychological, physical and emotional health are a few of the best prevention programs available to any person.

Health care benefits, wellness plans, EAP, etc. are plans that employers can provide to the workers to promote good health. Employers who participate in these programs should promote awareness of the benefits available under this program to all the workers. In promoting the services of these plans, the employer promotes good psychological, physical and emotional health or at the very least, the access to services that will assist any person in their pursuit for good health. Good health in turn will support a happier and healthier worker resulting in higher productivity, decrease in injuries and reduced costs in other areas.

Aligning objectives of the disability management program with corporate objectives such as decreasing costs will improve the company's positioning for profitability. One way to decrease costs is to decrease the number of lost time days. The advantages of decreasing the number of lost time days are:

- Decreasing costs in terms of premiums for the WSIB, STD, LTD programs;
- Decreasing costs of lost wages replacement in terms of claims costs;
- Decreasing lost productivity of injured workers;
- Decreasing lost productivity of coworkers covering the regular duties of the injured worker;
- Decreasing the need for overtime to cover injured worker's lost productivity;
- Decreasing the costs of lost productivity as the following activities are not required:
  - retraining a replacement;
  - costs of recruiting a replacement;
  - improving morale;
  - short shipments;
  - poor quality of a newly hired replacement; and,
  - workplace disruptions, etc.
- decreasing the potential legal fees for:

- counsel;
- tribunals for the WSIB and Labour Relations grievances;
- arbitrations; and,
- mediations.

Some best practices in disability management include:

- Statistics tracking;
- Trend analysis;
- Short term corrective actions;
- Long term preventative actions;
- Projections in claims costs vs. projections in health and safety program costs;
- Due diligence;
- Effective cost of claims;
- Document all communications;
- Establish medical networks;
- Functioning EHS Program;
- Root cause analysis process;
- Corrective Action Program;
- RTW Program;
- Stat tracking – identify trends, project trends, correct issues;
- Establish good communication/relationships between carriers and employees;
- Follow up;
- Premium negotiations where applicable;
- Strategic cost analysis;
- Projecting costs;
- Mitigating costs – return to work and NEER strategies; and,
- Prevention program including stretching program.

Any one of these best practices can assist a company in achieving targets and objectives in health and safety as well as disability management programs. To ensure compliance and realize greater returns on investment, the company should consider developing and implementing a combination of any of the best practices included in this text. These best practices are not meant to replace the existing EHS or disability management programs. However, the suggestions will complement the existing programs and promote continuous improvements.

Key Terms:

Best Practices
Lessons learned
Strategic planning

Questions:

1. Discuss the role of best practices in strategic planning.
2. List and explain five best practices for developing a health and safety program.
3. Describe five best practices for developing a disability management program including the advantages and disadvantages of each of the best practices.
4. Define the term best practices and discuss the advantages and disadvantages of implementing best practices.

GLOSSARY

A

Accident (WSIA 1997)
> –...includes,
>> (a) a wilful and intentional act, not being the act of the worker,
>> (b) a chance event occasioned by a physical or natural cause, and
>> (c) disablement arising out of and in the course of employment; ("accident")...

Accident Cost Statement
> – In Ontario, the workers compensation program, the WSIB, issues statements monthly that breaks down the costs by claim for each company. This is a tool to help company's monitor the cost of their WSIB claims.

Accommodation
> – to change the workplace environment, task, or station to enable a person to perform a task safely

Account number
> – Workplace Safety and Insurance Board assigns a number to a business in Ontario as they register for the insurance program within 10 calendar days of opening the operation.
> - This number is unique to the company, type of business and specific to the worksite.
> - A company may have several account numbers assigned to it depending on the type of work performed in the operation and the number of different worksites. The WSIB can assist an employer in making these determinations

Adjudication
> – decision-making process for insurance claims or benefits claims

Amalgamation
> – refers to re-opening an old claim instead of opening a new claim. the WSIB, Policy #15-03-01

Appeal
> — written submission requesting a decision to be reconsidered or re-evaluated based on new medical information

Arbitration
> — A neutral third party listens to both sides to determine the terms of the agreement. Used when an agreement could not be ascertained between the negotiating parties. The third party decisions are legally binding and final.

Auditor/Lead Auditor
> — From Wikipedia, the free encyclopaedia (en.wikipedia.org, 2009)
> - Performs "...an evaluation of a person, organization, system, process, project or product...to ascertain the validity and reliability of information; also to provide an assessment of a system's internal control. The goal of an audit is to express an opinion [on compliance or conformance] on the person / organization/system (etc.) in question, under evaluation based on work done on a test basis. Due to practical constraints, an audit seeks to provide only reasonable assurance that the statements are free from material error. Hence, statistical sampling is often adopted in audits..."

B

Best Practices
> — From Wikipedia, the free encyclopaedia (retrieved from: en.wikipedia.org, 2009)
> ...is a technique, method, process, activity, incentive or reward that is believed to be more effective at delivering a particular outcome than any other technique, method, process, etc. The idea is that with proper processes, checks, and testing, a desired outcome can be delivered with fewer problems and unforeseen complications. Best practices can also be defined as the most efficient (least amount of effort) and effective (best results) way of accomplishing a task, based on repeatable procedures that have proven themselves over time for large numbers of people.
>
> Despite the need to improve on processes as times change and things evolve, best-practice is considered by some as a business buzzword used to describe the process of developing and following a standard way of doing things that multiple organizations can use for management, policy, and especially software systems.
>
> As the term has become more popular, some organizations have begun using the term "best practices" to refer to what are in

fact merely 'rules', causing a linguistic drift in which a new term such as "good ideas" is needed to refer to what would previously have been called "best practices...

Bona fide requirement
- The "bona fide" requirements of the job are the essential tasks of the job that must be completed.

Budgeting
– setting targets for the amount of money to be spent or received on all operations of a business. The objective of a budget is to plan where the money will come from (receivables) and where the expenditures will be (costs) in order to reach a final targeted financial outcome (usually a profit)

Business Strategy
– plan(s) to achieve business targets and objectives

C

CAD7
– prevention incentive program from the WSIB in Ontario for the Construction companies only with an average annual the WSIB premium of more than $25,000. Essentially, the company will pay the respective premiums according to their payroll. Once a year, the WSIB will assess the health and safety record of the company of the review period to determine if the company receives a rebate or a surcharge. The company will receive a rebate if the company's health and safety record is good. However, if the company's health and safety record is poor, the company will receive a surcharge.

Cessation
– to stop

Claims Adjudicator
– decision maker regarding the disability claim from entitlement to termination, monitoring payments, medical information, recovery, return to work, etc.

Collective Agreement

  – a legally binding agreement between an employer and an Union negotiated between an appointed team of Management Representatives and an elected team of representatives for the membership of the Union. The Collective Agreement outlines rules and processes of managing labour issues, concerns, disciplines, training, wages, benefits, etc.

Communication

  - From Wikipedia, the free encyclopaedia (retrieved from: en.wikipedia.org, 2009)

  – ...is a process of transferring information from one entity to another. Communication processes are sign-mediated interactions between at least two agents which share a repertoire of signs and semiotic rules. Communication is commonly defined as "the imparting or interchange of thoughts, opinions, or information by speech, writing, or signs". Communication can be perceived as a two-way process in which there is an exchange and progression of thoughts, feelings or ideas towards a mutually accepted goal or direction.

  – Communication requires that all parties have an area of communicative commonality. There are auditory means, such as speaking, singing and sometimes tone of voice, and nonverbal, physical means, such as body language, sign language, paralanguage, touch, eye contact, by using writing...

Competent

  – Retrieved from: OHSA

  ...(a) is qualified because of knowledge, training and experience to perform the work,

  (b) is familiar with the Occupational Health and Safety Act and with the provisions of the regulations that apply to the work, and

  (c) has knowledge of all potential or actual danger to health or safety in the work;...

Compliance

  – Retrieved from Wikipedia, the free encyclopaedia
  (en.wikipedia.org, 2009)

  ...describes the goal that corporations or public agencies aspire to in their efforts to ensure that personnel are aware of and take steps to comply with relevant laws and regulations...

Confidentiality
 – Retrieved from Wikipedia, the free encyclopaedia
 (en.wikipedia.org, 2009)
 – ...ensuring that information is accessible only to those authorized
 to have access" and is one of the cornerstones of information security...

Conformance
 - From Wikipedia, the free encyclopaedia (en.wikipedia.org, 2009)
 - Comply to the requirements of any certification such as OHSAS
 18001 and ISO 14001

Cost Reduction
 – decrease the amount of costs or expenditures

Cost Relief
 – discount or amount of money subtracted from a claim

Cost Strategy
 – a plan to achieve a specific financial target or objective

Critical Injuries
 - Under the Occupational Health and Safety Act of Ontario
 (OHSA), it is an injury that occurs at the workplace which results
 in one of the following:
 1. Substantial loss of blood
 2. Fracture of an arm or leg but not a finger or a toe
 3. Unconsciousness
 4. Loss of sight in one eye
 5. Amputation but not a finger or a toe
 6. Places life in jeopardy
 7. Consists of burns to a major portion of the body
 - The Ministry of Labour (MOL) must be notified by the employer within forty eight (48) hours of the injury. The WSIB must
 be notified of the injury within three (3) business days.

D

Disability
 - ... impairments, activity limitations, and participation restrictions. An impairment is a problem in body function or structure; an activity limitation is a difficulty encountered by an individ-

ual in executing a task or action; while a participation restriction is a problem experienced by an individual in involvement in life situations. Thus disability is a complex phenomenon, reflecting an interaction between features of a person's body and features of the society in which he or she lives... Such impairments may include physical, sensory, and cognitive or intellectual impairments. Mental disorders (also known as psychiatric or psychosocial disability) and various types of chronic disease may also be considered qualifying disabilities. (Retrieved from: Wikipedia, 2009)

Disability Management Program (DMP)

– Retrieved from Wikipedia, the free encyclopaedia (en.wikipedia.org, 2009)

– ... used by employers to assist employees who are unable to work due to injury or illness. The DMP consists of several components, however not all DMPs have all possible components. Smaller programs may only include the basic components while larger programs generally have more components. The purpose of the DMP is to benefit the employer by returning experienced, trained employees to work quickly...

Discrimination

– Retrieved from Wikipedia, the free encyclopaedia (en.wikipedia.org, 2009)

– ...refers to treatment taken toward or against a person of a certain group that is taken in consideration based on class or category...

Disease

– Retrieved from: en.wikipedia.org, 2010

– ...to any condition that causes pain, dysfunction, distress, social problems, and/or death to the person afflicted, or similar problems for those in contact with the person. In this broader sense, it sometimes includes injuries, disabilities, disorders, syndromes, infections, isolated symptoms, deviant behaviours, and atypical variations of structure and function, while in other contexts and for other purposes these may be considered distinguishable categories...

Dispute Resolution

– method or mechanism for resolving conflict or disagreement

Due Diligence

– specified standard of care

- Due diligence is a "standard of care" to which a company has a legal obligation to provide. A more formal definition of due diligence can be found on the WSIB website. According to the WSIB, fact sheet on Internal Responsibility System and Due Diligence found on www.wsib.on.ca," due diligence refers to the employer's legal responsibility to take *every reasonable precaution* to prevent injuries and illnesses and prove that they have done this. This is in addition to complying with the provisions of the *Occupational Health and Safety Act* (OHSA) and Regulations and is not limited by them." In other words, due diligence refers to a standard of care that would include doing or not doing what a reasonable person would do or not do to prevent injuries or harm to others.

Duty to Accommodate

– ...Accommodation refers to the removal of potential barriers for access to employment. It consists of a series of steps taken to ensure that everyone is able to participate fully in employment and employment related activities. Accommodation means that the terms and employment conditions of the workplace may have to be modified. An accommodation is meant to address a person's needs in ways that are respectful of the individual's privacy and dignity; it is not a lowering of employment standards... (Retrieved from: Queen's Human Rights Office (613) 533-6886, Queen's University, www.queensu.ca/humanrights/accommodationbro chure.htm)

E

EAP – Employee Assistance Program

– A program designed to assist employees with professional services that may not be covered by the general health care benefits program. The standard EAP program will cover legal services, financial services, counselling services, etc.

Early and Safe Return to Work Program

- The company has a financial, legal, social and moral obligation to assist those workers injured at work to recover and return to their pre-injury job. Under the Workplace and Safety Insurance Act, the employer has an obligation to re-employ the injured worker and accommodate their restrictions. Reviewing the production lines and making modifications to them will allow the company to offer work within the injured worker's restrictions until the worker recovers and is able to return to regular duties. Medical updates are critical in obtaining accurate and current restrictions of the injured workers in order to assign suitable modified work during the recovery process. This will reduce the number and costs of lost time claims.

- the WSIB is now actively involved in assisting all parties in an ESRTW program.

- Process involves evaluating positions in the company to assess whether a restricted worker can safely perform the core essential duties of the job within their restrictions. Accommodations may be required to allow the restricted worker to safely perform the tasks.

- It is the duty of the employer to accommodate the worker

- It is the duty of the Union to cooperate and not add barriers to the return to work plan

- It is the duty of the worker to participate in the return to work and they cannot refuse a reasonable accommodation

Emergency Response Plan

- Being prepared for emergencies involves planning and practicing different situations to ensure that everyone knows their role during a real event to reduce chaos, confusion, and minimize chance of injury.

Employer

– Retrieved from: OHSA (June 2002)

– ...means a person who employs one or more workers or contracts for the services of one or more workers and includes a contractor or subcontractor who performs work or supplies services and a contractor or subcontractor who undertakes with an owner, constructor, contractor or subcontractor to perform work or supply services...

- Retrieved from the WSIA (1997)

– ... means every person having in his, her or its service under a contract of service or apprenticeship another person engaged in work in or about an industry and includes,

(a) a trustee, receiver, liquidator, executor or administrator who carries on an industry,

(b) a person who authorizes or permits a learner to be in or about an industry for the purpose of undergoing training or probationary work, or

(c) a deemed employer; ("employeur")...

Employer (as defined in the WSIA)

— ...means every person having in his, her or its service under a contract of service or apprenticeship another person engaged in work in or about an industry and includes,

(a) a trustee, receiver, liquidator, executor or administrator who carries on an industry,

(b) a person who authorizes or permits a learner to be in or about an industry for the purpose of undergoing training or probationary work, or

(c) a deemed employer; ("employeur")...

Employment Standards Act (ESA 2000)

— ...The ESA establishes basic employer obligations and employee rights with respect to rates of pay, hours of work and overtime, vacations, public holidays, various forms of leave and more. Every province and most industrialized countries have similar legislation. The ESA is enforced by officers who work for the Employment Standards (ES) Program, which is part of the Ministry of Labour. They visit businesses throughout Ontario...

Ergonomics

- The study of biomechanics will help workers, engineers and supervisors understand how to set up work stations that have low to no risks of injuries due to repetitive strain or poor layout. Knowledge of ergonomics assists workers in understanding the mechanics of their body and what to expect from the movements of their work station. Knowledge of ergonomics also empowers workers and allows them to be more accountable for their own safe actions. By reducing the risk factors through changes or improvements driven by understanding ergonomics, the company should realize a decrease in the number of repetitive strain injuries, decreased recovery time, decreased lost time and health care costs, and earlier return to regular duties.

Experience Rating Programs

— Retrieved from: www.wsib.on.ca

- These programs *"...provide financial incentives to improve health and safety in workplaces by issuing a rebate or adding a surcharge on an employer's annual premium..."*

F

FAE – Functional Abilities Evaluation

- an independent evaluation of the worker's abilities. It is a functional abilities evaluation to determine in depth what a worker can and cannot do based on objective physical activity testing. Usually a physiotherapist will conduct the testing and the testing takes about three (3) hours to perform. The worker is encouraged to communicate with the evaluator at all times during the evaluation process. The evaluator will carefully observe and monitor the restricted worker through a series of physical activities (including lifting, posture, walking, running, sitting, standing, reaching, etc.). The evaluator will then complete a comprehensive report to the requestor (usually the employer of the benefits carrier) detailing what the worker can perform safely and what restrictions continue to be appropriate at the time of the testing. This will assist the employer in developing and evaluating the return to work and return to regular duties plans. It also assists the benefits carrier to determine if the worker is capable of returning to work or if the worker has to be retrained for another career path more suitable to the worker's permanent restrictions. The employer would request this if there is a discrepancy between the worker's restrictions and what the worker says they can or cannot do.

FAF – Functional Abilities Form, the WSIB, Policy #19-02-04

...a worker must consent to the disclosure of functional abilities information to the employer by the treating health professional. The disclosure is specifically for the purpose of aiding in the worker's return to work.
- When requested to do so by an employer or worker, the health professional treating the worker must give the WSIB, the employer, and the worker such information as may be prescribed concerning the worker's functional abilities.
- used by the workplace parties to help identify suitable jobs consistent with the worker's functional abilities. Its purpose is to highlight what a worker can do and what limitations apply.
- does not contain either clinical or diagnostic information. It does not replace the health professional's reporting requirements to the WSIB. As well, the form does not replace the employer's initial-accident reporting obligations...

Firm number

– The WSIB assigns a number to a business in Ontario as they register for the insurance program. In cases where the company has several account numbers, a firm number joins all the account numbers under one firm so *"...All accounts registered by one employer are linked to ensure that the financial liability for each account is identified with the legal employer..."* (Retrieved from the WSIA, Policy #14-02-02).

Forecasting
— to project or predict costs and expenditures in order to develop a budget, financial plan with targets and objectives over a defined period of time.

Forklift Certification
- Forklift certification offers a foundation of practical knowledge and skills for safe forklift operation. The Ministry of Labour in Ontario has published a forklift operation guideline mandating licensing of all forklift operators as well as recertification every thirty six (36) months with a practical evaluation at eighteen (18) months.

Form 6 – Employee Statement – the WSIB form
- Allows the injured worker to document their side of the story on how they were injured in the workplace.
- For other wage replacement insurance programs due to disability that are non work related, have a form for the Employee to provide their statement.

Form 7 – Employer Statement – the WSIB form
- Allows the employer to document the facts that lead to the workplace injury
- For other wage replacement insurance programs due to disability that are non work related, have a form for the Sponsor or employer to provide a statement.
- All statements regardless of the origin of the disability should always be based on verifiable and reliable facts only.

Form 8 – Physician Statement – the WSIB form
- Allows the medical professional to document the objective medical condition and restrictions required for the injury.
- The physician is required by law to complete and send a copy to the WSIB. The WSIB uses this information to determine entitlement and length of claim.
- The employer is not entitled to a copy due to confidentiality (in Ontario and in Canada). However, if the worker volunteers to give

a copy of the form to the employer, the employer is bound to keep this information confidential and locked up.

Frequency

– the number of injuries over specific period of time normalized over the amount of work hours. This is a good measurable to track the effectiveness of corrective actions and health and safety programs in terms of the number of injuries that are occurring over time. It is also good to monitor any trends over time especially those relative to time like seasonal trends.

Future Concepts to Explore

- This section reviews concepts to explore for further continuous improvements and development to best practices in Health and Safety.

G

Goals

– see "Targets"

Graduated Hours

– gradual increase in time worked per day or per week in order to condition a worker's strength and endurance in order to return to working full time hours

Grievance Procedure

– process by which workers file complaints about workplace conditions, practices, procedures, treatment, etc. with their union or company in order to resolve a dispute. Usually found in unionized environments and this process is negotiated in the collective agreement.

H

Hazard Identification

- Identify risks that potentially could cause injury or environmental contamination

Health Care Benefits
- insurance benefits package for workers to be reimbursed for a defined portion of expenses from medical services. These services usually include dental, prescriptions, vision, hospital coverage, etc.

Health and Safety Policy
- written evidence outlining the company's commitment to health and safety in the workplace

Health and Safety Program
- Health and safety policies and procedures demonstrate the company's philosophy and commitment to health and safety of each worker. Effective policies and procedures should minimize or prevent injuries of everyone in the company.

Health Services Provider
- licensed medical professional providing medical services

Hearing Protection
- According to the Occupational Health and Safety Act of Ontario, hearing protection is another example of personal protective equipment. In order to reduce work related hearing loss injuries, develop and implement a hearing protection policy and procedure where hearing protection is mandatory where noise levels exceed the minimum standards as outlined in OHSA and engineering works towards keeping noise levels at a prescribed level within compliance of OHSA.

Historical Patterning
- trends realized through tracking statistics over years used to assist program planning and development to prevent future recurrences

Housekeeping
- Good housekeeping will not only ensure clean environment for increased productivity, tour readiness, but also assist in preventing injuries such as trips, slips, falls, fire hazards, and other hazards.

Human Rights
- fundamental rights of all people within the land of the law. The rights differ from geographical locations.

Human Rights Code
— Legislation both in Ontario and in Canada designed to protect the "basic" rights of Canadians and people living and working in Ontario. This legislation instructs companies in Canada and in Ontario respectively that workers cannot be hired or terminated based on the following factors:

- race — age
- gender — gender orientation
- family status — marital status
- ethnicity — religious beliefs
- disability — aboriginal status
- creed — citizenship
- Receipt of public assistance
- ancestry

I

IME – Independent Medical Evaluation
- the WSIA, Section 36, employer's request for medical assessment
- the WSIA, Section 35, the WSIB's request for medical assessment
- All wage replacement insurance due to a disability benefits carriers have the right in the policy underwriting to request the injured person to submit to medical evaluations at different points in the recovery process

Illness
— ...is a state of poor health. Illness is sometimes considered a synonym for disease.[1] Others maintain that fine distinctions exist.[2] Some have described illness as the subjective perception by a patient of an objectively defined disease." (Retrieved from: en.wikipedia.org, 2010)

Impairment
— restricted from movement or abilities due to injury or illness

Incentive Programs
— programs designed to promote prevention of both injuries and costs usually with financial rewards or punishments

Incident Reporting Process and Tracking
- All incidents should be reported to the employer immediately no matter how minor the situation in order to prevent future occurrences which might not be so minor as well as early signs of something more significant occurring. Early reporting and detection is the key to prevention as well as compliance to Workplace Safety and Insurance Act (Ontario).

Independent operator
– Essentially, it is the owner/operator of a business with no other employees. According to the WSIA, Policy #12-02-01, the an independent operator is "...a person who carries on an industry set out in Schedule 1 or Schedule 2 of the Act and who does not employ any workers for that purpose."
- To apply for this optional insurance, an Independent Operator must first complete and submit to the WSIB an Independent Operator questionnaire. The WSIB will decide if the applicant is in fact an Independent Operator and if the applicant qualifies for the insurance coverage at an additional premium. To access this questionnaire, the Independent Operator should contact the WSIB directly or visit the WSIB website at www.wsib.on.ca and search for independent operator.
- The chart below is copied from the WSIA. The chart illustrates the difference between workers and Independent Operators:
- According to the WSIA, below are the 2009 amendments concerning an Independent Operator definition and status for the WSIB insurance coverage.

Injury
- ...is damage or harm caused to the structure or function of the body caused by an outside agent or force, which may be physical or chemical, and either by accident or intentional. Personal Injury also refers to damage caused to the reputation of another rather than physical harm to the body... (Retrieved from: en.wikipedia.com, 2010)

Injury Statistics
- By identifying the areas that are causing the problem, the company can develop and implement corrective actions to remedy the problem. Trends are helpful tools in identifying and understanding risks in the business.

Internal Reporting Process
>   – process by which employees report injuries or incidents and corrective action plans are developed as a result of these reports from within the company.

J

Job Coaching or job mentoring
>   – a type of on the job training where a junior person is placed with a senior person to learn all about the job or business by shadowing the senior person

Job Rotation
>   - Job rotation minimizes the exposure level of repetitive strain through alleviating physical fatigue and stress as well as muscle/tendon group variation by changing the body movements frequent during the course of the shift. In variating the body movements over the course of the shift, exposure is minimized and the risk of repetitive strain injuries is reduced.

Joint Health and Safety Committee (JHSC)
>   - According to the Occupational Health and Safety Act of Ontario, a company is required to have health and safety representation. The size of the company and the number of employees will determine the size of the Committee. In general, the Committee should be made of equal numbers of members representing workers and management. This committee represents a group of people from all areas of the company coming together to support the health and wellness of all the workers and the company's health and safety objectives of reducing injuries by reducing or elimination hazards. This committee is an effective prevention tool to assist in identifying and resolving health and safety issues in the plant resulting in reduced injuries.

L

LMR – Labour Market Re-Entry program as outlined by the WSIA
>   - Retraining program for injured workers who cannot return to their pre-injury job to assist the worker to move forward with another career to become a productive member of society. The WSIB adjudicator will determine after the standard recovery if the

worker has permanent improvement resulting in permanent restrictions. If the permanent restrictions are such that the worker cannot return to work in their own occupation (or any available position with their pre-injury employer), then the adjudicator will refer the injured worker for an LMR assessment.

LOE – Loss of Earnings
– earning lost from not working due to a disability

LTD – Long Term Disability
- Long term wage replacement benefit insurance program designed to allow workers to collect a percentage of their earning while off work due to a medical condition. This is an insurance program and each case must satisfy all the criteria of eligibility before any lost wage payment will be approved. The benefit can be employer paid, combination of employer and employee paid or paid solely by the employee. The benefits have limits including the maximum amount of weekly benefits as well as for a number of weeks. It is important to note that people who prescribe to this insurance plan are not automatically entitled to these benefits, they must submit the appropriate amount of medical documentation supporting "total disability" that continue on passed the short term disability eligibility period.

Labour Relations Act – Labour Relations Act, 1995, S.O. 1995, c. 1, Sched. A:
...The following are the purposes of the Act:

1. To facilitate collective bargaining between employers and trade unions that are the freely-designated representatives of the employees.

2. To recognize the importance of workplace parties adapting to change.

3. To promote flexibility, productivity and employee involvement in the workplace.

4. To encourage communication between employers and employees in the workplace.

5. To recognize the importance of economic growth as the foundation for mutually beneficial relations amongst employers, employees and trade unions.

6. To encourage co-operative participation of employers and trade unions in resolving workplace issues.

7. To promote the expeditious resolution of workplace disputes. 1995, c. 1, Sched. A, s. 2...

Latency Period
– period of time that it takes for the virus or illness to manifest into symptoms. This is very similar to the incubation period.

Lessons Learned
– a collection of information compiled from the successes and failures of the actions of the company referred to for assistance in planning future development and growth – with by not repeating the same mistakes or improving on the system by building on the current systems

Lock Out Tag Out
- To achieve zero (0) energy while equipment is being maintained or repaired in order to avoid injuries. Where zero (0) energy is not possible, then a procedure is required in order to allow the worker to work safely around live energy.

Long Term
– over a long period of time

Long Term Disability
– see LTD

Lost Time
– day's absence from work due to an injury or illness

Lost Time Injuries
– injuries that result in time away from work after the initial date of injury
- the WSIB (Policy 11-02-02; website 2009) - "...claim is created when a worker suffers an injury/disease which results in
- being off work past the day of accident
- loss of wages/earnings, or
- a permanent disability/impairment."

M

Machine Safeguarding
- Proper machine safeguarding is critical in reducing work related injuries like pinches, body parts caught in machines, from falling objects, etc. Another critical practice for prevention.

MAP

– WSIB incentive program for employers in Ontario with less than $25,000 the WSIB premiums per year. A program focused on promoting prevention of injury and lost time based in financial rewards and penalties depending on the performance of the company's health and safety program or record

Mediation

– a form of negotiation where all the parties at the table try to reach an agreement. A neutral third party listens to both sides to propose an agreement – meet in the middle type of agreement.

Medical Network

- Establishing a standard medical network of medical professionals will help injured workers to get the health care they require for speedy and complete recoveries. Early diagnosis results in earlier specific medical interventions with therapies and medicine focused on correcting the problem which results in quick and complete recoveries, less down time for production, less lost time, less time in modified duties, increased proficiencies, consistent high quality health care for injured workers, and decreased claim costs.

Medical Professional (also the health services provider)

- a person who has completed the medical education and training standards as outlined by the governing body of the medical community
- "...Medical education and training varies around the world. It typically involves entry level education at a university medical school, followed by a period of supervised practice or internship, and/or residency. This can be followed by postgraduate vocational training. A variety of teaching methods have been employed in medical education, still itself a focus of active research.
- Many regulatory authorities require continuing medical education, since knowledge, techniques and medical technology continue to evolve at a rapid rate...." Wikipedia, December 2009

Metrics

– statistical representation or depiction of measurable units being tracked usually in the form of graphs and charts of compiled information relevant to a program's performance

Ministry of Labour – Relationship and Resource

- The Ministry of Labour is funded by the government to enforce legislation under the Occupational Health and Safety Act. However, the MOL can be a resource for assisting to make the workplace a safe working environment. The more congenial and respectful the relationship is with the inspector, the more the inspector is willing to provide assistance, advice and comments rather than written orders, fines and penalties.

MMR – Maximum Medical Recovery Period also referred to as the Standard Recovery Period

- As set out by the American Medical Association Guide, each type of injury has an "average" time frame "normal" for that type of injury. For example, a broken bone has a standard recovery period of about six (6) weeks. However, each person heals differently and at different rates of time. The average for each injury is designed to understand when the healing process is prolonged resulting in complications to the normal recovery process.

- WSIB, Policy #11-01-05

- "...*Workers reach maximum medical recovery (MMR) when they have reached a plateau in their recovery and it is not likely that there will be any further significant improvement in their medical impairment...*"

MOL – Ministry of Labour, Ontario, Provincial Government; www.labour.gov.on.ca

...Established in 1919 to develop and enforce labour legislation, the Ministry of Labour's mission is to advance safe, fair and harmonious workplace practices that are essential to the social and economic well-being of the people of Ontario. Through the ministry's key areas of occupational health and safety, employment rights and responsibilities, labour relations and internal administration, the ministry's mandate is to set, communicate and enforce workplace standards while encouraging greater workplace self-reliance. A range of specialized agencies, boards and commissions assist the ministry in its work...

Modified Work

– work or tasks that have been adjusted to accommodate a restricted worker.

N

NEL – Non-economic Loss

- Is a monetary award that the WSIB gives to workers who have a permanent impairment as a result of a workplace injury or illness

NEER – New Experimental Experience Rating Plan
- A program that monitors and measures the health and safety performance of an Ontario employer based on workplace injury and workplace injury costs
- If the employer's rate of injuries and injury costs are lower than expected, the employer may receive a rebate
- If the employer's rate of injuries and injury costs are higher than expected, the employer may receive a surcharge
- This program is designed to attempt to encourage the employers in Ontario to decrease the number of injuries and decrease the severity of injuries at the workplace
- This program measures the company's performance against the performance of other companies in the same industrial rate group.

New Hire Orientation – Health and Safety Section
- The significance to introducing the new hire to health and safety information before they start working is that the practical application of this knowledge result in lower number of injuries and the company proves compliance to legislation by teaching the new people of the risks associated to the tasks they are expected to perform. The new worker must be knowledgeable and trained to identify the risks they will be exposed to while working and how to work safely with the risks.

No Lost Time Claims
– injury claims that do not result in any days or time away from work

Non-occupational Injuries/Illness/Disease:
- An injury, illness or disease arising as a result of an event or exposure to risk not related to work or the workplace

O

OHSAS 18001
...- OHSAS 18001 is an Occupation Health and Safety Assessment Series for health and safety management systems. It is intended to help organizations to control occupational health and safety risks. It was developed in response to widespread demand for a recognized standard against which to be certified and assessed... (Retrieved from: www.ohsas-18001-occupational-health-and-safety.com)

Objection
     – dispute decision rendered

Objection Process
     – each insurance program has its own process by which a claimant
     (or employer) can object to any decision made in the claim. Usual-
     ly starts with the claimant submitting a written response illustrating
     the reason for the objection and any new evidence to support the
     claimant or employer's position.

Objectives – see "Targets"

Occupational disease (WSIA 1997)
     - ... includes,
     (a) a disease resulting from exposure to a substance relating to a
     particular process, trade or occupation in an industry,
     (b) a disease peculiar to or characteristic of a particular industrial
     process, trade or occupation,
     (c) a medical condition that in the opinion of the Board requires a
     worker to be removed either temporarily or permanently from ex-
     posure to a substance because the condition may be a precursor to
     an occupational disease,
     (d) a disease mentioned in Schedule 3 or 4, or
     (e) a disease prescribed under clause 15.1 (8) (d); ("maladie profes-
     sionnelle")...

Occupational Health and Safety Act (OHSA)
     - OHSA is government legislation outlining minimum standards
     for ensuring the health and safety of all workers. To demonstrate
     the company's commitment to health and safety of its workers, the
     company should build on these minimum standards through poli-
     cies and procedures of the daily operation of the business.

Onsite Physiotherapy Program
     - By offering physio therapy services on site to workers with
     workplace injuries and approved workers compensation claims,
     the benefits to the participants include: improved communication
     between the medical professional provider and the company in
     order to monitor progress of the injured worker, convenience for
     the injured worker, increased morale in the plant, decreased lost
     time from therapy appointments, increased productivity time for
     the injured workers, reduced claim costs through direct pay of
     health care and lost time costs, improved knowledge of the service
     provider of our facility and the jobs available, improved post re-

covery job placements and monitoring, early intervention before injury reaches acute phase which decreases recovery period and time away from regular duties, and technical knowledge resource for ergonomic improvements in the plant, etc. The program should realize cost savings through reduced severity, reduced costs, reduced recovery time, and reduced loss of production time.

P

PDA – Physical Demands Analysis

- Outline of all physical activity required to perform a specific task. Defines each job or task in each work station. Used to determine if an injury is compatible with the demands of the task. For example, if the person packs parts all day which requires bending at the waist every 60 seconds and the injury is low back then the repetitive motion of the bending at the waist could have caused the low back injury. However if the injury was for the ankle, the bending at the waist is not related to the ankle and ankle may not be a work related. The WSIB considers all such factors when determining eligibility.

PLOE – Partial Loss of Earnings

– worker is only able to work part time instead of full time due to a disability

Penalties

– surcharges and or fines that are designed to deter the employer or benefits subscriber from incurring costs or encourage the same for prevention of costs

Performance Index

- found on the WSIB NEER statement, this index is used by THE WSIB to monitor and measure the health and safety performance of a company. The index is calculated by dividing the NEER costs by the Expected Costs found on the NEER statement (N/E). The formula is found in the formula summary section in this book.

Permanent impairment (WSIA 1997)

- "...means impairment that continues to exist after the worker reaches maximum medical recovery; ("déficience permanente")..."

Personal Protective Equipment – PPE - Canadian Centre for Occupational Health and Safety

- Retrieved from: CCOHS, www.ccohs.ca/oshanswers/preven tion/ppe

...is equipment worn by a worker to minimize exposure to specific occupational hazards. Examples of PPE are respirators, gloves, aprons, fall protection, and full body suits, as well as head, eye and foot protection. Using PPE is only one element in a complete safety program that would use a variety of strategies to maintain a safe and healthy occupational environment. PPE does not reduce the hazard itself nor does it guarantee permanent or total protection...

Premiums

– set rate of money for specific insurance coverage for a predefined benefit; the upfront costs charged for the policy. Does not include any rebates or surcharges because of the performance or usage of the benefits.

Prevention

- The company's proactive approach to reducing injuries will prove to be the best counter measure as it will reduce the number of injuries, the severity of injuries, recovery time, workers compensation claims costs, and improve morale. Prevention is a critical tool in reducing injuries and costs of injuries. Prevention can include ergonomic adjustments, well maintained equipment, well trained workforce, solid hazard identification, good risk assessment, engineering follow up to equipment, etc.

Prevention Techniques

– programs developed and implemented to prevent injuries or illness

Privacy Act

– Freedom of Information and Protection of Privacy Act, R.S.O. 1990, c. F.31

...The purposes of this Act are,

(a) to provide a right of access to information under the control of institutions in accordance with the principles that,

(i) information should be available to the public,

(ii) necessary exemptions from the right of access should be limited and specific, and

(iii) decisions on the disclosure of government information should be reviewed independently of government; and

(b) to protect the privacy of individuals with respect to personal information about themselves held by institutions and to provide individuals with a right of access to that information. R.S.O. 1990, c. F.31, s. 1....

Progressive Discipline
– process by which to discipline workers for infractions of company policy and procedures. The gradual increase in severity of punitive measures for repeated offenses.

Projecting – see "Forecasting"

R

Rate Group
– According to the WSIA, industry is grouped into sections depending on the type of work performed. The companies are grouped into like industries together to determine the risk exposure, frequency and severity of injury (actual and potential) as well as usage of WSI to determine premium rates of the group. This allows for a company to compare their performance within like companies (in the same rate group).

Rating Factor
- The WSIB uses actuarial tables to determine reserve factors used to calculate to project the future costs of the claim. For employers that participate in NEER, claims are only assessed for three (3)* years (known as the NEER window). Therefore, the WSIB uses these reserve factors to project the future costs of the claim in order to attempt to charge the company as much as possible for the claim before the claim surpasses the NEER window (time limit the WSIB can charge the company back for the costs of claims). *As of 2009, the NEER window is 3 years after the year of accident. However, there is some discussion over the past several years to increase this NEER window to 5 or 6 years.

Reasonable
- is defined as moderate or rational. In Ontario and Canadian courts, the legal application of "reasonable" is the "average" or normal response; the expected response that would be within the average person's capabilities.

Reasonable person

- the standard of measurement used to determine a person's response against the response of an average person with the average education level and average capabilities. The standard measurement in its elemental form is simply, "to think and act as a normal person of normal education and capacity for reason would think or act where normal usually means average according to educational standards of the land"

Rebate

- the employer receives money back from the WSIB premiums the employer pays to the WSIB based on the employer's WSIB costs was less than the employer's Expected costs (see formula sheet for formula)

Recovery

– the healing process

Recovery Period

– the time it takes for the healing to begin to the time the injury is healed

References or Reference Material

- This section lists the information resources for both the information contained in this document as well as for health and safety networking resources.

Regulation 1101 – Retrieved from: WSIA, 1997, First Aid Requirements

– ...All places of employment must have workers trained in first aid and first aid boxes with the equipment they need to offer first aid service quickly and safely. Sections 8, 9, 10, 11 and 16 of Regulation 1101 list the items that must be included in the first aid boxes in workplaces of different types and sizes. The quantities of any item specified may be increased to suit the needs of a particular workplace. Personal protective equipment (for example, CPR mask and non-latex gloves) as prescribed by the first aid training should also be included in the first aid box. In a location where a physician or registered nurse is available, the employer may authorize them to expand the contents of the first aid boxes. Equipment outside of the scope of first aiders, equipment that may deteriorate or that is potentially dangerous (for example, medication and ointments) should not be included in a first aid box. Section 6 of the Regulation requires that the boxes and their contents be checked regularly, minimum four times a year, to ensure that everything is in good order...

Relationship between the company and the workers compensation provider

- Open communication with the worker's compensation provider will build and reinforce a relationship with professionalism, trust, and an open exchange of information. The provider will tend to work with the company resulting in improved disability management, timely claim closure, reducing lost time costs, early and safe return programs for injured workers, injured worker mediation, timely return to regular duties, etc.

Repetitive

– to repeat the exact motion or series of motions in a short period of time.

- "<30 seconds or >50% of work cycle" (*Silverstein et al., 1986 – Silverstein, B.A., Fine, L.J., Armstrong, T.J., 1986, Hand wrist cumulative trauma disorders in industry. British Journal of Industrial Medicine*).

Reportable Injuries (the WSIB, Policy 15-01-02, website 2009)

– In Ontario, "...Employers **must** report a work-related accident to the WSIB if they learn that a worker requires health care and/or
- is absent from regular work
- earns less than regular pay for regular work (e.g., part-time hours)
- requires modified work at less than regular pay
- requires modified work at regular pay for more than seven **calendar** days following the date of accident..."
- In the US, recordable injuries (US' OHSA 300 log) are defined as "...new cases of injuries or illnesses including those pre-existing conditions that have been significantly aggravated by workplace events or exposures that result in:
• Death
• Days away from work
• Restricted work or transfer to another job
• Medical treatment beyond first aid
• Loss of consciousness
• Significant injury or illness diagnosed by a physician or other licensed healthcare professional..." (S. Wood, *Risk Control Bulletin February 2008, OHSA Log 300 Reporting* Requirements, www.acwajpia.com, 2010)

Reporting Process
– a mechanism or method for reporting injuries or illness to the company

Restrictions
– a set of motions that must be avoided in order to safely perform a task to avoid further injury

Return to Work
– a plan outlining a specific set of tasks to be performed safely within a specific set of restrictions for a specified period of time

Risk Assessment
– Retrieved from Wikipedia, the free encyclopaedia (en.wikipedia.org, 2009)

...is a step in a risk management process. Risk assessment is the determination of quantitative or qualitative value of risk related to a concrete situation and a recognized threat (also called hazard). Quantitative risk assessment requires calculations of two components of risk: R, the magnitude of the potential loss L, and the probability p, that the loss will occur...

Roles and Responsibilities
– obligations for each party to perform as defined by the law, the contract, the procedure, the policy, best practice, etc.

Root Cause Analysis and Corrective Actions
- To identify the main cause of problems and develop a plan of action to correct the problems will reduce the risk of injuries. By studying trends and incident reports, we are able to evaluate and review tasks that are believed to be causing injuries.

S

SCAR Process
– system corrective action report process
- Process by which incidents are investigated and a plan is developed to correct the problem or prevent recurrence

STD – Short Term Disability
- Temporary wage replacement benefit insurance program designed to allow workers to collect a percentage of their earning

while off work due to a medical condition. This is an insurance program and each case must satisfy all the criteria of eligibility before any lost wage payment will be approved. The benefit can be employer paid, combination of employer and employee paid or paid solely by the employee. The benefits have limits including the maximum amount of weekly benefits as well as for a number of weeks. It is important to note that people who prescribe to this insurance plan are not automatically entitled to these benefits; they must submit the appropriate amount of medical documentation supporting "total disability".

Safety Awareness and Training
- It is everyone's responsibility to act and work in a manner that would not endanger themselves or any coworkers. Therefore, every employee in the company should have the knowledge and skill for working safely in their respective jobs. The knowledge and skill is acquired through safety awareness and training.

Safety Glasses
- Safety glasses significantly reduce risk of injury to the eyes from such risks as airborne objects, contaminated air, bright lights, parts, etc. Safety glasses are considered personal protective equipment. According to the Occupational Health and Safety Act of Ontario, safety glasses are required in many work environments such as manufacturing, assembly, etc.

Safety Group – WSIB prevention activity for employers,
Retrieved from: WSIB Policy #13-01-03:
... provides a premium rebate to groups that foster a corporate safety culture among their members and encourage the co-operative implementation and enhancement of prevention and return to work programs. The group rebate is dependent upon the completion of action plans and reduction in the frequency and severity of lost time injuries...The group rebate is distributed among group members and is not subject to adjustment after distribution...

Safety Review Program (SRP) and Pre-Health and Safety Reviews (PSR)
- The purpose of the Pre-Health and Safety Review is to ensure that the equipment has passed specific minimum standards of safety requirements in Ontario prior to its use in the workplace. This will assist in avoiding injuries.

- The SRP is an information resource committee or program developed to review the risks of equipment and procedures, make recommendations, and advise on safety regulations to ensure safe operation and compliance to legislation. The recommendations are presented to the responsible engineers in order for the engineers to develop and implement preventative measures prior to the launch of production to reduce risks of injury.

Safety Shoes

- According to the Occupational Health and Safety Act of Ontario, safety shoes are another example of personal protective equipment. In order to reduce work related foot injuries from falling objects, implement a safety footwear policy where the footwear is approved by CSA and in compliance with OHSA. Safety shoes are required in many work environments according to the minimum standards as outlined in OHSA of Ontario.

Severity

- the number of lost time days over specific period of time normalized over the amount of work hours. This is a good measurable to track the effectiveness of health and safety programs and return to work program in terms of the number of days lost in total and relative to each claim. Trends like seasonal and workstation design will allow Management to assess for preventive action development and implementation.

Short Term

- a specified period of time which is of a small amount of time

SIEF –Secondary Injury Enhancement Fund

– WSIB, Policy #14-05-03:

–...If a prior disability caused or contributed to the compensable accident, or if the period resulting from an accident becomes prolonged or enhanced due to a pre-existing condition, all or part of the compensation and health care costs may be transferred from the accident employer in Schedule 1 to the SIEF...The objectives of this policy are to provide employers with financial relief when a pre-existing condition enhances or prolongs a work-related disability. It thereby encourages employers to hire workers with disabilities...

Standard Recovery

– the average or normal healing

Standard Recovery Period
> – the average time it takes to recover from a specific injury, disease or illness. This period is determined or established by the medical professional community.

Strategy
> – plan to achieve a goal or the goal itself

Strategic Planning
> – development of a course of actions to achieve a predefined strategy

Substance Abuse Program
> – a program to help a person affected by addiction to substance(s) to receive medical treatment and work towards stop using the substance

Suitable – appropriate within restrictions

Supervisor Competency in Health and Safety
> - Supervisors can be an effective front line to improving the health and safety of the workers. To do this, supervisors have to be trained on the rules, policies, procedures, their roles and responsibilities, and how to identify, assess and prevent the hazards that cause injuries.

Surcharge
> - the employer is charged additional premiums because the employer's WSIB costs were more than the employer's Expected costs (see formula sheet for formula). Should a company receive high surcharges for a period of time, the WSIB and MOL will target the company for frequent MOL visits and Workwell Audits of the health and safety program.

Sustainable
> – provide for over a long term or long period of time

T

Targets
> – goals to achieve set by the coordinator of the health and safety program or disability management program. The goals can be

influenced by the injury statistics, corporate strategic goals, cultural environment, new legislation, safety group activities, etc. The goals should be reasonable and achievable. When possible, the goals should be linked to the corporate goals in order to become strategic partners with corporate in the normal business operations.

Technical Knowledge of workers compensation rules and regulations

- Clear knowledge of information required for decision making will enable the company to submit appropriately detailed and complete information on each claim, state the company's position clearly, and improve the quality of submissions supported with objective facts. This will result in more informed decisions by the service provider including claim denials.

Total Disability

– it has been determined by a medical professional that a person is incapable of working or functioning because of the impact of an injury, disease or illness. In other words, the wage earner is prevented from earning a wage due to the results of an injury, disease or illness.

Training

– Retrieved from: Wikipedia, the free encyclopaedia
(en.wikipedia.org, 2009)

...the acquisition of knowledge, skills, and competencies as a result of the teaching of vocational or practical skills and knowledge that relate to specific useful competencies. It forms the core of apprenticeships and provides the backbone of content at institutes of technology (also known as technical colleges or polytechnics). In addition to the basic training required for a trade, occupation or profession, observers of the labour-market recognize today the need to continue training beyond initial qualifications: to maintain, upgrade and update skills throughout working life. People within many professions and occupations may refer to this sort of training as professional development...

Transportation of Dangerous Goods

– Canadian Federal Legislation, SOR/2008-34 (Amendment 6)
- Federal legislation regulating the transport of chemicals or substance deemed dangerous. In the United States, the federal legislation is 49 CFR.

Tribunal – WSIAT – Workplace Safety and Insurance Tribunal
   1. Last stage of the appeals process.
   2. Board or panel of arbitrators reviews all the parties' arguments and decides the final resolution
   3. Decisions are legally binding and final

U

Undue Hardship

   - ...Accommodation can only be denied if an employer can provide quantifiable evidence that the required accommodation would pose significant and irreparable harm to the operation of the University. The considerations in determining undue hardship include: cost, outside sources of funding, if any and health and safety concerns, if any. Among the factors excluded are business inconvenience, and employee morale. (Retrieved from: Queen's Human Rights Office (613) 533-6886, Queen's University, www.queensu.ca/humanrights/accommodationbrochure.htm)

Unions

   – organization of workers with the objective to collective improve the compensation and working conditions of the workplace. Larry Suffield, "Labour Relations, Second Edition, PH Series in Human Resources Management" (2007)

V

Visitor/Contractor Safety Policy

   - To ensure that our employees and visitors (including contractors) are working in a safe environment and working safely while on the premises, the company should develop minimum standards for the visitors and contractors to observe while on company premises. All suppliers and their workers must perform their responsibilities in compliance with safety instructions, safe work practices, legislated requirements and regulations to minimize the possibility of injury to themselves or to others. The program should include a means to educate all people of the risks in the workplace as well as the rules and procedures of the workplace in order for their visit to be safe.

Vocational Retraining
        – training towards a new career
W

WSIA – Workplace Safety and Insurance Act of Ontario;
        In Ontario, the workers' compensation insurance program is regulated by legislation. This legislation is administered by a branch of the Ontario government called Workplace Safety and Insurance Board (WSIB).
        "...The purpose of this Act is to accomplish the following in a financially responsible and accountable manner:
        1. To promote health and safety in workplaces and to prevent and reduce the occurrence of workplace injuries and occupational diseases.
        2. To facilitate the return to work and recovery of workers who sustain personal injury arising out of and in the course of employment or who suffer from an occupational disease.
        3. To facilitate the re-entry into the labour market of workers and spouses of deceased workers.
        4. To provide compensation and other benefits to workers and to the survivors of deceased workers. 1997, c. 16, Sched. A, s. 1; 1999, c. 6, s. 67 (1); 2005, c. 5, s. 73 (1)."

WSIB – Workplace Safety and Insurance Board
        - Branch of the Provincial Government that administers and facilitates the regulations according to the WSIA.
        - Monitors workplace injuries and assists in the Early and Safety Return to Work (ESRTW)

WSIB Accreditation
        - graduates from the WSIB Prevention Program, Safety Group Program and continuing safety group activities by becoming industrial leaders in health and safety

WHMIS and MSDS
        - Workplace Hazardous Materials Information System (WHMIS) is a Canadian wide information resource system designed by business, labour and government so people who work with hazardous materials at the workplace have the necessary information about the product to work safely and protect their health
        - Material Safety Data Sheets (MSDS) are sheets of pertinent information for people to work safely with hazardous substances

Wage Replacement Program

– insurance program to replace lost wages usually due to a sickness, illness, or injury

Wellness Programs

– program designed to promote and encourage good health

Work hardening or work conditioning

- a gradual introduction of physical demands to a worker's set of tasks in order prepares the worker's muscles for the strength and endurance requirements to return to regular duties or to perform specific duties safely.

Worker

– According to the WSIA, Policy #12-02-01,

a worker is: "...a person who has entered into or is employed under a contract of service, or apprenticeship, written or oral, express or implied, whether by way of manual labour or otherwise, and includes

- a learner or student
- a member of a municipal volunteer fire brigade or a volunteer ambulance brigade
- a person deemed to be a worker of an employer by direction or order of the WSIB
- a person summoned to assist in controlling or extinguishing a fire by an authority empowered to do so
- a person who assists in any search and rescue operation at the request of and under the direction of a member of the Ontario Provincial Police Force
- a person who assists in connection with an emergency that has been declared by the Lieutenant Governor in Council or the Premier under section 7.0.1 of the Emergency Management and Civil Protection Act or by the head of council of a municipality under section 4 of that Act
- an auxiliary member of a police force
- a person deemed to be a worker under Section 12, or
- a pupil deemed to be a worker under the *Education Act*."

Workers Compensation Program

– insurance program designed to replace the wages and pay for the costs of an injury due to a workplace event.

Workers Compensation cost review and analysis

- Cost statements provided by the service provider can be a useful measurable to monitor the progress of the company's targets of reducing injuries and costs due to injuries as well as to strategize for reducing both injuries and costs.

Workplace Injuries or Occupational Injuries/Illness/Disease

- An injury or disease arising out of exposure to risk at the workplace. For example, tripping over a part on the floor and the worker breaks their arm

Workwell Program

— is an audit conducted by the WSIB due to poor health and safety performance or high injury frequency and severity rates. The program is designed to assist the employers with poor performance rates to improve their health and safety and prevention programs resulting in reduction of injuries both in terms of frequency and severity. The MOL could also get involved depending on the reason for conducting the audit. According to the WSIA, Policy #13-01-02, this program is in addition to any experience rating programs. This program charges an additional premium or premium rate adjustments. Employers are required to improve their compliance and performance rating within six (6) months. If the employer fails to comply or to improve, additional premium charges will be charged immediately. The employer has up to two (2) chances (audits) to provide evidence of improvements to their program. Furthermore, the criteria for becoming a candidate for a Workwell audit includes: "…

- the number and rate of Ministry of Labour workplace orders that have been issued and the degree of compliance with those orders,
- the type of order and the severity of the contravention of the *Occupational Health and Safety Act,*
- prosecutions initiated for failure to comply with Ministry of Labour orders,
- injury frequency information,
- injury cost information,
- severity of injury information,
- compliance with first aid regulations,
- complaints or referrals from workers or other parties, or
- any information concerning deficiencies or mitigating activities related to an employer's health and safety measures…."

FORMULAS

1. Frequency = (# of injuries X 200,000) / total # of hours worked

2. Severity = (# of lost time days X 200,000) / total # of hours worked

3. Premiums= $ rate group premium factor X $100 / payroll

4. NEER Rebate = (Expected costs – NEER costs) X rating factor
       = less than one

5. NEER Surcharge = (Expected costs – NEER costs) X rating factor
       = greater than one

6. Rating Factor = determined by rate group and the WSIB actuaries
       The greater total of:
       = 15% + (premiums / (premiums + (5 X Max Ins. Earnings)) X 100
       OR
       = 15% + (ins. earnings / (ins. earnings + (225 X max ins. earnings)) X 100

7. Claim Age = # of months from accident date to statement date

8. Performance Index = NEER costs / Expected Costs

9. Non Pension = Loss of Earnings (LOE) + Health Care + LMR

10. Projected Future Costs (PFC)= Discounted Costs X Reserve Factor

11. Limited Claim Costs = DPA + PFC + OC
       = subjective to claim cost limit = 4 X Max Earnings Ceiling

12. Expected Costs = Premiums X Expected Costs Factor

13. Expected Costs Factor =

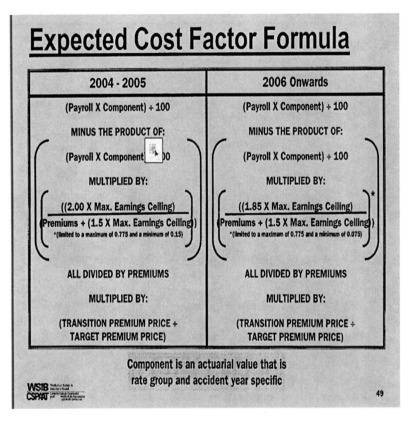

Expected Cost Factor Formula

2004 - 2005	2006 Onwards
(Payroll X Component) ÷ 100	(Payroll X Component) ÷ 100
MINUS THE PRODUCT OF:	MINUS THE PRODUCT OF:
(Payroll X Component) ÷ 100	(Payroll X Component) ÷ 100
MULTIPLIED BY:	MULTIPLIED BY:
$\frac{((2.00 \text{ X Max. Earnings Ceiling)}}{\text{Premiums} + (1.5 \text{ X Max. Earnings Ceiling)})}$ *(limited to a maximum of 0.775 and a minimum of 0.15)	$\frac{((1.85 \text{ X Max. Earnings Ceiling)}}{\text{Premiums} + (1.5 \text{ X Max. Earnings Ceiling)})}$ *(limited to a maximum of 0.775 and a minimum of 0.075)
ALL DIVIDED BY PREMIUMS	ALL DIVIDED BY PREMIUMS
MULTIPLIED BY:	MULTIPLIED BY:
(TRANSITION PREMIUM PRICE ÷ TARGET PREMIUM PRICE)	(TRANSITION PREMIUM PRICE ÷ TARGET PREMIUM PRICE)

Component is an actuarial value that is rate group and accident year specific

WSIB
CSPAAT

49

14. Pension = NEL + Survivors

15. NEER Costs = Claim costs X reserve factor + overhead costs

16. Overhead costs = claim costs X overhead factor
    = (discounted past awards + projected future costs) X overhead factor

17. Discounted Past Award (DPA) =
    Discounted Non Pension + Discounted Pension

REFERENCES

American Medical Association (AMA) (2010). Retrieved from: http://www.ama-assn.org/

Bird, Christopher (2008, July 22). "Hydro-Québec Makes employers A Bit Less Nervous About Employee Accomodation". Retrieved from: www.thecourt.ca

Canadian Centre for Occupational Health and Safety (2008, January 15). Due Diligence Self-Assessment. Retrieved from: http://www.ccohs.ca/

Canadian Standards Act (2010). Retrieved from: www.csa-international.org

Canadian Standards Act (2010). Retrieved from: www.csa.ca/cm/ca/en/home

Disability Association for Canada (2010). Retrieved from: www.ccdonline.ca/en/socialpolicy/fda

Disability Association for Ontario (2010). Retrieved from: www.ontario.ca/en/communities/disabilities

Employment Standards Act of Ontario (2000) (2009, December 15). Retrieved from: http://www.e-laws.gov.on.ca/html/statutes/english/elaws_statutes_00e41_e.htm

Freedom of Information and Protection of Privacy Act, R.S.O. 1990, c. F.31 (2008, October). Retrieved from: http://www.e-laws.gov.on.ca/html/statutes/english/elaws_statutes_90f31_e.htm

Human Resources Development Centre (of Canada) (2010). Retrieved from: www.servicecanada.gc.ca

Human Resources Professional Association (2008). "HRPA PLEASED WITH SUPREME COURT'S DECISION IN KEAYS VS. HONDA CANADA INC." *360 eNewsletter.*

Human Resources Professional Associations (2010). Retrieved from: http://www.hrpa.ca

Human Rights Code of Canada (2009). Retrieved from: www.chrc-ccdp.ca

Human Rights Code of Ontario (2009). Retrieved from: www.ohrc.on.ca

Labour Relations Act, (of Ontario) 1995, S.O. 1995, c. 1, Sched. A, (2009, December 15). Retrieved from: http://www.e-laws.gov.on.ca/html/statutes/english/elaws_statutes_95l01_e.htm

Lynk, Michael, Professor (2008). *"Disability and the Duty to Accommo-date in the Canadian Workplace".* Professor of Law at the Universi-ty of Western Ontario. Retreived from: http://www.ofl.ca/ up-loads/library/disability_issues/ACCOMMODATION.pdf

Ministry of Labour (2010). Retrieved from: www.labour.gov.on.ca.

National Institute of Occupational Safety and Health (NIOSH) (2010). Retrieved from: http://www.cdc.gov/niosh/

Occupational Health and Safety Act of Ontario (2009, December). Retrieved from: http://www.e-laws.gov.on.ca/html/statutes/ english/elaws_statutes_90001_e.htm

Occupational Health and Safety Management Systems (OHSAS 18001) (2009). Retrieved from: *www.ohsas-18001-occupational-health-and-safety.com*

Ontario Building Code (2009). Retrieved from: www.obc.mah. gov.on.ca.

Ontario Safety Electrical Code (2009). Retrieved from: www.esainspection.net

Queen's University Human Rights Office (2010). "Responsibilities of each party in the duty to accommodate". Retrieved from: www.queensu.ca/humanrights/accommodationbrochure.htm

Silverstein, B.A., Fine, L.J., Armstrong, T.J. (1986). Hand wrist cu-mulative trauma disorders in industry. *British Journal of Industrial Medicine.*

Suffield, Larry (2007). Labour Relations, Second Edition, PH Series in Human Resources Management.

Wikipedia (2009). Retrieved from: en.wikipedia.org

Workplace Safety and Insurance Board of Ontario (2010). Retrieved from: www.wsib.on.ca

Workplace Safety Insurance Act of Ontario (2009, December). Re-trieved from: http://www.e-laws.gov.on.ca/html/statutes/ eng-lish/elaws_statutes_97w16_e.htm

APPENDIX A

SAMPLE INCIDENT REPORT

Environmental Health and Safety Incident Report

Please complete ALL applicable sections of the report

Nature of Incident

Date of Incident: _____   Date Reported: _____

Time of Incident: _____ ( ) am ( ) pm   Time Reported: _____

Shift: S   M   T   W   T   F   S   ( ) Afternoons   ( ) Days   ( ) Midnights;   Overtime   Yes   No

Critical Injury: Yes   No   If so, time EHS Advisor called: _____   time MOL called: _____

Nature of Loss and immediate cause: _____

Where did Incident Occur: _____

Who was the Incident reported to: _____ Supervisor: _____

A   Personal Information: ( ) Employee   ( ) Contractor - Employer: _____
                                                    ( ) Visitor - Employer: _____

Name

| Family Name | First Name | Employee Number |

Address _____   City _____

Province _____   Postal Code _____

Telephone _____   Gender   ( ) male   ( ) female

Job classification during Incident _____

How long doing the Job? _____   Job Rotation? _____

Usual Occupation: ( ) Yes   ( ) No   If no, what is the Usual Occupation: _____

Union   ( ) Yes   ( ) No   **Union Local** _____

Work Centre _____   Workstation # _____ Part # _____

Consequence: ( ) Near Miss   ( ) First Aid   ( ) Medical Aid (Industrial Disease/Illness)
( )   Lost Time (Including Industrial Disease/Illness)   ( )   Fatality (Including Industrial Disease/Illness)

* As per section 5 of the Industrial Regulations

Witness(es)

Witness 1

| Name | Street Address | City | Telephone |

Witness 2

| Name | Street Address | City | Telephone |

Witness 3

| Name | Street Address | City | Telephone |

For non-injury incidents, continue on bottom of page 3. For detailed Witness Statement, go to page 8.

Document # _____   Version # (date) _____   Property of _____

(Company)

A. Personal Injury – Identifying Information

Part(s) of the body injured

Head ( )F ( )B	Eye ( )L ( )R	
Ear ( )L ( )R	Neck ( )L ( )R	
Back ( ) Lower	( ) Mid	( ) Upper
Shoulder( )L ( )R	Forearm( )L ( )R	
Elbow ( )L ( )R	Wrist ( )L ( )R	
Hand ( )L ( )R	Finger ( )L ( )R	
Chest ( )L ( )R	Abdomen( )L ( )R	
Leg ( )L ( )R	Knee ( )L ( )R	
Ankle ( )L ( )R	Foot ( )L ( )R	
Toe ( )L ( )R	Other _____	

R   L   L   R

Circle Area of Injury

Injury type   N/A ( )

( ) Bruise, contusion	( ) Puncture	( ) Burn
( ) Radiation	( ) Cut, abrasion, laceration	( ) Skin or eye irritation
( ) Discomfort	( ) Unconsciousness	( ) Fatality
( ) Strain	( ) Other _____	

Accident Agent   N/A ( )

( ) Caught between	( ) Hand tool power	( ) Contact with chemicals
( ) Lift truck involvement	( ) Contact with electricity	( ) Material handling
( ) Contact with foreign body	( ) Machinery involvement	( ) Contact with heat or cold
( ) Overuse or overexertion	( ) Fall from height	( ) Struck by
( ) Fall from same level	( ) Struck against	( ) Hand tool involvement
( ) Other		

Details of incident: Pictures taken   ( ) Yes   ( ) No

Supervisor to describe **what** happened, **who** was involved, **how** did it happen, **when** did it happen, **why** did it happen and **where** did it happen?

_____
_____
_____
_____
_____
_____
_____
_____
_____
_____
_____
_____
_____
_____
_____
_____
_____

Document #   Version # (date)   Property of

_____ (Company)

Medical & Return to Work Section	**Treatment** N/A ( ) ( ) First aid – in plant only ( ) Outside facility - specify _____ If worker left plant for treatment, time left _____ ( ) am ( ) pm time returned _____ ( ) am ( ) pm ( ) Family physician - name _____ Functional Ability Form (FAF) Package Provided? ( )Yes ( ) No Date _____ Time: _____ a.m. p.m. Transportation: ( ) via taxi ( ) via ambulance ( ) other: _____ **Initial Modified Work Offer (prior to leaving the plant for medical attention)** Based on the body part chart on the reverse side, circle modified work Supervisor offered. If not offered, explain: _____ Worker acknowledgement that modified work has been offered. _____ (worker initials) **Modified Work Offer (after worker returns with FAF, Supervisor reviews FAF with Worker)** **FAF restrictions:** ( ) Returned to regular work ( ) Off work balance of shift ( ) Returned to modified duties ( ) Off work for _____ days Worker acknowledgement that modified work has been offered. _____ (worker initials)

If it is only personal injury or near miss incident, go to page 5, supervisor follow up

B Property Loss	( ) Property Damage ( ) Theft/Vandalism ( ) Sabotage ( ) Violence/Harassment Estimated cost of damage ($): _____ Other Investigation attached ☐ Yes ☐ No Pictures taken ☐ Yes ☐ No

C: Environmental Incident	**Type of Environmental Incident:** ( ) Air ( ) Water ( ) Land **Consequence:** ( ) Minor Spill ( ) Major Spill ( ) Release to air / water Did the release/spill pose immediate risk to people, health or the environment? ( ) Yes ( ) No Date and Time the Municipality _____ and MOE was notified _____ Was a spill kit used? ( ) Yes ( ) No Location _____ If Yes, which type ( ) Regular ( ) Mercury ( ) Blood Borne Pathogen If used, was the spill kit replenished? ( ) Yes ( ) No Attach all related MSDS: ( ) Estimated cost of damage ($): Other Investigation attached ( ) Yes ( ) No Pictures taken ( ) Yes ( ) No

D: Emergency Situations	**Emergency Situations:** ( ) Fire ( ) Bomb ( ) **Power Failure** ( ) Other _____ Type of Emergency: _____ Estimated cost of damage ($): _____ Other Investigation attached ( ) Yes ( ) No Pictures taken ( ) Yes ( ) No

Body Part Chart

Body Part Injured	Standard Restrictions	Modified work within standard restrictions	Comments by Worker or adjustments due to FAF by Supervisor (initial each)
Shoulder	No above shoulder activity Limit reaching away from body with weight or against resistance Keep hands at waist to eye levels and between shoulders	No packing or retrieving from far side of bins (bin on spin table or cart) No welders Offline/self-paced work: -Grinder – light parts and w/hook - Tear downs - Boxing parts	
Hand/wrist	No forceful gripping and/or pinching No deviation of wrist (pronation or supination / ulnar or radial) No repeated flexion/extension of the wrist	No pushing of tubes No trimming No inspect and pack Offline/self-paced work: - grinder – light parts - tear downs	
Low Back	No lifting away from the body >10 lbs No side bending or twisting of lumbar spine No repetitive movements of the lumbar spine No sustained forward posture (stooping)	No packing into bins or retrieving from floor level bins Off line/self-paced work: - Grinder – light parts and with hook - Tear downs	

* This includes reference to Section 27 of the Occupation Health and Safety Act

Supervisor Follow up

Causes

Please identify the basic Information, in the chart below that may have contributed to the incident. Minimum, one item per box.

People	Equipment	Materials	Environment	Process/ Work Activity	State of Mind	Critical Error	Violence/ Harassment
					Rushing	Eyes Not on Task	
					Frustration	Mind not on Task	
					Fatigue	Line of Fire	
					Complacency	Balance/Traction/Grip	

Root Causes – (remember to circle the state of mind and critical error that is most applicable)

_____

_____

_____

Corrective and Preventive Action Plan

Short Term Corrective Action Implemented – (Supervisor has the obligation to implement this immediately)

_____

_____

_____

_____

_____

Short Term Corrective Action Recommended –

Person Responsible _____ Due Date: _____ Date Completed _____

_____

_____

_____

Review Section

I have reviewed the entire report and have completed all applicable sections:

_____ _____ _____
Signature of person reporting incident Signature of Supervisor Date Completed

Review by Safety Representative

_____ _____ _____
Safety Rep or designate (Signature) Name (Print) Date Completed

_____ **(Company)**

Long Term Preventive Action –
_____
_____
_____
_____
_____

Long Term Corrective Action Recommended –
Person Responsible _____   Due Date: _____Date Completed _____
_____
_____
_____
_____

Action Items Required			Violence/Harassment:
Hazards and Risk	☐ Yes	☐ No	Referred for TAT investigation: _____
Aspects and Impacts review	☐ Yes	☐ No	Copy of investigation sent to EHS ____
Emergency Preparedness and Response			
(Review & Revise Emergency Procedures)	☐ Yes	☐ No	Outcome of the investigation: _____
Business Continuity Plan	☐ Yes	☐ No	
Lessons Learned	☐ Yes	☐ No	
5 Why	☐ Yes	☐ No	

EHS Advisor Follow-up

Attachments
_____
_____
_____
_____

Reviewed by

EHS Advisor or designate: _____   Date _____
                          Signature

Worker Representative: _____   Date _____
                        Signature

Other Reviewers as Applicable: _____ Date _____
                                Signature

Employee/Visitor/Contractor Statement

_____
_____
_____
_____
_____
_____
_____
_____
_____
_____
_____
_____
_____
_____
_____
_____
_____
_____
_____
_____
_____

_____   _____
Signature of Employee/Visitor/Contractor   Date

If translator required I have provided translation assistance for the above statement.
I declare it to be true and accurate to the best of my knowledge.

_____ _____   _____ ____
Name of Translator (Print Name)   Signature   Date

BEST PRACTICES IN HEALTH & SAFETY

Witness Statement.

Name _____

      Family Name   **First Name**   **Middle Name**

Clock Number: _____   **Occupation:**_____

Employer if not (the company):

Address   _____   City   _____

Province   _____   Postal Code_____

Telephone _____   Gender ( ) male   ( ) female

Witness Statement

_____
_____
_____
_____
_____
_____
_____
_____
_____
_____
_____

_____   _____

Signature of Employee/Visitor/Contractor   Date

If translator required I have provided translation assistance for the above statement. I declare it to be true and accurate to the best of my knowledge.

_____ _____ _____

Name of Translator (Print Name)   Signature   Date

Appendix B

Sample Body Part Chart

Body Part Injured	Standard Restrictions	Modified work within standard restrictions	Comments by Worker or adjustments due to FAF by Supervisor (initial each)
Shoulder	No above shoulder activity Limit reaching away from body with weight or against resistance Keep hands at waist to eye levels and between shoulders	No packing or retrieving from far side of bins (bin on spin table or cart) No welders Offline/self-paced work: -Grinder – light parts and w/hook - Tear downs - Boxing parts	

Hand/wrist	No forceful gripping and/or pinching
	No deviation of wrist (pronation or supination / ulnar or radial)
	No repeated flexion/extension of the wrist
		No pushing of tubes
		No trimming
		No inspect and pack
		Offline/self-paced work:
		  - grinder – light parts
		  - tear downs	

Low Back	No lifting away from the body >10 lbs No side bending or twisting of lumbar spine No repetitive movements of the lumbar spine No sustained forward posture (stooping)	No packing into bins or retrieving from floor level bins Off line/self-paced work: - Grinder – light parts and with hook - Tear downs	

449

Sample Form 7

WSIB / CSPAAT

Mail To:
200 Front Street West
Toronto ON M5V 3J1

OR Fax To:
416-344-4684
OR 1-888-313-7373

Please PRINT in black ink

7

Employer's Report of Injury/Disease (Form 7)

Claim Number

A. Worker Information

Job Title/Occupation (at the time of accident/illness - do not use abbreviations)	Length of time in this position while working for you

Please check if this worker is a: ☐ executive ☐ elected official ☐ owner ☐ spouse or relative of the employer

Social Insurance Number

Last Name / First Name

Is the worker covered by a Union/Collective Agreement? ☐ yes ☐ no

Worker Reference Number

Address (number, street, apt., suite, unit)

Worker's preferred language: ☐ English ☐ French ☐ Other

Date of Birth: dd mm yy

City/Town / Province / Postal Code

Telephone

Sex ☐ M ☐ F

Date of Hire: dd mm yy

B. Employer Information

Fold here for #10 envelope

Trade and Legal Name (if different provide both)

Check one: ☐ Firm Number OR ☐ Account Number

Provide Number

Mailing Address

Rate Group Number

Classification Unit Code

City/Town / Province / Postal Code

Telephone

Description of Business Activity

Does your firm have 20 or more workers? ☐ yes ☐ no

FAX Number

Branch Address where worker is based (if different from mailing address - no abbreviations)

City/Town / Province / Postal Code

Alternate Telephone

C. Accident/Illness Dates and Details

1. Date and hour of accident/Awareness of illness: dd mm yy ☐ AM ☐ PM

2. Who was the accident/illness reported to? (Name & Position)

Date and hour reported to employer: dd mm yy ☐ AM ☐ PM

Telephone / Ext.

3. Was the accident/illness:
☐ Sudden Specific Event/Occurrence
☐ Gradually Occurring Over Time
☐ Occupational Disease
☐ Fatality

4. Type of accident/illness: (Please check all that apply)
☐ Struck/Caught
☐ Overexertion
☐ Repetition
☐ Fire/Explosion
☐ Fall
☐ Harmful Substances/Environmental
☐ Assault
☐ Other
☐ Slip/Trip
☐ Motor Vehicle Incident

5. Area of Injury (Body Part) - (Please check all that apply)

☐ Head ☐ Teeth
☐ Face ☐ Neck
☐ Eye(s) ☐ Chest
☐ Ear(s)
☐ Other

☐ Upper back
☐ Lower back
☐ Abdomen
☐ Pelvis

Left / Right: ☐ Shoulder ☐ Arm ☐ Elbow ☐ Forearm

Left / Right: ☐ Wrist ☐ Hand ☐ Finger(s)

Left / Right: ☐ Hip ☐ Thigh ☐ Knee ☐ Lower Leg

Left / Right: ☐ Ankle ☐ Foot ☐ Toe(s)

6. Describe what happened to cause the accident/illness and what the worker was doing at the time (lifting a 50 lb. box, slipped on wet floor, repetitive movements, etc...). Include what the injury is and any details of equipment, materials, environmental conditions (work area, temperature, noise, chemical, gas, fumes, other person) that may have contributed. **For a condition that occurred gradually over time, please attach a description of the physical activity required to do the work.**

0007A (11/05)   A guide to complete this form is available at   www.wsib.on.ca   Page 1 of 4

WSIB
CSPAAT

7 Employer's Report of Injury/Disease (Form 7)

Claim Number

Please PRINT in black ink

Worker Name	Social Insurance Number

C. Accident/Illness Dates and Details (Continued)

7. Did the accident/illness happen on the employer's premises (owned, leased or maintained)? ☐ yes ☐ no

Specify where (shop floor, warehouse, client/customer site, parking lot, etc.).

8. Did the accident/illness happen outside the Province of Ontario? ☐ yes ☐ no

If yes, where (city, province/state, country).

9. Are you aware of any witnesses or other employees involved in this accident/illness? ☐ yes ☐ no

If yes, provide name(s), position(s), and work phone number(s).

1. _____

2. _____

10. Was any individual, who does not work for your firm, partially or totally responsible for this accident/illness? ☐ yes ☐ no

If yes, please provide name and work phone number

11. Are you aware of any prior similar or related problem, injury or condition? ☐ yes ☐ no

If yes, please explain

12. If you have concerns about this claim, attach a written submission to this form. ☐ submission attached

D. Health Care

1. Did the worker receive health care for this injury? ☐ yes ☐ no   If yes, when: dd mm yy

2. When did the employer learn that the worker received health care? dd mm yy

3. Where was the worker treated for this injury? (Please check all that apply)

☐ On-site health care   ☐ Ambulance   ☐ Emergency department   ☐ Admitted to hospital   ☐ Health professional office   ☐ Clinic

☐ Other: _____

Name, address and phone number of health professional or facility who treated this worker (if known) _____

E. Lost Time - No Lost Time

1. Please choose one of the following indicators. **After the day of accident/awareness of illness, this worker:**

☐ Returned to his/her **regular job and has not** lost any time and/or earnings. **(Complete sections G and J).**

☐ Returned to **modified work and has not** lost any time and/or earnings. **(Complete sections F, G, and J).**

☐ **Has lost time and/or earnings. (Complete ALL remaining sections).**

dd mm yy — Provide date worker first lost time   Date worker returned to work (if known) dd mm yy ☐ regular work ☐ modified work

2. This Lost Time - No Lost Time - Modified Work information was confirmed by: ☐ Myself ☐ Other Name _____   Telephone ____   Ext ____

F. Return To Work

1. Have you been provided with work limitations for this worker's injury? ☐ yes ☐ no

2. Has modified work been discussed with this worker? ☐ yes ☐ no

3. Has modified work been offered to this worker? ☐ yes ☐ no

If yes, was it ☐ Accepted ☐ Declined   ☐ If Declined please attach a copy of the written offer given to the worker.

4. Who is responsible for arranging worker's return to work ☐ Myself ☐ Other Name _____   Telephone ____   Ext ____

0007A (11/05)

Page 2 of 4

WSIB
CSPAAT

Please PRINT in black ink

7 Employer's Report of Injury/Disease (Form 7)

Claim Number

Worker Name	Social Insurance Number

G. Base Wage/Employment Information - (Do not include overtime here)

1. Is this worker (Please check all that apply)

☐ Permanent Full Time ☐ Casual/Irregular ☐ Student ☐ Registered Apprentice ☐ Owner Operator or (Sub) Contractor
☐ Permanent Part Time ☐ Seasonal ☐ Unpaid/Trainee ☐ Optional Insurance
☐ Temporary Full Time ☐ Contract ☐ Other _____
☐ Temporary Part Time

2. Regular rate of pay $ _____ per ☐ hour ☐ day ☐ week ☐ other

H. Additional Wage Information

1. Net Claim Code or Amount Federal _____ Provincial _____

2. Vacation pay - on each cheque? ☐ yes ☐ no Provide percentage ____ %

3. Date and hour last worked dd mm yy ☐ AM ☐ PM

4. Normal working hours on last day worked From ____ ☐ AM ☐ PM To ____ ☐ AM ☐ PM

5. Actual earnings for last day worked $ _____

6. Normal earnings for last day worked $ _____

7. Advances on wages: Is the worker being paid while he/she recovers? ☐ yes ☐ no If yes, indicate: ☐ Full/Regular ☐ Other

8. Other Earnings (Not Regular Wages): Provide the **total of additional earnings** for each week for the 4 weeks before the accident/illness.

* For Rotational Shift workers - If the shift cycle exceeds 4 weeks, please attach the earnings information for the last complete shift cycle prior to the date of accident/illness.

Use these spaces for any other earnings ▼ (indicate Commission, Differentials, Premiums, Bonus, Tips, In Lieu %, etc..).

Period	From Date (dd/mm/yy)	To Date (dd/mm/yy)	Mandatory Overtime Pay	Voluntary Overtime Pay	Commission	Commission	Commission	Commission
Week 1			$	$	$	$	$	$
Week 2			$	$	$	$	$	$
Week 3			$	$	$	$	$	$
Week 4			$	$	$	$	$	$

I. Work Schedule (Complete either A, B or C. Do not include overtime shifts)

☐ **(A.) Regular Schedule** - indicate normal work days and hours.

Sunday	Monday	Tuesday	Wednesday	Thursday	Friday	Saturday

▶ **Example:** Monday to Friday, 40 hours

S	M	T	W	T	F	S
	8	8	8	8	8	

or,

☐ **(B.) Repeating Rotational Shift Worker** - Provide

NUMBER OF DAYS ON	NUMBER OF DAYS OFF	HOURS PER SHIFT(s)	NUMBER OF WEEKS IN CYCLE

▶ **Example:** 4 days on, 4 days off, 12 hours per shift, 8 weeks in cycle.

or,

☐ **(C.) Varied or Irregular Work Schedule** - Provide the total number of regular hours and shifts for each week for the 4 weeks prior to the accident/illness. (Do not include overtime hours or shifts here).

	Week 1	Week 2	Week 3	Week 4
From/To Dates (dd/mm/yy)	/	/	/	/
Total Hours Worked				
Total Shifts Worked				

J. It is an offence to deliberately make false statements to the Workplace Safety and Insurance Board. I declare that all of the information provided on pages 1, 2, and 3 is true.

Name of person completing this report (please print)	Official title

Signature	Telephone	Ext.	Date dd mm yy

THE WORKPLACE SAFETY AND INSURANCE ACT REQUIRES YOU GIVE A COPY OF THIS FORM TO YOUR WORKER

0007A (11/05)

Page 3 of 4

453

WSIB
CSPAAT

7 Employer's Report
of Injury/Disease (Form 7)

Claim Number

Please PRINT in black ink

Worker Name	Social Insurance Number

K. Additional Information

THE WORKPLACE SAFETY AND INSURANCE ACT REQUIRES YOU GIVE A COPY OF THIS FORM TO YOUR WORKER

0007A (11/05)

Page 4 of 4

454

SAMPLE FAF

WSIB
CSPAAT

Mail to:
200 Front Street West
Toronto ON M5V 3J1

or Fax to:
416 344-4684
OR 1-888-313-7373

Please PRINT in black ink

FAF

Functional Abilities Form
for Planning Early
and Safe Return to Work

Claim No.
if known?

A. Section A to be completed by the employer and/or worker.

Worker's Last Name	First Name	Telephone
Prefill Injured Worker's Name		

Address (no., street, apt.)	City/Town	Province	Postal Code
Prefill all injured worker info			

Employer's Name
Prefill Company Info

Full Address (No., Street, Apt.)

City/Town	Prov.	Postal Code

Date of Birth
(dd/mm/yyyy)

Date of Accident/
Awareness of Illness,
(dd/mm/yyyy)

Employer
Telephone

Employer
Fax No.

1. Type of job at time of accident (where available, please attach description of job activities)

Area(s) of injury(ies)/illness(es)

2. Have the worker and the employer discussed Return To Work ■ yes ☐ no

If no, will be discussed on   dd   mm   yyyy

3. Employer contact name

(only prefill if have rtw program)

Position

B. Worker's Signature

By signing below, I am authorizing any health professional who treats me to provide me, my employer and the Workplace Safety and Insurance Board (WSIB) with information about my functional abilities on the WSIB's "Functional Abilities for Planning Early and Safe Return to Work" form.

Signature

Date   dd   mm   yyyy

C. Health Professional's Billing Information
For billing purposes fax or mail pages 2 and 3 to the WSIB.

Health Professional's Designation
☐ Chiropractor ☐ Physician ☐ Physiotherapist ☐ Registered Nurse (Extended Class) ☐ Other

PROVIDER BILLING INFORMATION IN THE BOLDED AREA OF SECTION C SHOULD NOT BE PROVIDED TO THE WORKER OR EMPLOYER.

Are you registered with the WSIB?
☐ yes Please enter the **WSIB Provider ID.** in the box provided
☐ no Please call **1-800-569-7919** to register

▶

WSIB Provider ID.

Health Professional's Name (please print)

Your Invoice Number

Address (No. Street, Apt.)	Service Code **FAF**

City/Town	Province	Postal Code	Fax

I hereby declare that the information being submitted in Sections C, D, E and F of this form is true and complete. It is an offense to knowingly make a false or misleading statement or representation to the WSIB.

Health Professional's Signature	Telephone	Date dd mm yyyy

2647A2 (07/06)

page 2 of 4

WSIB CSPAAT

Mail to:
200 Front Street West
Toronto ON M5V 3J1
Please PRINT in black ink

or Fax to:
416 344-4684
OR 1-888-313-7373

FAF

Functional Abilities Form
for Planning Early
and Safe Return to Work

Worker's Last Name	First Name	Claim No.
Prefill Injured Worker's Name		if known?

D. The following information should be completed by the Health Professional to identify the patient's overall abilities and restrictions.

1. Date of Assessment dd mm yyyy

2. Please check one:
- ☐ Patient is capable of returning to work with **no restrictions.**
- ☐ Patient is capable of returning to work **with restrictions.** Complete sections **E and F.**
- ☐ Patient is physically unable to return to work at this time. Complete section **F.**

E. Abilities and/or Restrictions

1. Please indicate Abilities that apply. Include additional details in section 3

Walking:
- ☐ Full abilities
- ☐ Up to 100 metres
- ☐ 100 - 200 metres
- ☐ Other (please specify)

Standing:
- ☐ Full abilities
- ☐ Up to 15 minutes
- ☐ 15 - 30 minutes
- ☐ Other (please specify)

Sitting:
- ☐ Full abilities
- ☐ Up to 30 minutes
- ☐ 30 minutes - 1 hour
- ☐ Other (please specify)

Lifting from floor to waist:
- ☐ Full abilities
- ☐ Up to 5 kilograms
- ☐ 5 - 10 kilograms
- ☐ Other (please specify)

Lifting from waist to shoulder:
- ☐ Full abilities
- ☐ Up to 5 kilograms
- ☐ 5 - 10 kilograms
- ☐ Other (please specify)

Stair climbing:
- ☐ Full abilities
- ☐ Up to 5 steps
- ☐ 5 - 10 steps
- ☐ Other (please specify)

Ladder climbing:
- ☐ Full abilities
- ☐ 1 - 3 steps
- ☐ 4 - 6 steps
- ☐ Other (please specify)

Travel to work:
Ability to use public transit
- ☐ yes
- ☐ no

Ability to drive a car
- ☐ yes
- ☐ no

2. Please indicate Restrictions that apply. Include additional details in section 3

- ☐ Bending/twisting repetitive movement of (please specify)
- ☐ Work at or above shoulder activity:
- ☐ Chemical exposure to:
- ☐ Environmental exposure to: (e.g. heat, cold, noise or scents)
- ☐ Limited use of hand(s): Left / Right — Gripping / Pinching / Other (please specify)

- ☐ Limited pushing/pulling with:
  - ☐ Left arm
  - ☐ Right arm
  - ☐ Other (please specify)
- ☐ Operating motorized equipment: (e.g. forklift)
- ☐ Potential side effects from medications (please specify) Do not include names of medications.
- ☐ Exposure to vibration:
  - ☐ Whole body
  - ☐ Hand/Arm

3. Additional Comments on Abilities and/or Restrictions.

4. From the date of this assessment, the above will apply for approximately:
☐ 1 - 2 days ☐ 3 - 7 days ☐ 8 - 14 days ☐ 14 + days

5. Have you discussed return to work with your patient?
☐ yes ☐ no

6. Recommendations for work hours and start date:
☐ Regular full-time hours ☐ Modified hours ☐ Graduated hours
Start Date dd mm yyyy

F. Date of Next Appointment

Recommended date of next appointment to review **Abilities and/or Restrictions.** ► dd mm yyyy

I have provided this completed Functional Abilities Form to: ☐ **Worker** and/or ☐ **Employer**

2647A3 (07/06)

page 3 of 4

SAMPLE RETURN TO WORK PROCEDURE

Return to Work Program
Environmental Health and Safety Procedure

	Date	Page 1 /8
Id.-No.		Version

I. PURPOSE

1. This program has 2 components involving Early and Safe Return to Work after an injury and work hardening after prolonged absence from work. Each component addresses different requirements.

2. The Early and Safe Return to Work section addresses compliance with the Early and Safe Return to Work (ESRTW) requirements as set out in the Workplace Safety and Insurance Act, 1997. ONTARIO as well as any requirements under the Human Rights Code.

3. The work hardening section addresses preventative measures for incidents once any employee has returned to work after a prolonged period away from work.

4. To establish and implement a system designed to effectively manage the return to work of injured employees in an organized manner as well implementing preventative measures during the time the worker is re-acclimating to the work environment after a prolonged period away from work. The program is designed to reduce delays in returning an injured employee to his/her normal duties, minimize costs, minimize lost production hours, and reduce risk of injury.

5. The Early and Safe Return to Work section will assist an employee recovering from an injury or disease to make a safe and speedy return to their regular duties by providing appropriate modification to their work or work regime.

6. The work hardening section will provide a temporary work schedule involving a gradual increase in physical demands while performing duties within their restrictions until the worker has resumed full workload.

II. SCOPE

1. The whole program applies to all employees recovering from an injury or disease.

457

2. The work hardening portion will be reviewed for all employees returning to work after a prolonged period of absence from work.
3. The company will review accommodation requests and restrictions to identify an appropriate return to work program including work hardening.
4. The program will include a comparison between the physical demands of jobs and tasks with an employee's abilities. The individual program will be designed to provide the restricted employee with duties that encourages a gradual return to a full workload.

III. REFERENCE DOCUMENTS

3.1   Workplace Safety and Insurance Act (WSIA)
3.2   Ontario Occupational Health and Safety Act (OHSA)
3.3   Human Rights Commission
3.4   Short Term Disability/Long Term Disability Service Carrier Contract
3.5   Functional Abilities Form (2647A) - Workplace Safety and Insurance Board.
3.6   Form 7 employers Report of Accident, REO7 employers report of recurrence of injury (when issued by the WSIB),
3.7   F9 employers Subsequent Statement.
3.8   Incident Investigation Procedure
3.9   EHS Incident Report
3.10   Functional Abilities Evaluation (FAE)
3.11   Plant Collective Agreement

IV. DEFINITIONS

4.1   **Accommodation -** The qualified and objective process for removing the barriers that may prevent a person with restrictions from full participation in the workplace.

4.2   **Alternative Work -** Any job or set of tasks that have been specifically designated for a worker with temporary restrictions. This could be a modification to an employee's regular duties, or a change in duties, i.e. an off-line job. This designated work may consist of selected tasks whereby the worker, in the process of being rehabilitated, may be required to perform at the rate of production.

4.3   **Co-operation**   - The conduct and communication between the employee and the company throughout the period of disability that demonstrates the desire and willingness of both parties to develop and participate in a program that will enable a successful return to work.

4.4   **Functional Ability -** The information that identifies the range of activities a person is able to engage in without causing further injury. This may include a Functional Abilities

Evaluation to be completed by a regulated health care professional certified in the area of assessing an individual's functional ability.

4.5 **FAF -** Functional Abilities Form – This is a WSIB form completed by a health care professional which identifies restrictions for a worker with an occupational injury to enable the company to compare the worker's abilities and the physical demands of the tasks available and develop an appropriate return to work and work hardening program for the individual. The worker may request this or the company may request this form to be completed.

4.6 **Permanent Disability -** The extent to which a permanent impairment interferes with the employee's ability to be competitive in the job market. A permanent disability is identified by a health care professional.

4.7 **Personal Injury -** A non-occupationally related medical condition that affects any employee's ability to perform his/her normal job duties.

4.8 **Physical Demands Analysis (PDA) -** The information that identifies the functional requirements necessary to perform a specific job and includes information concerning the range of movement, force requirements, frequency of movements, sustained postures and dynamic activity associated with the work.

4.9 **Primary Physician -** Family Physician

4.10 **Regulated Health Professional -** Any person who is a licensed member of a Health Profession identified in the Table and/or Schedule 1 of the Regulated Health Professions Act.

4.11 **Undue Hardship -** Either the financial cost associated with accommodation or changes to workstation design, layout, tools or materials of such significance that the viability of the organization will immediately or inevitably be compromised. Note: Undue Hardship is a measurable and can be calculated in the short or long term but may not be expressed as an unqualified or unmeasured opinion. Reference Guidelines for Accommodating Disabilities – O.H.R.C.

4.12 **Work Hardening –** a program that assists the worker after returning from a prolonged period of absence from work to gradually build up their strength level. This will allow the worker to start with lighter load work, gradually increasing physical demands until the worker can perform full workload. This process normally happens over the course of 2 – 4 weeks which will be assessed on a case by case basis. This is meant to minimize risk of injury while the person is acclimating to the work environment again.

V. RESPONSIBILITIES

5.1 The Senior Location Manager will:

a) Ensure that the Return to Work Program required by this procedure is developed, implemented and maintained current by annual review.

b) Ensure that all managers and supervisors are informed of the program and the requirement to follow the steps set out in the procedure.

c) Appoint a qualified person to manage the claims and return to work program according to all relevant legislation.

d) Ensure that adequate resources are made available to obtain necessary information and to encourage production areas in the reintegration process.

e) Communicate support for return to work efforts and openly encourage return to work efforts so that negative attitudes toward functionally limited employees are not tolerated.

5.2 The Appointed Management (Claims Management)Advisor will:

a) Identify alternative work for employees and e-mail the Union office as to the location of the alternative work once determined. Alternative work will be assigned in accordance to information gathered from all required parties including the employee, company representatives, healthcare professional(s) and related insurance carrier.

b) Monitor the progress of employees placed in suitable work by scheduling requests for updated Functional Abilities to correspond with scheduled reviews by physiotherapists. This is done on a case by case basis.

c) Ensure that a process is in place to accurately track all Return to Work records and costs to achieve maximum recovery and restoration of physical ability.

d) Maintain regular contact with the applicable Claims Adjudicator and or Nurse Case Manager located at the insurance carrier so as to inform him/her of the ongoing status of any claim.

e) Contact the insurance carrier in the event that the Return to Work Program is prolonged or terminated either for medical reasons or a failure to co-operate on the part of the injured worker.

f) Coordinate and participate in any Return to Work meetings or mediations.

g) Be knowledgeable of the legal requirements regarding reemployment, human rights and accommodation.

h) Complete all required Workplace Safety and Insurance Board forms within the statutory time limits as prescribed in the Workplace Safety and Insurance Act.

5.3   The Employee will:

a) Attend proper medical treatment immediately following a work-related injury/illness and follow the recommendations of their health care providers. In cases where it is an occupational related injury, return the initial FAF to the workplace immediately after medical treatment so as to aid the employer in assessing the employee's capabilities regarding a safe return to work. In non-occupationally related injuries, restrictions listed on the medical professional's letterhead will be sufficient for the company to develop a safe return to work plan.

b) Report any injury to their Supervisor immediately.

c) Stay in contact with the company Appointed Advisor throughout their recovery period.

d) Provide the benefits carrier any information requested concerning their return to work.

e) Help the company Appointed Advisor and Supervisor identify suitable work that is available, consistent with his or her functional abilities, and restores pre-injury earnings when possible.

f) Cooperate in their return to work as per the legislated requirements.

g) Communicate and document any concerns to their Supervisor so those potential problems concerning the return to work can be resolved quickly. If unable to resolve the problem the Supervisor and the worker shall contact the appropriate company Appointed Advisor and a Union Health and Safety Representative to assist in further problem solving and potential resolution of the issue.

h) Communicate any treatment, medical assessment or change to an existing treatment program to the company and the benefits carrier.

i) Ensure that future Functional Abilities Forms (FAF) if required are completed and returned to the Supervisor within 7 days.
   NOTE: FAF distribution (beyond the original accident date) rests with the company Appointed Advisor and the employee only. Supervisors are not to provide a FAF for any employee who is on alternative work duties.

j) Schedule ongoing physiotherapy sessions outside of his/her regular shift schedule. Individuals will arrange their treatment sessions so as not to interfere with their work schedules. If there is a scheduling conflict with a medical appointment, discuss with the company Appointed Advisor prior to the appointment for resolution and approval.

5.4 **The Supervisor will:**

a) Meet with the employee on the first day of return to work in order to facilitate the process and establish reporting and monitoring measures.

b) Complete incident reports and the employee name section of the FAF. The supervisor shall offer modified work according to the set standard. Upon receiving completed FAF will reassess the modified work offered accordingly.

c) Facilitate communications and assist the claims management representative with the worker concerning all aspects of the alternative work or related issues.

d) Assist the Environment Health and Safety Coordinator or designate with data collection for job descriptions and task analysis, which will be used for the production of Physical Demands Analysis (PDA).

e) Assist with the implementation with measures of accommodation as well as corrective action.

f) Assist the company Appointed Advisor by monitoring the progress of employees in alternative jobs under their supervision.

g) A supervisor representative will be involved in the Return to Work meetings.

h) Maintain current copies of the Return to Work schedules in the Return to Work binder located in the leaders office and forward past work scheduled to the company Appointed Advisor.

5.5 **The Medical Consultant will:**

a) When required, provide independent medical assessments on the suitability of any alternative work being offered and any recommended treatment or diagnostic testing.

b) The Medical Consultant will provide at first a verbal report to the company. This report shall indicate the suitability of any work offered or for diagnostic examinations such as X- ray, ultrasound, CAT or MRI scans to be arranged for the worker.

c) Will forward reports as it relates to the workers restrictions.

d) Meet and/or discuss with the company Appointed Advisor as required to review any ongoing medical or medical administration issues concerning the Return Work Program.

e) When appropriate consent has been given the medical consultant will meet with any injured employee to assess their medical condition.

VI. PROCEDURE
6.1 Process

1. When an employee is injured at work the Supervisor shall complete an EHS Incident Report as per the Incident Investigation Procedure with the worker.

2. When an employee indicates at the time of incident they are seeking medical attention the Supervisor shall provide the documents contained in the Return to Work Package. The supervisor shall ensure:

   a) They Log the FAF number on the FAF log sheet in the Supervisor's Office.

   b) The employee and employer information is completed on the FAF.

   c) Offer modified work according to the set standard, document modified offer in the original EHS Incident Report

   d) The original incident report is forwarded to the EHS Coordinator immediately.

   NOTE: Under an emergency situation the priority is ensuring the worker receives appropriate first aid and emergency transportation to the nearest medical facility. It would be inappropriate to jeopardize these actions just for the purposes of form completion.

3. The Return to Work process will commence from the time an employee is unable to perform his/her normal occupation because of the injury. The process will continue regardless of whether there are employer concerns regarding causation of accident/injury.

4. When the company receives capabilities and limitations they will be reviewed to identify an appropriate job duty for the short and longer term.

5. As determined on a case by case basis, the work hardening portion may be progressive in both the number of hours performing the work and the workload itself, as dictated by health care professionals.

6. If there are any issues with the Return to Work process please log the issues on the employees Return to Work schedule and forward them to the EHS Coordinator or Claims Advisor.

7. In cases where more formal meetings (i.e. a conference room or office) are required to discuss any aspect of the employ-

ee's alternative work or injury status, the employee can request Union Representation to be present at these meetings.

8. The program will include a comparison between the physical demands of jobs and tasks with an employee's abilities. The individual program will be designed to provide the injured employee with duties that encourages a gradual return to a full workload.

VII. GENERAL

RECORD OF REVISIONS

Revision	Section	Changes	Date
I		New Procedure	

SAMPLE RETURN TO WORK PLAN

Work Hardening Program
Employee Name

Area of Concern
Injury:

- Left arm
- Lower back
- Right torso
- Both legs

Start Date:

Report Date:

List all the body parts affected by the restrictions

Status: Request for Modified Work

- Attempt work hardening program to gradually increase physical tolerance for work

Based on (benefits carrier) permanent restrictions

- No repetitive lifting,
- No repetitive bending or twisting movement of lower back
- Occasional lifting up to 50 lbs.

Ergonomic Concerns

- Avoid work on packing due to bending and pulling out of bins
- Avoid work as (specific job) due to forceful lifting/push/pull and awkward postures
- Avoid packing on high production lines

By signing this declaration you hereby acknowledge that you have reviewed and understand the intent of this plan.

_____   _____

Worker   Date

_____   _____

Claims Management Advisor   Date

PROPOSED SCHEDULE:
ROTATE TO DIFFERENT LINES DAILY

Week	Starting Dates	APPROVED Workstations *at production rates*
1		Light load line
2		*Additional workstations* • Light load line • Second light load line alternate days • Off line work (no Packing)
3		*Additional workstations* All work in previous weeks plus alternate days • Moderate load line (no packing) • Moderate load line 2 (no packing)
4		**Evaluate based on progress**

> Note the increase in physical demand within restrictions. The increase is inclusive meaning at each level of progression, the additional lines are assigned to the worker to rotate

NOTES:

_____
_____
_____
_____
_____
_____
_____
_____
_____
_____

A copy of this schedule has been provided to:
Claims Advisor, EHS Coordinator, JHSC or Union Representative, Floor Supervisors

APPENDIX G

SAMPLE ACCIDENT COST STATEMENT

This Statement lists WSIB awards and adjustments for claims recorded under your firm number. It has two main purposes:

- To enable you to check the accuracy of the information - dates, amounts, award types, allocation to the correct rate group, classification unit number, and so on - against your own records

- To assist you in monitoring your firm's occupational health and safety performance.

An explanation of the terms may be found on the reverse side of this statement.

Description	Awards and Adjustments	Date
RATE GROUP 421		
CLASSIFICATION UNIT 3256-000		
HEAD OFFICE		
Claim Number:		
Worker's Name:		
Accident Date:		
HEALTH CARE		
HEALTH CARE REFERENCE # 0066057711	$30.00	04/22/07
Total: Month	49.00	
: Year-to-Date	49.00	
Claim Total: Month	49.00	
: Year-to-Date	49.00	
Claim Number:		
Worker's Name:		
Accident Date:		
TEMPORARY COMPENSATION/BI-WEEKLY LOSS OF EARNINGS		
LOSS OF EARNINGS - ARREARS	108.38	03/06/08
Total: Month	108.38	
: Year-to-Date	108.38	
Claim Total: Month	108.38	
: Year-to-Date	108.38	
Claim Number:		
Worker's Name:		
Accident Date:		
HEALTH CARE		
HEALTH CARE REFERENCE # 0086492040C	24.00	03/03/08
HEALTH CARE REFERENCE # 0086492040C	24.00	03/10/08
HEALTH CARE REFERENCE # 0086492040C	24.00	03/29/08
HEALTH CARE REFERENCE # 0086492040C	24.00	03/17/08
HEALTH CARE REFERENCE # 0086492040C	24.00	03/05/08
HEALTH CARE REFERENCE # 0086402040C	24.00	03/17/08
HEALTH CARE REFERENCE # 0086402040C	24.00	03/14/08
HEALTH CARE REFERENCE # 0086402040C	24.00	03/12/08
Total: Month	192.00	
: Year-to-Date	192.00	

For Information Purposes Only. Please Direct Enquiries to (416) 344-1016 or Toll Free at 1-800-663-6639
Ces renseignements sont disponibles en français sur demande.

3431A (01/98)

467

APPENDIX H

SAMPLE NEER STATEMENT

—

 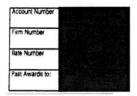

200 Front St. West
Toronto ON M5V 3J1

NEER Firm Summary Statement

Page No.   1

Account Number	
Firm Number	
Rate Number	
Past Awards to:	

Accident Year	Premium ($)	Expected Cost Factor (%)	Expected Costs ($)	NEER Costs ($)	Rating Factor (%)	Performance Index
2006	55,960.20	35.82	20,044.94	547.67	82.12	0.03
2005	109,018.44	38.47	41,939.39	316,717.24	82.85	7.55*
2004	111,411.03	38.37	42,748.41	13,229.26	83.60	0.31
2003	82,874.84	46.40	38,453.93	24,874.81	67.16	0.65

Refund/Surcharge Calculation			
Accident Year	Primary Adjustment ($)	Previous Adjustment ($)	Current NEER Adjustment ($)
2005	227,653.45	.00	227,653.45
2004	24,678.01CR	22,585.79CR	2,092.22CR
2003	9,119.74CR	3,802.76CR	5,316.98CR
		TOTAL SURCHARGE	220,244.25

* SUBJECT TO MAXIMUM SURCHARGE

This is your firm's NEER Quarterly statement for September 30, 2006.

***** PLEASE NOTE IMPORTANT MESSAGE ON THE BACK OF THIS PAGE *****
RE REBATES AND SURCHARGES

CLAIM TYPE AND CLAIM STATUS CHART (ONTARIO/WSIB)

Formulas and Claim Type Chart

BENEFIT TYPE	CLAIM TYPE
LOE less than or = to 1week*	01
Health Care only	02
Loss of Earnings (LOE)	
Less than 4 weeks of payment	
Active	03
Inactive	04
4 to less than 16 weeks of payment	
Active	05
Inactive	06
16 to less than 52 weeks of payment	
Active	07
Inactive	08
52 to 104 weeks of payment	
Active	09
Inactive	10
Permanent Disability Awards	
Non Economic Loss (NEL) Award	
Active	11
Inactive	12
LOE payment post 24 months after accident & Ret. Pen	
Active	13
Inactive	14
Fatality	15
Other	15

Claim Type:
- benefit types
- duration (= total LOE ÷ Weekly Rate)
- activity

Claim Age:
- number of months from Accident Date to NEER Statement's Past Awards to date (do not include month of accident but do include month of NEER Statement)

Non Pension:
- LOE + Health Care + LMR

Pension:
- NEL + Survivors

Discounted Past Awards:
Discounted Non Pension + Discounted Pension

Projected Future Costs:
Discounted Non Pension Costs X Reserve Factor

Overhead Costs:
(Discounted Past Awards + Projected Future Costs) X Overhead Factor (%)

Limited Claim Cost:
Discounted Past Awards + Projected Future Costs + Overhead Costs
- subject to a Claim Cost Limit, which is 4X the Maximum Earnings Ceiling for that accident year

40

APPENDIX K

DUE DILIGENCE SELF-ASSESSMENT

From www.CCOHS.ca:
What is an example of a due diligence checklist?

Yes	No	
		Do you know and understand your safety and health responsibilities?
		Do you have definite procedures in place to identify and control hazards?
		Have you integrated safety into all aspects of your work?
		Do you set objectives for safety and health just as you do for quality, production, and sales?
		Have you committed appropriate resources to safety and health?
		Have you explained safety and health responsibilities to all employees and made sure that they understand it?
		Have employees been trained to work safely and use proper protective equipment?
		Is there a hazard reporting procedure in place that encourages employees to report all unsafe conditions and unsafe practices to their supervisors?
		Are managers, supervisors, and workers held accountable for safety and health just as they are held accountable for quality?
		Is safety a factor when acquiring new equipment or changing a process?
		Do you keep records of your program activities and improvements?
		Do you keep records of the training each employee has received?
		Do your records show that you take disciplinary action when an employee violates safety procedures?
		Do you review your OSH program at least once a year and make improvements as needed?

STANDARD RECOVERY PERIOD CHART

	Usual healing times
Soft tissue injuries	all soft tissue
menisceal damage, knee	3 months
herniated disc, conservative treatment	3 months
Fractures	complex facial
upper limb	3-6 months
hand	3-6 months
simple vertebral, body compression all levels	3-6 months
spine, fractures or dislocations	6 months
pelvis, no reduction	3 months
pelvis, with reduction	12 months
femur and hip	6 - 12 months
tibia	6 - 9 months
other lower limb and foot	3 - 6 months
complex and/or complicated fractures	6 months
major joints fractures or dislocations (including wrist and ankle)	6 months
Infections	osteomyelitis
Nervous system injuries	peripheral nerve
minor head injuries	3 months
brain, with persisting neurological deficit	1 year
spinal cord and cauda equina injuries	1 year

	Post-surgical recovery times
Shoulder	acromioplasty
rotator cuff repair	6 months
Knee	
arthroscopy - diagnostic	1 week
- operative	6 weeks
arthrotomy	3 months
ligament repair	3 - 6 months
Ankle ligament repair	3 - 6 months
Spine herniated disc - operative	3 months
spinal fusion - single level	3 months
- multiple level	6 months
spinal stenosis decompression - single level	3 months
- multiple level	6 months
Nervous system	major nerve repair
minor nerve repair	4 - 5 months
carpal tunnel or other nerve repair	3 months
Tendon	flexor tendon repair or tendon transfer
extensor tendon repair	3 months
tendon release	3 months
Amputation	---
Reconstruction	digital re-implantation

LaVergne, TN USA
04 January 2011
211077LV00003B/2/P